The Student Teacher
in the Secondary School

The Student Teacher in the Secondary School

by

LESTER D. CROW, Ph.D.

PROFESSOR OF EDUCATION
FORMERLY DIRECTOR OF STUDENT TEACHING
BROOKLYN COLLEGE

and

ALICE CROW, Ph.D.

FORMERLY ASSOCIATE PROFESSOR OF EDUCATION
AND SUPERVISOR OF STUDENT TEACHING
BROOKLYN COLLEGE

DAVID McKAY COMPANY, INC.

NEW YORK

Preface

Because of the broadening interpretation of teaching, the task of educating a competent teacher is becoming increasingly difficult and time-consuming. As a college student who has decided on teaching for a career, you want to be a good teacher when you enter the profession. Hence you desire the kind of preparation that will enable you, from the start, to function at a high level of efficiency. All areas of your education are important. Student teaching is especially valuable to you in that it affords you the opportunity to discover at firsthand the problems that are involved in teaching and to learn how to handle them.

In order to assist you better to profit from your student-teaching experiences, the authors have undertaken through *The Student Teacher in the Secondary School* to alert you to the kinds of problems you are likely to encounter and to equip you to deal with them effectively. Throughout the book, emphasis is placed on the need and value of cooperation among all who participate in the professional activities associated with student teaching.

Your attention is directed to the various factors that are inherent in your orientation to student teaching. The personal and professional qualities that are significant attributes of good teachers are described. Since your effectiveness in the classroom depends in good part on your relations with your students, it is essential that you become acquainted with adolescent attitudes and behavior. To this end, the authors discuss young people's characteristics and present some approaches to the study of students that you may find helpful. Also important to achieving success in student-teaching experiences are the relationships you develop with your various colleagues.

Although you have learned about teaching methodology, you now are faced with the practical problems associated with meeting the learning needs of the students in your school. You may be helped to meet actual teaching responsibilities by the suggestions offered here concerning broad areas of planning in light of accepted educational objectives. The need for daily lesson planning is stressed along with the bases of such plans. Teaching techniques are presented in light of the learning needs of students. Special attention is given to the learning problems of rapid and slow learners. Suggestions are offered for the utilization of various supplementary teaching aids.

You further are alerted to the value of knowing how to deal with classroom management and what problems are associated with students' out-of-class activities. Considerable attention is given to the factors involved in the understanding of discipline and what is needed in furthering the development of self-discipline. The role of the teacher in these matters is carefully explored.

The importance of measurement and evaluation in teaching, and helpful hints concerning the evaluating and reporting of student progress are thoroughly explored with specific suggestions given for application to your teaching. Also, the problems of placement in a teaching position and of orientation to the new school are treated by means of numerous practical examples from various school systems.

The suggestions offered arise from Lester D. Crow's thirteen years' experience as the Director of Student Teaching at Brooklyn College and from Alice Crow's many years of experience as a college supervisor of student teachers.

The authors wish to thank all who have permitted the reprinting of material from their publications.

Lester D. Crow
Alice Crow

Contents

The Student Teacher
in the Secondary School

ORIENTATION TO STUDENT TEACHING

As a beginning full-time teacher, you will be likely to face many problems in adjusting to your new profession or lifework. Student teaching experiences, under wise guidance and supervision, are intended to help you adapt constructively to the various activities that constitute teaching responsibilities. Your experiences as a student teacher should result in your gaining an understanding of the many personal and professional aspects of your chosen lifework and motivate you to achieve a high level of teaching competence.

FUNCTIONS OF STUDENT TEACHING

To the present, you probably have viewed teaching from the point of view of a student. You have evaluated the worth of your teachers in light of their effect upon you and your educational progress. Now the situation is about to be reversed. You are being encouraged to evaluate teaching success according to the effect of your teaching procedures upon your students—their attitudes toward you, their classroom behavior, and their evidenced degree of success in subject-matter and skill mastery. The main functions or purposes of the student-teaching experience are to assist you (1) to achieve success in teaching-learning situations and (2) to achieve adequate control of teaching-learning conditions.

Some of the functional phases of teaching activities with which you can become acquainted as a student teacher are described here briefly. Later in the chapter, we shall discuss (1) the theoretical background of teacher education to which you probably have been exposed and (2) practical applications in student teaching.

Understanding Secondary School Objectives

One of the important purposes of secondary education is to build upon basic elementary education whatever further training is needed by individual young people either to become eligible for college entrance or to be prepared for specific vocational activity. Although you have studied about the aims of education on the junior and senior high school levels, your approach has been more or less academic. Now you are being given an opportunity to observe educational principles in action.

You can evaluate the ways in which and the extent to which educational purposes are being fulfilled in the school or schools with which you are associated. Your understanding of educational philosophy will be quickened. You will learn to apply those principles of secondary education that will enable you to become an effective teacher.

Need for Knowing Adolescents

How well do you understand and appreciate adolescent boys and girls? You probably are close enough to your own adolescence so that you believe that you know something about the joys and sorrows, the trials and tribulations, and the ambitions and interests commonly associated with this age period. Do you really understand adolescent behavior?

Your adolescent experiences were rooted in a specific family and personal background. Your attitudes and behavior, your interests and ambitions, and your school and social relationships have been uniquely your own. One finds many individual differences among adolescents, however. A secondary school teacher needs to understand these differences and adapt his own attitudes and behavior in light of those evidenced by his students.

As you work with young people during your student-teaching activities, you are enabled thereby to deepen your insight into the whys and wherefores of differences among them. What you learn during this training period will have value when later, as a regular teacher, you are responsible for the personal and academic development of the boys and girls whose learning you are attempting to guide.

Need to Appreciate the Total Concept of Teaching

In your own school experiences to the present, you may have envisaged the functions of the teacher to be those of assigning study units and then discovering how well the students master learning content. You may have conceded that some teachers, but not all, attempt to help students overcome learning difficulties. This, of course, is an immature point of view.

Your student teaching experiences should alert you to the various facets of the teaching process. You will come to recognize the many broad as well as specific duties that are included in the teaching concept. You will discover that the effective teacher:

1. Guides his students in the mastery of subject matter.
2. Helps his students improve needed skills.
3. Assists young people in the solution of their personal problems.
4. Organizes and conducts efficiently all of the many activities that constitute classroom management.
5. Develops satisfactory relationships with administrators, supervisors, fellow teachers, and parents.
6. Participates in out-of-class experiences.
7. Cooperates with the administration in all matters of school management.
8. Becomes acquainted with and cooperates with the community in which the school is located.
9. Learns to meet and work with parents.
10. Gives evidence of a love of teaching and a professional attitude toward teaching.

The foregoing list of teacher responsibilities covers broad areas of activities. You realize the fact that, during the school day, week, month, or year, a teacher can be called upon to participate in many specific situations that have for their purpose the furthering of pupil welfare. As a student teacher, you are afforded an opportunity to observe regular teachers in action as well as to share some of their many responsibilities. Student teaching is an excellent medium for alerting you to the important role of the teacher in the lives of young people.

ORGANIZATION AND CONDUCT OF STUDENT TEACHING

Various factors will affect your experiences as a student teacher. These factors include (1) the school to which you are assigned, (2) the classroom teacher (cooperating teacher) with whom you work, (3) the amount of time you spend in the student teaching activity, (4) your relationships with your college supervisor, and (5) the procedures employed in the school.

School Assignment

Colleges and other teacher training institutions differ in their arrangements for student teaching. Some colleges maintain campus schools to which teacher trainees are assigned for observation and, if the number of trainees is not too large, for actual practice as well. Consequently, some college students may complete their practice in the campus school while others are assigned to community schools.

Some colleges use neighboring public schools or send their student teachers to schools in communities that are removed from the college campus or are even in another town. If it is feasible, a trainee may be assigned to a school in a community in or near which he later may wish to serve as a full-time teacher.

Unless you are acquainted with your assigned school, you would be well advised to discover some things about it before you begin your practice period there. It would be helpful for you to know the following:

1. Location of the building
2. Size and age of the building
3. Number and types of students
4. Kinds and amount of teaching aids
5. Composition of the faculty
6. Attitude of faculty toward student teaching and student teachers

7. Curriculums offered
8. Community attitudes toward education

The more you know about the school and its environs the easier it probably will be for you to adapt yourself to participation in its activities. It is satisfying to feel wanted and to feel adequate in whatever you attempt.

Student Teaching Arrangements

The amount of time that you are expected to devote to student teaching and the manner in which the time is apportioned differ with college communities. You can check minimums required by various states in Table 1 and its footnotes. You may find also that individual colleges set a period of time for student teaching that is in excess of the minimum set by the state.

TABLE 1

SPECIFIC MINIMUM REQUIREMENTS FOR HIGH-SCHOOL CERTIFICATES
BASED ON DEGREES * †

State	Degree or College Years of Preparation Required	General Education Required, Semester Hours	Professional Education Required, Semester Hours	Directed Teaching Required, Semester Hours (Included In Column 4)
1	2	3	4	5
Alabama	B	36	24	3
Alaska	B	—	18	C
Arizona	5 a	—	18	6
Arkansas	B	48	18	5
California	5	40	22	6
Colorado	B	AC	AC	AC
Connecticut	B b	45	18	6
Delaware	B	60‡	18	6
District	5 c	30	18	6
Florida	B	45	20	6
Georgia	B	40	18	6
Hawaii	B	100	18	AC
Idaho	B	—	20	6
Illinois	B	104	16	5
Indiana	B d	30	18	5
Iowa	B	40	20	5
Kansas	B	50	20	5

TABLE 1 (*Cont.*)

SPECIFIC MINIMUM REQUIREMENTS FOR HIGH-SCHOOL CERTIFICATES
BASED ON DEGREES * †

State	Degree or College Years of Preparation Required	General Education Required, Semester Hours	Professional Education Required, Semester Hours	Directed Teaching Required, Semester Hours (Included in Column 4)
1	2	3	4	5
Kentucky	B [e]	45	17	8 [f]
Louisiana	B	46	18	4 [g]
Maine	B	39–48	12	0
Maryland	B	—	18	6
Massachusetts	B	—	12	2
Michigan	B	—	20	5
Minnesota	B	—	18	4
Mississippi	B	48	18	6
Missouri	B	25	20	5
Montana	B	—	16	AC
Nebraska	B	— [h]	18	3
Nevada	B	—	18	4
New Hampshire	B	—	21	6
New Jersey	B	—	24 [i]	6 [i]
New Mexico	B	48	18	6
New York	5 [j]	60	18	6
North Carolina	B	—	18	3
North Dakota	B	—	16	3
Ohio	B	100	17	6
Oklahoma	B	50	21 [k]	6
Oregon	B [l]	—	24	6
Pennsylvania	B	60 [m]	18	6
Puerto Rico	B	—	29	5
Rhode Island	B	—	18	6
South Carolina	B	45	18	6
South Dakota	B	—	20	5
Tennessee	B	40	24	4
Texas	B	45	24	6
Utah	B	48	22	8
Vermont	B	—	18	6
Virginia	B	48	15	4–6
Washington	B [n]	AC	AC	AC
West Virginia	B	36	20	5
Wisconsin	B	— [o]	18	5
Wyoming	B	40	20	C

LEGEND:—means not reported; AC means approved course; 5 means bachelor's degree and 30 semester hours of appropriate postbaccalaureate preparation, not necessarily completion of master's degree; B means completion of the bachelor's degree of specified preparation; C means completion of a course in the field.

Table 1, Footnotes

* From *A Manual on Certification Requirements for School Personnel in the United States,* 1961 edition, p. 28, National Commission on Teacher Education and Professional Standards, National Education Association, Washington 6, D.C., 1962. Reprinted with permission.

† Professional requirements listed are the basic requirements for degree or lowest regular certificates. Some variation from the professional requirements as stated in this table may be found in the requirements for specific certificates listed for the respective states in Chapter II of the Manual.

ᵃ Arizona. Secondary certificate: 5 years of college preparation. Presecondary certificate (valid for grades 7–12): bachelor's degree plus 6 semester hours of graduate work; valid for 2 years; renewable for second 2-year period with additional 12 semester hours of graduate credit; 4 years total life of presecondary certificate.

ᵇ Connecticut. For provisional certificate. Five years required for standard certificate.

‡ Delaware. Effective beginning 1962–63.

ᶜ District of Columbia. Master's degree required for permanent certificate.

ᵈ Indiana. Master's degree required for permanent certificate.

ᵉ Kentucky. For provisional certificate. Five years required for standard certificate.

ᶠ Kentucky. A teacher who has taught successfully 4 or more years is required to take only 4 semester hours in practice teaching or a seminar of 4 hours. A teacher who has had 2 years of successful experience may take a seminar dealing with professional problems instead of the 8 hours in practice teaching.

ᵍ Louisiana. Specified requirement in clock hours of actual teaching involved: 90 clock hours of actual teaching and observation, 45 hours of which must be in actual teaching.

ʰ Nebraska. Forty semester hours recommended by Nebraska Council on Teacher Education, which recommends approval of institutions of higher education to state commissioner of education for teacher certification purposes. Statutes require 18 semester hours in each of 2 recognized teaching fields.

ⁱ New Jersey. Practice teaching requirement is 150 clock hours, 90 of which must be in actual classroom teaching.

ʲ New York. A provisional high-school certificate is issued for the academic fields based upon completion of the bachelor's degree with 18 semester hours in education, including 6 semester hours of supervised practice teaching: valid for 5 years; nonrenewable; holder must complete requirements for permanent certificate; permanent certificate requires an additional 6 semester hours in education or in advanced study in the subject field.

ᵏ Oklahoma. For standard certificate; for temporary certificate the requirement is 12.

ˡ Oregon. For provisional certificate. Five years required for standard certificate.

ᵐ Pennsylvania. Plus 12 semester hours of postbaccalaureate work.

ⁿ Washington. For provisional certificates. Five years required for standard certificate.

ᵒ Wisconsin. Patterns for general education must be approved by state superintendent and on file in his office.

The student teacher can be assigned to a school for a block of time such as eight or ten weeks, during which he spends all of the school day in the school and engages in class and out-of-class activities. According to this arrangement, the trainee may observe and teach several classes in his field, give learning help to individual or small groups of students who need it, attend faculty meetings, assist in the conduct of cocurriculum activities, and work with parents. In fact, he is given an opportunity to get the feel of a total teaching situation.

Some colleges, especially those in large urban areas, prefer to utilize a split program—i.e., part of each day (two to three hours), throughout the entire semester, is devoted to student teaching in a laboratory school or a neighboring public school, and the remainder of the college day is spent in regular college classrooms where the trainees continue their academic study.

The following of the dual program mentioned in the foregoing has advantages as well as disadvantages. The trainee plays a dual role; he is both a student teacher and a student. Since his time in the practice school is relatively short, he is associated only with one, at the most two, teachers. He is denied full contact with the school as a community agency. Yet, his returning to college for part of a day affords him an opportunity to discuss his practical experiences with his college instructors and fellow trainees. He also can use this experience as background in class discussion to understand better the material he is studying.

Supervisory Personnel

During your practice teaching experiences you will be associated with members of both the college and the school personnel. In most education departments of colleges and universities or in other teacher training institutions, one member of the faculty is responsible for assigning student teachers to appropriate schools and classes. This usually is done in consultation with individual trainees and is concerned with matters such as subject-matter field, period of service, travel conditions, college program, and the like. If possible, the trainee is given some choice in the school assignment.

College supervisor. While you are on the job, you receive a certain amount of supervision and guidance of your activities. You will be assigned to a member of the college faculty who then becomes your college supervisor. Through regular visitations and conferences, this person aids you in your adjustment to your teaching responsibilities. This is discussed in greater detail later.

Cooperating teacher. The man or woman in whose classroom you are working usually is called the cooperating teacher. In your day-by-day association with him you can learn much by observing his attitudes and techniques and by attempting to follow them. This, too, is treated more fully later.

School Procedures

Schools differ in their educational outlook and modes of procedure. This difference is found in schools of the same as well as in widely separated communities. You may be assigned to a school in which traditional methods are employed, or you may find yourself in a school that follows modern educational principles. Since the latter approach probably is characteristic of the college in which you are studying, you may feel at a loss in a more traditional school.

To observe teaching procedures and to practice those that seem to be in opposition to the educational principles taught you at college may pose problems of adjustment. The situation is worsened if your college supervisor expects you to follow modern trends in your teaching, but the cooperating teacher insists that you fall in line with his mode of procedure.

Even though the situation is difficult, you need to keep in mind that you are a guest in the practice school. There is no compulsion for the school to accept student teachers. Moreover, your cooperating teacher is responsible for the academic achievement of his students. He is guiding their learning progress in light of school standards.

It is your obligation to help keep the wheels running smoothly by following the teacher's lead even though you disapprove of his teaching methods. Perhaps, in so doing, you can strengthen your own attitude toward proper teaching approaches to be utilized.

If any conflict or misunderstanding arises between you and your cooperating teacher, you probably can discuss the situation with your college supervisor, who is likely to understand the difficulty involved and be able to help you bring about a compromise between your educational principles and the practices you observe. You even may find that some so-called traditional approaches to learning are effective.

PREPARATION FOR STUDENT TEACHING

The question often arises as to whether teachers are born or made. The fact must be recognized that some people seem to have a flair for teaching. They are able, with a minimum of training, to assist others to learn. One also finds persons who, in spite of having experienced considerable teacher education, become and remain mediocre teachers.

Importance of Selecting Qualified Candidates

In order to insure for our young people the services of superior teachers, it is important that all college departments of teacher education and teacher-training institutions exercise care in selecting teacher trainees from among applicants. They need to select those men and women who seem to have an inherent aptitude for teaching, and then provide them with as extensive and intensive a program of teacher education as is possible.

We shall not dwell here at length upon the various techniques utilized for the selection of candidates. Do you recall on what basis you were chosen? In some training institutions, the selection is made when the student enters the freshman year. In most colleges, however, the final decision comes at the end of the sophomore year. Selection usually is based upon such factors as health and physical fitness, and personal qualities (including voice, academic achievement, and evidenced interest in the profession). We are concerned at this point with the kind of educational preparation needed for entrance into teaching.

Need for Liberal Arts Studies

The holding of at least a bachelor's degree is a generally accepted state requirement for secondary-school teaching. Some states require, in addition, thirty credits of graduate work. (See Table 1, pp. 5–7.) Anyone who is preparing to teach adolescents needs to possess a broad cultural background, as well as a thorough mastery of the subject matter in which he hopes to guide the learning of young people.

In most colleges, the freshman and sophomore years are devoted to what sometimes is referred to as "general education," with concentration on a major field that may or may not represent a subject to be taught later. Some students, of course, do not decide upon teaching until their junior or senior year. Regardless of when the decision to teach is made, a good background of liberal arts education is an asset to success in the teaching profession.

Need for Courses in Education

Until the recent past, a person was presumed to be fitted for teaching in the secondary school if he had mastered successfully the subject matter of his teaching. For a long time it was assumed that, although elementary school teachers needed to know something about child development and methods of teaching, these areas of study were not needed by the teacher of adolescents. Teaching them consisted more or less of pouring information into the heads of receptive young people. This philosophy of education has been found to be in error.

We now realize that motivating adolescent boys and girls to benefit from school learning requires an understanding and application of the fundamentals of adolescent psychology, sociological backgrounds, educational philosophy and principles, general and specific teaching techniques, and student teaching. Hence, college departments of education offer courses in educational theory, usually during the junior and senior years. These courses serve as a background of knowledge that you can apply during your student-teaching experiences. In fact, many regular teachers find it helpful to continue advanced or graduate study in these and related areas.

Need for Practical Experience

In the foregoing, we have seemed to stress theory at the expense of practice. This is not the situation, however. In an increasing number of colleges, teacher trainees are being given an opportunity to apply some of the theory that they are learning in the classroom before they begin actual student teaching. A few such experiences that precede student teaching are listed here.

Observation. If the college has a campus school, students, during the junior year or earlier, are assigned in small groups to observe young people in action in the laboratory school. If the college is in an urban community, groups of students visit neighboring schools, travel through the building, and sit in on classroom discussions. In either case, what has been observed is discussed later in the appropriate college classroom. In some colleges, the students are provided with a kind of questionnaire to guide their observation.

Community agency participation. Large cities have many welfare agencies, which, during the later afternoons and evenings, provide many activities for young people. These usually include athletics, crafts, dancing, and various social activities. Since these community agencies often are understaffed with paid personnel, college upper classmen are welcomed as volunteer workers.

Colleges in urban areas often cooperate closely with these agencies. During the junior year, teacher trainees are required, in connection with an appropriate course in education, to serve as volunteer workers in an assigned community agency. This is an integral part of the course and must be completed if the student is to receive credit for the course.

A trainee spends two or three hours weekly after the college day in an agency where he works with a group of the young people who frequent the agency. He works directly under the supervision of the personnel in the agency. His duties may include any one of the following—helping to supervise athletics activity, teaching arts or crafts, or sponsoring social activities.

The college student, by participating in the various activities and offerings of the agency, gains a more intimate knowledge of young people, including their behavior and attitudes. Through these experiences, he gets the feel of working with young people in these relatively unstructured situations. He also gains experience in working with experienced social workers and learns how to cooperate with fellow workers.

Value of Teacher Aides

Some colleges afford their students still another means of becoming acquainted with school procedures while they are mastering educational theory and before they begin student teaching. A student is assigned to a teacher in a neighboring public school as a teacher aide for a specific number of periods each school week.

The trainee's duties consist of helping the cooperating teacher with such matters as caring for routines associated with class management (such as preparing and distributing materials, proctoring tests, correcting papers submitted by the pupils, working with individual pupils or small groups of those who need help in their studies, and the like). Serving as a teacher's aide is valuable to the trainee in that it gives him an opportunity to become acquainted with the school situation. This experience gives him confidence in himself, thus minimizing the normal fear that he might experience when he begins his student teaching.

Other Areas of Valuable Experience

In addition to the experiences in dealing with young people provided by the college, some trainees engage in similar activities on their own.

Camp experience. An increasing number of young men and women are participating in camp activities. They serve as camp counselors. Living and working with young people in a summer camp provide them with excellent opportunities to study young people and to gain confidence in themselves as being able to meet and cope with individuals in these situations. These experiences prove to be invaluable to teacher trainees in their efforts to guide the various activities of young people.

Importance of participating in religious activities. Good practical preparation for teaching also can be obtained by your participating in religious work with children and adolescents. The informal relationship that exists between teacher and pupils in the religious day or Sunday school class enables you to gain some knowledge of young people's interests and ambitions as well as of the problems of growing up. If this experience is available to you, seize it as one to serve others as well as to receive your own personal rewards. *Value of home influences.* You also may be fortunate enough to have younger brothers and sisters with whose attitudes and behavior you are well acquainted. The meeting of youth problems in the home can serve you well as you encounter similar problems in the classroom. Although you may not have reflected on this before, you might evaluate some of those experiences as you go forward in your student teaching activities.

Conceptual Scheme for Teacher Education

The schematic representation proposed by Elizabeth Z. Howard [1] illustrates, in summary fashion, the important considerations and relationships that operate in a good teacher education program. It is presented in Figure 1.

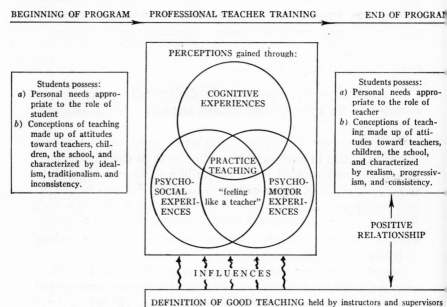

BEGINNING OF PROGRAM → PROFESSIONAL TEACHER TRAINING → END OF PROGRAM

PERCEPTIONS gained through:

Students possess:
a) Personal needs appropriate to the role of student
b) Conceptions of teaching made up of attitudes toward teachers, children, the school, and characterized by idealism, traditionalism, and inconsistency.

COGNITIVE EXPERIENCES

PRACTICE TEACHING

PSYCHO-SOCIAL EXPERIENCES   "feeling like a teacher"   PSYCHO-MOTOR EXPERIENCES

Students possess:
a) Personal needs appropriate to the role of teacher
b) Conceptions of teaching made up of attitudes toward teachers, children, the school, and characterized by realism, progressivism, and consistency.

POSITIVE RELATIONSHIP

INFLUENCES

DEFINITION OF GOOD TEACHING held by instructors and supervisors

Fig. 1.—Conceptual scheme for professional teacher education.

[1] Elizabeth Z. Howard, "Needed: A Conceptual Scheme for Teacher Education," *The School Review*, LXXI, No. 1 (Spring, 1963), 15. Copyright 1963 by The University of Chicago.

TEACHING AS A CAREER

As you begin the student-teaching phase of your teacher education, it might be well for you to evaluate yourself—your potentialities for and attitudes toward teaching as a lifework.

Your Selection of Teaching as a Career

When did you decide to become a teacher? Various studies have been made to discover answers to this question. According to one study,[2] in about 60 per cent of the replies the decision was made between the junior year of high school and the sophomore year of college (inclusive), with 16 per cent at an earlier time and 24 per

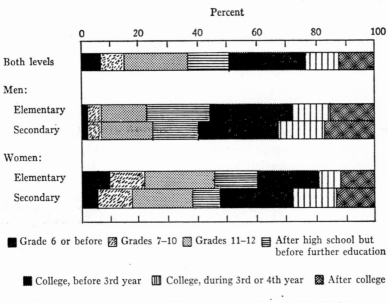

Fig. 2.—Educational level at which beginning teachers had decided to enter teaching, by sex and teaching level: 1956–57.*

[2] See Ward S. Mason, *The Beginning Teacher: Status and Career Orientations* (Washington, D.C.: U.S. Department of Health, Education and Welfare, 1961), pp. 96–98.
Ibid., p. 96.

cent at a later time. A very small percentage of decisions was made by the sixth grade or earlier. A somewhat larger percentage is indicated for "after college." (See Figure 2, p. 15.)

As you can see by studying Figure 2, women tended to decide earlier than men to go into teaching. One reason for this difference may be that men have a wider range of choice among occupations than do women.

Why did you decide upon teaching as a career? Perhaps you are not certain. Family members who either are or wanted to become teachers may have influenced your decision. Teaching may have seemed to offer greater security—both financial and emotional—than other fields. You may have been intrigued by working conditions—long vacations and relatively short working days.

Your actual vocational interest may lie in another field. Preparation for that field may have appeared to be too difficult, causing you to switch to teaching, or you may plan to engage in teaching while you are continuing to prepare yourself for another profession. Of course, the best motive for selecting teaching is a deep interest in working with people, especially young people.

Your Fitness for Student Teaching

Whatever the reason for your decision, you now have committed yourself, tentatively at least, to teaching as your lifework. As you evaluate your potentialities during your student teaching experiences, you can discover to some degree whether you have made a wise choice. The possession of certain qualities or characteristics is essential to success in student teaching as well as in full-time teaching.

Some of your teacher qualities are rooted in your basic personality pattern; others are outgrowths of your educational experiences. Regardless of whether your various characteristics are innate or acquired, they can be improved as a result of intelligent and serious application to your student-teaching obligations.

In the following, we list some of the essentials of good teaching. No attempt has been made to arrange the items in rank order, since all of them are significant. As you begin your student-teaching activities, try to assess your strong and weak points and resolve to achieve whatever improvement you believe to be needed. Be honest in your self-evaluation. "Know thyself" is an excellent motto to follow.

Interest in young people. Adolescents are extremely sensitive to adults' attitudes toward them. They seem to be able to recognize whether a teacher likes them and is concerned about their welfare. They respect the teacher who gives evidence of understanding them and their whims and foibles and who, patiently but firmly, attempts to encourage them to maintain high standards of conduct.

What is your attitude toward young people? Do you like them? Can you appreciate their problems of growing up? Have you a sincere desire to help them achieve the adult status toward which they are struggling? Are you perhaps somewhat afraid of them, believing that any uncooperative behavior displayed by them is aimed at you personally rather than a symptom of the adolescent urge for independence of action? The attitude you display in your dealings with secondary school students exercises a tremendous effect upon your degree of success as a teacher.

Knowledge of subject matter. How well-grounded are you in the content of the subject or subjects you are preparing yourself to teach? Are you enthusiastic about it or them and eager to share your enthusiasm with your students? Do you believe that you will be able to present the learning material so clearly and succinctly that young people will enjoy studying and will benefit from their learning experience?

It usually does not take long for secondary school students to evaluate their teacher's mastery of and attitude toward his subject. They know whether he is attempting to "bluff" his way through the presentation of a teaching unit because he is not sure of his facts. They judge his teaching in light of his ability to answer questions dealing with the subject that go beyond the requirements of the assigned unit of study. They are quick to discover whether the teacher enjoys teaching the subject or regards teaching as a chore.

We have stressed the fact that you should know your subject matter thoroughly. You need to be careful, however, that your mastery of the advanced phases of your subject has not caused you to forget the difficulties that can be present in the early stages of its study. Too often one hears students complain that a certain teacher knows so much about a subject that in his presentation of it to students he is not able to get down to their level of little or no acquaintance with it. It is important to present material on the learning level of the students.

Be careful not to become impatient with the apparent inability of learners to grasp the rudimentary principles that are involved. This often is the experience of beginning teachers. You can learn much about presenting subject matter as you observe skilled teachers in action.

Personal qualities needed for successful teaching. First impressions are important in the classroom. On your first day as a student teacher, you probably will come to a conclusion—either right or wrong—about the groups of students you are meeting. The young people too will be "sizing you up." They will respond favorably or unfavorably to your clothing, hairdo, voice, and manner. They tend to be severe critics. You need to behave properly to feel confident that you will meet this first test.

As you continue your student-teaching activities, you will give evidence of other personal characteristics that can affect the attitude toward you of those with whom you will be working. In Chapter 2, we discuss the assessment of teacher effectiveness. Hence, at this point, we shall do no more than list a few questions that you can use as a guide toward evaluating some of your personal characteristics as they may be rated by others.

1. Are your clothes appropriate and becoming?
2. Do you keep your clothes well pressed, clean and free from body odors, and your shoes shined and in good repair?
3. Is your hair neatly arranged, free from dandruff, and frequently washed?
4. Are your nails carefully manicured and your skin free from blemishes?
5. If you are a woman, do you avoid the excessive use of cosmetics?
6. Do you have an upright posture and a free-swinging walk?
7. Are your teeth in good condition, and is your breath free from unpleasant odors?

8. Is your voice resonant, distinct, clear, and properly modulated?
9. Do you have an adequate vocabulary, pronounce words distinctly, and employ correct English?
10. Do you avoid affected mannerisms, grimaces, loud laughter, and other unpleasant behavior habits?
11. Are you reliable? Can you be counted on to meet your obligations adequately and on time?
12. Have you a good sense of humor?
13. Do you regard yourself as patient, cheerful, and cooperative in your relations with other people?
14. Do you believe that students should be treated impartially but with kindness and consideration?
15. Are you prepared to maintain a democratic attitude in the classroom?

You may find it difficult to answer all of these questions in the affirmative. As you pass through student teaching experiences, keep them in mind and work toward effecting any improvement in your personal characteristics that seem to be necessary to achieving success in the classroom.

Your Attitude toward Criticism

You know that your student-teaching activities will be supervised by your college supervisor and your cooperating teacher. At times, a member of the administrative staff will observe you in action. What do you think your reaction will be to critical evaluations of you and your work?

When you are trying your best to succeed in an endeavor, it sometimes is disheartening to find that someone else is not completely satisfied with the results obtained. This situation is one that you may experience often during your neophyte days as a teacher. You are not perfect—no one is. No matter how sincere you are in your desire to do a good job, you still have much to learn about the many practical aspects of teaching. Constructive criticism of your activities is essential to your growth as a teacher.

Your attitude toward supervisory criticism will vary in light of your own evaluation of your purposes and behavior. You will accept some criticism without question, recognizing its validity. In some instances, you may believe that an unsatisfactory criticism is too harsh, that the critic did not fully realize what you were trying to accomplish.

A supervisory criticism may give evidence of serious divergence between educational points of view. This situation sometimes occurs when a student teacher attempts to apply educational principles learned in the college classroom. These principles may differ from those applied to the situation by a cooperating teacher. A conference in which the difference of opinion is aired can help clear the air in a situation of this kind. The two of you may find that you are not so far apart as you had thought when each clearly understands what the other had in mind.

Regardless of its emotional effect on you at the time, you should welcome constructive criticism and learn from it. It is important that you begin early to assess your strengths and weaknesses. A supervisor who is called upon to evaluate your work probably will find much to commend in what you do. He, thereby, is emphasizing your strengths. Cherish these comments. At the same time, heed well his suggestions for improvement. They are the foundation blocks upon which is built the structure of effective teaching.

When You Begin Your Student Teaching

You probably are beginning your student-teaching experience with ambivalent feelings. You are about to play a new educational role. In the past, you have been concerned with your own academic achievements; now you are about to take some responsibility for the academic achievement of others.

You probably are looking forward eagerly to practical participation in your chosen profession. You may believe (wrongly, of course) that to the present you have been no more than a passive recipient of educational materials and that now you will be actively engaged in proving yourself. Many young men and women tend to regard student teaching as the most, if not the only, professional experience that has value in teacher education. They underplay and misevaluate their previous study in the field.

College students often do not recognize the fact that mastery of theory is essential to effective practice. As you attempt to meet your student-teaching obligations, you will find yourself applying the principles of education that you learned in the college classroom.

In addition, no matter how interested you are in beginning your student teaching, you probably are approaching it with some degree of apprehension. You want to succeed in it, but it is a new experience. You may have doubts concerning your ability to meet adequately all the requirements of this period of training. An apprehensive attitude is not unusual and should not be regarded as undesirable. In fact, a little cautious fear may motivate you toward better achievement.

As you begin your student teaching, a certain amount of humility in your approach to the situation can indicate a degree of sensitivity that will serve you well as you continue your teaching efforts. Moreover, as a student teacher you are not entirely on your own. Experienced college and school personnel are prepared to help you as you encounter rough spots. In addition, a careful reading of this book and an intelligent application of its suggestions can aid you further in your preparation for teaching.

QUESTIONS AND TOPICS FOR DISCUSSION

1. Ask your college supervisor or another college instructor what he considers to be the chief function of student teaching. How does his opinion compare with what is said in this chapter?
2. On what bases have you been assigned to student teaching? Would you have prepared another plan? Why or why not?
3. With how many of the items listed on page 15 were you acquainted when you started your student teaching? How did you acquire the information?
4. If you have decided on the state in which you wish to teach, consult Table 1 for the requirements for teaching in that state. To what extent are you fulfilling those requirements?
5. What is your present attitude toward the teaching procedures utilized in your school? How do you plan to adjust to them?
6. What prestudent teaching experiences with young people have you had? How can these help you now? Be specific.
7. Why did you select teaching as a career? Be honest in your answer.
8. Assess your personal qualities according to the list on page 18. In which of them do you believe you need improvement? What can you do about them?

SELECTED REFERENCES

BROWN, T. J. *Student Teaching in a Secondary School.* New York: Harper & Row, Pub., Inc., 1960.

———. *Guiding a Student Teacher.* New York: Harper & Row, Pub., Inc., 1960.

CARTER, W. L., HANSEN, C. W., and MCKIM, M. G. *Learning To Teach in the Secondary School.* New York: Macmillan Co., 1962.

GRIM, P. R., and MICHAELIS, J. U. (eds.). *The Student Teacher in the Secondary School.* Englewood Cliffs, N.J.: Prentice-Hall, Inc., 1953.

HAINES, A. C. "Role Dilemma in Teaching," *Journal of Teacher Education,* 1957, pp. 365–68.

SCHORLING, R., and BATCHELDER, H. T. *Student Teaching in the Secondary Schools* (2nd ed.). New York: McGraw-Hill Book Co., Inc., 1956.

SCHULTZ, R. *Student Teaching in the Secondary Schools.* New York: Harcourt, Brace & World, Inc., 1959.

STEEVES, F. L. *You'll Have Fun in Student Teaching.* Minneapolis, Minn.: Burgess Pub. Co., 1955.

WIGGINS, C. P. *The Student Teacher in Action.* Boston: Allyn & Bacon, Inc., 1957.

2

THE EFFECTIVE TEACHER

During your years in school, you have met various kinds of teachers. Some you will remember for many years, either because you liked them very much or because you disliked them intensely. Others you have forgotten or will soon forget since your attitude toward them was neutral; they made little or no impression on you.

YOUR IMPRESSION OF GOOD TEACHING

Try this little project. Jot down the names of those secondary school teachers whom you remember well. How do you explain the fact that these names come to your memory so quickly? Check the names of those teachers who leave pleasant memories. Cross the names of those teachers in whose classes you were not happy. What is at the root of your evaluation of these men and women? What were the differentiating characteristics?

Select one teacher who might serve as a model of the kind of teacher you would like to be. Do you have any reservations about the person you have chosen? You realize, of course, that what you have just done is to evaluate those qualities that make for a good or a poor teacher, according to your personal standards of what constitutes teaching competence.

The personal and professional attitudes and behavior of teachers probably have already been discussed in some of your college education courses. You have formed some conclusions concerning the kind of teacher you would like to be. You also have answered the questions about yourself as a potential teacher that appear in Chapter 1. Now you are having an opportunity to observe secondary school teachers in action as you meet them and work with them during your student-teaching experiences. Perhaps what we say in this chapter will enable you better to discriminate between a more or less effective teacher.

PRESENT CONCERN ABOUT TEACHING COMPETENCE

The educational facilities available to young people are matters of extreme importance to all of the citizens of the United States. In our fifty states as well as in our many local communities, more and more financial support is being made available to schools. The federal government is allocating an increasing amount of money to meet evidenced educational needs throughout the country.

Curriculum modifications and special programs are being constructed by school people to provide for the special schooling needs and interests of our large and diverse school population. Moreover, it is being recognized that the achieving of worthwhile educational results depends not only on the content of school offerings but also on the teaching skill by which young people are motivated to learn. Hence teachers, buildings and equipment, and learning materials are important if learners are to be helped to develop their capacities to the fullest.

The Importance of the Teacher

The present century is notable for the interest displayed by educators and the lay public in attempts to find an answer to the question: Who is an effective teacher? Many informal and more formal studies have been conducted to ascertain the attributes of apparently successful leaders of young people's learning. The significance of the teacher in the complex totality of the teaching-learning process cannot be minimized. We quote:

A good teacher and the quality of his teaching have always been of paramount importance to free men and to a free society. As society increases in complexity and as the concept of democracy strikes a responsive note in the culture of peoples throughout the world, the need for good teaching is accentuated. This need can be met only as we draw on our warehouse of research findings to improve teacher competence everywhere.[1]

[1] From "Foreword" in *Who's A Good Teacher?* written by Anita Ruffing, President, NEA Department of Classroom Teachers; Theodore C. Sargent, President, National School Boards Association; Benjamin C. Willis, President, American Association of School Administrators, in *Who's A Good Teacher?* eds. W. J. Ellena, M. Stevenson, and H. V. Webb (Washington, D.C.: American Association of School Administrators, Department of Classroom Teachers of the NEA, and National School Boards Association, 1961).

The many studies of teacher efficiency that have been conducted during the present century (and earlier) have been affected somewhat by the purposes and points of view of those who undertook the particular study. You, as a beginner in the teaching field, want to know what you should be and do to earn success in the profession. Administrators, students and parents, and other members of the lay public have specific goals in mind as they attempt to discover what constitutes effective teaching. Let us analyze briefly some of these specific purposes.

Qualities administrators want in teachers. Although certain educational principles can be applied generally to all learning situations, each school community is likely to present teaching-learning conditions that differ somewhat from those of other communities. Educational needs may differ from school to school, especially in large urban communities. Hence administrative personnel, such as superintendents, principals, and other men and women associated with school administration and supervision tend to evaluate teacher services in light of the educational needs of their districts and schools.

Administrators of secondary schools want teachers who are well-grounded in the content of the subject that they are teaching. They expect their teachers to understand and like adolescents and have the ability to earn the respect and cooperation of their students. Administrators also appreciate teachers who can get along amicably with their colleagues, and who are willing to submit intelligently to constructive supervisory evaluation of their teaching efficiency.

In the modern secondary school, a teacher's responsibilities go beyond the immediate classroom. He is expected to participate in out-of-class school activities, to establish a good relationship with parents, and to be actively interested in community welfare. Administrators approve of the teacher who is able to meet the more or less noninstructional aspects of his total teaching responsibilities.

An important duty of a school administrator or supervisor is to rate or assess the efficiency of his teachers. He can do this by (1) observing a teacher functioning in the classroom, (2) evaluating, by means of standardized or school-constructed tests, the progress in learning achievement of the teacher's students, and (3) alerting himself to the attitudes displayed toward a teacher by students, their parents, and other persons within and outside the school with whom the teacher is professionally associated.

It is evident that an administrator's evaluation of teacher competence is influenced by his own concept of what a good teacher is like in his particular school or school system. We need further to keep in mind that an administrator or supervisor, like any other human being, can be influenced in his rating of teacher effectiveness by personal bias or prejudice. His evaluation also can be affected by his own earlier experiences as a teacher.

Community attitudes toward teaching and teachers. Many teachers are dedicated members of their profession. They are sincere in their desire to meet the demands of teaching as effectively as is possible for them to do. Their difficulty is that they do not always understand fully what is expected of them. They are sensitive to students' attitudes toward them, to administrative criticism of their activities, and to public opinion concerning their status in society. They cannot help resenting such popular evaluations of their worth as "Those who can, do; those who cannot, teach."

Attitudes toward teachers vary with communities. Among some of our communities, the teacher is treated with great respect. In fact, he may be regarded as a superior being who can bring about all the desirable changes in their children that they themselves cannot effect.

In larger cities, the teacher has not always been accepted as a worthy member of the community. Rather was he regarded as a kind of public servant who should be willing to subsist on a low living wage and be subservient to the will of community leaders. It is no wonder that many teachers of the past found it difficult to maintain self-respect and evaluate rightly their teaching effectiveness.

Fortunately, with increased public emphasis on the value of continued education for American youth has come a new appreciation of the part played by the teacher in the educational progress of young people. Earlier community restrictions on the social activities, for example, of a teacher have gradually been withdrawn, and teacher salaries are increasing. The teacher is coming to be a respected member of most community groups. This general change in attitude toward teachers and teaching has helped the members of the profession to view themselves as solid citizens who have a worthwhile contribution to make to society.

Qualities teachers want to possess. Their newly won status often makes it increasingly difficult for teachers to assess objectively the qualities that are essential to efficiency on the job. In too many communities, school programs are set up by lay and professional "higher ups," and the classroom teacher is expected to follow a curriculum, for example, which, in light of his teaching experience, is inadequate or inappropriate. How well can he function in a situation of this kind? What are the teacher qualities needed by him to perform effectively? The teacher does not know—he is confused. His one hope is that eventually he may be included among members of a planning committee for school programs, as is now the situation in some progressive school systems.

It is satisfying for a teacher to be afforded an opportunity to discover the extent to which he has the ability to work effectively in an educational framework that he has helped to erect. Yet, since the master teacher is likely to have set high standards of accomplishment for himself, more often than not he is unsatisfied with his work; he tries in various ways to motivate young people to want to learn.

The serious-minded teacher thrills to his successes, but becomes depressed if he believes that he has failed in his endeavors. More and more, teachers are evincing a serious interest in research concerning teacher effectiveness and are attempting to rate themselves honestly on the various teacher rating scales that are being made available for their use.

Attitudes of students toward teachers. Secondary school students differ in their attitudes toward teachers. Many adolescents take their teachers for granted. During the growing-up years, a teen-age girl may become emotionally involved with a woman teacher who usually is young, who possesses personal characteristics that are admired by the girl, and who gives evidence of liking the student. The girl attempts to imitate the favorite teacher's dress and manners, and in various ways call the teacher's attention to herself. An adolescent boy may develop a strong liking for a male teacher, especially his physical education teacher, and try to model his own attitudes and behavior according to those of the teacher. You, as an enthusiastic and outgoing student teacher, may be faced with the problem of striving to develop a friendly but objective relationship between yourself and some young people. You are young enough that members of the opposite sex may become emotionally involved. You will need to be objective and meet this situation in such a way as not to hurt the student.

In general, secondary school students have a favorable attitude toward teachers in whose classes they are earning academic success. Even though adolescents approve of their teacher, they are likely to refer to him or her among their friends by a term other than his correct name, and mimic certain personal characteristics. For example, Miss Beckwith, a teacher of social studies who was liked by most of her students, was known in private among these adolescents as "Becky, the Third, of England." They also derived much fun from imitating her manner of looking at them over her eyeglasses. Yet, these young people defended her staunchly if anyone attempted to criticize her adversely.

Qualities of teachers preferred by students. When students are asked to list the characteristics that they would like a teacher to possess, they usually include all or most of the following traits:

Interest in students	Ability to control class
Patience	Sincerity
Adaptability	Enthusiasm and cheerfulness
Knowledge of subject matter	Friendliness
Good organization of subject matter	Consideration of others
Daily preparation	Tactfulness
Attention to the needs of individuals	Cooperation
	Sense of justice
Stimulation of thought	Sense of humor
	Impartiality

You will notice that many of these characteristics have to do with human relationships. The rank order of these characteristics varies with student groups. Adolescents rarely approve of the easy-going, overly-permissive teacher or the teacher who "plays favorites." Even though the adolescent may seem to want independence from adult control, he has little respect for the teacher who disregards or overlooks displays of youthful whims.

Among the studies made to determine teacher traits liked and disliked by students is one in which many senior high school students participated. This study, made by Frank W. Hart,[2] revealed some of the reasons given by high school seniors for liking and for disliking their teachers. The three most important reasons given for liking "Teacher A" best were in the area of helpfulness, cheerfulness, and friendliness. Reasons given for liking "Teacher Z" least are in the area of personal attitude toward students, failure to help with schoolwork, and display of favoritism.

Results of a more recent study of student ratings of teacher personality reveal the data presented in Table 2. These results include the weighted opinion of both men students and of women students.

Interest in school by parents and other community members. In general, parents tend to be very much interested in the elementary schools that their children attend. For many years, Parents Associations have worked in close cooperation with elementary school people. These groups have been active in assisting principals and teachers in furthering their children's early education. Class mothers have served in various ways to lighten teachers' work. Parents also show concern about teacher attitudes, characteristics, and behavior.

Up to the recent past, parents have not been displaying a similar interest in the schools attended by their adolescent sons and daughters. The purpose of the secondary school was accepted as the inculcation of subject matter. The teacher's main function was regarded to be that of seeing to it that the adolescent mastered learning material. Too many parents whose sons and daughters were not achieving successfully blamed the teacher for youthful failure in schoolwork. Hence a teacher was rated "good" or "poor" in light of the academic success of the student.

Fortunately, school people have become increasingly able to convince parents that secondary schools are concerned with various aspects of adolescent development in addition to the mastery of subject matter. The school and the home have been brought closer together as teachers, guidance counselors, and administrative personnel have given evidence of their interest in students' physical and mental health, social adjustment, and vocational planning.

[2] Frank W. Hart, *Teachers and Teaching by Ten Thousand High-School Seniors* (New York: Macmillan Co., 1934), pp. 250–51.

TABLE 2

Five Factors Obtained from the Student Evaluations in the Spring of 1961 and the Item Which Loaded Highly on Them *

Factor and Item	Loading	
	Men students	Women students
I. Skill		
Put materials across in interesting way	.863	.847
All-around teaching ability	.818	.859
Stimulated intellectual curiosity	.755	.812
Explained things clearly and concisely	.782	.706
Skillful in observing student reactions	.568	.645
Changed approach to meet new situations	.689	.674
Tried to increase interest of class in subject	.640	.487
Class time well spent	.626	.674
Made clear how each topic fit into course	.561	.471
Overall value of course	.341	.589
Explained why he did things	.556	.442
Anticipated difficulties before they arose	.572	.550
Improved ability to understand deviant individuals	.534	.423
Improved ability to deal with personal problems	.485	.528
Was aware when students failed to keep up	.281	.348
Explained reasons for his criticism	.560	.463
High degree of cultural attainment	.574	.568
II. Overload		
Assigned a great amount of reading	.704	.666
Assigned difficult reading	.679	.699
Asked for more than students could get done	.537	.675
III. Structure		
Planned class activities in detail	.585	.727
Had everything going on schedule	.613	.698
Followed an outline closely	.645	.680
Decided in detail what and how things should be done	.417	.598
IV. Student Rapport		
Invited criticisms of his acts	.463	.250
Told students when they had done a good job	.428	.366
Complimented students in front of others	.424	.490
Able to get personal help in course	.315	.199
Improved ability to deal with personal problems	.184	.322
Criticized poor work	−.006	.225
Was sensitive to students' desire to ask questions	−.010	−.016
Anticipated difficulties before they arose	.283	.171
Permissive and flexible	.075	.108

* Robert L. Isaacson, Wilbert J. McKeachie, and John E. Milholland, "Correlation of Teacher Personality Variabilities and Student Ratings," *Journal of Educational Psychology,* April, 1963, p. 114.

TABLE 2 (*Cont.*)

Factor and Item	Loading	
	Men Students	Women Students
V. Group Interaction		
Students argued with each other and instructor without hostility	.383	.486
Students frequently volunteered own opinions	.302	.494
Students felt free to express own opinions	.556	.280
Students were friendly	.384	.189
Instructor was aware when students failed to keep up	.425	.012

Interest of parents in good teachers. Parents have begun to assume a more realistic point of view toward the men and women who teach their teen-age children. They recognize and appreciate the worth of the teacher who displays a sincere interest in young people, who can motivate them to profit from their school experiences, and who cooperates with parents in helping adolescents develop mature attitudes and behavior patterns.

There continues to be a growing appreciation among lay people of the value of high school and college education. Social expansion and technological advances are demanding that our young citizens achieve increasing "know-how" in many areas of activity. Hence communities are committing themselves to the task of providing the best possible education for their youth. Graduation from senior high school rather than from elementary school is being regarded as the completion of fundamental education.

This increasing interest in the nation's schools is accompanied by concern about the kind and number of teachers needed for the guidance of young people's learning. State and local communities demand that their teachers be persons who are interested in and understand their students, are well-grounded in subject matter, and find satisfaction in teaching.

Various approaches are utilized to insure the obtaining of competent teachers. The lay public is demanding that secondary school teachers, for example, receive an adequate preteaching education, increasing mastery of subject content, cultural backgrounds, and sufficient study in the field of teacher preparation to enable them to motivate adolescents' learning progress effectively. The majority of teacher trainees are educated in state and/or community-financed colleges and universities. Many communities also offer an in-service program aimed at alerting teachers to eductional changes and advances, and to ways of improving their teaching approaches and techniques.

Increasing birthrates, especially during the past twenty years, have resulted in a serious teacher shortage. Communities not only wish to procure well-trained beginning teachers but they also want to keep them. Hence, within their financial ability to do so, they gradually have been increasing teachers' salaries and in other ways are attempting to make teaching an attractive profession for ambitious and able young men and women.

Local boards of education, as well as educational leaders, recognize the fact that teaching is a complex, demanding vocational field. Consequently, they are cooperating in efforts to lighten the teacher's burdens. These include the provision of good pensions, hygienic teaching conditions, adequate supplies, helpful teaching aids, and other personal and social advantages.

Growing public concern with teachers and teaching is evidenced also in an increasing attempt to discover what constitutes teacher efficiency. Competent teachers are wanted; but who is a competent teacher? Public and private organizations are devoting considerable time, energy, and money to research projects in this field of investigation. Informal studies are giving way to attempts to measure objectively and scientifically those personal and professional attributes that differentiate the effective teacher from the less competent teacher.

DISTINGUISHING ASPECTS OF TEACHER COMPETENCE

As we have indicated earlier in the chapter, many investigations of teachers' personal and professional competencies have been constructed. We now shall consider the items included in some of these studies.

Lists of Teacher Qualities

If you were to analyze the many questionnaires that deal with teacher evaluation, you would find that certain broad areas of personal and professional characteristics appear on many of them. There is agreement among most researchers that the successful teacher has achieved proficiency in (1) guiding the learning process, (2) motivating students to learn, (3) improving teaching techniques, (4) encouraging young people to develop desirable attitudes, (5) encouraging young people to develop desirable behavior, and (6) developing those personal and social traits that are conducive to effective teaching.

As you read the foregoing list of six areas of teaching responsibilities, you might comment on them somewhat as follows: "I agree that these items represent important activities and attributes, but they do not indicate how they are to be achieved. How shall I guide or motivate students? What are 'desirable' attitudes? Which teaching techniques can or shall I improve? How do I know whether my particular traits are conducive to effective teaching?" These general fields need to be so analyzed that anyone rating a teacher's competence can apply them in practical situations.

It is desirable that all important areas of teacher competence be considered in the evaluation of teachers and teaching effectiveness. A teacher should display an understanding of learning procedures and know how to utilize them in the teaching function. The competent teacher should:

1. Understand the accepted principles of education and how to function within their framework.
2. Understand the areas for service and demonstrate ability to perform those services.
3. Understand the value of planning and of using those plans in his teaching.
4. Understand the principles of healthy living and how to apply those principles to his teaching.
5. Understand adolescent development and how to adapt his teaching accordingly.

6. Understand differences among individuals and how to meet these individual differences in his teaching.
7. Understand the guidance function and how to apply its principles in the education of adolescents.
8. Understand teaching-learning material and how to present this material to his learners.
9. Understand the function of extracurricular activities and what he can do to incorporate them into his teaching.
10. Understand the nature and use of evaluation in the education of students.
11. Understand the interrelating functions of the community and the school in the education of students.
12. Understand the utilization of audio-visual and other aids in the teaching-learning situation.

It will be noted that in the construction of this list an attempt was made to explain the connotation of each general aim by means of its possible applications.

Significant studies of teacher characteristics. A well-known investigator of the literature dealing with teacher characteristics was A. S. Barr, who, before his death, was at the University of Wisconsin. Barr found that, in general, constructors of lists of teacher characteristics tend to use three differing approaches:

1. Personal qualities.
2. Behavior of the teacher.
3. The teacher's knowledge, special skills and attitudes.[3]

In his discussion of "Characteristics of Successful Teachers," Barr presents the following succinct points of view:

When one attempts to describe the successful teacher in terms of personal qualities one is confronted with an overwhelming wealth of descriptive terms. One of the problems that confronts the worker in this field is to telescope and organize these many qualities to a more manageable shorter list. Several years ago the author proposed some twelve qualities, as follows:

[3] See A. S. Barr "The Measurement and Prediction of Teacher Efficiency: A Summary of Investigations," *Journal of Experimental Education*, XVI (June, 1948), 202–8; and A. S. Barr, "Characteristics of Successful Teachers," *Phi Delta Kappan* (March, 1958), pp. 282–84.

1. *Resourcefulness*
Originality, creativeness, initiative, versatility, imagination, adventurousness, progressiveness.
2. *Intelligence*
Foresight, judgment, intellectual acuity, understanding, mental ability, intellectual capacity, common sense.
3. *Emotional Stability*
Poise, self-control, steadfastness, sobriety, reserve, dignity, non-neuroticism, emotional maturity, adjustment, constancy, loyalty, easy-going realism in facing life, not excitable, stable, integrated character.
4. *Considerateness*
Appreciativeness, kindliness, friendliness, courteousness, sympathy, tact, good-naturedness, helpfulness, patience, politeness, thoughtfulness, tolerance.
5. *Buoyancy*
Optimism, enthusiasm, cheerfulness, gregariousness, fluency, talkativeness, sense of humor, pleasantness, carefreeness, vivaciousness, alertness, animation, idealism, articulativeness, expressiveness, wit.
6. *Objectivity*
Fairness, impartiality, open-mindedness, freedom from prejudice, sense of evidence.
7. *Drive*
Physical vigor, energy, perseverance, ambition, industry, endurance, motivation, purposefulness, speediness, zealousness, quickness.
8. *Dominance*
Self-confidence, forcefulness, decisiveness, courageousness, independence, insensitiveness to social approval, self-sufficiency, determination, thick-skinnedness, self-reliance, self-assertiveness.
9. *Attractiveness*
Dress, physique, freedom from physical defects, personal magnetism, neatness, cleanliness, posture, personal charm, appearance.
10. *Refinement*
Good taste, modesty, morality, conventionality, culture, polish, well-readness.
11. *Cooperativeness*
Friendliness, easy-goingness, geniality, generosity, adaptability, flexibility, responsiveness, trustfulness, warm-heartedness, unselfishness, charitableness.
12. *Reliability*
Accuracy, dependability, honesty, punctuality, responsibility, conscientiousness, painstakingness, trustworthiness, consistency, sincerity. . . .
There are hundreds of illustrative behaviors associated with buoyancy. Only five illustrations have been given here.
If one considers the successful teacher from the point of view of observable behaviors, one might center attention upon items such as:

1. Behaviors associated with identifying pupil needs.
2. Behaviors associated with setting and defining goals.

3. Behaviors associated with creating favorable mind sets and motivation.
4. Behaviors associated with choosing learning experiences.
5. Behaviors associated with providing for individual differences.
6. Behaviors associated with making activities meaningful.
7. Behaviors associated with the analysis and organization of learning experiences.
8. Behaviors associated with the direction of group activities.
9. Behaviors associated with the use of learning aids.
10. Behaviors associated with teacher-pupil relations.
11. Behaviors associated with the evaluation of pupil growth and achievement.

Much has been written on all the above items. It is not enough to list them. They must be defined, preferably in an operational way.

A third approach to the characteristics of the successful teacher is through the knowledges, attitudes, and special skills that teachers need to be considered competent. Among the knowledges there are four that are usually listed as essential to successful teaching:

1. Good cultural background.
2. Substantial knowledge of the subject taught, or of some area of specialization.
3. Substantial knowledge of human development and learning.
4. Substantial knowledge of professional practices and techniques.

Among the generalized skills the following are frequently emphasized:

1. Skill in the use of language, spoken and written.
2. Skill in human relationships.
3. Skill in research and educational problem-solving.
4. Effective work habits.

Among the interests and attitudes frequently emphasized are the following:

1. Interest in pupil.
2. Interest in a subject or area of specialization.
3. Interest in teaching.
4. Interest in the school and the community.
5. Interest in professional cooperation.
6. Interest in professional growth.[4]

Note carefully the various items on Barr's list. Ask someone who knows you well to give you some idea where you stand in reference to the teacher traits mentioned. Note the traits on which you are

[4] A. S. Barr, "Characteristics of Successful Teachers," *Phi Delta Kappan* (March, 1958), pp. 282–84.

not considered to be very proficient. Discuss with the rater the reasons for the evaluations given. Do you find it difficult to accept adverse comments? It probably was not easy for your friend to give you an honest appraisal of what he considers to be your strong and weak characteristics for teaching. This experience should be helpful to you when later you are officially rated by your supervisors.

We need not remind you that when supervisors rate you, their judgments are based on your observable modes of behavior. You need constantly to be aware of the kind of impression you are making on those with whom you work. Moreover, it is practically impossible for a rater to be completely objective. Personal interest or bias is likely to affect the evaluation of a teacher by a supervisor.

It is essential that, as a student teacher and as a regular teacher, you engage in periodic self-analysis. The following teacher self-rating scale can be utilized by you as a means of discovering to what extent and in what ways you meet some of the requirements of effective teaching. From time to time, refer to this checklist. Note the items that seem to indicate the need of self-improvement. Consult your supervisors for help in determining what you can and should do to bring about needed improvement in any area of competence.

Differentiation among Teacher Trait Values

Various possible aspects of teaching competence are included in the many lists of teacher characteristics that now are available. It probably is a fact that the possession of these characteristics contributes to teaching effectiveness, yet it also is probable that some qualities and behavior reactions are more valuable as predictors of teacher competence than are others.

More than a quarter of a century ago, a study of teacher qualities was completed that attempted to distinguish between the more significant and the less significant of fifty traits as having predictive value in rating teacher effectiveness.

Each of sixty supervisors, two hundred teachers, and three hundred fifty student teachers rated two excellent and two ineffective

TABLE 3
TEACHER SELF-RATING SCALE *

(Directions: For each item, place a check in the appropriate column.)

NAME_____

	Low	Average			High
PERSONAL QUALITIES	1	2	3	4	5
Accuracy					
Adaptability					
Cheerfulness					
Cooperativeness					
Dependability					
Desire for self-improvement					
Effective use of English and voice					
Emotional stability					
Enthusiasm					
Forcefulness					
Friendliness					
Good health					
Good judgment					
Honesty					
Industriousness					
Interest in community affairs					
Interest in teaching					
Kindness					
Loyalty					
Neatness					
Open-mindedness					
Optimism					
Patience					
Resourcefulness					
School spirit					
Sense of humor					
Sense of justice					
Sincerity					
Sociability					
Tactfulness					
GUIDANCE OF LEARNING	1	2	3	4	5
Ability to develop pupil self-control					
Ability to direct study					
Ability to maintain pupil interest					
Ability to measure pupil achievement					
Ability to sponsor out-of-class activities					
Ability to stimulate thinking					
Ability to meet individual needs					

* L. D. Crow, H. E. Ritchie, and Alice Crow, *Education in the Secondary School* (New York: American Book Co., 1961), p. 286. Reprinted with permission.

TABLE 3 *(Cont.)*

TEACHER SELF-RATING SCALE

(Directions: For each item, place a check in the appropriate column.)

NAME_____

	Low	Average			High
	1	2	3	4	5
UTILIZATION OF TEACHING MATERIALS					
Definiteness of aim					
Knowledge of community resources					
Knowledge of improved teaching techniques					
Knowledge of special teaching aids					
Knowledge of subject matter					
Organization of material					
Preparation of material					
School and class management					
Skill in making assignments					
Skill in motivating work					
Skill in questioning					

teachers they knew on each of the fifty listed items using the following seven-point scale.

Almost totally lacking	Notice- ably below average	Slightly inferior to average	In no way unusual	Notice- ably superior	Unusually superior	Nothing left to be desired
1	2	3	4	5	6	7

A rater might be so enthusiastic about an excellent teacher that he would rate him 7 in each item (a total of 350 points) or disapprove so heartily of a poor teacher that he would rate him no more than 1 in each item (total 50 points). Since no one tends to be perfect in all characteristics and no one probably is almost totally lacking in them, the raters were limited to a total of 275 points for the excellent teacher and 125 points for the poor teacher. These limitations compelled the rater to place special emphasis on those traits that in his estimation were the most predictive, thereby understressing relatively unimportant items.

The fifty items then were arranged in rank order, according to the *point divergence* between respective arithmetic means. The greatest divergence between judgments of exceptional and poor teachers was 3.51 (*Ability to develop pupil's self-control*) and 1.96 (*Health*). These figures can be interpreted to mean that the raters considered the *Ability to develop pupil's self-control* as the most significant difference between the excellent teacher and the ineffective teacher, and *Health* as the least predictive.

According to the findings, the ten most significant and the ten least significant items are given in Table 4.

TABLE 4

THE TEN MOST IMPORTANT AND THE TEN LEAST IMPORTANT TRAITS TO DIFFERENTIATE GOOD FROM POOR TEACHERS

Most Significant Traits	Least Significant Traits
1. Ability to develop pupil's self-control	41. Interest in community
2. Personal influence	42. Punctuality, attendance
3. Ability to teach how to study	43. Intellectual capacity
4. Enthusiasm	44. Posture
5. Ability to stimulate thinking	45. Voice
6. Skill in questioning	46. Use of English
7. Ability to discipline	47. Care of light, heat, etc.
8. Ability to motivate students	48. Economy of using material
9. Definite aim	49. Dress
10. Care of individual needs	50. Health

Correct interpretation of these data is very important. One should not conclude that the last ten qualities are unimportant. They are, but, by comparison, they are not so significant as the first ten in distinguishing between the competent and the less competent teacher.

We shall illustrate our point. A teacher should have good health, but most teachers do, regardless of the quality of their teaching. Of course, a teacher should possess superior intelligence. However, a young person having inferior or mediocre mental ability would scarcely be able to achieve successfully in his many years of study before he becomes a teacher. Similarly, good posture, proper dress, correct use of English, and pleasantness of voice are attributes that result from general educational experiences. A teacher's interest in the school community is desirable, but may have comparatively little effect upon his efficiency in the classroom. You will notice also that the ten most significant characteristics are closely associated with individual attitudes and behavior.

This early study and others like it that have been conducted through the years indicate the direction being taken by recent research in this area. The three national associations, mentioned earlier, expressed a similar point of view in *Who's a Good Teacher?* The traits listed in this publication as being closely associated with teacher competence include:

> . . . intelligence, knowledge of subject matter, scholarship, educational background, age and experience, professional knowledge, cultural background, socio-economic background, teaching attitude and interest, and voice and speech characteristics.[5]

The authors then proceed to assess the relationship of each of these traits with observable teacher success. They conclude their discussion of effectiveness as an elusive quality with this statement:

> In most of the studies of unsuccessful teachers, poor maintenance of discipline and lack of cooperation tend to be found as the chief causes of failure. Health, educational background, preparation, age, and knowledge of subject matter, on the other hand, appear to be relatively unimportant factors in terms of teacher failure.[6]

In light of what is now known, educators might wish to give different weights to different items in evaluating teacher competence. If we turn to the fifty items used to discover the differences between "good" and "poor" teachers and consider how each might be weighted in the evaluation of teachers, we would be able to construct a scale that might be meaningful. We present a teacher rating scale with appropriate weights assigned to each item on the scale. In this type of scale, provision for only three evaluations (Poor–1) (Average–2) (Good–3) is sufficient to arrive at the index for each teacher. This approach, if adopted, would make it possible to compare one teacher with another by use of a single index.

[5] W. J. Ellena *et al., op. cit.,* p. 22.
[6] *Ibid.,* p. 26.

TABLE 5
WEIGHTED RATING SCALE FOR TEACHERS

Student's Name_____	Poor	Average	Good	Weight	Total
Trait for Evaluation	1	2	3		
Ability to develop pupil's self-control				2.5	
Personal influence					
Ability to teach how to study					
Enthusiasm					
Ability to stimulate thinking					
Skill in questioning					
Ability to discipline					
Ability to motivate students					
Definite aim					
Care of individual needs					
Ability to develop good habits				2.0	
Ability to understand the learner					
Attention to responses of pupils					
General growth					
Adaptability					
Skill in making assignments					
Interest in pupils					
Ability to organize subject matter					
Growth in subject					
Cheerfulness					
Ability to be tactful					
Choice of subject matter					
Practice of self-control					
Ability to be sympathetic				1.5	
Sincerity					
Sense of justice					
Attention to health of pupils					
Daily preparation					
Initiative, self-reliance					
Ability to cooperate					
Professional interest					
Attention to punctuality of pupils					
Sense of humor					
Accuracy					
Industry					
Interest in school					
Grasp of subject matter					
Care of routine					
Attention to neatness of room					
Promptness with reports					

TABLE 5 (*Cont.*)

WEIGHTED RATING SCALE FOR TEACHERS

Student's Name_____ Trait for Evaluation	Poor	Average	Good	Weight	Total
Interest in community	___	___	___	1.0	___
Punctuality, attendance	___	___	___		___
Intellectual capacity	___	___	___		___
Posture	___	___	___		___
Voice	___	___	___		___
Use of English	___	___	___		___
Care of light, heat, ventilation	___	___	___		___
Economy of using material	___	___	___		___
Dress	___	___	___		___
Health	___	___	___		___

Total Index

CODE OF ETHICS FOR STUDENT TEACHERS

In order to assist student teachers to understand their professional responsibility, the California Student Teachers Assocation, in 1963, revised its *Code of Ethics for Students of Education.* We present it in this chapter along with the specific suggestions for implementing its provisions. Likewise, as a means of pinpointing a teacher's responsibility in relation to students, the community, and the profession, and to acquaint you with professional employment practices, the Committee on Professional Ethics of the National Education Association drew up the *Code of Ethics for the Education Profession* that appears in Chapter 16.

As you consult these codes you realize that basic to their construction are various teacher characteristics that have been stressed in the foregoing discussion. Each Code sets down in practical terminology those professional qualities that are important in effective teacher relationships. Note, especially, your responsibility to pupils, to the teacher education institution, to the profession, and to society as outlined in the "applications of the student teachers' code of ethics."

CODE OF ETHICS
STUDENT CALIFORNIA TEACHERS ASSOCIATION

A CODE FOR STUDENTS OF EDUCATION: The objectives of the Student of Education are to gain insight into teaching skills and to develop professional integrity; therefore, it is necessary that he accept these responsibilities:

RESPONSIBILITY TO THE PUPIL

The first consideration of the Student of Education is the welfare of his pupils and future pupils. He seeks to gain a firm foundation in all subject matter in order to make himself an informed, prepared person. As a Student Teacher he respects the judgment of and assists the Supervising Teacher in guiding the pupil toward mature responsibility in the school, the home, and the community.

RESPONSIBILITY TO THE TEACHER EDUCATION INSTITUTION

The Student of Education observes the professional and personal standards expected by his college and welcomes the guidance of its representatives. As a Student Teacher he becomes informed on and supports the policies of the school in which he is doing his Directed Teaching and develops satisfactory rapport with the Supervising Teacher and other personnel.

RESPONSIBILITY TO THE PROFESSION

The Student of Education strives to develop his professional skills and attitudes and maintains a constructive and cooperative relationship with his associates.

RESPONSIBILITY TO SOCIETY

The Student of Education recognizes the concern of society for the education of its youth and is ready to preserve the social heritage and promote the democratic way of life.

APPLICATIONS OF THE STUDENT TEACHERS' CODE OF ETHICS

The following applications of the preceding Code are designed to implement the interpretation of each of the four general responsibilities.

I. RESPONSIBILITY TO PUPILS

    1. The Student of Education, realizing that he has a responsibility to

his future pupils, prepares himself with a sound foundation in the liberal arts, as well as in his technical professional preparation.

2. The Student Teacher respects the confidence of a pupil; information given in confidence should be passed on only to authorized persons or agencies that are attempting to aid the pupil.
3. The Student Teacher is an example to his pupils physically, mentally, intellectually, morally, and ethically.
4. The Student Teacher refrains from indoctrinating his pupils with his religious or political views.
5. The Student Teacher recognizes the need for understanding child growth and development. On the basis of this understanding, he develops:
   a) a learning program oriented to the individual capacities of his pupils, and
   b) a social climate which encourages personal integrity and societal responsibility.
6. The Student Teacher deals sympathetically with each pupil without prejudice or partiality.

II. RESPONSIBILITY TO THE TEACHER EDUCATION INSTITUTION

1. Having established an affiliation as a student with a college, the Student of Education upholds its academic standards.
2. The Student of Education approaches all of his opportunities for academic and professional preparation with a constructive attitude.
3. The Student of Education appreciates the assistance of the school in which his student teaching is done.
4. Realizing that the supervising teacher is legally responsible for the class, the Student Teacher assumes only the authority which has been delegated to him.
5. The Student of Education respects the rights and the dignity of all members of the profession and conducts himself so that he is worthy of equal respect.

III. RESPONSIBILITY TO THE PROFESSION

1. The Student of Education shows pride in and considers himself a member of the profession and he acts according to professional ethics.
2. The Student of Education continues to inform himself about academic, professional, and current affairs.
3. The Student of Education is informed on the legal aspects of his profession.
4. The Student of Education includes the professional organization as an instrument for solving the problems related to education.
5. Placement: The Student Teacher

   a) uses only professional methods in obtaining a position.
   b) does not apply or underbid for a position held by a qualified teacher.
   c) will be honest in the statement of his competencies in order that the employing district may best utilize the prospective teacher's abilities.

IV. RESPONSIBILITY TO SOCIETY

   1. The Student of Education maintains an open mind toward the attitudes and activities of the community and takes an increasing interest in community life.
   2. The Student of Education assumes the responsibility of informing society of the purposes and activities of the American schools.

As you reflect on the material in this chapter, keep in mind that all of the qualities and attributes listed are important, but that some have a higher degree of significance in distinguishing between the good and the poor teacher than do others. You already possess many of the success-encouraging characteristics; others you are achieving through your teacher training experiences. Much that follows in this book can aid you in developing, through practice, whatever strengths you need to acquire.

QUESTIONS AND TOPICS FOR DISCUSSION

   1. Write a description of the teacher whose attitudes and behavior you would like to emulate when you are a teacher.
   2. What are some of the factors inherent in present-day concern about teaching and teachers?
   3. What do you think administrators can do to foster among teachers the teaching qualities they desire?
   4. What are the general attitudes toward teachers in your home community?
   5. Why do teachers find it difficult to meet present high standards of teaching?
   6. What were your relationships with your teachers when you were a secondary school student? Be specific.
   7. Reread the list of teacher qualities on page 42. Rearrange them according to your judgment of their importance.
   8. What was your parents' attitude toward your secondary school and your experiences in it?
   9. What evidences have you of an increased interest in education on the part of your home community or elsewhere?
   10. How well do you think you meet Barr's list of teacher characteristics?

11. In what ways can lack of cooperation militate against effective teaching? Illustrate.

SELECTED REFERENCES

ADAMS, H. P., and DICKEY, F. G. *Basic Principles of Student Teaching.* New York: American Book Co., 1951.

ALEXANDER, W. M., and HALVERSON, P. M. *Effective Teaching in Secondary Schools.* New York: Holt, Rinehart & Winston, Inc., 1956.

BARR, A. S. "The Measurement and Prediction of Teacher Efficiency," *Journal of Experimental Education,* June, 1948, pp. 202–8.

CARTER, W. L., HANSEN, C. W., and McKIM, M. G. *Learning to Teach in the Secondary School.* New York: Macmillan Co., 1962.

CROW, L. D., and CROW, ALICE. *Mental Hygiene for Teachers: A Book of Readings.* New York: Macmillan Co., 1963.

CROW, L. D., RITCHIE, H. E., and CROW, A. *Education in the Secondary School.* New York: American Book Co., 1961.

CURTIS, D. K., and ANDREWS, L. O. *Guiding Your Student Teacher.* Englewood Cliffs, N.J.: Prentice-Hall, Inc., 1954.

HASKEW, L. D., and McLENDON, J. C. *This Is Teaching* (rev. ed.). Chicago: Scott, Foresman & Co., 1962.

RICHEY, R. W. *Planning for Teaching* (3rd ed.). New York: McGraw-Hill Book Co., Inc., 1963.

MASON, W. S. *The Beginning Teacher: Status and Career Orientation.* Washington, D.C.: U.S. Department of Health, Education and Welfare, 1961.

THOMAS, L. G., KINNEY, L. B., COLADARCI, A. B., and FIELSTRA, H. A. *Perspective on Teaching.* Englewood Cliffs, N.J.: Prentice-Hall, Inc., 1961.

VAN DALEN, D. B., and BRITTELL, R. W. *Looking Ahead to Teaching.* Boston: Allyn & Bacon, Inc., 1959.

WIGGINS, S. P. *Successful High School Teaching.* Boston: Houghton Mifflin Co., 1958.

3

RELATIONSHIPS WITH YOUR STUDENTS

You are hoping that your student-teaching experiences will help prepare you to guide effectively the learning activities of secondary school boys and girls. You want to gain confidence in the ability to work cooperatively with the many young people whom you will be meeting in various school situations. In order to achieve your purpose, it is essential that you know something about them—their abilities, their likes, and dislikes; their attitudes toward themselves and toward other people; their aims and ambitions.

The college courses you have taken to this point probably included a course in adolescent psychology in which you traced the pattern of adolescent development and adjustment. Now you are beginning to work closely with these adolescents about whom you have studied. You find that no two adolescents are exactly alike.

You know as never before that each of your students has a unique personality. This fact requires that you (1) recognize the differences that exist among adolescents, (2) know how and to what exent your students differ from one another, and (3) learn how to deal effectively with the differing attitudes and behavior patterns that they exhibit. We now shall consider these three areas of student-teaching responsibilities that can help you achieve good relationships with your students.

THE DEVELOPING ADOLESCENT

People are prone to refer to a young person between the ages of about twelve and nineteen as a "typical adolescent." There is little, if any, truth in a statement of this kind. The one common experience of adolescents is that they all are passing through a period of growth from so-called childhood to adult maturity. The progress of this development varies from adolescent to adolescent and represents the emerging of traits or qualities either rooted in original nature or based on earlier childhood experiences.

Differences among Adolescents

Some adolescents are tall, others are short; some are physically robust, others are delicate; some are mentally superior, others have average intelligence, and still others are slow learners; some are rapid maturers, others mature slowly; some possess a rich experiential background, others have had meager social experiences.

Although young adolescents tend to be unsure of themselves and somewhat unstable emotionally, some are less insecure and unstable than others. With the passing of the teen years, most adolescents gain greater control of their emotions. Also, attitudes and appreciations gradually take on a more mature form of expression.

To a greater or lesser degree, young people experience problems of adjustment to their "in-between" status. They differ, however, in the ways in which they display some of the characteristics usually associated with this age period. Many adolescents tend to have strong loyalties; but there may be conflict, for example, between loyalty to adults, like parents and teachers, and the companionship of peer-age individuals or gangs. Social approval is important, but from whom—adults or other teen-agers? Adolescents often have ambivalent feelings toward adult control of their behavior. They have the urge to be independent, yet, in emergencies they need adult support and protection.

The Young Adolescent

Some young people pass through the early pubescent stage with relative ease. If they have been wisely prepared for the physical changes that they will experience, they can accept them in their stride and gradually acquire new interests and a wholesome degree of self-dependence. Other pubescents can become very much disturbed by the changes that are taking place within them. They come to realize suddenly that they no longer are children, but they are not quite certain what their present role should be.

Former interests and activities of young adolescents are spurned by them as "childish" or "silly." They begin to recognize within themselves a new attitude toward members of the opposite sex. The fact that girls tend to mature earlier than boys may give rise to conflict between the sexes. Younger adolescent boys especially seem to be interested in same-sex group activities, although they are willing to share some of their activities with girls who are "good sports."

Rate of anatomical growth differs among young adolescents. In too many instances, this growth is uneven. Hands and feet may seem to be inordinately large in comparison to the growth pattern of other parts of the body. This condition causes awkwardness of movement. You may find that a junior high school student or a high school freshman constantly stumbles over his feet or drops books, or other things, to the amusement of his classmates. At this age, young people often are cruel in their appraisal of one another's peculiarities. The young adolescent girl who suddenly "shoots up" like a weed, or the short, dumpy young adolescent boy may suffer much embarrassment in the presence of more evenly growing young associates.

The more you know about your learners, the more confident will you become in dealing with them. Some schools help teachers and guidance counselors learn about their pupils so that they can better work with them. For example, in one of the junior high schools of Vancouver, Washington, various characteristics of learners on each school level are made available to teachers and guidance counselors. The list we present here pertains to the pupils of the seventh, eighth, and ninth grades. You may want to study these suggestions so that you can compare the characteristics exhibited by your students with this list:

Some Characteristics of the Seventh-Grader

The twelfth year brings an unmistakable clearing of the air, and seventh-graders are more self-contained and self-competent than they were only one year earlier. The twelve-year-old protests that he does not wish to be considered a "baby" any longer. The outstanding characteristic of this age is enthusiasm.

There is a wider range of differences in rate of physical growth than there was among the ten- and eleven-year-old boys.

For girls this is the period of most rapid adolescent growth. Menstruation occurs most often toward end of this year. Initial periods may be irregular in occurrence.

Sex is really interesting to a twelve-year-old, and he tends less to think of it as dirty. Wants accurate information.

He is becoming aware of appearance, and of what the crowd wears. Rarely goes against the crowd.

Emotionally he is "smoothing out," and on the whole will listen to reason. Anger however is not under good control for many.

Likes double meanings and seems to spot them with—or without—the least provocation.

When controls are too rigid or he is expected to do something he does not understand, the negative side of the seventh-grader may come to the fore.

Much shifting of interest from one friend to another. Usually is common knowledge among a group which boy likes which girl and vice-versa. Most boys still prefer boy friends, however.

Most want to be part of the group, and are heavily ruled by group. Also enjoy "fooling around" and "sitting around" while life just happens to them.

Tend to like their teachers and to admire the teacher who holds them in line, and demands much of them.

Many still love tales of adventure and are partial to those which combine facts and fancy. Some are beginning to enjoy lighter adult books where human drama unfolds.

Most argue to win a point, not just for the sake of argument.

Enthusiasm may carry them in many different directions. Need help in channeling it and giving it expression.

Some Characteristics of the Eighth-Grader

The thirteenth year is rather complex because adolescence is now well under way. This is a reflective stage when a boy or girl is very sensitive to criticism, and keenly perceptive of the emotional states of others. Typically, he is fond of school—a good school—with fair and efficient discipline. He appreciates a teacher who stresses factual knowledge and he has a prodigious capacity to assimilate knowledge when his interest is aroused.

The average girl will have menstruated before her fourteenth birthday, and at thirteen she has 95 per cent of her mature height.

For middle group of boys this is a period of rapid growth of genitalia. Most boys have started sudden spurt of growth in height.

Sometimes not too good natured, and may be nicer away from home than at home. Periods of marked moodiness may occur.

More likely to be annoyed or irritated than really angry. Rarely cries in public, but may do so in own room.

An age of inward absorption, of thinking things over. Reticent in asking questions about growing up, but definitely concerned about changes which are taking place in themselves.

The "gang" isn't as important to girls as is the friendship of one or two classmates. Boys are likely to cluster in groups of four or five.

Girls dating older boys, but few boys are "single" dating, and may be very self-conscious in company of girls.

Time is better organized and concentration more sustained. Better sense of responsibility, but he almost begs for an authority which says "There are some things in life which you have to do whether you like it or not."

If teacher does not command respect, eighth-graders "try to get away with things," usually practical jokes.

Boys prefer stories about athletics or adventure, and girls, stories about people their own age.

Much interest in trying new things. Have a broadened outlook of world affairs and enjoy the newspaper.

Long-term projects catch him short of time. This may throw him in a sudden panic, for his task seems interminable.

Fuller knowledge of what relative truth is. Tries to be truthful, but sometimes tells only part of the truth.

Some, boys especially, swear a lot. Others condemn it as a mark of being ill-bred, and girls generally disapprove of the bad language used by the boys.

Some Characteristics of the Ninth-Grader

The fourteen-year-old feels that he is coming into his own. The shyness, touchiness, and vagaries of the thirteen-year-old give way to a robust, vigorous expressiveness. He tends to be friendly and outgoing in his interpersonal relationships. He abounds in energy, exuberance, and expansiveness. Albert Schweitzer holds the fourteen-year-old youth in high regard and says: "If all of us could become what we were at fourteen, what a different place the world would be."

Maturity features in girls now approximate those of young adulthood. Most are becoming aware of premenstrual symptoms. Girls may feel an actual physical involvement in response to boys.

Boys continue to look more like boys than like adults. By fifteen, most will look like men.

Period of most rapid height growth for greatest number of boys. May be very trying for slow maturer.

Happy moods far outstrip sad ones. May drop into the depths occasionally but bounce back rather quickly. Less inhibited than he was about his temper and may get angry quickly, but not often.

Crying is not common at fourteen, but when it occurs it may be a call for help, and should not be treated lightly.

Fourteen likes to compete in that in which he excels. He wants above all to do well.

May be quite aware of outward apperance, but clothes are more often chosen to suit them and express their personalities.

Trend toward increased feelings of confidence in parents, even though approval may not be expressed.

Fourteen has a real drive toward the opposite sex, boys being as interested in girls (though in a milder way) as girls are in boys.

Great admiration for athletes, and boys like to put their muscular ability to the test. Girls more influenced by goal of artificial rewards.

Criticisms of teachers are more closely related to fact than they were. Appreciate teachers who can sense the need for a change of pace when it arises.

Prone to talk very loudly, and to want their music at top volume.

Very receptive to suggestions which throw light on his individual traits. Interested in "personality" and simple "psychology."

Experiences pleasure in asserting new command of language. Words are very important to ninth-graders. They help to broaden his outlook for seeing things whole and in totality.

Boys still like to "gang up," and they have a good time together. Girls tend to have "cliques" or "circles" of friends. Outsiders may find it difficult to get in.[1]

During early adolescence, young people react differently to their changed social status. Some are very active. They develop many new interests and want to participate in as many as are possible. They become avid joiners of various groups. Their interest in any one of these may be short-lived, however, and they discard it for another form of zestful activity.

Young adolescents tend to live in an imaginary world. They engage in daydreams about the wonderful things that they would like to have happen to them or the daring or romantic deeds they would like to perform. They are extremely active—physically, mentally, and emotionally.

The Older Adolescent

Older adolescents tend to pattern their behavior and attitudes according to what they consider to be conformity to adult standards. Here again, differences among individuals are apparent. Some may give evidence of a gradualness of development that was characteristic of their earlier teen-age years, keeping a good balance between the enjoyment of adult privileges and the assumption of adult responsibilities.

[1] R. E. Jongeward, "Guidance Services, Lewis Junior High School," in L. D. Crow and Alice Crow (eds.), *Readings in Guidance* (New York: David McKay Co., Inc., 1962), pp. 402–5.

Other older adolescents exhibit a strong desire to "grow up" too quickly. Before they are mature enough to handle themselves effectively, they demand that they be treated like adults. Too often, these young people overemphasize the procuring of adult privileges and disregard their present responsibilities.

Boy-girl group activity gives way to twosome dating. Some of the senior high school boys and girls become so involved with particular members of the opposite sex that they tend to neglect their school obligations. Time spent in class is devoted to gazing at or attempting to attract the attention of the current object of affection.

Often, during later adolescent years, some of your students become very much concerned with their choice of vocation; others give little thought to their future lifework. These latter are content to spend their time, perhaps fritter it away, in satisfying temporary interests, which may or may not include mastering learning material.

The adolescent usually tries to solve his problems in one of three ways: (1) adjust his ideals to those of the group, (2) ignore or defy group standards, or (3) modify group attitudes so that they conform more closely to his own ideals. It is gratifying when teen-agers possess those wholesome life values that enable them to have the inner strength to influence the ideals of their associates for the better.

The Adolescent in School

Teen-agers differ in their attitudes toward school and school responsibilities and activities. You need to understand these differences. Most adolescents give evidence of curiosity about the world about them and their relationship to it. Yet their interest may not lie in learning about those areas of knowledge that constitute the school curriculum.

In the same class you may find some students who are intensely interested in mastering the content of your subject and others who, because of other strong interests or inability to grasp the subject, regard the study of the subject to be an unpleasant chore. Some are college bound, others are planning to go to work as soon as they are graduated, and still others are waiting impatiently for the time when they will be old enough to leave school.

Some adolescents display a friendly, cooperative attitude toward you; others derive considerable pleasure from "baiting" you in various ways. You must learn early that you cannot utilize the same method of motivating all of your students to want to learn. Even though the class may be relatively homogeneous from the point of view of achievement or intellectual capacity, you may find differences in their attitudes toward your subject.

Your Adolescent Experiences

In the foregoing pages, we have reviewed some of the differentiating characteristics of your secondary school students. You recall your own adolescent attitudes and interests. During that period you recognized the fact that some of your schoolmates differed from yourself, but you did not think too much about these differences. You may have experienced some difficulties of adjustment, but you probably were able to solve them satisfactorily. Now you are viewing young people from a different point of view. It is your responsibility as a teacher to recognize differences among them and to do what you can to help all of your students become fine, upstanding adults.

You need to be careful to refrain from judging your students' behavior according to standards that you and/or your parents set up for you during your adolescence. You represented a specific social and economic status that was accompanied by adherence to certain mores and customs according to which you charted your life course.

Some of your students are the products of homes that may differ much from that in which you grew up. You need to avoid snap judgments about these young people. Rather should you attempt to discover and take into account all of the factors that are basic to adolescents' displayed modes of conduct. The various techniques and approaches utilized in studying and evaluating adolescents' developmental progress are discussed at some length in Chapters

4 and 14. At this point we survey briefly some of the media you can employ to learn about students.

LEARNING ABOUT YOUR STUDENTS

To face a class of secondary school students with the realization that included in the group are many differing personalities can be a fear-producing experience. You realize that if you are to be effective in your guidance of their learning you need to know as much as you can about their differing abilities, interests, and attitudes. This requires that you become acquainted with each of them and discover all that you can about him.

You are limited, of course, in what you are able to discover about your students by the amount of time your total college and practice program permits you to devote to this project, as well as by the availability of material on students. If you meet several classes during the weeks or months of your student-teaching experience, you probably will not be able to learn everything or even much about every student with whom you work; but you can make a good beginning by gathering data about some of them, thereby gaining practice in performing an activity that is an important responsibility of the regular teacher.

Suggestions for Getting Acquainted

At your first meeting with the class, prepare a seating chart or utilize one prepared by your cooperating teacher. By referring to the chart during class discussion, you can begin to associate names with the proper individuals. Watch their reactions to you, the class teacher, and teaching procedures. After several sessions, you probably will discover differences in their attitudes. You may decide early that you need to know more about some of them, if you are to deal with them effectively.

You now are ready to obtain some helpful information about these students. You know what they look like; you have memorized their names; and you have observed some of their class behavior. What else can you discover about them? Where can you go to obtain needed information?

Utilize Various Sources of Information

Your cooperating teacher can be helpful by (1) acquainting you with the cumulative record of your students, and (2) supplying pertinent information concerning the home background of a student, any serious problems he may be experiencing, or his relations with other students, for example. You also can learn much about a student's attitudes toward you, his studies, the school, and life in general through friendly, informal little conferences with him, if you have the time and opportunity to arrange with him for them outside regular class hours. On occasions, you may need to consult the student's guidance counselor to obtain personal help in dealing with him.

Maintaining a Confidential Attitude

Perhaps, a word of caution is in order. Remember that any information you gather about a student or obtain from him should be treated as confidential material. Too often, enthusiastic student teachers become so much interested in some of the young people whom they meet in the practice school that they are moved to discuss them with their college classmates, and with their family or friends. To do so is highly unethical.

Even though you may believe that a particular student has a personal problem with the solution of which you would like to help, seek advice from authorized members of the school personnel. Consult such individuals as your cooperating teacher and the school guidance counselor, or an administrator. Do not gossip about the situation with other people—not even with your most intimate friends. You cannot know who may report your gossip to someone who is acquainted with the student. Anyone to whom you speak may report the matter to the young person or to the family, with undesirable results.

Two examples of such betrayal of confidences come to mind. A student teacher in physical education was told in confidence by Donald, a healthy-appearing boy, that he very much wanted to join the basketball team but that his father had forbidden him to do so, without giving any reason for his decision. This young man who was helping to coach the team did not take the matter up with his cooperating teacher. Instead he discussed the matter with a friend, accusing the parent of being a "stick in the mud." The matter eventually came to the attention of the other man who was incensed by the student teacher's attempted interference. What the student teacher did not know was that Donald had an incipient heart condition and was to refrain from any strenuous exercising for the present. Donald's parents had not told the lad about this lest he worry about his health.

Another situation concerned Jane who, in a burst of confidence, admitted to a student teacher that she was very much in love with one of her classmates but that he did not give her a "tumble." This story of adolescent love amused the student teacher who repeated it at home. Her own adolescent brother, equally amused, repeated it to a friend of his who was a fellow student of Jane and the object of her affection. The news spread and both Jane and the boy became the victims of youthful "joshing."

These stories of actual occurrences represent what can happen to young people if they find that teachers do not respect what is told them in confidence. It is equally serious for a teacher to give out indiscriminately information that is in a student's folder, such as intelligence status, teacher's notations, and similar recorded data about the student. Student teachers do not always appreciate the seriousness of revealing information that they either receive in confidence or get from confidential files. Now is the time to practice the professional approach in these matters.

DEALING EFFECTIVELY WITH SECONDARY SCHOOL STUDENTS

You may recall that in the previous chapter we listed the characteristics that secondary school students would like their teacher to possess. Here we shall indicate briefly how you can apply, in practice, some of these qualities admired by students.

Show a Genuine Interest in Students

Remember that an adolescent wants to be regarded as an individual. He does not want to be lost in the crowd. One way of helping him maintain his individuality is to know his name and address him by it. In so doing, follow the custom prevalent in the school in which you are doing your student teaching. In most junior high schools, the student's first name is used. Senior high schools differ in their practice, however. In some schools, a girl is called Miss _____, and a boy is referred to by his last name only. Some schools continue the use of the first name. Others use both the first and surname, as *Edith Coyle* and *George Grant*.

There are senior high schools in which teachers differ in their mode of addressing students. For example, in an all-girls' school in which the students generally were referred to as Miss _____, one teacher of English called the members of her Honors classes by their first names, using the more formal approach for other students, except for senior students with whom she used first names. Whatever your preference in this respect, always follow the procedure of your cooperating teacher. Also, be careful to avoid calling some members of a class by their first names and addressing others more formally. This procedure is likely to arouse resentment among some students.

You can give expression to your interest in your students in various little ways. Be quick to commend an especially fine bit of behavior, but do not expand upon it to the extent that other members of the class come to believe that you are "playing favorites." Spread your commendations among the entire group insofar as this is possible. Be ready to lend a sympathetic ear to any reports of students concerning interesting things that are happening to them.

Be willing to help your students when they bring some of their simple problems to you for your advice. You must keep in mind, however, that your time is limited. You cannot afford to give any one student more attention than you give to others, unless the need is great. Then, as already indicated, you should seek the help of other qualified personnel in solving a problem.

Most students are careful not to be too demanding of your time and attention, but they do want to be assured of your interest in them and your desire to be helpful in suitable ways. Interest in your students is closely associated with other personal attributes. We shall refer to some of these briefly.

Show Friendliness and Consideration to Students

Many opportunities arise in the classroom for you to display attitudes of friendliness and consideration. As your students enter the classroom, they like to be greeted with a friendly smile. Adolescents are extremely sensitive to adult attitudes toward them. No matter how independent they may seem to be or how casual their treatment of you, they want to feel that your attitude toward them is one of friendliness and consideration of their interests. This does not mean, of course, that your face during the recitation period should continue to resemble that of the famous Cheshire cat in *Alice in Wonderland,* but they do appreciate your maintaining a pleasant attitude toward them.

The tone of voice you employ is important. Requests usually are better than commands. "Please" or "Will you?" is likely to be heeded promptly. At times, such directives as "Open your textbook to page —" may be desirable. You can either utter these words so sternly or harshly as to imply that you do not expect them to obey or indicate by your friendly, businesslike approach that you expect them to comply with your request as a matter of course.

You can gain the respect and admiration of your students by displaying consideration for their feelings. Do not harangue a student for a misdeed in the presence of his classmates. When a young person engages in a bit of mischief or is otherwise uncooperative, you cannot permit him to interfere with the study activities of his classmates or disrupt the class, but, as we suggest in Chapter 12, in which we discuss discipline, let him know that you are aware of his undesirable behavior by a glance in his direction or a word of admonition. Speak further with him about the matter in a private conference. If his class behavior does not improve, his conduct should be reported to the cooperating teacher who then will either settle the issue or consult the guidance counselor or someone else in authority.

Most classes usually include at least one member who is so much interested in the class discussion that he wants to preempt an undue amount of class time. He may blurt out answers, without raising his hand or waiting for you to call on him or on another member. You realize that he does not mean to be officious—he is being carried away by his enthusiasm. To reprimand him publicly might cause him to feel that you do not appreciate his study efforts; his feelings are hurt.

A good way to handle a situation as described in the aforementioned is to say quietly something like this, "Not now, John. You know the answer, but let us hear what Max has to say about it." Several repetitions of this kind of treatment usually are sufficient to convince him that he needs to employ self-restraint. Especially is this so if, on occasions, you call on him to summarize what other students have said or to add a point that they have omitted. In addition, you can explain in private to a too active student that everyone in the class has the same rights that he has.

There are many other ways through the following of which you can convince your students of your friendly and understanding consideration of their feelings. For example, you have requested a student to read to the class a paper that you have assigned on a specific topic or to place on the chalkboard a diagram or outline that he has prepared. He is having some difficulty in finding the material. It is extremely embarrassing for the adolescent to have you, the teacher, sit in silence while he fumbles through his books to find his material. Better results are obtained if you fill the gap by addressing some pertinent comments to the group until he is ready. He will appreciate your helping him out in this way.

Again, a student enters the classroom late, or fails to submit required written work on time. Your first impulse probably is to reprimand him publicly for his tardiness, since one of your responsibilities as a teacher is to encourage promptness in the fulfillment of obligations. Yet, the student may have a good reason for his apparent negligence. A wise procedure for you to follow is to note the offense mentally and, at the first opportunity, give him a chance to explain his conduct to you in private. Of course, if lack of promptness is a habitual failing of the student, he needs to be suitably penalized for his uncooperative behavior.

Display a Sense of Justice

We often hear young people say of a teacher, "He's not fair!" They thereby are giving expression to the difference between adolescents' and adults' attitudes concerning what should be considered to be right and just. Teen-agers tend to evaluate adult attitudes toward them in light of their own subjective interpretation of what is due them. Most adults have learned to view their experiences more objectively. They have learned that, although rules and regulations, for example, do not please them personally, such regulators of behavior are aimed at the common good. The immature adolescent cannot always project his thinking beyond his own immediate interests and desires.

The administrators of the school in which you are doing your student teaching have established certain rules of conduct to which the students are expected to conform. These may include directives concerning matters such as smoking, mode of dress in school, passing through corridors, punctuality in meeting school responsibilities, respect for authority, and similar aspects of behavior. It is your obligation to know these regulations and to make certain that your students obey them.

You cannot afford to permit any student to flout prescribed school dicta in your presence. Perhaps, because of your youth and newness in the school, a student may attempt to "get away" with a form of forbidden conduct that he would not attempt in the presence of one of his regular teachers. You must be alert to the possibility of such an attempt to try you out.

Be mentally prepared to let any miscreant individual know that you are aware of his intentions and warn him that you will not tolerate a repetition of undesirable behavior. You may need to penalize any individual who repeats the offense. If he persists in his misbehavior, you should report him to your cooperating teacher. It usually is better for you, yourself, to handle infraction of rules, however. Too much reporting of misdeeds to a person higher than yourself in authority may earn for you a reputation among the students of being an unfair talebearer.

Another area of class procedure concerning which students may accuse their teachers of injustice is that of the administration of tests. In order to give you practice in evaluating learning progress, your cooperating teacher may permit you to construct, administer, and mark class tests. Although you consult him in the preparation of testing material, you are more than likely to include questions that will be disapproved by some members of the class.

You may safely assume that one or more students will complain that the material on the test had not been covered in class, that the test was so long they could not complete it, or that the questions were too difficult or stated too broadly or vaguely. In addition, some students will accuse you of marking their papers unfairly. They may insist that their answers were similar to those of other students to which you assigned a higher rating than you did to theirs. This is a common experience of most teachers. It often is difficult for students to evaluate their own performances. Hence they are likely to blame you for their failure to achieve desired success in a test.

Since the evaluation of learner progress is discussed in later chapters, here we do no more than suggest the following testing procedures. Adherence to them will be helpful to you.

1. Be certain that the content of the test does not include anything that has not been assigned for study. If a thought question is included, it should be based on a background of learned material.

2. After you have constructed the questions, put them aside for a while. Then read them to make sure that their meaning is clear.

3. Write an answer to each question, noting the length of time it took you to do it. Multiply that time by three, allowing that much time for the student to complete it. Doing this will avoid your constructing too long a test.

4. Before you start to mark any student's answers, read all the papers through quickly in order to discover the general trends in the answers. If the test includes several essay questions, a good plan is to grade one question on all of the papers before you start on another question. In this way, you can keep in mind what you expect to find included in the answer and can assign grades on a relative basis.

5. No matter how carefully you mark papers, you may make mistakes. You can misinterpret an answer that is correct but differs somewhat from the answer you wanted. If a student calls this fact to your attention, be willing to admit your error and make correction by reevaluating the answer. Do not let this situation occur too often, however, lest you be bombarded with demands for reconsideration of many other papers. If it happens occasionally and you are gracious in your attitude toward giving a student all the credit he deserves

for his performance, you soon earn the reputation of being a fair and just teacher.

During your day-by-day contacts with students, many incidents occur that cause adolescents to rate you as just or unjust. The best you can do is to display a *sincere attitude* of interest in the welfare of every student in the room. Inadvertently, you may seem to single out one or a few students to the exclusion of others. You may commend one student for work well done, for example, but disregard others who have performed equally well.

At one time you may call a student to account for a wrongdoing but, at another time, fail to notice that another student is engaging in the same kind of behavior. You may grant a request to one student but deny the same request to another. In justice to all students, you need to be consistent in your behavior toward each of them.

Importance of Being Tactful

In dealing with your students much tact is needed. You know that young people are easily aroused emotionally. Their feelings are hurt if they believe that anyone is belittling them in the opinion of their peers. An adolescent is sensitive to the recognition of any way in which he may seem to be inferior to other members of his group. You therefore need to handle tactfully any situation in the classroom that may cause one student to be criticized adversely by his classmates, especially if the condition is not of his own making. We cite a few examples.

Speech defects, such as stammering or stuttering, are not uncommon among adolescents. A tense, high-strung young person finds it difficult to enunciate clearly when he is called upon to recite. The attitude of the other members of the class toward the defect reflects your own attitude toward it. Do not frown or give evidence of impatience. Encourage him with a smile to try to answer the question, warning the others with a glance to desist from laughing at him.

Young people can be cruel to their peers, but they also can be sympathetic and willing to take their cue from your leadership in situations of speech difficulties. If the defect is serious, the student probably is receiving therapeutic treatment from a special speech teacher. Your cooperating teacher will acquaint you with this fact and tell you how you best can help the student. Be sure to follow any such suggestions given you.

Again, a student, who usually is alert to what is going on in the classroom and responds well in discussions, offers a contribution that is patently incorrect. The class bursts out in uncontrolled laughter to the student's great embarrassment. For example, a senior high school girl when asked the average rainfall in a certain relatively rainy locality responded quickly, "Six or seven feet." The class started to laugh and the teacher added to their merriment by remarking sarcastically, "Oh, then you would keep your canoe handy." The fact that this girl, now an older woman, still recalls the incident unpleasantly indicates the embarrassment she experienced at the time of its occurrence. It would have been much more tactful for the teacher to have said quietly, "You don't really mean that. Think again."

In a cosmopolitan high school, there can be found some students who do not have many of the advantages enjoyed by others among their classmates. For example, they may not be able to afford to wear as attractive clothes as those worn by other young people. These students, especially girls, are keenly aware of such differences. In one high school, a girl remarked to a teacher that she wished the school would require the wearing of uniforms so that there would be no apparent differences among the clothes of students.

In order to achieve recognition from others, an underprivileged young person may come to school dressed in cheap, inappropriate clothing or, if a girl, wearing too much costume jewelry. This may give rise to much amusement among class members. As the teacher, you can help in a situation of this kind by talking to the student in private, tactfully suggesting that clean, simple clothing and little or no adornment are the correct dress for school wear. If you yourself make it a practice to dress simply in school, you not only will set a good example for all students but your advice to particular students is likely to be heeded.

Use Tact in Personal Situations

In your dealings with your students, you experience many opportunities for the display of tactfulness. One of these has to do with your personal relations with students. Sometimes, because they like you, young people want to know all they can about you. Hence they are motivated to ask you questions about yourself. How old are you? Do you live at home? What is your address? What does your father do?

Once students are given an opening they will continue to ply you with questions. They might continue with such questions as the following. Do you have brothers and sisters? How old are they? Do you dance and/or go to parties? Have you a girl friend (boyfriend)? There sometimes seems to be no end to the personal questions they ask you.

You need to realize that usually students are not trying to be pert or "fresh." They just want to know. You need to be tactful in your answers to their questions, however. Some matters are none of their business. Yet, you cannot put them off completely. Answer truthfully whatever you think they have the right to know. Give a general answer to others.

It usually is unwise to give students your address unless you would welcome them in your home as visitors. Some regular teachers invite their students to their homes for special purposes. It usually is better for a student teacher not to encourage any visiting between himself and his students. If you are in a school that is close to your home and a student's parents are friends of your family, you cannot avoid meeting this student socially. Be careful, however, to avoid discussing with him either members of the school faculty or his classmates.

Use Tact in Social Situations

You need to be tactful in the matter of socializing with your students. You may be asked to assist in arranging and conducting student social events, club activities, and the like that take place in the school. In such relationships, you need to exercise considerable discretion. You want to maintain a pleasant attitude toward them, thereby assuring them of your friendly interest in their activities. Yet, you must preserve your dignity as a teacher.

When attending school social events you may dance with a student, but take care not to dance with some to the exclusion of others. Give preference to those young people who seem to lack

dancing partners. Do not engage in extreme forms of dancing, however. In your conversations with them at a school social gathering,
remember that you no longer are a teen-ager; refrain from the kind
of light badinage that sometimes is characteristic of the adolescent
years. If you find yourself in a situation of this kind, you can
always get away from it with the excuse, offered pleasantly, that
you are needed elsewhere. Adolescents usually are quick to recognize
your position.

There are many other sets of circumstances requiring the application of tact to meet them. Students may attempt to draw you into
social relationships outside the school. As a result of your friendly
interest in them and your cooperative attitude toward them, you
earn their respect and admiration. They learn to like you as a
person and come to think of you as an honored member of their
group. This is a high accolade, but they may be stimulated by their
feelings toward you to want to include you in their out-of-school
interests and activities. They have the urge to become better acquainted with you and to "show you off" to their friends.

Avoid Entangling Social Situations

Adolescents' attitudes toward their proper relationships with you
may be unrealistic. Hence, without meaning to do so, they can place
you in embarrassing situations. Students may offer you expensive
gifts that you tactfully must refuse to accept. During out-of-class
hours, they may start to address you by your given name. The first
time this happens, it is best to ignore it or to act as though you
were unaware of the fact that you were being spoken to. If it
persists, you may have to speak, in private, to the leader of the
group about the inappropriateness of using your first name without
your permission. A cooperating teacher occasionally sets the stage
for the students to develop this practice by referring to his student
teacher by his given name. Emotionally charged young adolescents,
especially, are not always able to distinguish between adult privileges and adolescent rights.

Your students may be eager to share their social activities with
you. For example, Dick Gavin, as a student teacher, had succeeded
in establishing cordial relations between himself and his class. One

of the girls in the class, a fine cooperative student, invited him to attend a party at her home. Without thinking much about it, the young man accepted the invitation. When he arrived, he discovered to his amazement and chagrin, that he was supposed to be the "escort" of his hostess and was expected to participate in all of their adolescent activities. He did not want to hurt their feelings by leaving the house abruptly. He compromised by helping the girl's mother prepare and serve refreshments, and he spent much of the evening talking with the parents. The next day, the girl apologized to him for the fact that her parents had monopolized his time so that he missed all the fun.

The sequel to the story is that he received many other such invitations, which he refused because of other engagements, pressure of study, and the like. At the end of his stay in the school, the students admitted to him that they had attempted to draw him into their social life, and they expressed the hope that they would remain friends.

Ethel Gray had a somewhat similar experience as a beginning teacher in an all boys high school. She was an attractive, friendly young woman who soon won the admiration of her students. The senior class boys tried in many ways to win her friendship. One day a box of candy appeared on her desk. She opened it and offered its contents to the students with the smiling comment, "How good it was of somebody to realize that you all like candy." No more candy was forthcoming. Someone else sent flowers to her home. She brought these to school and placed them on the desk "so that everyone can enjoy them." That was the end of flower sending.

Ethel Gray was a teacher of English. The class was reading Shakespeare's *Hamlet*. One of the boys informed her after class one day that he was able to get free tickets for *Hamlet* at one of the theaters. She let him know that she thought he meant to obtain these for the class. Embarrassed, he admitted that he had access only to a pair of tickets and that his plan was for him to take her to see it. She thanked him for thinking of her. Fortunately, she was able to say honestly that she had seen the play. She added "Why don't you take one of the girls? You would enjoy that much more than you would going with me." The boy understood what she meant by her remark and accepted her advice, reporting to her later that he and Doris had enjoyed the evening immensely.

An adolescent's attempted involvement with a young attractive teacher may represent the beginning of interest in members of the opposite sex. You can do service to a young person by accepting this point of view and tactfully steering his or her attention in the direction of peer-age associates. At the same time, you need to convince all of the students of your desire to cooperate fully with them in wholesome adult-adolescent relationships.

IMPORTANCE OF SUBJECT MATTER

Immediately following the advent of Sputnik, subject matter began to receive added attention from educators. Today subject matter commands a position of considerable importance in the pursuit of an education. Much important subject matter can be learned through reading what is written on the printed page. Hence to acquire needed knowledge, students must first master the tools of learning, such as ability to read. With ability to read, students are enabled to further their education at an acceptable pace; without this ability to read they experience great difficulties in getting ideas from the printed page.

Your Knowledge of Subject Matter

If you hope to earn success as a secondary school teacher, it is not enough to know your students and how to deal with them. It is equally important that you are well grounded in subject matter. This fact takes constant repetition. At one time, it is true, subject matter mastery was emphasized as the basic, if not the only, prerequisite for teaching on the secondary school level. Other aspects of teaching effectiveness were almost totally disregarded.

During the recent past, educators came to realize that teaching adolescents requires an understanding of certain psychological and sociological factors that are fundamental to achieving positive teacher-student relationships. The significance of methodology also has received much attention. As teacher education has come more and more to stress these areas of preparation, there has been some danger that the thorough mastery of teaching content be somewhat neglected.

Your primary goal as a teacher is to guide the learning progress of young people in a given body of learning content to the end that they may apply what they have acquired—knowledge, skills, or attitudes—in the conduct of their lives. Other aspects of teacher education represent means to an end.

No matter what their own attitudes toward study materials may be, secondary school students expect their teachers to know their subjects thoroughly. They will not tolerate half knowledge. They want to feel that they can bring any of their questions to a teacher and receive a satisfactory answer. As we have suggested earlier, you may find occasionally that you cannot supply an answer on the spur of the moment. You should know, however, where to find it. Admit this fact to the students and, either alone or assisted by them, obtain the correct data.

Do not hedge. Do not give a vague or incomplete answer to a question and expect your students to be satisfied. Keep up to date in your subject. Many adolescents read voraciously, especially in a field of special interest. They can embarrass you by referring to new developments in your field, unless you keep one step ahead of them. Be acquainted with the magazines that they read. In fact, they often appreciate your bringing an interesting article to their attention.

No matter how thorough your mastery of subject matter has been during your preteaching education, you probably will need to continue your studies during your entire teaching career. Consider, for example, the situation in which a teacher of physics would find himself today if he attempted to rely on the knowledge of his subject that he had gained during college study twenty, ten, or five years ago. So much has happened and is happening in science these days that what was learned even last year may not be sufficient for teaching purposes this year.

The changing knowledge holds for almost every field of teaching. New information, improvement of techniques and skills, greater understandings, and more realistic appreciations challenge you from day to day and require that you continue to be a student as well as a teacher. Moreover, as you yourself engage in continued learning, you are enabled to maintain a student point of view and become increasingly aware of the learning problems of your students.

Your Organization of Subject Matter

Later we shall discuss lesson planning and all that it entails. We want here to stress the importance of so organizing your presentation of learning materials that your students can get a clear understanding of relationships between various phases and units of study. Keep in mind that they probably begin the study of your subject with only a meager background of related material.

You need to help your students build each unit of knowledge or skill on a thoroughly recognized and understood base. You must avoid rambling from one topic to another or leaving a topic hanging in midair. Your own thinking needs to be clear and well organized in order to help the students follow you step by step in the learning process of the subject under consideration.

Your Daily Preparation

As a student teacher, you probably will receive considerable assistance from your cooperating teacher and your college supervisor in the matter of preparing the material that you expect to teach each day. There are certain suggestions that, if you follow now, will develop habits that can be valuable to you as a beginning teacher.

Know exactly *what* and *how much* you expect to cover during recitation. This you learn from experience. The beginning teacher is likely to attempt to include either too much or too little material. If he tries to do too much, he will find the period ending with important points left dangling. If not enough material is included, the teacher may find his lesson finished before the end of the class period. To the inexperienced teacher, this time is not easy to fill fruitfully.

The points to be included in the lesson should follow a well-thought-through sequence. You may find that questions arise in class that indicate lack of understanding of the material on the part of some students. If you are well prepared for the lesson, you probably have foreseen such difficulties and will be able to meet them.

What we have said here will be treated in greater detail when we discuss lesson planning. The important point is that your students recognize the fact that you are well prepared in your subject as well as in general education. You start the day's work promptly, and you are able to carry it through the period in an interesting and worthwhile fashion.

Your Attitude toward Your Subject

Attitudes are caught rather than taught. If you bring to the teaching of your subject a high degree of enthusiasm born of your deep interest in it, you are more than likely to engender in your students a similar attitude toward their learning activities. High school students often are heard to say about one or more of their teachers "It's fun to go to _____ High School" or "The teacher enjoys his subject so much that he makes us want to learn."

You probably are enthusiastic about teaching your subject. That is why you selected teaching and the teaching of your particular subject. You need to take care, however, that, as you continue teaching it through the years, you do not let your work become so routinized that you lose your earlier interest and enthusiasm.

QUESTIONS AND TOPICS FOR DISCUSSION

1. Recall four fellow students (of about the same age) in secondary school. List ways in which these young people differed from one another.
2. What were your experiences as a preadolescent?
3. Why do some educators consider the junior high school years the most difficult age period to teach?
4. Select three students in your class about whom you would like to have more information. Ask permission to consult their cumulative records and study them. To what extent did the data help you understand these students better?
5. If you have had a conference with any of your students, write a brief report of what transpired at it.
6. Cite examples of your cooperating teacher's consideration of his students' feelings.
7. Have you had any difficulties with student behavior? If so, how have you handled such situations?

8. If you have been the victim of a tactless teacher, explain how his behavior affected your attitude toward him.

SELECTED REFERENCES

BARUCH, D. W. *How to Live with Your Teen-ager.* New York: McGraw-Hill Book Co., Inc., 1953.

BLOCK, H. A., and FLYNN, F. T. *Delinquency.* New York: Random House, Inc., 1956.

COLEMAN, J. S. *The Adolescent Society.* New York: Free Press of Glencoe, Inc., 1961.

CROW, L. D., and CROW, ALICE. "The Expanding Interests of Adolescents," *The High School Journal,* October, 1962, pp. 14–22.

JERSILD, A. T. *Psychology of Adolescence* (2nd ed.). New York: Macmillan Co., 1963.

LANDIS, P. H. *Understanding Teen-Agers.* New York: Appleton-Century-Crofts, Inc., 1955.

LINDGREN, H. C. *Psychology of Personal and Social Adjustment* (2nd ed.). New York: American Book Co., 1959.

SLATON, T. F. *Dynamics of Adolescent Adjustment.* New York: Macmillan Co., 1963.

GENERAL ASSESSMENT OF STUDENTS

Throughout your teacher training courses you have had your attention called to the need to understand students as individuals. As a student teacher, you find yourself face-to-face with situations in which you must be able not only to distinguish one individual from another but to understand what the differences are among individuals, how they occur, and what can be done to meet them.

You have already seen how individual differences affect student-teacher relationships. During your observation of your cooperating teacher, you have noticed how differences have been met by him, how he has handled deviant behavior, and what can be done for students who suffered serious problems of adjustment.

VALUE OF STUDYING STUDENTS

You will find as you enter the teaching profession that the more you know about learners the better are you able to help them individually. If you wish to be most effective in your stimulation of learners toward a well-rounded education, you will want to learn the extent of their mental, emotional, and social development.

An understanding of the psychological factors involved in human development and learning enables you to deal effectively with the class as a whole and with members individually. It is your duty to identify and concern yourself with those individual differences that exert a significant influence on learning and necessitate adequate differential treatment in the teaching-learning situation. You will need to know the kinds of information available and how to evaluate the qualitative effect of each on effective learning.

Ability Differences among Students

Every teacher knows that no two of his learners are alike. The ways in which and the extent to which these differences occur may

74

be difficult to discern. You soon discover, however, that the more nearly equated your students are in ability to achieve in your subject the better teaching-learning climate will there be in your classroom. Before long, school administrators may realize that optimal learning conditions prevail in those classrooms in which the learners are able to cope with a subject of study without too wide a gap among their basic potentialities in that area of learning. In other words, recitation classes will be organized according to levels of ability or extent of achievement.

We have known for a long time that every measurable trait of individuals tends to distribute itself according to a normal curve of distribution. (See Figure 3.) This seems to be true whether the trait is one of height, weight, mental ability, or other measurable human quality. For example, if mental ability is measured, we find a wide range of capacity for those individuals having low ability to those displaying superior ability, with the larger number clustering near the middle or average. (See Figure 3.)

Again when norms are established for the determination of a reading grade level in the seventh grade, for example, the median score obtained from administration of a reading test to a large number of learners in that particular grade is used as its norm. However, the results of a Reading Test administered to all of the seventh grade students indicate that the range of responses probably will vary from third to twelfth grade norms. A similar wide spread of abilities usually can be found in any heterogeneously grouped class. If your class is organized according to ability or achievement level, you should find a smaller range of differences in reading ability and mental capacity. You also should encounter fewer problems as you attempt to meet the learning needs of all of your students.

Behavior Differences among Students

You soon become aware of the overt behavior characteristics of your students and realize their significant differences. You need to learn to recognize and identify behavior differences and come to appreciate the extent to which these young people are alike and different in their ways of responding to classroom procedures. Moreover, you know a student's personality characteristics do not consist of a single entity but represent a combination of traits.

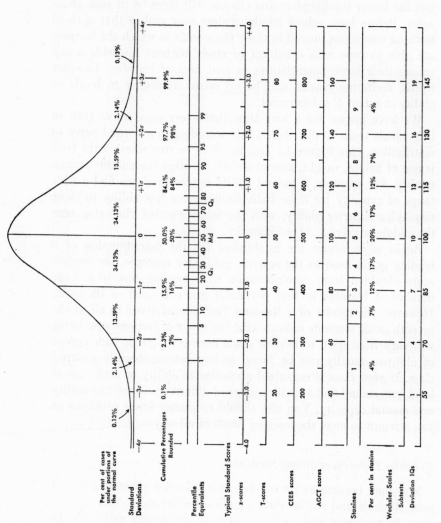

Fig. 3.—Normal curve of distribution. Shown are per cent of cases, Standard

To be alert to your students' daily behavior in the classroom is a valuable teaching asset. It not only will make you aware of present behavior but may be an indication of what can be expected in the future. Also, usually anticipated behavior follows a pattern of past practices. To have information regarding a student's past as well as present behavior should be helpful to you in your attempts to encourage him to bring about needed improvement in his behavior.

Student Attitudes as Revealed in School Setting

In addition to observing a student's commonly displayed behavior, it often is necessary to try to discover why he behaves as he does. He may exhibit a deep prejudice or a noncooperative attitude. When these traits are discovered, it is worth while to study the student's characteristics intensively in order to discover how any undesirable trait fits into his total personality pattern. As we suggested earlier, you may find it profitable to learn all that you can about such characteristics as his physical structure, health, mental ability, special aptitudes, interests, and emotional and social status.

Effect of Out-of-School Environment

If you wish to achieve a well-rounded understanding of the forces and influences that have an impact on the students in your class, you will need to know something about the kind of homes from which they come, the types of clubs available in the immediate neighborhood, the level of training of the parents, the economic level represented in the community, and numerous factors that affect the out-of-school life of your students. You need to realize that you do not deal with learners in a vacuum, but rather with young people who are constantly interacting in their school and out-of-school environment.

You will discover that classroom behavior of most learners is markedly affected by environmental factors, both within and outside the school. As a teacher, you have some influence over the behavior of students within your class or within the confines of the school; you have little or no control over the outside influences to which they are exposed. Yet, your ability to evaluate the school behavior of your students will be enhanced to the extent that you are acquainted with such factors. Your greater understanding of an adolescent's total life pattern has value in helping you work effectively with him.

Sources of Information about Learners

It is not difficult for you to understand the value of studying your students in order to provide them with appropriate learning conditions. It is essential that you know where and how significant information about them can be obtained. In Chapter 3, we surveyed briefly ways in which you can learn about some adolescent characteristics. In this chapter we treat in greater detail some general study approaches and other more specific areas of study in which you might participate and the results of which would have value for you. Among the sources of information available to you are (1) the results of major studies of adolescent development and adjustment, (2) cumulative records of pertinent data, and (3) evaluative techniques, some of which can be used by you in the classroom.

GENERAL APPROACHES TO CHILD AND ADOLESCENT STUDY

In your psychology and education courses you have reviewed some of the major studies that have been conducted by researchers in the field of child and adolescent development and adjustment. These studies, for the most part, are general in that they stress common developmental trends, although individual differences are not neglected. In fact, some studies deal specifically with the problems of individual differences.

In many instances, the results of studies reveal to you the extent to which certain characteristics can be expected to show themselves at specific stages of growth. An understanding of the general trends can help you determine the ways in which and the extent to which specific students in your class differ from a more or less to-be-expected pattern. There are various approaches to the study of young people. They may be studied individually or in groups of differing sizes.

As a teacher in the classroom, you should be well acquainted with the results of valid and reliable research studies so that you can evaluate your students, both individually and as a group, according to derived norms or standards of behavior. You should know also the study approach utilized by a researcher for arriving at his conclusions.

A developmental or adjustment study may be based on either (1) the *cross-sectional* approach (horizontal study), or (2) the *longitudinal* approach (vertical study). The cross-sectional approach is a normative study and usually involves large numbers of individuals at one time. For example, same-age or same-grade young people are studied to discover various facts about "normal" or average characteristics of the particular group studied. These data are valuable for teachers dealing with students of this age or grade to use as standards of comparison. The longitudinal approach is employed when the purpose of the study is to discover the sequential developmental pattern of an individual or group of individuals during a more or less extended period of time.

Interpretation of Horizontal Studies

The results of many adolescent studies with which you are acquainted were obtained by means of the utilization of the horizontal or cross-sectional approach. To the extent that you have familiarized yourself with general growth or developmental trends of same-age students, you can "spot" the individual or individuals among them who deviate from the expected "average" and therefore are atypical. In a ninth-grade class, for example, you may find that the majority of its members vary little from the height norm for their age, but that a few of them may be extremely short and several others are as tall as or taller than average twelfth graders.

Students who deviate in height require special consideration in the matter of seating arrangements. You also may find that the height deviation of your students affects their attitude toward their classmates and the latter's behavior toward them. The very short boy is denied participation in some of the sports activities of his classmates. The tall boy may be regarded as a leader, even though he possesses little or no leadership abilities. The extremely tall ninth-grade girl may display awkwardness of movement and feel ill at ease among the average height boys and girls in her class.

As you work with your students, you are likely to discover young people in the class who appear to be atypical in one or another aspect of development—physical, physiological, mental, or emotional. It is your responsibility, of course, to attempt, insofar as you are able, to meet the needs of the deviate. At the same time, you must be reasonably certain that the standards according to which you are evaluating your students represent conclusions from horizontal studies that are based on samplings inclusive of a sufficient number of the population to make them valid for general application.

In addition, the usability of the results of a cross-sectional study as a standard of comparison depends on the extent to which the research involved has followed strict scientific procedure. Much information now is available on various traits of adolescents that has been obtained through horizontal studies.

Interpretation of Vertical Studies

School people as well as parents are interested in knowing something about the developmental history of young people. They want to know what to expect at the different stages of the total growth and developmental pattern. The results of well-organized and scientifically conducted vertical or longitudinal studies can answer some of their questions.

Several vertical studies have been made to provide us with information concerning developmental and maturational processes and progress over a long time, such as during the first eighteen years of life. You may recall reading about some of these studies. A valid and comprehensive vertical study usually takes many years to complete and involves the utilization of various techniques of evaluation. Significant longitudinal studies have been completed at Harvard University in the Center for Research in Child Health and Development by Shuttleworth, and at the University of California in the Institute of Child Welfare by Jones and Bayley.

When a sufficient number of the same individuals are included in the longitudinal study, the cross-sectional or horizontal approach can be utilized to obtain information about them at the respective stages of their development. This is particularly true of the study of 134 children made by Reed and Stuart on height and weight over a period of eighteen years.[1] It should be noted that a relatively complete research study of child and adolescent development usually employs both the vertical and horizontal approach.

As a student teacher, it is unlikely that you will be asked to participate in a vertical study or even in a horizontal study. However, you should know about such research activities and apply their findings in your practice teaching and later in your regular teaching assignments. There are many cross-sectional studies to which you can have access.[2] An excellent source of a collection of longitudinal studies can be found in Stone and Onque, *Longitudinal Studies of Child Personality.*[3]

AVAILABLE RECORDS OF PERTINENT DATA

By the time a student enters a secondary school he has, in most school systems, a record of achievement that accompanies him on his journey through school. This often is known as a cumulative record and will provide whatever has been recorded about the student. It may be meager or it may be rather complete, including not only his academic record but also pertinent data on his behavior and acceptance by his peers.

Learn to Use the Cumulative Record

In an appropriate office of the school, you will find for each student a cumulative record of various items of interest about him as well as a record of his school progress. The record may be contained in a folder with other pertinent data. As a student teacher, you probably will be permitted access to this confidential material. By consulting the record card of a student, you can obtain information about him, such as his age and school grade; his record of attendance; the results of standardized tests that have been admin-

[1] See R. B. Reed and H. C. Stuart, "Patterns of Growth in Height and Weight from Birth to Eighteen Years of Age," in *Supplement to Pediatrics* (Springfield, Ill.: Charles C Thomas, Pub., 1959).

[2] See Paul H. Mussen (ed.), *Handbook of Research Methods in Child Development* (New York: John Wiley & Sons, Inc., 1960).

[3] See A. A. Stone and G. C. Onque, *Longitudinal Studies of Child Personality* (Cambridge, Mass.: Harvard Univ. Press, 1959).

istered to him, including some or all of the following—intelligence, special aptitudes and interests, emotional and/or social status, or any other areas of personal adjustment; his general achievement record; and his progress in your subject and others in which he is enrolled.

Other significant data that may be recorded on the cumulative record form are the student's educational and vocational plans, work experiences, cocurricular and extracurricular activities, and personality ratings assigned to him by his various teachers. Notations concerning the health status of a student may be very valuable. Some student folders also include anecdotal reports concerning his behavior and attitudes.

During your student teaching assignment, you should learn to study these records so that you learn what they contain and how to make use of the information you find there. We present a sample of what might be found on one of these cards.

CLASSROOM PROCEDURES FOR THE STUDY OF LEARNERS

Fortunately, school people are concerned with evaluating more than merely the school achievement of a secondary school learner. Modern emphasis on the development of the "whole" individual implies the need to evaluate all aspects of an individual's personality. We now concern ourselves with the nature and extent of the student's physical, intellectual, emotional, and social characteristics. Human traits developed in the classroom almost defy your ability to measure them objectively. Yet, although subjective elements are involved in evaluating approaches, you should get some training and experience in their use during your student teaching activities.

Need for the Utilization of Various Procedures

You will need to utilize various study procedures in your efforts to carry on student appraisal activities. Whatever evidence you obtain concerning the degree of progress of individual students in the development of knowledge, skill, and behavior attitudes tends to improve your effectiveness in your working relations with your students. Young people like a teacher who is expert in evaluating

PUPIL'S NAME

FATHER'S NAME

MOTHER'S MAIDEN NAME

OLDER BROTHER   OLDER SISTER

YOUNGER BROTHER   YOUNGER SISTER

GUARDIAN

ADDRESS

PHOTOGRAPH

YEARS IN GRADES 1-6   CIRCLE ONE   5   6   7   8

TRANSCRIPT SENT TO   DATE

ADMISSIONS — TRANSFERS — DISCHARGES

DATE	FROM	TO	REASON	ATTENDANCE TO DATE		
				PRES.	ABS.	LATE

SCHOOL GUIDANCE COUNSELOR J.H.S.

SCHOOL GUIDANCE COUNSELOR H.S.

SCHOOL GUIDANCE COUNSELOR H.S.

PERSONALITY RATING

CODE
O-OUTSTANDING
S-SATISFACTORY
N-NEEDS IMP'VMENT
U-UNSATISFACTORY

TEACHERS — COURTESY · EFFORT · RESPONSIBILITY · SELF-CONTROL

SEVENTH YEAR

EIGHTH YEAR

NINTH YEAR

TENTH YEAR

ELEVENTH YEAR

TWELFTH YEAR

THIRTEENTH YEAR

MAJORS EARNED			
YR.	TERM ENDING	MAJORS	AD-JUSTED
			CUMU-LATIVE
9			
10			
11			
12			
13			
TOTALS			

RATING — DATE | ORIG. | REV.

REGENTS CITY — WIDE

R C W — C W

SUMMER SCHOOL AND OTHERS

SCHOOL | SUBJ. DATE MARK

SCHOLASTIC RECORD	
FINAL AVERAGE	
STANDING IN CLASS	
QUARTILE	
NO. IN GRAD. CLASS	

SUBJECT & TERM	PDS. WK.	
ENG. 7	5	
TEACHER		FINAL
A.W. BALDWIN		

EXPLANATION OF ENTRIES IN SCHOLASTIC RECORD
GRADES 10-13

9TH | JUNE 19— | JAN. 19— | SCHOOL YEAR

13TH JUNE 19— | JAN. 19— | 12TH JUNE 19— | JAN. 19— | 11TH JUNE 19— | JAN. 19— | 10TH JUNE 19— | JAN. 19—

R | PDS | R | PDS

SCHOOL YEAR | TERM ENDING | 7TH 19— | 8TH 19— | 9TH JAN. 19— | JUNE 19—

Column labels (right section):

CAL. YEAR
ENGLISH
SPEECH
SOCIAL STUDIES
MATH
SCIENCE
FOREIGN LANGUAGE
ART
MUSIC
HEALTH EDUCATION
HYGIENE
ABS. LATE
OFF. TERM CLASS AVER.
OFFICIAL TEACHER

Column labels (left section):

CAL. YEAR
ENGLISH
SOCIAL STUDIES
MATH
SCIENCE
FOREIGN LANGUAGE
IND. ARTS
HOME ECO.
ART
MUSIC
HEALTH EDUCATION
HYGIENE
ABS. LATE
OFF. TERM CLASS AVER.
OFFICIAL TEACHER
FAMILY NAME
GIVEN NAMES

Right side fields:

DIPLOMA-CERTIFICATE
GRADUATION DATE — JHS / SHS
ADMISSION DATE — JHS / SHS
NAME OF SCHOOL — JHS / SHS
DATE OF BIRTH
BIRTHPLACE

PERSONALITY PROFILE (WORK EXPERIENCES, RECREATIONAL ACTIVITIES, SPECIAL INTERESTS, ETC.)

COMMENTS — RECORD OF INTERVIEWS, ETC., WITH DATES AND SIGNATURES;

INCLUDE — EDUCATIONAL AND VOCATIONAL PLANS. PUPIL'S & PARENTS' PLANS — COUNSELOR'S RECOMMENDATIONS — CHOICE

YEAR: 7   8   9

NMSQT

COLLEGE BOARD

IOWA TEST

ACHIEVEMENT TESTS	DATE	GRADE	RATING	INTELLIGENCE TESTS	DATE	GRADE	I.Q.

their behavior and achievement; they lose confidence in one who seems to lack this facility.

The teacher has many avenues available to him that he may utilize in his discovery of the differences and likenesses among his students. Among the informal procedures that are helpful in studying students are: (1) observing student behavior, (2) writing anecdotal reports, (3) having the students write autobiographical sketches, (4) using sociograms, (5) assigning individual or group projects, and (6) stimulating challenging class discussions.

You will find it helpful to develop skill in the utilization of various evaluative techniques during your student-teaching experiences. The first step toward success in their use is to adopt a positive mental set (attitude) toward their value as a teaching aid. Unless you believe that these techniques can improve your teaching effectiveness, they may be a burden rather than a help.

Observation of Student Behavior

The teacher has a continuous opportunity to observe student behavior. The alert teacher attempts to keep informed concerning whatever is transpiring in the classroom. Try as he may he does not always know all that is happening, however. He may observe deviant behavior, overhear an unusual comment, or note a questioning expression on the face of a student. These observations are important to him in learning about student reactions to classroom procedures.

You should be interested in the various patterns of behavior that are displayed in the classroom. However, you need to evaluate these overt expressions objectively, realizing that some may have no more than momentary significance but that others may be symptomatic of behavior that needs to be corrected. Your ability to assess classroom incidents correctly can be helpful to the students involved as well as to yourself.

The student teacher and observation. It may seem to you that to expect a teacher to be aware of what every student is doing at every minute of the recitation period is assigning him an almost impossible task. The teacher is concentrating on his presentation of subject matter and evaluating student responses to his questions. At the same time, he needs to know what John (who is sitting in the rear of the room) is doing, that Jane (at the side of the room) may be trying to whisper to her schoolmate, that Ethel is writing, or why George is fussing under his desk. Yet, you have known teachers who have been able to carry on learning activities and also keep aware of student behavior.

Education departments in colleges and universities in teacher-education institutions realize the fact that student teachers need training in multiple-attention giving. Hence, before you are assigned the responsibility of teaching a class under supervision, you have opportunities to observe teachers and their classes in action. In these experiences, you can observe teaching approaches and watch student behavior. This is good practice since, when you are teaching a class (especially as a beginner), you can overlook many student activities that you can detect as a visitor whose objective is to note the teacher's and the students' behavior.

When you begin your observations of teaching methods, student responses, and general classroom behavior, you may not know to what matters you should direct your attention. You need to be helped to develop skill in observation. In order for you to keep alert to students' reactions, you can be asked to employ the open-end approach by using a class seating chart to record any observed behavior characteristics of individual students during the class period. Another approach is to supply you with a prepared list of more or less typical behavior responses on which you can check your observation of students' attitudes and behavior. By utilizing both the seating chart and a list of suggested activities, you can spot the particular activities of individual students.

Suggested list of student activities. Various lists have been devised to guide student teachers in their beginning participation in observation of student behavior. You may find the following list of suggestions helpful. The list includes:

1. Manner of entering classroom and taking seat
2. Promptness in coming to attention
3. Specific kinds of behavior displayed in attempts to gain peer attention or teacher approval
4. Extent of participation of individual students in class discussion
5. Types of student responses

6. Tendencies of students to dominate the discussion
7. Tendency to engage in irrelevant activities or to tease class-mates
8. Care with which students have prepared assigned work
9. Nature and extent of displayed interest in subject
10. Types of questions, if any, asked by students
11. Ability of individual students to read with understanding
12. Nature of observable physical handicaps
13. Speech or language problems of students
14. Displayed tendency toward leadership
15. Individual reaction to deserved punishment
16. Attempts to monopolize the attention of the teacher
17. Attempts at cheating or other forms of dishonesty
18. Work or study habits displayed by individual students
19. Special cooperative or noncooperative acts
20. General social atmosphere in the classroom

As you learn to observe student behavior and make notations, you can become proficient in utilizing ways of discovering much about each learner. Your interest in your students tends to increase as you come to know more about them and their displayed attitudes.

Observation of Teaching Procedures

Watching students and student responses is only one aspect of your total observational activity. You need also to discover what is being done by the teacher and to note the skill with which he conducts the lesson. You should attempt not only to discover what he does to increase his understanding of his students but also to observe the respective steps taken by him in his development of the ideas associated with the learning experience.

A list of suggestions that you can use to guide your observation during your early observational experiences may prove helpful. We suggest that as you observe your cooperating teacher you can be rewarded greatly by noting such aspects of his procedure as:

1. The manner in which the teacher starts the lesson
2. The intrinsic and extrinsic rewards utilized to motivate the students to learn the subject

3. The use made of visual aids; chalkboards, charts, slides, film-strips, motion pictures, programmed learning, and the like
4. The ways in which the teacher helps the learners draw upon their previous experiences
5. The extent to which students are stimulated toward the development of mental readiness for engaging in a specific unit of study
6. The number of students who are drawn into the class discussion
7. The means used by the teacher to engender self-discipline
8. The ways in which students are encouraged to develop good habits of work
9. The way in which full use is made of available time
10. The influence on students of the teacher's attitude and behavior
11. The extent to which the lesson is developed step-by-step
12. The variations that are made in methods of presentation that are in accord with differences among learners

As you observe a teacher conduct a lesson, you must keep in mind that your function is not to criticize adversely what you observe. In Chapter 8 we note that, in spite of college courses in methods of teaching, you can learn much from watching a teacher in action. You may not agree with everything that is done. If time permits, you will find it helpful to discuss with the teacher whom you observed his reasons for employing certain techniques rather than others.

Writing Anecdotal Reports

The recording of information concerning an individual student is referred to as an anecdotal report. During your observation of your cooperating teacher and his class, you will have many opportunities to make entries of specific characteristics of individual students. You can take notes on types of responses displayed, such as actual behavior during recitation, span of attention, willingness to participate in the discussion, interest in the subject, attempts to converse with a neighbor, tendency to daydream, and the like. You then can report the incident in the form of an anecdotal report.

Before you write an anecdotal report you should evaluate the data and decide what you want to keep on record and what you may wish to discard. Although this phase of evaluation may not seem to be important to you, it may be one of the most important steps in student evaluation. It represents what you believe to be important in student responses.

Need for accuracy in reporting. You must learn to be accurate and objective in what you record and make every effort to avoid any personal biases or prejudices. This suggests the recording of everything that you observe happening in connection with a particular student in a particular situation. You should not select only certain aspects of the situation. Record the facts as you observed them. However, after you have made your preliminary notes you should evaluate their worth. Decide whether they are important enough to be retained as a permanent record.

In your observation of behavior, try to be accurate and reliable. As you rise above an injection of personal bias in your interpretation of an incident, to that extent will you become objective in dealing with student behavior. When these records are kept, from year to year, by teachers of various subjects there is built a cumulative record that tends to inscribe a profile of the student.

Some teachers seem to believe, mistakenly, that anecdotal records are to be used only to report incidents that reflect undesirable or uncooperative behavior. This is not the only purpose of such reports. Rather are they intended to record unusual incidents concerning a student or students. They may represent behavior that is superior or inferior to the average. All entries should be made in light of student's assets or liabilities in a given situation.

It takes time and considerable thought to write a good anecdotal report. As you practice writing them, develop the habit of reporting a significant incident as soon after it occurs as is possible, thus avoiding a failure to include significant aspects of the situation (which you may forget if you allow too much time to elapse between the incident and your reporting of it). Include the date on which the incident occurred and sign the report. Also, be terse and to the point. Your job is to report and not to evaluate the incident or give your personal opinion concerning it. Here are several examples of anecdotal reports.

During the week of September 16 to 20, 1963, Henry, one of the boys, was absent from school because of a badly sprained ankle. John Graves volunteered to take to Henry the daily assignments so that he could keep up with the classwork. When the latter returned to school, John stayed with him after school to brief him on some of the class discussion he had missed.

On October 14, 1963, George Drake stuck his foot out into the aisle, causing a passing student to stumble and fall. This had happened on earlier occasions. When George was spoken to about it, his answer, with a laugh, was "My legs are too long for this desk." He himself had selected this seat. When it was suggested that he change to a seat that might be more comfortable, he replied, "This seat suits me. Let them be careful." He has continued to keep his feet in the aisle. (This incident needs the immediate attention of a member of the school personnel who is authorized to deal with serious behavior problems.)

December 19, 1963. Joan Forbes submitted her science notebook today. The notes were carefully and neatly prepared. Her diagrams and other illustrative material were accurate and attractively executed. She gives evidence of special ability in drawing.

Value of anecdotal records. Anecdotal reports can be extremely valuable to you as a teacher and to other members of the school personnel. If your students know that you keep pertinent records concerning them and their school performance, they realize that you regard them as individuals in whose strengths and weaknesses you are interested.

Students thrill to the knowledge that you recognize their cooperative behavior by recording it in writing. For a student to know that you have written an honest report about his lack of adherence to school regulations, his uncooperative behavior, or other misdeed may help deter him from engaging again in that form of undesirable conduct. Any subsequent improvement in his behavior should then be noted specifically in another anecdotal report, and he should be informed of this fact.

Anecdotal reports also have value in conferences with parents. A counselor or you as the teacher may be conferring with the parent of a student who is not achieving satisfactorily in his studies, in spite of his ability to do so. You can help the parent discover reasons for his poor work if you have available reports of his behavior—such as coming to class without having prepared home assignments, giving attention in class to something else rather than to the subject of discussion, and the like. Again, a parent may consult you about his child's plans for the future. Records that you have kept of some of the student's displayed interests can be helpful in advising the parent.

Anecdotal reports also are valuable to members of the school faculty who are charged with recommending students for holding offices in a school organization or for part-time vocational placement or a full-time job after graduation. An accumulation of reports (usually not only one single report) can offer good evidence of a particular student's habitual attitudes, interests, or observed behavior. In addition, some colleges request from the high school a brief statement concerning an applicant's special strengths and weaknesses. Honest reports of his behavior as a high school student can provide the basis of the statement sent to the institution.

The various uses to which anecdotal records can be subjected should convince you of their importance in the school life of students. Hence you need to be careful that you do not write an adverse report in a moment of anger caused by a student's display of a relatively insignificant uncooperative act. Be certain that you have viewed the incident objectively and unemotionally before you submit in writing something that may affect his reputation in the school and outside it.

One function of the high school is to guide young people in their development of desirable personal characteristics. A high school freshman may be guilty of misdeeds that, with the help of his teachers, gradually stop. This fact should receive recognition. The faculty of one high school has adopted a sensible attitude toward anecdotal records. All of the teachers are encouraged to submit special notations about students. These are accumulated in student folders. At the end of a student's junior year, his guidance counselor reads all of the reports, discarding those that deal with a single unimportant incident. Those that appear to represent a habitual behavior trend are kept and evaluated at the end of the senior year in light of reports entered during that year. Commendatory records as well as those indicating serious weaknesses are then filed as part of the permanent record of the student.

The degree of value of anecdotal records depends on the attitude toward them of the teachers who submit them. Some teachers use them sparingly; others write many. The worth of various reports differs. Some teachers seem to observe and report only commendatory behavior; others appear to emphasize undesirable conduct. The alert teacher who is truly interested in all of his students tends, of course, to evaluate behavior intelligently and reports either praiseworthy behavior or behavior that needs improvement. In addition to reporting, this teacher also attempts to help the uncooperative student change his attitude, or solicits the services of school personnel and parents to bring about needed improvement.

Cautions in the use of anecdotal records. To help you in your use of anecdotal records, we shall summarize some of the cautions to be observed. The keeping of accurate anecdotal records is a sizable undertaking. Their value depends somewhat on the attitude of the school toward them. Even when the school administration is committed to them there are many limitations in their development and use. We present here some difficulties confronted by a teacher who conscientiously writes and uses anecdotal reports. In working with these records you may find it difficult:

1. To be accurate and correctly record information so that the record becomes more valuable than harmful.
2. To write reports objectively so that you avoid giving expression to your opinion—simply to record behavior.
3. To avoid using these records in defense of your own weaknesses.
4. To record all significant behavior incidents, good as well as bad.
5. To be alert to the danger of misinterpretation after you are no longer in the social setting in which the act occurred.
6. To write the kind of report that will not be damaging to the student, if, later, it falls into the hands of irresponsible persons.
7. To follow up on discovered undesirable behavior practices.
8. To avoid submitting too many negative reports and too few positive ones.
9. To differentiate between a student's typical and atypical behavior.

10. To provide a set of anecdotal records that can be used by the entire faculty of the school or school system.

In spite of the limitations of anecdotal records, you will be able to function at a higher level as a teacher to the extent that you become skilled in the keeping of significant records. The greatest obstacle to the keeping of these records will be your attitude toward their worth. When you have faith in them you are likely to become proficient in their use.

Significance of Autobiographical Reports

An effective device to obtain data directly from an individual concerning his attitudes, interests, and general behavior and ideals is the autobiography. The student who takes the time to write a comprehensive statement about himself, and his interests and aspirations, is likely to provide important insight into his thinking and general personality. When it is studied carefully, an autobiographical report reveals much about the student. This is characterized by what he includes as well as what he omits. It is not easy to stimulate an adolescent to write freely about himself. He often is suspicious of the purpose of the assignment and therefore hesitates to portray his real self.

Autobiographical sketches are more easily obtained in a normal setting such as writing a composition in an English class. Here it does not become a project that is looked upon as one to delve into a student's past but rather as a means of giving him an opportunity to express his ideas in good English. Nevertheless, it is not easy for most secondary school students to write freely about their interests, attitudes, aspirations, and past experiences. Rather do they tend to set down what will be supportive to their status among their peers.

Any attempt to write an autobiography requires some form of self-evaluation. A biography that is based on entries in a diary is likely to give greater accuracy to the story than is one based on memory of past happenings. Then, too, the method used to motivate the student to write his story may affect what he eventually writes. Some adolescents are helped by supplying them with an appropriate topic such as "My Most Interesting Experience during the Past

Year." Once this has been written, it can be followed by adding supplementary data, such as personal attitudes toward experiences.

Another topic for a composition that can have autobiographical overtones is "My Plans for the Future." Some adolescents have given thought to what they plan to do after graduation from high school. Those who expect to continue their education on the college level usually are more realistic about the future than are those who expect to leave high school as soon as age permits or to complete their formal education with high school graduation. In any case, you can discover much about a young person's expectations and interests by having him write on this topic. Of course, you must realize that what an adolescent reveals about himself in autobiographical form may be fancy as well as fact. At least you can discover how his imagination functions.

You need to use caution in the matter of having autobiographical reports read to the class. A young person may be moved to include confidential information in his report that he would prefer not to have shared with classmates. Another young person may deliberately "pad" his report in order to impress you and the other members of the class. At times, the content of such a report can well be the subject of a private conference between you and the writer of the autobiography.

Stories that are partially autobiographical can be undertaken on a regularly planned basis. In an English class, each student might be asked periodically to write on "My Most Interesting Experience This Month." These compositions are then accumulated and placed in individual folders. Toward the end of the term you might read each student's offerings, set by set. A student can reveal much about himself and his personal qualities through a series of such compositions. Your own evaluative reports of what you discover can be filed in the student's folder where they will be available for use by other school personnel, such as the principal and the guidance counselor.

Significance of Sociograms

The dynamics of human nature are not easy to understand. The more aids we have at our disposal the better able shall we be to make value judgments on individual behavior. There are those who believe that any good teacher knows his students so well that an application of the principle of the sociogram will not reveal anything that he does not already know. Teachers who have used the sociogram in their classes are quick to point out that they can discover much about their students through the use of this device that otherwise would not have been discovered by them.

Before you attempt to utilize the principle of the sociogram you should have a purpose or problem in mind to which its application will help give you an answer. You may have observed that one of your students is behaving strangely among his peers and that he is not succeeding in his work. You may wish to discover by means of the sociogram the extent to which he is being accepted by the members of his class. This can be done in one of several ways.

You might organize a class project and ask each student to list the names of three students with whom he would like to work on it. Or you can use a more simple problem such as asking each student to write the names of three of his best friends on a sheet of paper. From this you might be able to obtain valuable information to enable you to gain insight into a young person's personality problem. The extent to which he is an *isolate* tends to be revealed through the use of the sociogram approach. It is important that the information obtained be kept confidential by the teacher. Figure 4 illustrates how a sociogram is constructed. Study it to determine how it can be of help to a teacher.

Significance of Individual or Group Projects

With our present focus on the full development of the individual and of ways and means of dealing with differences among learners, opportunities should be provided for students to plan and develop special learning projects on which a group of students can work together. These can be set up in the science laboratory, the language laboratory, as well as in English classes, mathematics classes, and so on.

Whatever special project is approved must be within the capacities of the students involved. There also should be adequate materials and equipment for successful completion of the project. The teacher has the responsibility of giving the kind of super-

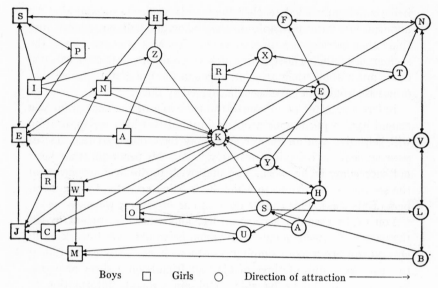

Boys □   Girls ○   Direction of attraction ——————→

Fig. 4.—Sociogram showing the choices of students to work on a committee on a social studies project (three choices).

vision that encourages every student to participate in the project. When completed, the project needs to be evaluated. It should be presented to the class and be understood so that all students will feel a part of what is being done by everyone.

It is through many of these well-planned projects that your students can be given opportunities to apply and reveal their special talents. Students need a variety of activities through which they can give expression to their creative urges. As you observe students at work on these special projects during your student-teaching experiences, you can learn much concerning ways in which the students work on such assignments. Thus, when you are a regular teacher you will be able to guide their learning activities in these projects.

Significance of Holding Informal Conferences

You often can make good use of a face-to-face meeting with a student. Technically, this is not considered to be a formal interview situation, but much can be achieved through its utilization. An informal talk can help you gain a better understanding of what motivates certain types of behavior by discovering more about the individual's interests, attitudes, and modes of thinking. What you gain from such an informal talk depends on your skill in interrelating with the student concerned.

The outcomes of the informal conference with a student usually depend on its underlying purpose, and whether it was sought by the student or held at your invitation. If the student, because of his confidence in you, requests an opportunity to discuss an immediate problem that bothers him, the establishment of rapport between the two of you is easily achieved.

An informal conference might be held for the purpose of bringing greater understanding to the student instead of scolding or berating him for some act. The discussion should represent a give-and-take relationship. If the conference is to be considered successful, the student should feel that he has been benefited in some way by it.

Adolescents sometimes tend to be secretive about themselves and have a tendency to respond with suspicion to a student-teacher conference initiated by the latter. If you wish a student to reveal much about himself, it is up to you to convince him that you are sincerely interested in his welfare. You are likely to find the informal conference valuable as a result of asking significant questions and assuming the role of a good listener.

As a student teacher, you often are in a good position to talk informally with students. Through these experiences you can discover something of their value and, at the same time, get practice in the development of the technique utilized in these informal relationships with students. We now present some guiding principles that might help you during these face-to-face personal conferences. In an informal conference with a student, you are likely to find it important:

1. To meet in a place that provides privacy.
2. To assume a friendly attitude toward the student so that a free exchange of ideas may flow between the two of you.
3. To assume an attitude of learning from the student as well as imparting information to him.

4. To be concerned that the liking becomes mutual between the two of you.
5. To make a conscious effort to minimize your own talking in order that the student may reveal as much as possible of the problem that is under discussion.
6. To respect the confidences given to you during the conference.
7. To avoid any discussion of extraneous matters unrelated to the issue at hand.
8. To keep the conference within reasonable limits of time.
9. To help the student develop the feeling that he has gained something from this meeting.
10. To invite the student to talk with you whenever he has a problem on which you might be able to enlighten him.

Much good can result from these conferences. As you develop skill in their use you will find that they are excellent teaching aids. You will find great differences among students concerning what they are willing to tell you during a conference. You will discover also that some students will tell you what they would not tell another teacher or that they will reveal to another teacher what they will not tell you.

Through face-to-face talks, you can discover many individual differences in the area of learning ability and in behavior patterns. Take care, however, that you do not attempt to help a student resolve a deep-seated personal problem but encourage him to seek the assistance of the guidance counselor. In fact, as a student teacher, you should not use any of these interview procedures for studying students without the approval of your cooperating teacher.

QUESTIONS AND TOPICS FOR DISCUSSION

1. List some of the values to you as a teacher of recognizing various differences among your students.
2. Differentiate between horizontal and longitudinal studies. Give an illustration of each.
3. As you examine the cumulative records of your students, note which items are not filled in. How do you explain these omissions?
4. What have you gained from observing your cooperating teacher and his class at work? Be specific.

5. Practice writing several anecdotal reports of student behavior. Submit them to your cooperating teacher for evaluation.
6. Have your students write autobiographical reports. Read them carefully. What do you learn about some students that you did not know?
7. Ask your students to list the names of three classmates with whom they would like to work on a project. Arrange the results in the form of a sociogram. What information does this give you about individual students? What can you do for the isolates? Consult your cooperating teacher about this.
8. Set a simple project for small group participation. Observe students' attitudes toward the activity.
9. After you have had an informal conference with a student, review the important points of a conference presented in this chapter. Check those to which you adhered. Note those that you forgot. Try to remember them in your next conference with a student.
10. Why should you not hold conferences with students without first consulting your cooperating teacher?

SELECTED REFERENCES

ADAMS, G. S., and TORGERSON, T. L. *Measurement and Evaluation for the Secondary-School Teacher.* New York: Holt, Rinehart & Winston, Inc., 1956.

BRAFIELD, J. M., and MOREDOCK, H. S. *Measurement and Evaluation in Education.* New York: Macmillan Co., 1957.

COHEN, D. H., and STERN, V. *Observing and Recording the Behavior of Young Children.* New York: Teachers College, Columbia Univ., Bureau of Publications, 1958.

DUROST, W. N., and PRESCOTT, G. A. *Essentials of Measurement for Teachers.* New York: Harcourt, Brace & World, Inc., 1962.

FROELICH, C. P. *Studying Students.* Chicago: Science Research Associates, Inc., 1953.

GREENE, H. A., JORGENSEN, A. N., and GERBERICH, J. R. *Measurement and Evaluation in the Secondary School.* New York: David McKay Co., Inc., 1954.

JENNINGS, H. H. *Leadership and Isolation.* New York: David McKay Co., Inc., 1950.

———. *Sociometry in Group Relations* (rev. ed.). Washington, D.C.: American Council on Education, 1959.

LINDVALL, C. M. *Testing and Evaluation: An Introduction.* New York: Harcourt, Brace & World, Inc., 1961.

MAIER, N. R. *The Appraisal Interview: Objectives, Methods and Skills.* New York: John Wiley & Sons, Inc., 1958.

NOLL, V. *Introduction to Educational Measurement.* Boston: Houghton Mifflin Co., 1957.

SCHWARTZ, A., and TIEDEMAN, S. C. *Evaluating Student Progress in the Secondary School.* New York: David McKay Co., Inc., 1957.

THOMAS, R. *Judging Student Progress.* New York: David McKay Co., Inc., 1954.

TYLER, LEONA. "The Initial Interview," *Personnel and Guidance Journal,* April 1956, pp. 466–73.

WENDT, E., and BROWN, G. W. *Essentials of Educational Evaluation.* New York: Holt, Rinehart & Winston, Inc., 1957.

WHITE, VERA. *Studying the Individual Pupil.* New York: Harper & Row, Pub., Inc., 1958.

WRIGHTSTONE, J. W., JUSTMAN, J., and ROBBINS, I. *Evaluation in Modern Education.* New York: American Book Co., 1956.

5

RELATIONSHIPS WITH YOUR COLLEAGUES

You bring to your student teaching a personality pattern, a degree of individual ability, and a body of background of experience that differentiate you from every other student teacher. You want to prepare yourself to be a successful teacher. During this apprenticeship period you will experience many conditions peculiar to your student-teacher status in addition to those you will encounter when you become a regular teacher.

YOUR PROFESSIONAL RELATIONSHIPS

As a student teacher you perform in an educational environment that enables you to gain confidence in yourself so that later as a regular teacher you can work effectively with young people, and school and community personnel. You need to be helped to make a good social adjustment to the many differing persons with whom you will be associated—students, teachers, supervisors, and administrators, as well as other members of the school and college personnel. In addition, you will meet and work with parents and community leaders. Also, you will need to become acquainted with the social mores of the practice school and of the community.

Student Teaching as an Interacting Process

Your successful induction into student teaching is a two-way process. It necessitates the display of a spirit of cooperation between yourself and all others with whom you associate during the critical period of student teaching. You will respond favorably to any show of sympathetic understanding of your problems of adjustment by the members of the school to which you are assigned and by your college supervisor who is guiding your observational and teaching activities.

Your effectiveness in the classroom is strengthened to the degree that the students and the faculty members learn to respect you and cooperate with you. Consequently, you need to keep in mind that what you do or do not do affects the extent to which you are accepted by all of those with whom you are associated. The building of friendly attitudes of others toward you depends upon your attitudes and behavior toward them. At the same time, your attitude toward student teaching and the persons with whom you work affects the extent to which you are helped by them in practical ways to recognize the value to you of your various experiences.

Areas of Relationships

Your relationships with students were discussed in Chapter 2. These relationships stand at the top of the list of valuable interactions for effective teaching-learning conditions. Yet, of great importance also are the working relationships that are established from the start of your practice experiences with all of the persons who, to a greater or lesser degree, are responsible for the extent of your success in your student-teaching activities.

You soon discover that this educational experience involves professional contacts with various people both within and outside the school or schools to which you have been or will be assigned. You realize that personal adjustments need to be made to the philosophy and practices of such individuals as your college supervisor, your cooperating teacher, the school principal, and other members of the school personnel.

You also will want to become acquainted with the educational ideals and the attitudes toward the school of the parents of the students and of the community as a whole. Your closest relationships probably will be with your cooperating teacher and with your college supervisor. There will, however, be occasions when you will need to interact in a constructive fashion with other individuals or groups. In this chapter we present concrete descriptions of some of the basic professional relationships that you will experience as a student teacher.

PROFESSIONAL HELP NEEDED

As we suggested in Chapter 1, your introduction into student teaching involves your assuming of new responsibilities and the changing of your attitude from that of a student to that of a teacher. This metamorphosis does not take place overnight, nor can it be brought about without the intelligent assistance of experienced and understanding professional associates.

You must be willing and able, of course, to profit from whatever help is afforded you in this critical phase of your teacher education program. You also should know just what help you need in order to get a good start in this new experience and to continue to meet your student teaching obligations effectively and successfully.

Inez Ahlering of the Reitz High School, Evansville, Indiana, was interested in obtaining an answer to the question, "What are the reactions of student teachers to their practice teaching in the high schools?" To this end, a questionnaire was administered to a group of student teachers who had done their student teaching at different schools and who had come from different colleges.

According to the report of this study:

> Students were very complimentary of the schools and teachers with whom they worked; however, they were frank in their other comments, too. Questionnaires indicated that some teachers were very helpful, made an effort to give students varied experiences, and held frequent conferences where frankness was encouraged in discussing problems and where students found solutions that were satisfying and encouraging.[1]

We now present the eight questions asked in the questionnaire with a list of student responses for each. Note that the term *supervisory teacher* has the same connotation as *cooperating teacher*.

I. What help from the teacher or school would have made you better acquainted with the school when you began your student teaching?

A student handbook on student-teacher responsibilities, rights, and so on. Guidance on how far one can go with one's own ideas in the classroom. General knowledge of facilities available to the student teacher—records, forms, and so on.

[1] Inez Ahlering, "Reactions by Student Teachers," *The Clearing House*, February, 1963, p. 337.

General layout of the building—knowing where the library, cafeteria, and other rooms are located.

Information about school policies on absences and tardiness.

A guided tour of the building.

Provision by the college for an introductory meeting with the teacher before actual student teaching began.

II. What help from the teacher would have been useful at the time you began your teaching?

Introduction to the class by the supervising teacher.

Introductions to other teachers in the school's cafeteria, where there is a relaxed attitude.

A schedule of what I was going to teach before I started my student teaching.

Some definite information concerning student-teaching responsibilities. My duties at first were rather vague.

Background material on the students—physical handicaps, problem students, and so on.

Knowing what material the class was using.

A complete understanding of what was going to be required of me.

Type of lesson plans required, whether extensive or merely for personal use; how far in advance lesson plans were required; length of time to spend on each unit.

Some place where a teacher could practice writing on the chalkboard before getting in front of the class.

Duties that are expected—bulletin board, cafeteria, clubs, signing in, and so on.

III. Did you visit the school and talk with the supervising teacher previous to your teaching assignment? Was this visit valuable? In what way?

No. I did not visit in advance, but I did telephone the teacher.

No. I think this would have been valuable, but I was told there was nothing that I was to do prior to the first day of school.

(A few other students answered "No" to this question.)

Yes. I visited the class several times a few months earlier. I felt less uneasy and more confident when I began my teaching.

Yes. I became somewhat familiar with the room, facilities, etc.

Yes. It acquainted me with my assignment, the teacher, and the students.

Yes—my own volition. I saw the room and met my supervising teacher. I didn't have to begin from scratch.

Yes. I knew where classes were scheduled, learned where materials were kept, and observed how classes were conducted.

Yes. I learned what texts would be used, was given texts and materials, was told what material would be covered when I returned, and where I should begin.

IV. What help from the supervising teacher would have made your student teaching easier?

More sessions to answer problems.
Greater helpfulness on the part of the teacher.
An opportunity to start planning my lessons sooner. I was given the units. I was to teach only a few days before starting.
More help in planning and evaluating.
Greater willingness on the part of the teacher to explain "why" something was done.
Help in making reports.
Use of a teacher's manual a few weeks prior to my teaching.

V. What help from your supervising teacher was valuable to you in your teaching and adjustment to teaching?

Watching me teach and making comments.
Giving me background information on pupils.
Pointing out aspects of teaching that are sometimes overlooked—the homeroom, class, and so on.
Giving hints on how to organize.
Having conferences daily and evaluating my work.
Praising me for things well done.
Observing me teach and making comments on what I did.
Giving constructive criticism of daily lesson plans in advance in order to eliminate problems, avoid embarrassment, and insure effective instruction.
Knowing that the supervising teacher always backed me up. When I was wrong, she told me later.
Having the supervisor in the room helped.
Being friendly, enthusiastic, understanding, and interested.
Helping me gain confidence in myself.
Evaluating my work daily.

VI. What help that you received from the teacher or school do you consider the most important?

Comments on my teaching, together with constructive suggestions.
Pointing out different teaching techniques.
Giving information on grading procedures.
Suggesting good related material to read.
Helping me to have confidence in myself and my teaching.
Being willing to have questions asked without making me feel ignorant as a result.
Inviting questions.
Helping me in a regularly scheduled conference period where I had an opportunity to discuss planning, organizing, teaching, evaluating, discipline, and so on.

Guiding me in planning lessons and units.

Learning ways of handling discipline problems.

Leaving me alone for certain lessons.

Working in the friendly atmosphere of the school.

Feeling of acceptance by all the teachers and administrators.

Being introduced to teachers and administrators and being shown around the school, which made me feel a part of the school.

Willingness of other teachers to have students observe classes.

VII. What helpful suggestions do you have for the supervising teacher?

Have a definite time to talk things over.

Give the student teacher an opportunity to be alone at times.

Be a good listener and willing to answer questions.

Give the student teacher something to do at the beginning of the assignment with you.

Give a picture of the teacher's responsibilities.

Try to be on the level with the student teacher.

VIII. List problems you encountered in your student teaching.

(Student teachers were quick to recognize some of the problems that experienced teachers have not yet solved.)

Grading papers.

Arguing over test answers.

Restlessness of students.

Handling discipline problems.

Attending college and doing student teaching at the same time.

Introducing new ideas to stimulate discussion.

Planning lessons to accomplish definite goals.

Cheating.

Being criticized for going ahead and doing what I wanted to do after I had been given instructions to do so.

Having to rely on my own judgment as I started to teach when advice from supervising teachers, college instructors, books, and pamphlets was conflicting.

Motivating students who don't care so long as they pass and some who just don't care at all.

Handling absenteeism.

Budgeting time.

Presenting subject matter.

Being able to ask questions on a high school level.

As I mentioned in the beginning of this article, there were many complimentary remarks made that are worthy of note:

Student teaching, I believe, is the most valuable training one receives in preparing for teaching.

It was an ideal situation.

The supervising teacher was most helpful.

The supervising teacher tried to acquaint me with the school as quickly as possible. I think she did a good job.

On the first day, my supervising teacher introduced me to the principal, assistant principal, counselors, and dean of girls: this I appreciated.

The supervising teacher did a fine job.

My situation was fortunate. I was given all the help I needed.

I couldn't have asked for a better teacher.

The comments of students indicated that supervised teaching differs by schools and teachers; however, this is no serious criticism. Responses showed, too, that supervised teaching may be made more vital. Improvement, naturally, rests with the college, the high school, and the teacher.

The supervising teacher has an opportunity to build the profession and to encourage and help capable young people to become competent teachers. A student teacher's experience may inspire his entrance into the profession, or it may discourage the individual forever. Working with student teachers requires time, understanding, and patience; but the rewards in building a profession of dedicated teachers who play major roles in the lives of young people cannot be measured.[2]

You can profit from reading these questions and responses carefully and comparing the reported situations with your own experiences. Furthermore, you probably will find that these student teachers recognize areas of needed help of which you may not yet be aware. You can be alerted thereby to some of your own responsibilities to the students and the school. If you find that you are experiencing problems similar to those reported, do not hesitate to bring them to the attention of your cooperating teacher or college supervisor.

BUILDING PROFESSIONAL RELATIONSHIPS

Your first appearance at the school is important. You are in the school, including the classroom and the corridor, and are being observed by students and others, as well as being there to observe what you can about school matters. If the school is in a small community you also are making an impression on some members of the community outside the school personnel. To the students, to the faculty, and to the community you are a teacher—not a college student. You need to conduct yourself as such.

As you go about the school in the performance of your various

[2] *Ibid.*, pp. 337–40.

activities, your appearance, attitudes, and behavior are noted by those whom you meet or with whom you work. You impress them either favorably or unfavorably. They are quick to recognize your evidenced strengths and noticeable weaknesses, and they tend to treat you accordingly. You are being evaluated as a future teacher.

Most members of the school personnel, as well as your college instructors, are more than willing to meet you on a professional basis and give you whatever help you need to achieve success in your chosen lifework. In fact, it often happens that a cooperative student teacher is invited by his practice school to continue there as a regular teacher. The ability to build good professional relations can become one of your strongest assets.

Your Relationships with Your College Supervisor

The person whom you ultimately must satisfy for a final evaluation of your teaching effectiveness is your college supervisor. He serves as the link between the college and the high school in which you work. Either he or a director of student teaching has the responsibility of assigning you to a school. He may have something to say concerning the cooperating teacher to whom you will be assigned to work. However, this usually is the duty of the school principal.

Importance of the college supervisor. The college supervisor has his theories of education and his own ideas about the teaching approaches to be employed by you. These can serve as background information for you. Yet, you must give careful attention to the plans and procedures utilized by your cooperating teacher. If you attempt to deviate widely from the methods utilized by the class teacher, you may confuse rather than help the students in their continued learning.

The college supervisor can be an excellent support-provider to you and to the cooperating teacher. To do this, he needs to help the cooperating teacher understand the purposes of student teaching and the need for providing you with at least a minimum of teaching opportunities. Your college supervisor should be available to you whenever he is needed. You should be able to go to him for help in planning your work as well as to discuss any problems that arise in connection with student teaching. You can benefit from his careful analysis of lessons that he observes you teach. You will want to know what he considers to be your strengths and your weaknesses. You will appreciate his suggesting ways in which you can bring about needed improvements rather than merely calling attention to your faults.

Functions of the college supervisor. In the performing of his duties, the college supervisor functions in the capacity of serving the student teacher, the college, and the school and its students. He acts as a kind of liaison between you, your college methods instructor, the school, and your cooperating teacher. You are likely to find that your college supervisor is concerned with most of the following functions:

1. Serving as the professional link between the school and the college
2. Acting as liaison between the student teacher and the cooperating teacher, between college instructors of education courses and your cooperating teacher, and between present educational policy and the way it affects your student teaching
3. Recommending the proper placement of student teachers
4. Assisting the procurement of professional materials for the student teacher
5. Critically evaluating the student teacher's classroom teaching
6. Facilitating various forms of communication between the college and the cooperating teacher
7. Alerting the cooperating teacher to the bases of selection of students for student teaching
8. Advising the cooperating school on personal strengths and weaknesses of individual student teachers
9. Keeping the cooperating school informed on the college courses a student teacher is enrolled in during his student teaching
10. Providing the cooperating teacher with a tentative schedule of his official visits to a student teacher
11. Being sensitive to the interests and needs of the cooperating teachers and to the administrators of cooperating schools
12. Helping the student teacher plan his lessons for teaching
13. Helping the student teacher relate his experience to his teaching

14. Evaluating the student teacher's teaching based on personal observation of his teaching
15. Utilizing the cooperating teacher's evaluation of a student teacher in his own final judgment of teaching effectiveness

Your Relationship with the Administrators of the School

If you have not already learned it, you soon will discover that the principal is the most important person on the school staff. You perhaps have heard that as is the principal so is the school. This is more than an expression. The principal sets the overall tone of the school. He, with his staff, determines school policy. Whatever *esprit de corps* prevails in the school emanates from his influence.

Your contact with the principal is likely to be limited. There may be occasions when you help prepare refreshments for a staff meeting or assist in the planning of assembly programs or other general school activities. Such situations may afford opportunities for you to meet the principal in more direct relationships. You may be certain, however, that he is aware of your presence in the building and gives indirect supervision to your student-teaching activities. Sometimes he brings himself directly into the student-teaching experience by observing you teach and conferring with you about the lesson.

The way in which you are inducted into the school often rests with the principal. Some principals welcome the opportunity to be able to engage in the training of students. They believe that they have something to offer and do all they can to see that you are afforded every advantage possible in the school. These receptive attitudes enable you to build feelings of security and belongingness. They encourage you to want to teach.

Large secondary schools have other school administrators who fill important roles in providing supplementary administrative relationships with you. These activities vary with schools, especially with the size of the school. Probably, more than you realize it, all administrators are aware of your presence in the school and are devoting energy to the success of your student-teaching activities. These are among the incidental professional values that accrue to you without your being aware that they operate in your behalf.

Your Relationships with Your Cooperating Teacher

The cooperating teacher probably is the person with whom you will work most closely during your student-teaching experiences. You should realize that having a student teacher increases his already heavy load of duties. He must assume a double role, since he is responsible for the successful progress of both his class and yourself. His teaching effectiveness is evaluated in terms of the success of his students in mastery of learning materials.

Responsibilities of the cooperating teacher. When a cooperating teacher takes on the added responsibility of guiding your teaching activities, he is faced with the need of devoting extra time and energy to planning for his regular classwork and, at the same time, to providing you with constructive and worthwhile activities. You should keep this point in mind if you are tempted to think that your cooperating teacher is not meeting your needs as well as he might.

Whether your student teaching is being done in a college-operated laboratory school or in a cooperating public school, your cooperating teacher performs similar functions. He has the responsibility to make certain that the students are given good coverage in their curriculum material. He becomes both a teacher of his students and a supervisor of your activities during your stay with him.

Cooperating teachers in laboratory schools are selected because of their ability to meet this dual role. Regular classroom teachers in public schools often are asked to perform this double function on short notice and without any special training for it. You have the responsibility of assisting this person with whatever plans are projected and to adopt a positive attitude toward what is being done. This attitude should be one that will permit you to approach your observation and teaching with an open mind.

Ways in Which the Cooperating Teacher Can Help You

The alert cooperating teacher recognizes your need for growth on the job and does what he can to help you use your special competencies to their best advantage. He attempts to enable you to grow in the process of relating to students and others in ways that are unique to you as a student teacher. Your induction into student teaching can be eased through the efforts of a sympathetic and understanding cooperating teacher.

The cooperating teacher can be especially helpful to you to the extent that he is willing and able to do the following:

1. Meet and confer with you before the first day of class.
2. Acquaint you with the organizational structure of the school.
3. Arrange for you to meet other faculty personnel, especially other teachers of your subject.
4. Introduce you to the class in such a way as to help you feel important and needed.
5. Regard you as a member of the faculty.
6. From the start, provide opportunities for you to participate in class activities—a kind of team approach.
7. Alert you to the details of classroom management.
8. Assist you to discover the students' interests by giving you access to available student records and by sharing with you his knowledge of the students.
9. Help you in your personal observation of learners and in your interpretation of gathered data.
10. Help you become aware of and meet learning differences among the students.
11. Explain his teaching approaches to you.
12. Acquaint you with his planning procedures and assist you in your own lesson planning.
13. Encourage you to participate in the evaluation of students' learning progress and in the recording of these data.
14. Make it possible for you to have private conferences with him whenever these seem desirable.
15. Evaluate your teaching activities critically and constructively.

Value of Conferences with Your Cooperating Teacher

You will find it valuable to confer frequently with your cooperating teacher. These conferences may be held during definite times set aside for them. If you wish a specific answer to a simple question, however, this can be taken care of either just before or after the class period.

You also will become involved in three-way conferences with your cooperating teacher and your college supervisor. In these, let the others take the lead, and try not to display a defensive or belligerent attitude. You are there to learn and to benefit from all the suggestions that you can receive from these two individuals. Even though you believe that you can justify your procedure, you should hear out the others before you present your views, unless you are invited to clarify the situation by presenting your ideas pertaining to it.

The cooperating teacher often will ask you for your opinion about one or another class procedure or about a student. If you have ideas based on observations, feel free to express them. You may be invited to give your opinion about a specific learning experience or to evaluate the learning progress of students. Do not hesitate to present your ideas, but do not force them into the situation. When you listen to the ideas of your cooperating teacher, you may find that you want to revise your judgments to conform more closely to those expressed by him.

It is through conferences with your cooperating teacher that you can receive such help as:

1. Discovering relationships between theory and practice
2. Developing an understanding of the role of the cooperating teacher and that of the school in the community
3. Growing in self-analysis and self-improvement
4. Developing a worthwhile professional attitude that serves you well
5. Learning to work with fellow teachers
6. Discovering that there is no one easy solution to many classroom problems
7. Learning to ask those questions that will enable you to grow in your profession

Display a Good Attitude toward Your Cooperating Teacher

As a student teacher you need to be ever alert to ways and means by which your cooperating teacher is attempting to help you. You may have a tendency to accept many of his efforts in your behalf as routine activities. You may fail to appreciate the fact that he probably has devoted much time and thought to how best to help you grow in your profession. Often when your activities run smoothly you may not realize that they represent well-thought-through plans made by others for your benefit.

When your cooperating teacher gives evidence of respect for your personal integrity, his attitude should be reflected in your behavior toward him. When you are invited by him to seek his assistance and advice, take advantage of his offers. If he suggests your planning a lesson or working out a specific activity on your own, be sure to do so. He thereby is attempting to give you practice in meeting situations independently. He is trying to strengthen your self-confidence.

You must learn through observation of teacher-planning procedures how to meet classroom situations. You need experience in decision making in these situations. You will grow in making correct decisions under the guidance of your cooperating teacher and college supervisor. Hence keep an open mind and listen carefully to all suggestions offered rather than become defensive toward them.

You can improve your effectiveness as a student teacher when you display an attitude of willingness to discover new and better ways of dealing with learners and with subject content. Remember that it is one experience to observe an expert teach a lesson, but another to teach similar material as effectively as he does. Skill in the teaching-learning situation comes only with practice. Although you may believe that in your first attempts you performed well, it may be that there is more clumsiness in your approach than you realize. Fortunately, your beginning ineptitudes are likely to disappear as you continue to practice.

Do not hesitate to ask questions that will give you further understanding concerning teaching procedures and school routines, rules, and regulations. It is better to ask than to assume to know that about which you have only a vague idea. A careful study of the school handbook can be helpful. It gives you much information known to your students, which, if understood by you, reveals to learners the fact that you know what to do in various situations.

This inspires them to have confidence in you. Many undesirable situations can be averted before they start.

The Importance of School Services

Just as a teacher is a member of the faculty and works on the school team, so must you become one of the group with functional relationships that reach beyond the classroom. You need to develop sensitivity to the working relationships that exist among the various personnel in the school. You also need to become a part of whatever extensions the school may have into the community.

The modern secondary school includes the services of many trained persons in addition to the administrative staff and the regular classroom teachers. During your student-teaching period in a school, you need to become acquainted with these services and utilize them as the opportunity arises.

As a student teacher you should maintain the attitude of a learner. Regard the various service personnel as experts in their field from whom you can gain much that will improve your teaching effectiveness. Your cooperating teacher is in the position of acquainting you with the services offered in the school and of encouraging your utilization of them and of those in the community with which the school has some dealings.

Your Relationships with Guidance Counselors

Most modern secondary schools have developed well-organized guidance services and include trained counselors among their staff members. You need to know who these counselors are and how they function in the school. You should understand the relationship of these counselors with classroom teachers and their students.

For a school guidance program to be effective, there is needed close teamwork between counselors and teachers. It usually is in the classroom that individual needs become apparent. You become sensitive to these needs as you observe your cooperating teacher and engage in your own teaching. If a student seems to have a serious problem, his teacher needs to confer early with the guidance counselor to explore possible causes of the difficulty and to develop workable plans of action. You should participate in some of these conferences so that you learn about the services offered and also achieve a background of dealing with a particular problem.

Counselors need the cooperation of teachers in working with disturbed or uncooperative students. They cannot and should not attempt to work alone. Guidance is a team approach in which the feelings and attitudes of the teacher are respected by the counselor. You will be fortunate if you are given an opportunity to participate in a conference between your teacher and a school counselor concerning members of the class. You need training in building these guidance interrelationships. Make certain that, before you complete your student-teaching assignment in a school, you become acquainted with its guidance facilities and learn something about what is being done to help in student adjustment.

You need to appreciate the fact that it is the function of the school counselor to bolster your teaching, not to undermine it. If you have an opportunity to work closely with a school counselor during your student-teaching experiences, you will come to understand that counselors have a definite role to fill in the school organization. Most teachers want to cooperate with counselors but need help to know how to work together. At first, you may regard consulting with a counselor to be a drain on your time; but, with practice, you will need less time to work with counselors. Also, the help you receive from the counselor reduces your responsibility for trying to solve a problem.

You may be fortunate enough to be assigned to do your student teaching in a school in which there is a good program of group guidance. If so, ask permission to observe in one or more of these classes. Here you will see practical applications of attempts to meet many of the personal needs of students. These group guidance classes have been more completely organized on the junior high school level than on the senior high school level, however.

As you observe these classes in action, you will discover that an attempt is made to help students recognize and understand types of problems with which they are faced during adolescent years. Each student is encouraged to learn to assume responsibility for his thinking and behavior. Consideration is given to such matters as (1) ways to earn a living—selecting a vocation in light of interest and ability, (2) kinds of problems to be met in various types of occupations, (3) need for constructive personality qualities, (4) importance of maintaining good interrelationships between self and parents, school personnel, schoolmates, and other associates, and (5) value of being willing to seek help when and where needed.

Your Relationships with Other School Personnel

There are various other members of the school personnel whose services are needed to keep the school functioning as a well-organized, unified educational institution. You are likely to come into more or less direct contact with each of these groups. In so doing, you can gain some appreciation of their value in helping to keep the school a smoothly running organization.

The school secretary. You need to understand the precise functions of the school secretaries. They are responsible for taking care of teachers' attendance reports, sorting and delivering mail appropriately, preparing some reports and typing those prepared by other members of the school faculty, and caring for all the many other details that may need attention during the school day or week. You can lighten their work, for example, by submitting to them any documents about yourself that need filing and by recording promptly and accurately your arrival and leaving of the school each day.

The custodial staff. The custodial staff is responsible for the care of the school plant. Their work includes the making of simple repairs and the daily cleaning of the building. You can help them by making certain each time you meet a class that any litter that accumulates during a class period is removed from desks and the floor before you and the class leave the room. Also, you should not remain in your room or keep students there so long after the day's school session is ended that you delay the staff in the task of preparing the room for the next day's session.

The school nurse. You should know where the office of the school nurse is located and the conditions under which you can make use of her services. You may find it annoying, on occasions, to have the school nurse or the dental assistant send for students in your class while you are in the midst of a lesson. You should cooperate with them graciously, however. They do not want to interrupt lessons, but it often is impossible for them to see students only during the latter's unassigned periods.

Workers in the school cafeteria. The workers in the school cafeteria are important members of the school's service personnel. The cafeteria is likely to be crowded during the scheduled lunch periods. Groups of hungry young people can be noisy and inconsiderate in their demands for immediate service. If you are asked to assist in lunchroom duty, you can be helpful by keeping the students in an organized line at the lunch counter, by trying to control any over-exuberant behavior, and by seeing to it that the students clear their tables properly after they have finished eating.

Your Relationships with Parents

You will soon discover that you can learn much from parents. You also will learn that to confer with parents about a particular student's problem is not an easy matter. When no particular problem is to be considered, you may be able to carry on an informal conversation with most parents without any difficulty. Therefore, in order to promote growth in these functions, you need to be placed in situations that give you considerable contact with parents. If these situations are frequent and varied, your confidence in dealing with problems through them will be strengthened.

Your role with parents is likely to be indirect for most of the time you are doing your student teaching. Nevertheless, you can learn from parents how they feel about the school, the kind of education they want for their sons and daughters, and, perhaps, what their attitude is toward you as an inexperienced person leading their offspring in educational matters. These experiences can be invaluable to you.

You will want to share the responsibility of meeting parents and of preparing reports that go to parents describing the learning progress of their adolescents. As a student teacher, you should not attempt alone to discuss a student's progress with his parents. Rather should you start by sitting in on a teacher-parent conference. The welfare of the pupil, the teacher, the parent, and yourself is involved. It sometimes takes long years of practice to avoid using expressions that give a negative effect to parents and to develop speech patterns that will give the more positive effect. The following expressions will illustrate this point: [3]

Negative Expressions	More Positive Expressions
Must	Should
Lazy	Can do more when he tries
Troublemaker	Disturbs class
Uncooperative	Should learn to work with others
Cheats	Depends on others to do his work
Stupid	Can do better work with help
Never does the right thing	Can learn to do the right thing
Below average	Working at his own level
Truant	Absent without permission
Impertinent	Discourteous
Steal	Without permission
Unclean	Poor habits
Dumbbell	Capable of doing better
Help	Cooperation
Poor	Handicapped
Calamity	Lost opportunity
Disinterested	Complacent, not challenged
Expense	Investment
Contribute to	Invest in
Stubborn	Insists on having his own way
Insolent	Outspoken
Liar	Tendency to stretch the truth
Wastes time	Could make better use of time
Sloppy	Could do neater work
Incurred failure	Failed to meet requirements
Mean	Difficulty in getting along with others
Time and again	Usually
Dubious	Uncertain
Poor grade of work	Below his usual standard
Clumsy	Not physically well coordinated
Profane	Uses unbecoming language
Selfish	Seldom shares with others
Rude	Inconsiderate of others
Bashful	Reserved
Show-off	Tries to get attention
Will fail him	Has a chance of passing, if

If you are invited to assist in the preparation of reports to parents, make sure that you understand the reporting system, and know

[3] *Conference Time for Teachers and Parents: A Teachers' Guide to Successful Conference Reporting* (Washington, D.C.: National School Public Relations Association and Department of Classroom Teachers, NEA, 1961), p. 13.

what types of things to include and what to omit. Follow the practices of the school, not those utilized by the secondary school that you attended.

The following report cards are representative of those used in reporting to parents:

SEMESTER REPORT
Benson High School
Omaha, Nebraska

Name ....

Subject .... H.R. ....

Semester beginning .... 19 ....

Teacher ....

	MID SEMESTER	FINAL AVERAGE
SCHOLARSHIP		
CREDIT EARNED		
DAYS ABSENT		

The figures used on this card indicate the teacher's estimate of the pupil's work according to the following statement:

Mark "1" 93 - 100%
Mark "2" 85 - 92%
Mark "3" 78 - 84%
Mark "4" 70 - 77%
Mark "5" below 70%

Signature of Parent or Guardian

Paul A. Miller, Superintendent
Howard R. Sorensen, Principal
(over)
SHS. 30-10-62-162M-332

Teacher's Comment:

Parent's Comment:

Dear Parent:

This card is a progress report in a particular area of endeavor. It is a sample of your child's educational growth. You are encouraged to form a bond of friendship and helpfulness with the school, so that your child may do his best.

At this point in school life, it is exceedingly important for parents to look not only at the student's present pattern of development, but well into the future in preparation for events that will concern him beyond the high school.

Consider this a personal invitation to attend your school to get more complete details.

Paul A. Miller
Superintendent of Schools

HORACE MANN JUNIOR HIGH SCHOOL

Report of..

Grade....................HR....................School Year 19................- 19..............

Homeroom Teacher..

To the Parent:

This report for junior high school pupils will be sent home six times during the school year. If the pupil's work is unsatisfactory, special reports may be sent to you calling the difficulty to your attention and requesting a conference.

The scholastic marks in the various subjects and certain personal and social traits are indicated in this report because they are deemed essential to happy, successful growth.

We hope you will discuss this report with your son or daughter, and that you will commend and encourage improvement. Remember that children differ greatly in the way in which they learn or mature. Each child should be guided as an individual whose problems and needs differ from those of other children.

Pupils make the best progress when parents and teachers understand each other fully. Feel free to come in for a visit or a conference, or call LAkewood 1-9220.

C. C. CLARK, *Principal*

WILLIAM B. EDWARDS, *Superintendent of Schools*

MU-J-9

PERSONAL AND SOCIAL TRAITS

(See page 4 for explanation)

1. Exercises self control
2. Cooperates well with others
3. Is courteous in speech and manner
4. Is dependable
5. Respects rights of others
6. Respects authority
7. Is active and alert
8. Observes school regulations
9. Shows improvement
10. Assumes responsibility
11. Accepts constructive criticism

12. Begins and completes work promptly
13. Follows directions carefully
14. Is critical of own work
15. Gives satisfactory attention
16. Is making commendable effort
17. Brings necessary materials to class
18. Works in neat and orderly manner
19. Completes homework assignments
20. Makes up work
21. Participates in class discussion
22. Contributes beyond assignments
23. Makes good use of time

ATTENDANCE RECORD

	Report Period						
	1	2	3	4	5	6	TOTAL
DAYS ABSENT							
TIMES TARDY							

Regular and prompt attendance is necessary if the pupil is to make satisfactory progress and maintain an interest in his school work. When health permits, see that your child attends school regularly.

PARENT'S SIGNATURE

1st Period...

2nd Period...

3rd Period..

4th Period..

5th Period..

Name _____

SCHOLARSHIP MARKS AND PERSONAL-SOCIAL TRAITS

Subject	Scholarship Marks							Personal-Social Traits					Teacher
	1st Per.	2nd Per.	3rd Per.	4th Per.	5th Per.	6th Per.	FINAL	1st Per.	2nd Per.	3rd Per.	4th Per.	5th Per.	
Homeroom	x	x	x	x	x	x	x						
English													
Spelling													
French													
German													
Latin													
Spanish													
Mathematics													
Algebra													
Science													
Social Studies													
Art													
Typing													
Industrial Arts													
Drafting													
Woodworking													
Graphic Arts													
General Metal													
Home Economics													
Clothing													
Foods													
Music													
Physical Ed.													
Health													
Band													
Choir													
Orchestra													

EXPLANATION OF SCHOLARSHIP MARKS

The marks given on page 3, in the columns headed "Scholarship Marks," are based upon the pupil's growth toward the objectives of the course as shown by written work, class work, recitations, contributions to discussion and class projects, individual projects, and test scores. The quality of the work is important, but the amount of work is also considered in determining a mark.

H - Honors - Superior and/or Creative Achievement
A - Excellent
B - Good
C - Average, most frequent mark
D - Below average, but passing
P - Passed on Effort or Placed
E - Failing
Inc. - Incomplete

EXPLANATION OF PERSONAL-SOCIAL RATINGS

On page 2, personal and social traits deemed important in school success are listed and numbered. Each number identifies a particular trait. On page 3, the columns headed "Personal and Social Traits," may contain one or more of these numbers opposite the subjects studied.

1. When the number is not circled, the pupil should be commended by the parents and teacher for noticeable success in the trait.

2. If the number is enclosed within a circle, it means that the teacher of that subject believes there is a definite need for improvement in the trait. The cooperation of the parent, the pupil, and the school toward improvement is urged.

3. If no number appears opposite a subject, the pupil is considered to be satisfactorily adjusted. Therefore, most of the spaces will contain no numbers.

For example, if a 3 and a 14, with a circle drawn around the 14, appear opposite Mathematics, it means that the teacher of mathematics feels that the pupil should be commended by the parent for courtesy and good manners, but that he should be more critical of his own work. The need for parental cooperation toward improvement of the latter trait is thereby indicated.

Semester

Pupil's Last Name			First Name				Grade			Home Room	

PD	Course & Number	ROOM	1st Report		2nd Report		3rd Report		FINAL		Teacher's Signature
			Sch.	Cit.	Sch.	Cit.	Sch.	Cit.	Sch.	Cit.	
1.											
2.											
3.											
4.											
5.											
6.											
7.											
Honor Points											
Home Room Citizenship											Next Semester's
Days Absent											
Times Tardy											Grade_____

Signatures:

Home Room Teacher
13-168 80 150M 7-1-57

Principal

Grade Counselor

E 83

EXPLANATION OF CARD
Subject Marks

A—Superior   B—Above average   C—Average
D—Barely passed   F—Failed   Inc.—Failure; but work may be made up

Citizenship Marks

The recording of citizenship marks by the teacher is at the option of the principal. Such marks, when given, are registered by the following letters:

E—Excellent   W—Warning
S—Satisfactory   U—Unsatisfactory

Remarks:_____

_____

_____

Signature of Parent or Guardian

First Report   Second Report   Third Report   Final Report

COPY OF REPORT CARD USED IN THE JUNIOR HIGH SCHOOLS OF THE
SAN FRANCISCO SCHOOL SYSTEM

PROGRESS REPORT

GARDEN CITY
HIGH SCHOOL

SCHOOL YEAR 19........ - 19........

* * *

Pupil's Name........................

TO THE PARENT OR GUARDIAN

Progress reports are issued once every ten weeks. The most common causes of unsatisfactory work are frequent absences and lateness, inadequate provision for home study, too numerous social and other engagements.

In high school a student should do at least two hours of homework a day.

Parents are earnestly requested to confer with teachers concerning the work of their sons and daughters. You are cordially invited to visit the school. Conferences may be arranged through the office at the convenience of the parent and the teacher.

Please examine this report carefully, sign it, and have it returned promptly.

Each subject taken five times a week and passed, counts one unit toward graduation.

17 units required for graduation
12 units required for senior classification
8 units required for junior classification
4 units required for sophomore classification

Signature of Parent or Guardian

First Quarter...

Second Quarter...

Third Quarter...

Name..................

GENERAL RATING IN COURSE

Subject..................

MARKING PERIODS	MARK		
First Quarter			
Second Quarter			
First Term			
Third Quarter			
Fourth Quarter			
Second Term			
Year			
Regent Examination			

KEY: A+ (100-95); A (94-90); B+ (89-85); B (84-80);
C+ (79-75); C (74-70); D (69-65); F (Below 65).
FF (Below 55).

Passing Mark — 65   College Certification Mark — 80

Teacher..................

PROGRESS OF PUPIL

Social Studies Department

I. Class Work

1. Ability to read and organize Social Studies material.

2. Test Achievement.

3. Use of texts reference reading, maps, and charts.

4. Initiative and independence of work habits.

5. Evidence of open-mindedness.

6. Participation in class discussions.

II. Citizenship Traits

1. Neatness

2. Punctuality in fulfillment of assignments.

3. Effort to improve quality of work.

4. Class conduct

KEY: G (Good); S (Satisfactory); U (Unsatisfactory)

DES MOINES PUBLIC SCHOOLS
Junior High Report Card — Advanced Track

Pupil _____ Home Room _____

Subject _____ Grade level _____ Semester Ending _____

MARK	9 Weeks	Semester

Absences from this class

1 — Excellent
2 — Very Good
3 — Average
4 — Poor Work, But Passing
5 — No Credit

Listed below are important attitudes and work habits.
Absence of a check shows satisfactory growth or better.
A check indicates that improvement is needed.

------ Brings materials
------ Works to ability
------ Shows active interest
------ Uses time effectively
------ Accepts responsibility
------ Completes work on time
------ Is courteous and considerate
------ Cooperates with teachers and students

_____ Signature of Teacher

_____ Signature of Parent

Use reverse side for remarks

Teacher's Remarks

Parent's Remarks

BASIC TRACK—Meets minimum standards of school achievement
GENERAL TRACK—Meets average standards of school achievement
ADVANCED TRACK — Meets highest standards of school achievement

Teaching methods and or materials increase in difficulty from basic track to advanced track. For further information please call your principal.

Form 91B (Salmon) 6M-7-62 D. M. Tech Press

Your Relationships with the Community

In many communities you will find that the teacher's activities do not end when he leaves the school building. Varying with the size of the community, the professional status of the teacher receives differing degrees of recognition. You will find, however, that there is constant interaction between the school and the community. Often, what goes on in the community vitally affects the school, and school activities influence community plans and projects. You will want to become a part of that influence.

Seek opportunities to participate in those activities that are community centered and have significance for the students in the school. The afterschool activities mentioned in Table 6 are representative of the kind of things you can undertake in the community in which you are doing your student teaching. This is not to suggest that you should attempt all or even a large number of them. The important thing is that you know that there are things to which you might turn, and then do something about it.

Your acceptance in the community will depend in part on your willingness to become active in one or another community project. Some of these activities can be provided in the school building itself, as in the case of parent-teacher meetings. Rather than to disregard these meetings, make every effort to attend them so that you know what is happening. Such meetings also can provide opportunities for you to meet and talk with parents and other community leaders.

The better you understand the community and its goals and aspirations, the better will you be able to work with the learners and interpret the school to anyone who is interested in knowing about its purposes and offerings. There are many civic, religious, and cultural activities that might be commended to you. Become acquainted with them and associate with as many as your time permits.

YOUR PROFESSIONAL RESPONSIBILITIES

Throughout this book, we stress the various approaches to your duties as a student teacher that are basic to your achieving a full

TABLE 6

AFTER-SCHOOL ACTIVITIES OF STUDENT TEACHERS *

Attended

Student teachers' dinners, parties, and teas.
Faculty dinners, picnics, and teas.
Interviews for news releases concerning student teaching.
Practice sessions for athletic events, musical programs, and plays.
School census meetings.
Service-club dinners and luncheons.
Community functions such as church meetings and scout meetings.

Assisted

Students with science fair projects.
Students with schoolwork.
Students with the distribution of the school paper.
Students with Y-Teens' Christmas projects.
Students with social studies projects.
Students preparing reports.
Teachers taking school census.
Teachers in the guidance program.
Teachers with the school beauty review.
Teachers with the May Day program.
Teachers constructing final examinations.

Visited

Public libraries.
School systems.
Community bakeries.
Manufacturing concerns.
Bookstores.

General

Cleaned hats for the band uniforms.
Coached baseball, basketball, football, tennis, and track.
Constructed posters, reading charts, and St. Patrick Day displays.
Decorated stage for "Who's Who" and the gymnasium for junior proms.
Directed boys' quartet.
Entertained students waiting for late school bus.
Gave talks on the "Ole Miss" band trips to Brussels, Belgium.
Judged students' science fair projects and student debates.
Modeled for community style show.
Observed band parade and parent-teacher conference.
Packed and moved band equipment.
Prepared food for athletic events, material for bulletin boards, and material for
    exhibits.
Repaired drum for the school band.
Shopped for classroom supplies.
Sold tickets at athletic events.
Supervised students in detention classes.
Taught students folk dancing.
Took trip with school band.
Tutored students absent because of prolonged illness.

* A. W. Scrivner, "Professional Laboratory Experiences," *The Journal of Teacher Education,* XII, No. 1 (March, 1961), 52.

and rich educational experience. Hence here we do no more than list some of the professional activities in which you can engage and some of the attitudes you can display in order to gain the approval and respect of your professional associates.

Ways in Which You Can Cooperate

It is essential that you begin your student teaching with the understanding that during your stay in the school you are there to serve in whatever ways you can. You should not assume that the responsibility for your success as a student teacher lies wholly with the persons who guide your activities. You need to take the initiative in discussing ways in which you can exhibit a cooperative attitude.

There are certain minimal activities in which you must engage. These include arriving promptly at the designated time, observing the cooperating teacher and his class at work, and planning and teaching a minimal number of lessons, some of which are observed by your cooperating teacher and your college supervisor. If your efforts do not go beyond these minimums, it is likely that you will not learn what is involved in carrying a full teaching load. You must be willing to help whenever, wheresoever, and however you can if you wish to grow professionally during your student-teaching experiences.

When you meet your cooperating teacher, indicate to him that you appreciate whatever he does for you and that you want to help him in as many ways as you can. The display of this attitude will get you off to a good start. As you participate in various class routines, you will get the feel of what to do as a teacher as well as how to perform these activities expeditiously.

At first, you probably will not know what you can do to help your teacher and will need to ask him to assign you odd jobs. If you are alert, however, you soon can find various ways to be helpful. For example, if you are assigned to the school sufficiently early to be present at the first meeting of the class, you can offer to prepare a seating chart for the teacher and another one for your use. Then, during the course of your stay in the class, you can assume much of the responsibility for the following aspects of a teacher's duties:

1. Record attendance
2. Monitor the bulletin board
3. Care for the cleanliness of the chalkboard
4. Regulate light and ventilation
5. Locate supplementary material
6. Distribute and collect materials
7. Set up demonstrations
8. At the end of a lesson, collect materials used and return to proper files or cabinets
9. Keep record of written material of the students and correct as much of it as the teacher encourages and your time permits
10. Supervise classroom study
11. Construct quizzes under teacher guidance, administer them and correct them, recording the results
12. Hold conferences with students
13. Supervise remedial activities
14. Assist with the preparation of report cards
15. Write evaluative reports of students' attitudes, behavior, and learning progress
16. Participate in fire drills
17. Sponsor students' out-of-class activities
18. Assist in supervising students in the lunchroom or cafeteria
19. Become active in meeting the school's organizational routines
20. Accompany your cooperating teacher and his class on trips to points of interest outside the school
21. Attend faculty meetings
22. Be present at as many parent-teacher association meetings as your college obligations permit

The foregoing are some of the activities in which you can participate. As you become increasingly aware, during your stay in the school, of the many differing duties of a teacher, you can find other ways in which you can give evidence of your cooperative attitude. Do not try to undertake more jobs than your time or energy permits, however.

If you are combining student teaching with college study, you may be carrying a heavy load of work. It is not enough to be willing to assume extra duties. Whatever you do to assist your teacher must be done well. Otherwise, you will be more of a nuisance to him than a help.

Assess Your Own Strengths and Weaknesses

You know that your cooperating teacher has the responsibility of evaluating your attitudes and behavior in light of your degree of displayed aptitude for teaching. He needs to recognize and report to the proper authorities your outstanding strengths and weaknesses. It might be helpful to you to know those traits that have been found to be the strong and weak points of student teachers.

Recently, Rachel D. Wilkinson published a report of the personal strengths and weaknesses of thirty-two student teachers as these were reported by their cooperating teachers. The number of persons involved is small. Moreover, the study was made in elementary schools. Yet, you probably can find much in the report that is applicable to yourself as a student teacher.

Strengths of student teachers. According to Wilkinson, the strengths seem to involve personal attributes, manners, and attitudes of the student teacher, evidence of planning, and teaching procedures. We present her findings:

Personal strengths. With regard to personal strengths, pleasing personality, appearance, and voice were the main phrases listed. The personality was described in the following terms: good appearance, attractive appearance, neatness, dress, attractive and friendly, and simply the word "appearance." The word "voice" was used alone to describe strengths along with "firm but friendly voice, voice and speech, tone of voice, good voice, and voice well modulated."

Some of the strengths depicting desirable manner and attitude were mentioned more often than others: mature, sincerity, enthusiasm, and rapport. Specific wording of these attributes is listed below, with similar items grouped together:

1. Cheerful, sense of humor, calm and happy, ability to joke, happy about work
2. Positive attitudes, use of positiveness and courteous manner, use of praise
3. Sweet and gentle, manner is gentle and assuring, gentle manner
4. Mature, poised, patient
5. Alert, industrious, willing, competent, capable, cooperative, works hard,

seriousness toward work, hard worker, conscientious, willing and good natured
6. Manner, natural manner, sincere, professional manner, punctual
7. Enthusiasm for teaching, enthusiasm, curiosity about teaching
8. Gets along well with superiors
9. Likes children, respect for children, comfortable with children, and they with her, manner with children, well liked by children, understanding and sympathy, superior understanding, desire to work with children, rapport, ease with children
10. Patient, wonderful with children, warmth toward children
11. Willingness to accept criticism and learns quickly, willingness to learn, willing to follow suggestions, willingness to take suggestions
12. Self-evaluation, awareness of difficulties

With regard to the background of the students, the strengths noted included these: superior understanding of children, good background, writes well, artistic ability, expert pianist, command of subject matter, good at record keeping.

Teaching strengths. The descriptions involving planning for teaching indicated that the supervisor liked the planning techniques, careful planning, thorough planning, selection of teaching material, and charts and attractively prepared teaching aids.

The supervisors described the observed strengths in teaching as follows:

Excellent teaching, splendid, superb lesson, outstanding lesson

Fine motivation, creative, resourceful, original and enthusiastic

Use of illustrative material, use of objective material

Routines, moved about, transition from one activity to another, thorough, reviews

Timing, alert to need for change of pace, adjustment to situation

Questioning, explanations

Ability to handle a class, no trouble with discipline

Character development, use of praise, mature judgment, sensitive to emotional problems, recognition of needs of children

Participation of children

Board writing clear, no errors

Weaknesses of Student Teachers

The improvements which the supervisors suggested that the student teachers needed to make were almost the opposite of the strengths which were observed by them. The improvements needed may be classified as weaknesses in personal qualifications, background, manner, and teaching techniques.

Personal weaknesses. The comments with regard to weaknesses in personal qualifications included: untidy appearance, overweight, poor health, and inadequate speech or voice defects.

The backgrounds were inadequate due to lack of information regarding teaching methods, poor handwriting, and a need of insight into how children learn.

Manner and attitude showed a lack of self-confidence, an unwillingness to accept suggestions, lack of poise and maturity, tardiness, irregular attendance, and inability to adjust to the children and to peers.

The complete list follows:

Manner, immature attitude, lacks spark and vitality

Lacks confidence, not assertive enough, negative approach, authoritarian, does not relax, tense, not sure of herself, feels inferior and lacks self-confidence, does not assume responsibility

Not punctual at school, attendance irregular, personal problems and illness interfered

Criticizes other teachers, an "apple polisher"

Unwilling to follow suggestions, unwilling to accept criticism

Sarcastic manner with children, emotionally involved with students

Too sensitive and reads trouble into situations where none exists

Teaching weaknesses. The weaknesses in teaching seemed to stem from these inadequacies: preparation for the lessons, use of teaching materials, motivation techniques, sense of timing, skill with questioning, routines, and adjustment to class and to individual children. The complete list of needed teaching improvements follows:

No plan, planning inadequate, duplicated material would have helped, does not plan for slow and bright students.

Tried to cover too many concepts in one lesson, poor timing, lesson too long, might use duplicated material to save time

Need to use concrete materials, techniques and methods, teaching skills, techniques of teaching

Does not know how to motivate, poor motivation, no ingenuity

Not challenging, does not require children to think

Directions not clear, questioning skills, questions and comments not suited to age level, vocabulary above children, repeats answers of children, does not allow children to talk enough, repeats what they say

Routines, untidy with classroom routines, does not adapt to rules and methods of class, attention to details, writes too low on board, careless habits with board work, overuse of O. K.

Participation of children, no participation by some children, needs to involve children in process, called on some children too often, some children too soft spoken

Did not have children put away objective material before going on

Discipline, getting attention of whole class, lets other groups get restless, does not get total attention, starting lesson without getting attention at the beginning

Insists on formal behavior

Maintains stationary position

The writer feels that the factors included under strengths and weaknesses found by the supervisors working in one term with 32 student teachers are revealing. Perhaps such a list might be made available to students as a checklist for self-evaluation. If over the years the same weaknesses are apparent in each group, it may mean that the screening process for the selection of student teachers is inadequate.

It was most interesting that the supervisors involved used similar terminology in describing the strengths and weaknesses of the student teachers. These comments were submitted without any previous discussion of what should be listed. Each comment was therefore an individual matter on the part of each supervisor.[4]

General Comment

In the following chapters of this book, suggestions are offered for the overcoming of weaknesses common to beginning student teachers. You will find that to the extent that you throw yourself wholeheartedly into meeting the many areas of your professional relationships, you will increase your self-confidence and develop those attitudes and activities that will serve you well as you continue in your chosen life work.

QUESTIONS AND TOPICS FOR DISCUSSION

1. Which of the items in Ahlering's questionnaire do you consider to be most significant?
2. Which of the problems included in question VIII of the questionnaire have you encountered to date?
3. What is your relationship with your college supervisor?
4. In what ways is your cooperating teacher being helpful to you?
5. Compare the report card used in your school with the models presented in this chapter. Of all of them, which one do you prefer? Why?
6. How effective is the guidance program in your school? Be specific.
7. In which of the activities listed in Table 6 are you participating?
8. In what special ways are you assisting your cooperating teacher?
9. Show your cooperating teacher Wilkinson's list of the strengths and weaknesses of student teachers. Ask him to evaluate you honestly according to the items listed. Do the same for yourself.

[4] Rachel D. Wilkinson, "Evaluation Based upon Observation of Reports of Supervisors of Student Teaching," *The Journal of Educational Research,* January, 1963, pp. 266–67. Reprinted by permission of Dembar Publications, Madison, 3, Wisconsin.

SELECTED REFERENCES

BURTON, W. H. *The Guiding of Learning Activities* (3rd ed.). New York: Appleton-Century-Crofts, Inc., 1962.

CURTIS, D. K., and ANDREWS, L. O. *Guiding Your Student Teacher.* Englewood Cliffs, N.J.: Prentice-Hall, Inc., 1954.

DIXON, P. T. (chairman). "Some Guiding Principles for Student Teaching Programs," *The North Central Association Quarterly,* XXXII (October, 1957), 193–96.

GREEN, C. C. "A Professional Partnership," *The Indiana Teacher,* CII (February, 1958), 258–59.

Improving Instruction in Professional Education, Thirty-seventh Yearbook. Lock Haven, Pa.: Association for Student Teaching, State Teachers College, 1958.

MILNER, E. J. *You and Your Student Teacher.* New York: Teachers College, Columbia Univ., Bureau of Publications, 1954, reprinted, 1962.

STRATEMEYER, F. B., and LINDSEY, M. *Working with Student Teachers.* New York: Teachers College, Columbia Univ., Bureau of Publications, 1958.

The Supervising Teacher, Thirty-eighth Yearbook. Cedar Falls: Association for Student Teaching, Iowa State Teachers College, 1959.

PLANNING FOR EFFECTIVE TEACHING

Throughout this book, we stress the primary function of the teacher to be that of guiding the learning activities of secondary school students. We assume that as a result of their learning experiences on the elementary school level, young people have attained some competence in fundamental education.

Insofar as their maturational growth has permitted, young learners have achieved basic knowledge about themselves and the world about them, and have developed simple positive attitudes toward their social and civic responsibilities. They now are ready, within the limits of their abilities and interests, to further their educational attainments in light of their goals and ambitions and according to the educational objectives of the secondary school or school system of their community.

NEED FOR CAREFUL PLANNING

To the present, you have benefited from the learning guidance given you by many teachers. Some teachers seemed to you to be better equipped than others to help you master learning materials. You probably recognized differences among your teachers in their ability to handle subject content and to impart their knowledge of it to you. In some classes, learning proceeded smoothly and was pointed toward the achievement of specific purposes; in other classes, little constructive activity took place and you often left a lesson period without any clear idea of what the work was about. In other words, some of your teachers knew what they wanted to do and how to do it; others were not sufficiently prepared to guide learning activities.

Now, as a student teacher, you are beginning to realize that a successful teacher needs to do more than master the subject matter of his teaching and gain some understanding of his students, important as these two aspects of his teaching responsibilities are. He must be able so to plan his work that every one of his students benefits from participation with him in the learning.

You are no stranger to planning. You constantly are making plans for your long-range and immediate activities. You are aware of the *what, why,* and *how* of your many life activities. So it is with the teacher. He should know *what* learning activities need to be planned, *why* he includes what he does in his teaching, and *how* the learning process can best be developed, term by term, week by week, and day by day.

IMPORTANCE OF PLANNING

Effective planning has many facets. It includes (1) an understanding of the general educational objectives of the secondary schools, (2) an appreciation of the contribution of a particular subject area to the general purposes of education on this level, (3) a comprehension of what is or should be included in a term's or a year's study of the subject, (4) a knowledge of the appropriate units into which the subject can be divided, and (5) facility in planning for short-range instruction.

Attitudes toward Planning for Teaching

At one time, emphasis was placed on the preparation of elaborate daily lesson plans that adhered strictly to administratively imposed formats. The teacher was not expected to concern himself with the relation of his subject to others taught in the same school. In fact, he might not have been aware of any ultimate goals to be attained by the study of his subject, except that the mastery of it was necessary for the student to become an educated person.

To a student's question, such as "What am I supposed to get out of this subject?" or "Why are we studying it?" the teacher often could give no more than a vague or inconclusive answer. Also, the teaching of the subject followed a more or less unrelated sequence of steps, with little or no effort taken to group these steps into logical or psychological units of learning.

Today, constructors of secondary school curriculums, or of programs of study, attempt to include in their offerings those areas of learning that can prepare young people to meet effectively their responsibilities for their own well-being and for the welfare of other people. Moreover, teachers are expected so to organize and plan subject materials that the learning needs of their students can be fulfilled.

Areas of Planning

Curriculum construction is a shared responsibility of teachers, supervisors, administrators, and boards of education. Working together as a team, the teachers of a particular subject, often with the help of other experts in the field, establish the educational purposes to be served by the subject, set broad limits to the content to be covered, and develop the teaching-learning units to be included. The individual teacher, preferably in cooperation with his students, determines appropriate approaches to the development of each unit.

Finally, the teacher, building on the foregoing basic aspects of planning, prepares his day-by-day lesson plans, perhaps again bringing students into the planning process. In this chapter we consider the objectives of secondary education and the fundamental areas of curricular planning. The daily lesson plan is discussed in Chapter 7.

SECONDARY SCHOOL OBJECTIVES

As you probably know, secondary schools of the past were known as preparatory schools or academies. Their chief purpose was to prepare young people for college entrance. Relatively few elementary school graduates continued their education on the secondary level. Although many modern secondary schools still continue to offer a college preparatory curriculum, education on this level is fast becoming an extension of fundamental learnings and serves the great majority of the nation's adolescent population.

Significance of Educational Objectives

Constructors of secondary curriculums are guided in their work by ever-expanding statements of educational objectives that are concerned with providing for the present and future personal, social, civic, and vocational needs of our adolescent population. Secondary school offerings are being geared to constantly changing economic conditions. During the present century, various sets of secondary school objectives have been and continue to be formulated.

Civic and educational associations, governmental leaders, boards of education and committees of secondary school administrators, supervisors, and teachers are engaged in preparing educational aims and objectives that embody those areas of learning concentration that can help provide for every adolescent the learning experiences that have value for himself and society. Whatever your subject field may be, it needs to find a place for itself in an existing or projected program of secondary school education. This is a must if your subject hopes to survive as a serviceable area of study for young people. We now shall review some well-known statements of secondary school objectives.

Cardinal Principles of Education

Early in the twentieth century, the Commission on the Reorganization of Secondary Education was appointed by the National Education Association to study the educational needs of young people, the social and civic functions of secondary schools, and the learning offerings of existing schools. As a result of their investigation, the Committee submitted its report, *Cardinal Principles of Secondary Education,* in which were included seven general objectives for education on the secondary level.

These are:

1. Health
2. Command of fundamental processes
3. Worthy home membership
4. Vocation
5. Citizenship
6. Worthy use of leisure
7. Ethical character

The objectives as stated are broad in their connotation. The Committee broke them down into specific areas of application to school offerings.[1] Can you justify the inclusion of your subject in the secondary school curriculum in light of one or more of these objectives?

The Needs of Youth as Objectives

Other statements of objectives have been formulated from time to time. Each of these formulations has attempted to incorporate the primary values to be achieved by adolescents through their study experiences on the junior and senior high school levels. One of the most clearly and definitely stated lists of guideposts for study programs is *Imperative Needs of Youth of Secondary School Age* published in 1947 by the National Association of Secondary School Principals. Read this list carefully and decide which of them apply to your subject.

1. All youth need to develop salable skills and those understandings and attitudes that make the worker an intelligent and productive participant in economic life. To this end, most youth need supervised work experiences as well as education in the skills and knowledge of their occupation.
2. All youth need to develop and maintain good health and physical fitness.
3. All youth need to understand the rights and duties of a citizen of a democratic society, and to be diligent and competent in the performance of their obligations as members of the community and citizens of the state and nation and of the world.
4. All youth need to understand the significance of the family for the individual and society and the conditions conducive to successful family life.
5. All youth need to know how to purchase and use goods and services intelligently, understanding both the value received by the consumer and the economic consequences of their acts.
6. All youth need to understand the methods of science, the influence of science on human life, and the main scientific facts concerning the nature of the world and of man.
7. All youth need opportunities to develop their capacities to appreciate beauty in literature, art, music, and nature.
8. All youth need to be able to use their leisure time well and to budget it wisely, balancing activities that yield satisfactions to the individual with those that are socially useful.
9. All youth need to develop respect for other persons, to grow in their

[1] See *Cardinal Principles of Secondary Education*, U.S. Bureau of Education, Bulletin No. 35, 1918, pp. 5--10.

insight into ethical values and principles, and to be able to live and work cooperatively with others.

10. All youth need to grow in their ability to think rationally, to express their thoughts clearly, and to read and listen with understanding.[2]

Objectives of Secondary Education at State Levels

Goals for Junior High School Students, Washington State

A close study of the following objectives in the state of Washington will reveal that, although specific in their application, they fit into the general purposes of education stated by national bodies:

1. All junior high school youth need to learn the fundamental skills necessary to observe, listen, compute, read, speak, and write with purpose and appreciation.
2. All junior high school youth need to develop and maintain abundant physical and mental health.
3. All junior high school youth need to develop an understanding of the democratic way of life and the benefits derived through individual freedoms.
4. All junior high school youth need educational experiences which contribute to personality and character development; they need to develop respect for other persons and their rights and to grow in ethical insight.
5. All junior high school youth need appropriate experiences and understandings as foundations for successful home and family life.
6. All junior high school youth need to learn about natural and physical environment and its effect on life, and to have opportunities for using the scientific approach in the solution of problems.
7. All junior high school youth need to be participating citizens of their schools and their community with increasing orientation to adult citizenship.
8. All junior high school youth need to develop a sense of values of material things and rights of ownership.
9. All junior high school youth need to explore their own interests and aptitudes and to have experiences basic to occupational proficiency.
10. All junior high school youth need to have a variety of socially acceptable and personally satisfying leisure-time activities which contribute either to their personal growth or their development in wholesome group relationships, or to both.

[2] The National Association of Secondary-School Principals, "Imperative Needs of Youth of Secondary School Age," *Bulletin,* Vol. 31, No. 145 (March, 1947), entire issue. See also The Educational Policies Commission, *Education for All American Youth: A Further Look* (Washington, D.C.: National Education Association, 1952), p. 216.

11. All junior high school youth need the enriched living which comes from appreciation of an expression in the arts and from experiencing the beauty and wonder of the world around them.
12. All junior high school youth need to develop respect for adults and their parents without undue dependence upon them.[3]

Educational Goals: New York State

Education—An American Heritage

We, the people of New York State, believing in the equality of opportunity for all and realizing that education is fundamental to our democratic way of life, do hereby recognize and accept these basic premises:

- that every youth shall be afforded the opportunity to obtain at least a high school education;
- that every youth shall have the fullest opportunity for moral and ethical development in keeping with our American heritage;
- that every youth has certain needs and responsibilities that are common to all youth and to the perpetuation of our democratic society;
- that every youth, as a person of inherent worth, differs from every other young person in respect to health, mental ability, interests, and background.

Since these premises are self-evident to those who have faith in our democracy, it becomes necessary that our high schools provide:

- a program of studies in general education that will insure the unity of our people for the common good;
- diversified experiences and educational services that will meet the educational, vocational, and avocational needs of our youth;
- a variety of standards flexible enough to permit each to succeed according to his own ability;
- counseling that will help young people make intelligent choices beneficial to self and society;
- those services that will assist youth to be physically and mentally healthy;
- qualified teachers, extended research, and expanded facilities to meet more effectively the changing demands on education.

Recognizing that the school is but one segment of our complex society requiring the full support of the community, we conceive it our duty as citizens of New York State to provide for the full support of these schools to guarantee each youth his American Heritage.[4]

[3] Jongeward, *op. cit.*, p. 401.
[4] *The Schools We Need: Now and for Tomorrow*, Regents Council on Readjustment of High School Education, New York State, 1954, p. 13. Reprinted with permission.

Educational Goals for Ohio, as Revised in 1963 [5]

The prime concern of the State Board of Education of Ohio is to improve the quality of education. Through various policy statements and the prescription of minimum standards, it has attempted to develop an educational program that will provide for the fullest possible development of the talents and potentialities of all young people in order that they may participate effectively in the cultural, political, social, and economic life of our democracy.

The State Board of Education announces the following urgent goals that it is striving to reach by 1970:

I. A professionally prepared and competent person in every educational position for which certification is required by Ohio law.

II. A program of in-service education for all school employees aimed at growth in ability to work with others in a variety of activities that improve the quality of instruction.

III. A program of guidance and counseling services staffed with a sufficient number of fully qualified counselors to meet the needs of all students.

IV. A program of child-study services, staffed with fully qualified school psychologists in sufficient number to meet the needs of children.

V. An immediate and continuing overall appraisal and revision of the curriculum from the kindergarten through the twelfth grade and in all teacher-education programs.

VI. A systematic and orderly organization of school districts, adequately financed, which will provide schools enrolling at least 500 students in grades 9 to 12, inclusive, in those communities where topography and density of population permit, so that they are capable of maintaining an efficient and complete educational program.

VII. A widespread experimentation with new media of instruction and fuller utilization of those of proved merit.

VIII. A post-high school public educational system, properly coordinated and articulated with other facets of education, which will better serve the youth and adults of Ohio by providing course offerings for advanced standing in college level programs, as well as serve their need in vocational and technical programs.

IX. The development, expansion, and improvement of the program of vocational rehabilitation, so that every Ohioan handicapped by disability may have prompt skilled help in achieving rehabilitation.

[5] Furnished by the Office of the Superintendent of Public Instruction of the State of Ohio and reprinted with permission.

X. A program of parent and community education, aimed at the development of attitudes toward education that will result in improved motivation of students to take full advantage of improved educational opportunities.

XI. A closer working relationship with other departments of government and community agencies having responsibilities that affect children.

Summary Considerations

As you read and meditate on the foregoing sets of secondary school objectives and recall others with which you are acquainted, you no doubt become aware of the all-embracing nature of secondary education and its application to the life interests and activities of developing adolescents.

Every young person needs to master those knowledges and gain those understandings that are appropriate to his life pattern. He also must be helped to acquire such skills and competencies as will increase his proficiency in meeting his responsibilities as an active and constructive member of his family and of his occupational and community groups. In addition, if a young person is expected to become a worthy citizen of his country, he should be guided toward the achievement of an intelligent outlook on world affairs, a constructive point of view toward life experiences, a wholesome set of values, and a sound philosophy of life.

Any subject included in the curriculum design of a secondary school probably does not place equal emphasis on all of the three inclusive areas of educational objectives—knowledges, skills, and attitudes. Yet, no one of them can be disregarded. As you examine formulated sets of purposes to be considered in the teaching of your subject, note the ways in which and the extent to which these relate to accepted objectives of secondary education.

PROBLEMS OF LONG-RANGE PLANNING

Before a teacher attempts to prepare plans for the teaching of his subject, he needs to appreciate its aims or purposes in light of generally-accepted secondary school curriculum objectives. He also should know how much and what content is to be covered during the course of a term, year, or longer period. He must be able to view the subject in perspective—to recognize the significant aspects to be mastered by his students.

Preparation of Courses of Study

There still are schools in which teachers use the sequentially arranged material of a well-organized textbook as the basis of their long-range planning. The present trend, however, is for qualified school personnel, working as a team, to organize a body of material that will meet appropriate educational objectives and that can be used as a guide to the subject teacher in his unit preparation and daily planning.

Long-range teaching guides usually are called courses of study. They include the teaching-learning objectives and the topics or units to be taught, arranged in logical or psychological order. It is unlikely that during your student-teaching experiences you will be asked to participate in the preparation of a course of study for your subject. Moreover, you probably will find that one already has been prepared for use in your school. Your cooperating teacher will help you become acquainted with it and assist you in using it as you plan for your teaching under his supervision. Your responsibility is to understand it and to use it.

The course of study for a particular subject may be prepared by statewide committees. In large cities, a committee of experts, selected from among members of the school system, often are responsible for the preparation of the document. In small school communities, the teachers of the subject may develop their course of study according to state-formulated objectives for its teaching.

A Comprehensive Course of Study

A well-organized, detailed course of study represents a comprehensive piece of work that includes the activities of a large group of qualified persons. To illustrate this point, we shall describe the construction of the Course of Study in World History (Regents Course of Study) published by the Board of Education of the City of New York.[6]

[6] *World History for High Schools: Regents Course of Study,* Curriculum Bulletin, 1958–59 Series, No. 11, Board of Education of the City of New York.

The members of the committee consisted of five teachers of social studies, a senior high school principal, and a junior high school principal. The work of the committee was supervised by three Assistant Superintendents and the Director of the Bureau of Curriculum Research. Helpful suggestions were offered by various other committees and organizations. You can readily recognize the fact that the preparation of this course of study represents a tremendous task of research and organization.

To acquaint you further with the value to a teacher of a well-prepared piece of long-range planning, we shall briefly describe the contents of the Course of Study in World History as prepared by the Committee.

Objectives of the Course in World History

The aims of the course of study in World History are as follows:

1. To develop an understanding of the background and origins of present institutions and customs.
2. To develop an appreciation for the values of democracy.
3. To develop a sense of ethical values which are part of the heritage of civilized man.
4. To awaken a realization of the ever-present danger of totalitarianism to man's liberty.
5. To instill an appreciation of the value of solving international disputes by peaceful means.
6. To foster an understanding of the interdependence of men and of world resources and to further a knowledge of other people's cultures and problems and an appreciation of human values.
7. To develop an understanding of the importance of technology in raising living standards.
8. To show the influence of Western civilization on underveloped parts of the world.
9. To develop critical thinking, suspended judgment, objectivity, an understanding of cause-and-effect relationships, and research techniques.
10. To show the importance of the historical method and historical evidence in problem solving.
11. To foster ability to read and interpret the printed page and other mass media of communication.
12. To promote skill in reading and interpreting charts, graphs, maps, and statistics.

More detailed accounts of the aims will be found in the introductions to individual units.[7]

[7] *Ibid.*, pp. 2–3.

Two Approaches to World History

The committee developed two approaches to World History—the *chronological* and the *topical*. We present them as follows:

The Chronological Approach

Units and Suggested Time Allotment

The chronological approach is organized into seven major units with the following suggested time allotment:

Unit I   — How to Introduce the Study of World History—1 or 2 weeks

Unit II   — Western Civilization from Ancient Times to the Renaissance—5 weeks

Unit III — The Emergence of National States and Democratic Institutions —6 weeks

Unit IV — The Industrial Revolution and Its Consequences—3 weeks

Unit V   — The Meeting of East and West—8 weeks

Unit VI — The Threat of the Modern Totalitarian State—5 weeks

Unit VII— Modern International Relations—Diplomacy, Wars, Quest for Peace—5 weeks

This allotment allows time for current developments, tests, visual aids, and reviews.[8]

The Topical Approach

Units and suggested Time Allotment

The topical approach is organized into six major units with the following suggested time allotment:

Unit I   — How to Introduce the Study of World History—1 or 2 weeks

Unit II   — How Men Have Struggled to Achieve Democratic Rights and Human Dignity—9 weeks

Unit III — How Men Have Tried to Satisfy Their Economic Wants through the Ages—4 weeks

Unit IV — How Men's Cultures and Political Systems Have Influenced Each Other in Modern Times—10 weeks

Unit V   — How Men Have Been Attracted by and Oppressed under Totalitarian Rule—5 weeks

Unit VI — How Men Have Fought Wars but Have Tried to Achieve Peace —5 weeks

[8] *Ibid.*, p. 5.

This allotment allows time for current developments, tests, visual aids, and reviews.[9]

Reasons are presented for the inclusion of these two approaches.[10] Also included for each approach is a description of the way in which each unit can be treated including: Problems, Notes on Methods, and Suggestions for Biographical Enrichment and Review.

Value of a Course of Study

As you read this brief review of the course of study in World History, you are able to appreciate its usefulness to a teacher, especially a beginner, in planning for his teaching. Not all courses of study are as comprehensive as the one described. Some include no more than a listing of the topics to be included; others are organized according to a plan—such as objectives, understandings, skills, attitudes, and suggestive units. You are fortunate if you find in your school a relatively complete, well-organized plan that can guide you in your own planning.

Most good courses of study are flexible. They allow for the meeting of specific student needs. During his years of working with young people of differing abilities, the experienced teacher learns what in a given course of study needs special emphasis. He works out his own long-range plans in light of his background of experience. He is careful to achieve the specific learning goals of his subject and to include appropriate topics or units of the course of study. Your cooperating teacher will encourage you to work with him in making any needed changes in the planning for the particular group of students with whom you are working.

Contextual Aspects of Planning

There is another aspect of long-range planning to which you should give attention. As a beginner, you may believe that you need to be concerned only with the work of the term in which you are involved. This is not enough. You also should be cognizant of what your students have studied to the present in your subject and what

[9] *Ibid.,* pp. 24–25.
[10] *Ibid.,* pp. 1–2.

lies ahead of them. For example, you are teaching English to an eleventh year high school class. What have they had in the ninth and tenth years, and what is the course of study for the twelfth year? How is economics related to the entire program of secondary school social studies? In brief, what learning experiences have your students had in preceding terms in the study of your subject, and what learning experiences can be expected to follow?

You probably have gained some understanding of long-range objectives and teaching approaches in your college methods classes. Now it becomes your responsibility to apply what you have learned in light of the philosophy and teaching approaches of the school in which you are student teaching.

THE UNIT APPROACH IN TEACHING

In the past, most teachers were accustomed to place major emphasis on day-by-day lesson planning. The many sequentially organized topics of a detailed course of study or the chapter contents of a textbook served as the bases of daily lesson plans. Following this procedure might result in segmented, unrelated teaching. The unit approach in teaching provides the teacher and his class an opportunity to center attention on a series of comprehensive learning wholes that, insofar as they represent the functioning of broad unifying principles, improve learners' retention of subject materials.

Interpretation of Unit Teaching

A unit of work can be interpreted as a series of teaching-learning experiences that are centered in and unified around an appropriate topic, a practical project, or a problem of interest to a particular group of students. Much of secondary school teaching centers around each of the various topics included in the course of study. However, more and more consideration is being given to the utilization of problem and project units that, as they are developed by the teacher and students planning together, can serve to meet the life needs of adolescents as these are presented in present-day formulations of educational objectives for the secondary school.

We present here a comparison of topical units and problem or project units from various subjects. These are representative of the kinds of topics that can be treated in the subject.

TABLE 7

ILLUSTRATIONS OF TOPICAL UNITS AND PROBLEM OR
PROJECT UNITS IN VARIOUS SUBJECTS

Subject	Topic Unit	Problem or Project Unit
Biology	A study of bacteria	How are we fighting polio?
English	The composition of a newspaper—contents, format, etc.	Appreciating the background of others from newspaper reports
World History	The development of labor unions	Do we still need labor unions?
Composition	The social letter	Corresponding with a "pen pal"
American History	The Monroe Doctrine	Our relations with Latin American countries

Some subject materials, especially those in which sequential treatment is needed, lend themselves better to topical treatment than to the problem approach, such as grammar, higher mathematics, accounting, shorthand, and typewriting. Other areas of study can well include the problem-unit approach, such as the language arts, the social studies, some aspects of science, artistic appreciation, and other materials that may have a direct bearing on students' experiences and relationships.

Value of the Unit Approach

Student interest is a prime motivator of learning progress. Since the unit approach is relatively flexible, it can be adapted to meet changing interests of adolescents. For example, a unit such as "Our Civic Responsibilities" would receive slightly different treatment in the tenth year of high school from that accorded it in the twelfth year. Also, practical learning outcomes can be stressed rather than only the mastery of subject content. Hence learning can become more meaningful.

In addition, through the unit approach, the teacher can make provision for learning differences among his students. There is more opportunity for remedial work. The work of the class is geared toward a better relationship between subject content and educational objectives. As teachers and students plan together, the classroom takes on the nature of a laboratory.

Some educators believe that the unit approach is more applicable to the junior high school than to the senior high school, since on the latter level, the students are engaged in the mastery of advanced learning materials, some of which, at least, may not be directly related to their present life experiences. This point of view may or may not be tenable. It is a fact, however, that much of learning content in the upper secondary school years seems to follow a more or less sequential pattern of presentation.

Curriculum guides vary considerably. Yet, if you examine the following curriculum design for the junior high school, you probably will realize that the broad concepts included might well apply to all levels of secondary education. These curricular concepts are:

1. Continuing and strengthening the streams of basic learnings and skills.
2. Exploratory, enrichment, and creative activities.
3. Personal development—physical, spiritual, social, and moral.
4. Special experiences to meet individual needs or interests.[11]

The Core Curriculum

Some secondary schools have been experimenting with a form of organization that usually is referred to as the core curriculum. According to this form of organization, a ninth grade class, for example, is scheduled to meet with one teacher for several periods per day. Two or more subjects are programmed under the same teacher. In most schools where the core is used, the subjects include the language arts, social studies, and science (although art, music, or the industrial arts may be added). Units of work tend to cross subject lines.

Since the core teacher often is the homeroom or official teacher, he can give guidance to the group, thereby being enabled to help his students meet their personal needs. Other subjects, such as mathematics, a foreign language, and physical education are taken in regular class situations.

In core classes, as in other unit teaching approaches, essential

---

[11] *Guide to Curriculum Improvement in Grades 7–8–9,* Curriculum Bulletin, 1955–56 Series, No. 10, Board of Education of the City of New York, 1957, p. 48.

knowledges and tool skills must receive proper attention. Much can be done, however, in the development of wholesome and positive student attitudes and in meeting young adolescents' needs and interests as they participate in the development of learning units similar to the following:

1. Problems related to orientation to the school and the community
2. Problems related to how people make a living; modern industrial processes and development; consumer and worker information—budgeting, saving, and investing
3. Problems related to the air age, the atomic age, scientific progress, and world communication
4. Problems related to health and growth; personal planning; behavior standards; living in the home and family; friendships, recreation and social activities; developing satisfying interests
5. Problems related to the American heritage and the rights and duties of citizens in a democratic society; the development of freedom and our obligations to maintain freedom; interrelationships—racial, national, cultural, religious; leaders in art, science, government, military; the development of values and activities that strengthen idealism
6. Problems related to expression in the language and related arts; great writers, their ideas, times, and influence; appreciation of good writing—personal and professional; relation to music, art, dancing, drama, and mass media of press, radio, movies, television.[12]

To illustrate the ways in which the study of a unit can cross subject lines, we present the following organizational pattern of a study unit to be included in a core program:

SUGGESTIONS FOR A STUDY UNIT [13]

By Eugenie G. Nadelman

I. PROBLEM: WHY DOES THE CARIBBEAN HAVE ECONOMIC AND GEOGRAPHICALLY STRATEGIC IMPORTANCE TO THE UNITED STATES?

A. Reasons for Selection:

1. Current interest in Cuba and Puerto Rico especially, as well as in the other islands.
2. More detail on the voyages of Columbus. The discovery of America had its beginnings in the Caribbean.

---

[12] *Ibid.,* pp. 63–64.

[13] Eugenie G. Nadelman, "Suggestions for a Study Unit," *Classroom Clipper,* XXX, No. 4, Pan American Airways, New York (April–May, 1963), 10–11.

3. Great amount of advertising done by tourist agencies creates a desire to know more about the islands.
4. Many students and their parents have visited the islands, which have been brought so close to us by the jet airplane.
5. Many economic and political situations concerning the United States and the islands are of interest to the students, and a background of knowledge is needed to discuss them intelligently.
6. This region is considered an important trading center for the U.S.

II. PROBABLE DURATION: Two weeks.

III. LAUNCHING THE UNIT:

A. Approach:
1. The use of travel folders would be an interesting and direct way to create curiosity.
2. Current news about some of the islands would be helpful in arousing curiosity.
3. The voyages of Columbus could be studied in detail to highlight the many islands he and other explorers visited.
4. Books from the Bibliography could be used as a starter.
5. The use of the suggested Audio-Visual material would also create a desire to know more.
B. Subsidiary Problems:
1. What are the most significant cultural contributions of the Caribbean islands?
2. How has the fact that these islands seem to be a "magnet for visitors" affected their own economic problems as well as their relationship with the United States?
3. Of what importance is their proximity to the United States?
4. What has been the effect of the exploitation of their natural resources?
5. As the islands grow economically and politically, what effect may they have on future relations with the United States and other countries?
6. Which products have formed the bulk of trade between the U.S. and the islands?

IV. EXPECTED OUTCOMES:

A. Social Studies:
1. Cuba—largest and most populous island in Antilles; entrance to Gulf of Mexico, location significant in historical and economic development of island; about 200 harbors: Guantanamo, Santiago de Cuba, Cienfuegos, leading ones; Capital, Havana; discovered by Columbus in 1492; last Spanish colony to obtain independence; incident of the *Maine*, McKinley, President; Treaty of Paris, 1898, Spain relinquished Cuba to U.S. in trust; 1901, Platt Amendment, leased naval station, Guantanamo, to U.S.; Palma, first President, 1902; Batista, Castro, sugar, 87% of

exports, tobacco, second in importance; pineapples, avocados, meat produce and dairying, pepper, manganese, copper, nickel; dependent on commerce and tourism, both cut down in recent trouble with Castro; Bahía Honda, Matanzas, Cárdenas, Nuevitas, other cities; proximity to great population centers of the world.

2. Dominican Republic—formerly Santo Domingo; capital, Ciudad Trujillo; Santiago and La Vega, cities; Juan Pablo Duarte, national hero; St. Lucia, safe harbor, called "Beachcombers Paradise"; sugar, coffee, limes; although small, plays an important role in international politics; commands main sea routes from Europe and Eastern North America; Samana Bay, good harbor; first European colony in America, established 1493; Columbus' burial ground and castle; Ramirez, Jimenez, Vasquez, General Trujillo.

3. Haiti—Port au Prince, capital; discovered by Columbus, 1492; Toussaint L'Ouverture, statesman; Cape Haitien, oldest city; La Belle Creole, famous free port; coffee most important product; sugar cane, mahogany; rich in unexploited minerals.

4. Jamaica—largest island in British West Indies; "Isle of Springs"; discovered by Columbus in 1494; great slave market; Kingston, capital; Port Royal, Spanish Town, Montego Bay, Port Antonio; bananas, formerly most important product, now surpassed by sugar; tourists, most important industry; one of largest producers of bauxite; ginger, pimento; only island completely surrounded by Caribbean.

5. Puerto Rico—island dependency of U.S.; discovered by Columbus in 1493, actually the only time he trod on U.S. soil; San Juan, capital; 1917, Puerto Ricans awarded citizenship; Ponce, second largest seaport and industrial city; more surfaced roads per square mile than any other area on earth; crossroads of the Caribbean; Arecibo, home of Ron Rico rum; sugar, pineapples, vanilla, coffee (orange trees used as shade for coffee).

6. Martinique—discovered by Columbus in 1502; Empress Josephine born here; capital, Fort-de-France; sugar, bananas, pineapples, cacao, coffee, rum.

7. Curaçao—part of Netherlands Antilles; Willemstad, capital; oil refining, chief industry, one of largest oil refineries in the world situated here; used by Allies in World War II; calcium phosphate; orange liqueur (Curaçao).

8. Trinidad—second largest island in British West Indies; 99-year lease to U.S. for naval and air base; Port-of-Spain, capital; Angostura Bitters, oil, cacao, sugar, coconuts; pitch lake, asphalt.

9. Barbados has been continually under British flag since 1625.

10. Antigua—Island of Nevis, birthplace of Alexander Hamilton.

11. Grenada—capital, St. Georges; one of prettiest miniature harbors in Caribbean; nutmeg and mace.

12. Virgin Islands—100 small islands, 14 inhabited; St. Thomas, largest

population; bought by U.S. because of strategic location; U.S. air base on St. Croix, submarine base on St. Thomas; Charlotte Amalie, capital of St. Thomas; Bay rum; Governor appointed by U.S.; people are citizens.

B. Health:
ill health on many islands because of lack of balanced diet, need for animal and vegetable protein, more fish and dairy-products, better storage methods; health conditions in Trinidad good; mountain climate of Jamaica good for people afflicted with tuberculosis and rheumatic diseases; Carlos Finlay helped rid Cuba of yellow fever, malaria, smallpox.

C. Science:
coral reefs, natural harbors, volcanic eruptions, mud volcanoes in Princes Town, Trinidad; Tobago, sanctuary for birds of paradise; mogotes rocks in Cuba look like organ pipes; matanzas, red clay soil in Cuba; royal palm, characteristic tree of Cuba; starch from Yucca, tapioca from cassava, indigo from saffron; sponges; many bats in Cuba; butter-flies in Haiti; white limestone in Jamaica; climate, chief attraction of Jamaica; home of moths and butterflies; one of deepest chasms on the globe, Brownson Deep, in Puerto Rico.

D. Art and Music:
most significant cultural contribution is song and dance; drum, steel band, stringed band, calypso.

E. Mathematics:
units of money; distance from island to island; comparison graphs of population, exports and imports; time differences; length of time by ship and by air.

F. Language Arts:
a. new words in this issue.
b. literature—outgrowth of singing stories.
c. oral and written communication:
sharing information by reporting; comparing information; debating current political issues; discussing economic problems; writing to people on the islands for further information; planning tours; interviewing people who have visited the islands; outlining notes for reports; review-ing books and movies.

V. SUGGESTED ACTIVITIES:

A. Things to do:
1. Prepare a map showing the location of the islands and the routes by ship and by airplane.
2. Make a chart listing the products of each of the islands.

3. Display products from the islands.
4. Plan a sightseeing trip—"island hopping."
5. Trace the history of the islands, the changes in ownership and in leaders.
6. Discuss present-day situations, particularly in Cuba, Haiti, and Puerto Rico.
7. Explain the West Indian Federation and give reasons for its failure.
8. Read some of the books listed and show some of the movies.
9. Interview people who have toured the islands.
10. Arrange a bulletin board, keeping it up to date with news of the islands.
11. Trace the routes of Columbus on his various voyages.

B. Culmination:
1. Arrange a songfest featuring island music and dances.
2. Take your audience on a tour of famous places for vacationers and sightseers.
3. Make slides about the islands and show them to other classes.
4. Any item listed under "Things to Do" can be used as a culmination.

VI. LEAD TO NEW UNITS:

Having studied the islands, it might be interesting to study about the countries which own some of them.

I. General Questions:
1. Who referred to Cuba as "The Key to the New World"?
2. What does the Caribbean area include?
3. What islands compose the Greater Antilles? The Lesser Antilles?
4. What are the two main products of Cuba?
5. What is the principal export of Haiti?
6. Which fruit is grown extensively in Jamaica?
7. Which trees are used mainly as shade for coffee crops in Puerto Rico?
8. Name five spices which are important exports from the islands.
9. From which islands does vanilla come?
10. On which islands is oil an important product?
11. Which island is well known for valuable deposits of calcium phosphates?
12. Which island is one of the largest producers of bauxite?
13. On which island is "Operation Bootstrap" being carried out?
14. Which two islands, of the European territories, are the most highly industrialized?
15. Why has the tourist industry become one of the largest sources of income for the Caribbean?
16. From which area of the arts have the most significant cultural contributions come?
17. What does "Jamaica" mean?
18. Which is the only island completely surrounded by the Caribbean?
19. Of which island is Kingston the capital?
20. What is the capital of Trinidad?

21. Which island is described as the "little England of eternal summer"?
22. Which island did George Washington visit before the American Revolution?
23. Of what island is St. Georges the capital?
24. Where was Alexander Hamilton born?
25. Which island is known as the "gateway to Latin America"?
26. What is the capital of Puerto Rico?
27. Why was this region called the West Indies?
28. Who discovered the majority of the islands?
29. How many voyages did Columbus make?
30. Which of the islands are the three independent republics?

II. Discussion Questions:

1. How has the location of Cuba been significant in its historical and economic development?
2. Discuss the attitudes of Presidents Franklin Pierce and James Buchanan toward Cuba.
3. How did sugar, more than any other single factor, shape the Caribbean economy?
4. Discuss the changes in the lives of the "sugar workers."
5. Why has the growth of cotton increased and that of cocoa decreased on the islands?
6. Discuss what "Operation Bootstrap" has done for Puerto Rico, and the future plans in this program.
7. Why do the islands of the Caribbean act as a "magnet for visitors"?
8. Discuss the rise and fall of the West Indies Federation.

III. What did the following have to do with the history of the Caribbean?:

1. Columbus
2. Balboa
3. Cortes
4. Pizarro
5. Arawak Indians
6. Sam Lord
7. Lord Nelson
8. Alexander Hamilton
9. Henri Christophe
10. Oliver Cromwell
11. Carib Indians
12. The battleship *Maine*
13. Castro
14. Batista
15. Carlos Finlay
16. Juan Pablo Duarte
17. Jimenez

18. Toussaint L'Ouverture
19. Ponce de Leon
20. Brooke

IV. To which island would you go to find:

1. The birthplace of Empress Josephine
2. The ruins of St. Pierre
3. The Morne Rouge rain forest
4. "The land of Wood and Water"
5. International society at Montego Bay
6. The pitch lake of La Brea
7. Maracas Bay
8. The Caroni Swamp
9. The flying fish fleet at Bathsheba
10. Pigeon Island
11. Nelson's Dockyard
12. The birthplace of Alexander Hamilton
13. La Belle Creole, famous free port center
14. Burial place of Christopher Columbus
15. El Morro, largest and strongest Spanish fort
16. Casa Blanca, residence of Ponce de Leon
17. San Cristo Chapel, smallest public chapel in the world
18. Guantanamo Bay
19. Anegada Passage

Noting the meanings of the words below will help in the understanding of the reading matter.

allocated	set apart for a specific purpose
bisect	divide; cut in two
consecutive	following in order without interruption
decadence	period of decline; deterioration
decorous	showing good taste
disdain	attitude of contempt
diversification	variety
elite	choicest
encompasses	surrounds; encircles; contains
enhanced	made greater in value
expedients	means to an end; resources
exuberance	high spirits
façades	fronts of buildings
facet	a side or aspect
ferocious	fierce; savage
fiscal year	a 12-month period for financial accounting
fluctuations	rise and fall
galleons	large, heavy Spanish ships

indenture	a contract binding one person to work for another for a given length of time
interlopers	those who intrude on another's rights or privileges
interlude	anything that fills time between events
mitigated	softened; moderated
monoculture	the raising of only one crop
myriad	a very large number
oligarchy	a state governed by only a few persons
petrified	changed to a stony substance
proximity	nearness
pulses	edible seeds of peas, beans, lentils, etc.
ramie	plant, fiber of which is used in the making of fine cloth
rampant	widespread; unchecked
satirical	sarcastic
subjugated	brought under control of; subdued
submerged	underneath the water
subsidiaries	companies controlled by others
subsistence	means of support or livelihood
synonymous	same meaning
tenacious	persistence; stubborn
topography	surface features
unviable	not able to live
zenith	highest point

Planning for the Unit Approach

Planning for the unit approach to teaching requires a considerable amount of preliminary preparation. The term's or year's work can be divided into a series of related units. For example, the following theme content might represent the work of the tenth, eleventh, and twelfth years in English.

TENTH YEAR

Theme: The Individual as a Member of the Group
1. Learning to Live With the Family
2. Our School:
    a. It's Better to Work Together Toward an Education
    b. Participating in the Extracurricular and Co-curricular Programs
    c. Teams and Sports: Fair Play—the American Way
    d. Out-of-school Organizations for Teenagers
3. Making and Keeping Friends
4. As One Generation to Another
5. Appreciating the Backgrounds of Others
6. Finding One's Way into the World of Work

7. Out-of-School Organizations for Teenagers
8. What Is Fun and What Isn't Funny
9. United We Stand, Divided We Fall: Many Groups of People Make America
10. Making the Most of Oneself
11. Around the World in New York City

ELEVENTH YEAR

Theme: The Individual and the American Heritage
1. Westward Ho!—the Pioneer Spirit
2. Great Americans and Their Legacy to Us
3. Let's See the Funny Side: American Humor
4. The Regions of America Contribute to Her Heritage
5. America in Song and Story
6. Guideposts to Liberty
7. The Union: Storehouse of Treasures from All Lands
8. Tell All the People: Mass Media
9. American Literature: Ideals in the American Heritage
10. New York City: Focal Point of American Culture
11. Secession vs. Union: A Drama of Human Relations—Many Became One

TWELFTH YEAR

Theme: The Individual's Quest for Universal Values
1. Heroes and Heroines of All Nations and Ages
2. The Search for Values in the Community of Work
3. Educational Values: To Go or Not to Go to College (Technical School, Trade School, Secretarial School)
4. Your Country Needs You: The Armed Forces and the Dignity of Man
5. The U.N.: An Experiment in the Living-Together of All People
6. World Understanding Through Literature
7. Standards for Appreciation: TV, Motion Picture, Radio, and Theatre
8. The Arts in Modern Living
9. The Literature of the Newspaper, Magazine, and Paperback
10. Land of the Free, Home of the Brave: The Development of Civil Liberties in America
11. Man's Struggle for World Peace
12. Truth vs. Falsehood: Stereotypes, Smears, Slogans, Insinuations, and Fallacies
13. The Good Life [14]

The preliminary step of dividing the course of study into appropriate units often is the responsibility of a group of teachers of that subject. Then, either the committee as a whole or the individual

[14] Reprinted from *English-Speech: Language Arts for Senior High Schools,* Curriculum Bulletin, 1955–56 Series, No. 12, by permission of the Board of Education of the City of New York, pp. 63–64.

teacher organizes the aims, the materials, and the activities for each unit. The information to be mastered and the skills to be improved are noted.

Student participation in the determination of the activities to be included often is encouraged. Appropriate individual and group projects are planned and conducted by students under teacher guidance. Other activities may be dramatizations; demonstrations; oral or written reports based on reading, on other research, or on project construction; and whole class discussions. The final step is an evaluation by the teacher and students of the value of the unit of learning.

In planning unit activities with your class you serve as the chairman, giving the group intelligent leadership. The unit may be simple or relatively complex; but you know the aims that you hope to achieve, and you view these in light of students' interests and purposes. You attempt to motivate their thinking through questions that can arouse their interest or through involving them in challenging experiences, as you observe the various students at work on unit activities. You thus can learn much about their attitudes and their strengths and weaknesses.

The following expansion of three central themes in English offer many suggestions concerning various activities associated with these units.

LEARNING TO LIVE WITH THE FAMILY. The adolescent is groping his way towards a new relationship with his family. The inevitable tensions, conflicts, and misunderstandings with parents or with brothers and sisters can be lessened by the insights and attitudes resulting from a well-conceived unit of study in family relationships. Many books, plays, short stories, as well as television and radio programs, are concerned with the rights and responsibilities of young people with respect to the family group. Books like *The Yearling, Life with Father, Giants in the Earth,* and *Silas Marner* may be used for group study depending upon the abilities of the group. Questions relating to allowances, dating, working after school, selecting and entertaining friends, choosing a career, minding younger brothers and sisters, helping with household chores, contributing earnings to the family, decorating one's own room, choosing family vacation places, using the family car, and many others lend themselves to round-table, panel, and forum discussions in which the exchange of opinions and experiences as well as the opportunity to read books and newspaper or magazine articles contributes to a fairer and more impersonal appraisal of these problems. Creative expression in the form of biographies, diaries, and stories of family life can be closely integrated with the reading and discussion. Real or imaginary family situations and problems may be used for impromptu or prepared conversations and dramatizations and as the theme of original short stories, plays, or radio scripts.

OUR SCHOOL: IT'S BETTER TO WORK TOGETHER TOWARD AN EDUCATION. For the increasing number of junior high school graduates in our tenth year classes, this unit can assist in their orientation to a new school environment; for others, it becomes an occasion to assess their success in utilizing all the opportunities for growth provided by the school and to evaluate their contributions to the school. A study of the school newspaper might well be the approach to a serious consideration of such issues as cheating, the problem of homework, good study habits, planning for a college or occupation, opportunities for service and opportunities to develop talents, hobbies, and interests in the school, G.O. campaigns and elections, assembly programs, and so forth. Letter writing should be an important part of this unit, e.g., letters to grade advisers, teachers, and other school officials; correspondence with students or clubs in other schools and in other countries; letters to the school newspaper; letters to parents inviting them to be guests at or to participate in school or class activities. An effort should be made to give instruction in the social amenities and conventions involved in letters of inquiry, letters of apology, thank-you notes, invitations, requests for assistance or favors, and letters of complaint or commendation. The preparation of a school or department handbook, a code of behavior, or a guide to new students might well be one of the culminating activities involving group writing and editing.

OUR SCHOOL: PARTICIPATING IN THE EXTRA-CURRICULAR PROGRAM. The value to the individual and the place in the total educational program of extra-curricular and co-curricular activities are not always completely understood by students. The individual's responsibility to serve his group should be stressed as strongly as the advantages accruing to him from participation. Qualifications for leadership and the ethics and loyalties involved in selecting officers and leaders should be considered. Some instruction and practice in the elements of parliamentary procedure would seem a necessary part of this unit. Writing simple minutes of meetings is within the power of most tenth year students; the more able classes may try their hand at writing a constitution for an organization.[15]

The Resource Unit

Preplanning for the utilization of the unit approach to teaching and learning may include the preparation of resource units or col-

[15] Reprinted from *English-Speech: Language Arts for Senior High Schools,* Curriculum Bulletin, 1955–56 Series, No. 12, by permission of the Board of Education of the City of New York, 1956, reprinted 1961, pp. 64–65.

lections of materials and activities that can be helpful in the actual development of subject aims. The suggestions included in a resource unit center around a specific topic, problem, or project that fits into the general outline of the course of study. In their preparation of a resource unit, individual teachers or committees of teachers differ somewhat in the format that they follow.

A comprehensive resource unit can include all or most of the following areas:

    I. Topic or problem
   II. Relation to objectives of the subject and students' interests
  III. Content or appropriate activities
  IV. Research to discover appropriate source material
   V. Developmental approach to the conduct of the unit
  VI. Possible media for evaluating worth of the unit

A well-organized, comprehensive resource unit probably contains much more material than can be utilized with any one class or group of students. For example, a planned resource unit may recommend the use of the following sources: much reading material, many community resources, and various audio-visual aids. A long list of possible learning activities also can be included.

The teacher is not expected to employ every suggestion appearing in the outline of the resource unit. He is enabled, however, to select from the wealth of material at his disposal whatever would seem to be best suited for meeting the educational needs, interests, and abilities of a particular group of students. The resource unit is flexible. It provides ideas or suggestions upon which the teacher can build his teaching unit.

As a student teacher, you may be asked by your cooperating teacher to carry through a unit in your subject. He may have available a resource unit that he will review with you, helping you to select those sources and activities that would seem best fitted for use with the class.

If your cooperating teacher does not have a resource unit, he and you can prepare one. He may permit you to do most of the work under his supervision. He probably will suggest some sources of materials that are in the school. You may be able to obtain others from books and other materials available in your college. Your college supervisor can be of considerable help to you in your development of the unit.

As an example of the contents of a resource unit, we present the following treatment of a unit in World History:

HOW DOES OUR LIVING STANDARD COMPARE WITH THAT OF OTHER PEOPLES OF THE WORLD?

Introduction

Living standards are conditioned by many factors, the most significant of which are the modes of production and the use of natural resources. Prior to the Industrial Revolution, people toiled long hours with primitive tools in the hope of eking out a frugal livelihood. The advent of the power-driven machine made available a variety and abundance of goods hitherto unobtainable by the mass of people. As industries developed, productivity increased, often raising standards of living. The people of the United States have one of the highest standards of living in the world because their industrial system is efficient, and the country is endowed with varied and abundant natural resources.

It should be remembered that a general statement concerning standard of living cannot adequately describe living conditions of all people in any particular country. Thus there are many people in our country who live under sub-standard conditions. On the other hand, in Iran, for example, where the mass of people do not enjoy a high standard of living, some people live at a standard comparable to the highest in the Western world.

In evaluating standards of living, consideration must be given to varying values and needs of different people.

There is an interrelationship among the economies of the world; and it is therefore in our natural interest to encourage expanding economies in the other parts of the world.

The flexibility of a free society often makes possible improved living standards.

Aims

a. To understand the various factors which determine a standard of living.
b. To study the relationship among the following factors: resources, industrialization, and a standard of living.
c. To understand why our standard of living is higher than that of most other people.
d. To appreciate the relationship between a democratic system and a high living standard.
e. To appreciate that archaic and rigid political systems militate against economic growth.
f. To realize that some people in the United States still do not enjoy an adequate standard of living.
g. To show the interrelationship of the American and the world economies.

Content

1. *How do we measure standard of living?*
   (AIMS: *a, b*)
   a. Necessities: food, clothing, shelter
   b. Education, leisure time, recreation
   c. Economic security, health, longevity
   d. Services, home comforts, communications
   e. Increased real income

2. *Why is the standard of living in other parts of the world low? (Case study:* standard of living in any underdeveloped area.)
   (AIMS: *a, b, c, f*)
   a. Economic factors
   Lack of resources, such as minerals, water
   Use of primitive tools and methods; lack of industry
   b. Social factors
   Overpopulation
   Concentration of land
   Ownership
   Mass illiteracy
   Disease, malnutrition
   Survival of feudal privileges and practices
   c. Failure to apply modern science to economic and social problems
   d. Instability of government

3. *What evidences do we have that our standard of living is high?*
   (AIMS: *a, b, e, g*)
   a. Variety, quality of goods and services in terms of criteria in 1 above
   Availability of world-wide products
   Recreational opportunities
   Increase in services, such as: laundry, installment loans, prepared foods
   Wide use of modern industrial products, such as: auto, electrical appliances, modern homes with central heating
   b. Security of people
   Modern social and medical services, longevity
   Economic security through social security, insurance, unions
   Potentialities for improving living standards in modern industrial economy
   Stable, responsible government

Approaches and Activities

1. This unit can be launched by presenting a chart on comparative standards of living found in various economics texts, data from the U.N. Statistical Office, and the *Miracle of America,* prepared by the Advertising Council.

   In the absence of the complete chart, the teacher can present the following facts: The average annual purchases of an American are about $1500, but only $495 for Europeans; $155 for Latin Americans; $118 for Africans; $89 for the people of the Middle East; and $30 for South East Asians. There is one auto for every American but only one for every 93 Italians and one for every 252 Russians. What other information can be deduced or figured out from this simple statement of fact? What questions does it lead you to ask? This approach can be used to develop an interest in comparative living standards, and the reasons for the differences.

2. To launch or develop this theme, other approaches can be used, such as: stories of hunger in underdeveloped areas from Wm. Vogt, *Road to Survival,* and from Jose de Castro, *Geography of Hunger;* stories of living standards in the U.S.S.R. from H. E. Salisbury, *American in Russia;* and stories of unprecedented consumer demand in the U.S. in journals like *Consumer News,* or *Federal Reserve Survey. Our World and Its People,* by E. Kolevzon and J. Heine, contains a readable survey of the reasons for America's high living standard. To demonstrate that living standards vary within as well as among nations, use the chart showing the distribution of income in the U.S., found in *America's Needs and Resources,* Twentieth Century Fund.

3. Use a film to develop the living standard theme, such as: *Productivity— Key to Plenty* (#497.3); *Fate of a Child* (UN); *Battle for Bread* (UN, #46.5); *On to Jupiter* and *American Harvest* (GM free loan).

4. Use a film strip, such as: *Assets of the Free World* (NYT); *Power— Servant of Our Nation* (Curr.); *Economics* (McGraw) on national income; *Machine Power Means Plenty* (McGraw); *Machines and Human Plenty* (J.A.).

5. Have students prepare maps of the world's arable land, distribution of mineral resources, population, important railroads, navigable rivers and canals, industrial centers, large cities.

6. Ask pupils to make a scrap book or bulletin board display from current magazines, showing what people from each of the following income groups would buy: persons on the wealth level, persons on the comfort level, persons on the health and decency levels. Current motion pictures also serve as sources which illustrate standards of living. Publications from the various embassies can be used to compare the American standard of living with those of the European and the underdeveloped areas.

7. Ask pupils to prepare a family budget, assuming that each as head of the family earns a given income. (The teacher can suggest a figure in keeping with the socio-economic level of the school.) Use the budget as a motivation for items to be included and as basis for discussion of standard of living.

8. Prepare a glossary of words: standard of living, poverty level, bare subsistence level, health and decency level, comfort level, wealth level, real income, per capita income, mass purchasing power, conspicuous consumption.

9. Read selected passages: F. L. Allen, *The Big Change;* T. R. Carskadon, *U.S.A.—Measure of a Nation;* Stuart Chase, *Rich Land, Poor Land; Men and Machines;* Fred Clark, *How We Live.*

10. Conduct forums on the following subjects: Is a great difference in living standards good or bad for a community? Should the government act to eliminate sharp differences in living standards? to eliminate poverty? Should the U.S. government grant more extensive Point Four aid to underdeveloped areas? (See Colonialism unit.)

11. Have students use the living newspaper technique or radio skit to dramatize the "good life" 100 years ago and the "good life" today. Another comparison that can be made is between life in underdeveloped areas and in industrialized areas. Develop the program around a theme, such as: science has affected longevity; a poverty standard of living today is much better than an average standard of living 100 years ago; electricity has been harnessed for the good life.

12. Use adult speakers on the theme of comparative living standards.

13. Thought questions can be developed on the basis of matter within the experience of the pupils.

    a. Explain how each of the following affects standard of living:
    The establishment of a free university in India
    The development of atomic power for fuel
    The discovery of cures for many diseases of old age—cancer, heart ailments—greatly extending longevity
    The distribution of land in underdeveloped areas
    The enactment of anti-discrimination laws with respect to employment and education
    The adoption of required course in home economics for all girls

    b. Explain the possible reasons for each of the following statements:
    In the past 50 years more and more people have left villages and farms to live in the cities.
    There are more people earning very high incomes from city than from farm occupations.
    The Pacific states have a higher per capita income than the Southern states.
    It took a larger income to buy a health and decency standard in 1947 than in 1935.

    c. What is the significance of the facts that 50 years ago most of the bread consumed in the U.S. was baked at home; today almost none of the bread is baked at home? that there is one radio for every seven Americans and one for 55 Russians?

14. Visit the New York Historical Museum or the Museum of the City of New York to see the articles used in 1700. Make a list of ten articles we use today that could not be found in the early days. Make a list of ten articles we do not have today that might be found in advertisements in a newspaper in A.D. 2000. What changes in life would these articles bring to the people?

15. Make a chart of synthetic products indicating the raw material from which they were taken.[16]

You realize that this resource unit includes a tremendous number of possible approaches and activities. Within the time limit allocated to the development of a teaching unit it would be inadvisable, if not impossible, to utilize all or even many of the suggestions offered. The inclusion of all of this material in the resource unit affords the teacher an opportunity to select those approaches and activities that he deems to be best suited in light of the interests of his students and the teaching aids available for his use. In fact, the richness of the offerings makes it possible for the teacher to vary his presentation of the topics from term to term or year to year.

In many school communities, groups of teachers of respective subjects participate in college or school-sponsored workshops (often during the summer vacation) for the purpose of developing full and challenging resource units based on an appropriate course of study. The resource unit is not static, however. From time to time, it may need to be revised in light of newer subject findings, improved techniques, and the like.

QUESTIONS AND TOPICS FOR DISCUSSION

1. List the activities you have planned for the coming week.
2. Recall the subjects you were required to take in the secondary school. What purpose was each supposed to serve?
3. Compare the purposes to be served by your particular subject field with the general objectives of secondary education. Which of these objectives apply specifically to your subject?
4. Is there a course of study of your subject available in your school? By whom was it constructed? What do you think of it?
5. According to what type of organization do you think the teaching units of your subject could best be planned? Why?
6. Select one unit of your subject and list the various activities that could be associated with it.
7. Prepare a resource unit for your subject. What are some of the difficulties you encounter?
8. List the possible values to the teacher and the students of utilizing the unit approach to teaching.

[16] Reprinted from *Resource Units in World History,* Curriculum Bulletin, 1958–59 Series, No. 12, by permission of the Board of Education of the City of New York, 1959, reprinted July, 1961, pp. 60–64.

SELECTED REFERENCES

ALEXANDER, W. H., and HALVERSON, P. M. *Effective Teaching in Secondary Schools.* New York: Holt, Rinehart & Winston, Inc., 1956.

BROWN, T. J. *Student Teaching in a Secondary School.* New York: Harper & Row, Pub., Inc., 1960.

CARTER, W. L., HANSEN, C. W., and McKIM, M. G. *Learning to Teach in the Secondary School.* New York: Macmillan Co., 1962.

Guide to Curriculum Improvement in Grades 7–8–9. New York: Board of Education, 1956. (*See also* Curriculum Guides in other cities.)

LEE, J. M. *Principles and Methods of Secondary Education.* New York: McGraw-Hill Book Co., Inc., 1963.

McKEAN, R. C. *Principles and Methods in Secondary Education.* Columbus, Ohio: Charles E. Merrill Books, Inc., 1962.

RISK, T. M. *Principles and Practices in Secondary Schools* (2nd ed.). New York: American Book Co., 1959.

SCHORLING, R., and BATCHELDER, H. T. *Student Teaching in Secondary Schools.* New York: McGraw-Hill Book Co., Inc., 1956.

SCHULTZ, R. *Student Teaching in the Secondary Schools.* New York: Harcourt, Brace & World, Inc., 1959.

WIGGINS, S. P. *The Student Teacher in Action.* Boston: Allyn & Bacon, Inc., 1957.

7

LESSON PLANNING

The planning of an effective lesson is an essential skill of teaching. As a beginning teacher, you probably will find the making of an adequate lesson plan to be a difficult and frustrating experience. Hence during your student teaching experiences you will need considerable practice in developing daily lesson plans under the guidance of your cooperating teacher and college supervisor.

THE STUDENT TEACHER AND LESSON PLANS

Planning procedures are much more flexible at present than they once were. This in no way detracts from their importance. The teacher needs to know exactly what he hopes to accomplish in a lesson and how he plans to develop the subject material. An experienced teacher may find it sufficient to prepare his written plan in the form of notes or a short outline. Much of his planning is done mentally. It is essential, however, that, as a student teacher, you begin to develop skill in the writing of carefully prepared lesson plans for the meeting of your daily teaching responsibilities.

Observation of Cooperating Teacher in the Utilization of His Plans

You can learn much about lesson planning by observing your cooperating teacher at work and by conferring with him concerning the concomitant aspects of teacher preparation as well as the specific areas of the daily lesson plan. You probably will find that a good teacher not only plans for the teaching of his subject, but also gives careful thought to the management of all of his daily class and out-of-class duties. He is prepared for any eventuality that may occur.

If you are a careful observer, you probably will find as you watch and listen to your cooperating teacher and his class at work on any one day that:

1. There is a purpose to the lesson that is made clear to the students
2. The lesson is conducted step by step in such a way that good learning progress takes place
3. If a discussion seems to veer away from the topic at hand, the teacher skillfully brings the thinking of the students back to the matter under consideration
4. The period ends with a brief summarization of what has been accomplished
5. An assignment for home study is definite and is given at that point in the lesson when it is most effective

Your Responsibility in Lesson Planning

You cannot expect to be as proficient as an experienced teacher in conducting a smoothly running lesson. You can develop skill in planning and teaching, however. As you assist your cooperating teacher in conducting lesson procedures, some of your beginning activities in the classroom may be: helping to prepare and distribute materials, proctoring class tests, correcting test papers and recording their results, engaging in remedial work with individual students or small groups, and similar activities. After you have become acquainted with the total class situation, you will be given the opportunity to participate in the actual teaching of lessons.

Before you attempt to guide the learning experiences of the students for an entire class period, it is essential that you prepare a well-organized lesson plan. Your cooperating teacher can give you considerable assistance, but the plan itself must be yours. It should be based on your understanding of certain factors that are basic to good lesson planning and should incorporate those elements that have value in determining what shall be done during the class period and how teaching-learning experiences should be conducted.

BASES OF LESSON PLANNING

Many background elements combine to assist you in meeting the teaching responsibility of lesson planning. You are acquainted with the objectives of secondary education and the general and specific aims or purposes of study in your field of teaching. You have access to the course of study in your subject that is followed in the school in which you are a student teacher. Available to you also may be resource units from which you can glean suggestions for the development of your subject.

In your college classes you probably have discussed lesson plans and perhaps have written some as a class exercise. You have seen some of your cooperating teacher's plans. As we suggested earlier in the chapter, you have observed this teacher put his plans into operation. All of these activities are helpful in that they acquaint you with fundamentals of lesson planning. They are only preparatory, however. No one of them is a substitute for the actual writing of a plan of procedure that you yourself will use as a guide toward stimulating student learning in the classroom.

FACTORS TO BE CONSIDERED IN LESSON PLANNING

Your lesson plan must be so organized that when you meet your class you are fully prepared to start the lesson promptly and carry it through to a successful conclusion. You need to know the *what, why,* and *how* of your presentation. Hence you consider thoughtfully the various factors that are inherent in a good lesson, and plan accordingly.

An experienced teacher may be able to use some shortcuts, especially if he has taught the subject many times. He may be able to do some of his planning mentally. Even he, however, often finds that his various classes differ in their ability to master the subject matter and in their attitude toward it. Consequently, he adapts his plan to meet the learning needs and interests of each particular class.

Since you are inexperienced, it is essential that you prepare in writing a full and complete plan of procedure. You want to enter the classroom with confidence in your ability to make the lesson a rich and rewarding learning experience for all of your students.

Young people are quick to recognize whether you are well prepared for the day's lesson. Any hesitation on your part in getting started, any fumbling for materials, and the like, will cause them to give their attention to irrelevant matters. You have lost them, and may find it difficult to regain their attention. Hence there are various factors that need to be considered as you prepare your daily lesson plan.

Importance of Sequential Treatment

A specific lesson must fit into a sequential pattern of development. Rarely can you afford to have a lesson stand alone, unrelated to what has preceded it or what will follow. As you plan a lesson, you need to review the material covered in the last lesson, decide what you expect to do in this lesson, and think ahead to what should be incorporated in the next lesson.

For example, you and your class may be studying the unit in biology on "How Biology Explains Our Behavior." Your last lesson dealt with "How Can Our Behavior Be Conditioned?" This leads into today's topic, "How Does the Problem of 'Growing Up' Affect the Behavior of Adolescents?" In the next lesson you might well consider "How Can Adolescents Attempt to Solve Their Behavior Problems?" You can realize that a common thread runs through these three lessons but that they build up from a generalized concept to a specific behavioral situation. In your planning and teaching, you need to make this relationship apparent to the students.

Importance of the Time Element in Lesson Planning

The inexperienced teacher usually has difficulty in adjusting his lesson plan to the rigid requirements of the time element. Either he has included so much in his plan that the dismissal bell rings before he has completed half of what he expected to cover, or he has finished the lesson and has extra time that must be filled. The former situation is likely to occur more often than the latter. You are encouraged to prepare a *full* plan, but during the class period (commonly about 40 to 50 minutes in length) caring for extraneous matters such as reading notices, clarifying of a special point in the lesson, and other unavoidable delays interfere with the smooth progress of the lesson.

Your lesson plan should be so clearly outlined that you are aware of the important points that must be considered and realize that certain details, worthwhile as they seem to you, may need to be omitted or given only passing recognition. You need to budget your material to meet your time allocation. As you gain in experience, you will achieve skill in budgeting your time in light of the activities to be included in the lesson.

THE COMPONENTS OF A LESSON PLAN

After you consider some of the important factors inherent in lesson planning, your next question is "What should be included in the plan itself?" The form of the lesson plan varies with teachers or schools. Your college supervisor probably has suggested a form that he favors. Your cooperating teacher may use another form. Eventually, you will decide for yourself the kind of plan that best meets your purposes. The following plan covers, in a general way, the various aspects of your lesson that you need to consider as you prepare yourself to teach it:

A Lesson Plan

Subject   Date
School Level or Grade
  Aim or Purpose
  Content
  Motivation or Introductory Approach
  Development or Procedures
    Activities
    Budgeting of Time
    Supplementary Materials
    Pivotal Questions
    Assignment
    Summary
    Evaluation or Comments

Aim or Purpose in a Lesson Plan

Aim or purpose is an extremely important aspect of the lesson plan. Your first consideration is to decide *why* you are planning to teach this lesson. How do you expect the students to benefit from it? In what ways does the purpose or aim of this lesson fit into the recognized objectives of the course of study in your subject?

State your aim simply and briefly. Here are a few examples of aims:

1. To develop an understanding of the role of the American government in our economy.
2. To appreciate the importance of water conservation.
3. To develop an understanding of the forms of the adjective and adverb, the comparison of adjectives and adverbs, and their effect and meaning in the sentence.
4. To develop skill in extracting square root.

Content in the Lesson Plan

It is not enough to have a definite, clearly stated aim or purpose for your lesson. You need also to include in your plan the subject matter upon which you expect to focus in your purpose in teaching the lesson.

In some plans, the content is included under the caption "materials." What is included in the content or material depends on the kind of lesson you are teaching. If your aim is to develop skill in extracting square root, it would be well to decide ahead of time the numbers of which the square root is to be extracted and include these in your plan.

In dealing with a subject such as the social studies, you should set down in your plan the subtopics that you expect to include. These should be arranged in logical or psychological order. For example:

Aim: To show that if a democracy is to be effective, each individual must accept responsibility.

Content: 1. The citizen's responsibilities to local community, state, and nation
      a. Participating intelligently in primary and general elections
      b. Giving attention not only to personal well-being but also to the general welfare

    c. Maintaining high moral attitudes and appreciating governmental ethics

    d. Respecting the rights of both majority and minority groups

2. The high school student's obligations to his parents, his school, and his community

Motivation of the Lesson

You have learned from your own experiences and probably have often heard in your college education classes that interest is a prime motivator of activity. When interest is aroused in a project or situation, the learner tends to stay with it as long as his initial interest continues to function. This is a well-known psychological principle that applies to the teaching-learning process. Hence, as you plan your lesson, you need to consider ways in which you can "catch" your students' interest in the content of the lesson, so as to help them utilize their experiences in their struggle toward its mastery.

In planning your approach to a lesson, you must consider the present interests of your students (but you also should keep in mind the specific aims of your lesson and the amount of time available for its coverage). One motivating technique is to start the lesson by asking a challenging question that will encompass the material and be closely related to current adolescent interest. Your task in motivating learners is to steer the discussion from students' responses to your question to the actual material of the lesson. The students may become so interested in discussing the question raised, however, that the inexperienced teacher finds it almost impossible to make the transition from the initial motivating effort to the consideration of lesson content.

Assume, for example, that your aim is to have the students become acquainted with the joust as described in Scott's *Ivanhoe*. Adolescents tend to be interested in present-day sports. The World Series in baseball is in progress. You might start the lesson with "Who do you think will win the World Series?" "Why?" Such questions probably will arouse an animated kind of debate among the members of the class concerning the relative merits of the two teams. How long shall you permit the discussion to continue? How will you go about transferring their attention to a consideration of the factors involved in sports in general and in the joust in particular, and yet maintain their interest? To do this successfully requires considerable teacher ingenuity. Perhaps for an inexperienced teacher this motivating introduction is a little too challenging.

A common mistake of an inexperienced teacher is to use motivation as a kind of "gimmick" to arouse student interest. As soon as the students are interested, he delves into the lesson with no further reference to the interest-arousing approach. In such cases, the students are likely to fall into a kind of lethargy, showing little or no interest in what the teacher is trying to do. They experience a feeling of being "let down." To serve as a stimulator of learning progress, interest must not only be aroused, it must be sustained and maintained throughout the conduct of the lesson.

Degree of student interest in your subject depends on the presence of various factors. It is relatively easy to motivate the individuals in those lessons that constitute progressive steps in the development of a unit of study in the planning of which the students have participated. They are interested in seeing the project through to its conclusion. The extent to which individually, or in groups, they can share in its developmental activities predicates their continued interest in it.

Also, secondary school programs of study include both required and elective subjects. If you are teaching a required subject, you are likely to be faced with the problem of "selling" it to the students. Rarely can you convince them of its value by telling them that it is good for them or that they will find it useful later in their lives.

For example, young adolescents sometimes object to being required to take algebra to obtain an academic diploma. Hence you need to introduce specific lessons in such a way that the students enjoy meeting the mental challenge of mastering their content. On the other hand, the fact that a student has elected a particular course usually presupposes interest on his part in its content. It therefore should be easier for you to motivate the arousal and maintenance of his interest in the sequential steps of its development.

Degree of maturity also is a factor of student interest in a subject. It usually is more difficult to encourage a junior high school student to participate in learning activities than it is to motivate an older adolescent student. The younger teen-ager is concerned with himself and his present environment. He needs to be shown that what he is studying is associated with his current interests, ambitions, and activities.

Because of his more mature point of view, the senior high school student is better able to project himself into the future and to recognize the possible value to himself of his formal learning experiences than is the junior high student. Yet, regardless of secondary students' background of experience and degree of maturity, each lesson in a series of developmental steps needs to be so introduced and conducted that the learner recognizes it to be a vital and stimulating learning experience.

The motivation of students in a lesson can take various forms. We have referred to the asking of a challenging question. The teacher can read, or have a student read, a brief, pertinent excerpt from a recent newspaper or a current magazine. A student may have been asked to prepare and read to the class a short report on a current incident or condition that refers directly to the subject of the lesson. The teacher or a student can present a simple and appropriate demonstration. An interesting picture or diagram, or a short film related to the subject matter can be shown and discussed briefly.

Some teachers occasionally administer a short objective review quiz that the students correct on the spot. The discussion of errors, if held to a minimum, can serve as the starting point of the day's lesson. An ingenious teacher can think of many ways to focus student interest on the lesson. Whatever technique he employs, his introductory motivation:

1. Should be geared to the experiences and current interests of the students.
2. Should lend itself to easy application to the content of the lesson.
3. Should not be accorded an undue amount of class time.

The Lesson Activities

We already have stressed the importance of maintaining student interest throughout the class period. You know from your study of psychology that the attention span of most people, especially young people, is relatively short. We tend to crave change of activity. You need to keep this psychological principle in mind as you plan classroom procedures.

A class period devoted entirely to the question-answer technique is likely to induce daydreaming or the giving of attention to extraneous matters on the part of some students. There are times, of course, when a lively discussion of a topic of common interest is in order. You may have observed your cooperating teacher conduct just such a lesson. You probably noticed, however, that not all of the questions were propounded by the teacher. Student enthusiasm ran high; students asked questions of one another or disagreed among themselves. Part of the discussion may have taken on something of the nature of an informal debate. The skillful teacher encourages this kind of student participation. He is careful to lead the discussion in such a way that it does not become rambling or stray too far afield.

You can plan to include various types of activities in the conduct of the lesson. Some of these activities are:

1. Oral reports by individual students or student committees
2. Demonstrations by teacher or students
3. Reading aloud of pertinent material by the teacher or by students who read well
4. A short debate
5. Examination of illustrative material on bulletin board, etc.
6. Role playing or dramatization
7. Viewing of slides or short motion pictures
8. Radio listening or televiewing
9. Panel discussions
10. Construction of projects
11. Consulting reference material
12. Discussion of errors in a test previously taken by the students
13. Review drill
14. Supervised study

You probably can think of other activities that are appropriate to teaching-learning experiences in your subject. Of course, we are not suggesting that you attempt to utilize all or even many of the foregoing types of activities in any one lesson. You may be surprised, however, to discover the extent to which you can vary the work of a lesson so that the interest of all the members of the class can be aroused and sustained.

The Budgeting of Class Time

Little need be said about the importance of budgeting class time. As you list the activities that you expect to carry out during the period, note the approximate amount of time in minutes that should be devoted to each. Try not to depart from your schedule. Allocate some time to matters that deal with classroom management, but organize these matters in such a way that they can be executed efficaciously.

Do not take time to call the roll for attendance; use a seating chart. Have materials to be distributed so arranged that students can pass them out quickly. If there is writing on the chalkboard when you enter the room, have it erased before the lesson begins. In this connection, be sure that when you and the class leave the room, the chalkboards are ready for the next class or group of students.

Read important notices promptly at the beginning of the period. Do not use class time to discuss irrelevant matters with individual students or groups. You should maintain a businesslike attitude toward routine duties. Your students will appreciate your avoidance of wasting time.

Prepare and Ask Pivotal Questions

During the course of a lesson, you may need to ask many and varied questions that grow out of the activities being conducted. For example, after a student presents a report, you may need to ask a question in order to have him clarify some of the points of the report. Such questions usually cannot be formulated ahead of time. Hence it would be foolish for you to try to predict all of the questions that you probably will raise and to incorporate them in your plan.

You will find it helpful to include in your plan a short list of significant or pivotal questions arranged in sequential order. The content of the lesson revolves around these questions. Regardless of the various activities of the lesson, these pivotal questions should be included at such time and in such form that they will challenge the students to engage in reflective thinking as they discuss relationships and arrive at conclusions.

Inexperienced teachers often have difficulty in the formulation of thought-provoking questions. The "Yes" or "No" question should be avoided. For example, in a study of Scott's *Ivanhoe* the question "Do you like Rowena?" does not ask the student what he really thinks about Rowena. Better questions would be "Why do you like or dislike Rowena?" "Compare your attitude toward Rowena and Rebecca," or "How do you explain the fact that some people consider Rebecca rather than Rowena to be the real heroine of *Ivanhoe?*"

Questions dealing with facts sometimes are necessary, yet they tend to emphasize mastery of subject matter rather than critical thinking. Both content-oriented and thought questions may be included among pivotal questions. Note the following sets of questions.

1. Explain what is meant by habit.
   How important are motivation and practice in habit formation?
   What are desirable study habits?
   Why should you develop effective study habits?
2. Explain what is meant by public utilities.
   Why are public utilities significant in our lives?
   How are publc utilities regulated?
   What are some of the problems associated with public utilities?
   What is your opinion concerning private ownership of transportation, communication media, etc.?
3. Explain what is meant by heredity.
   Why do offspring tend to resemble one parent more than the other with respect to a certain trait?
   How do we explain the inheritance of traits?
   What happens when hybrids are mated?

As you were reading and thinking through the foregoing sets of questions, what were your conclusions concerning their value as pivotal questions? What might be the implied aims of the respective lessons? To what extent do they follow a sequential order? How clearly stated are they?

Value of Providing Supplementary Material

You may want to use various kinds of source material in order to illustrate or emphasize significant points of the lesson or to present additional information. Included among such materials could be: motion picture films; slide projectors; tape recorders; articles from newspapers, magazines, or reference books; charts, maps, or pictures; materials for an experiment; or any other form of resource material that can arouse student interest or help clarify subject content.

The utilization of resource material should not be a haphazard undertaking. Whatever is to be utilized during the presentation of the lesson should be prepared ahead of time for ready reference when needed. If you plan to use a story to illustrate a point, be sure that you are sufficiently acquainted with the story to tell it without hesitation and in such a way that it holds the interest of the students. Make certain that you can operate audio-visual machines correctly. If you plan an experiment, have all the needed materials available and follow the steps of the experiment accurately.

Care must be taken that all students can see any samples of visual material. Students also must be led to understand the relationship of source material to the subject of the lesson. If you have sufficient copies of the material for individual study, have them so arranged that they can be distributed quickly and efficiently. Use of the chalkboard by teacher or students for outlining points in the lesson, drawing diagrams, and the like also can be valuable learning aids. Remember, however, that the utilization of supplementary aids has for its purpose the *helping* of students to improve their learning. Hence you must avoid devoting an undue amount of time to their presentation, lest consideration of them becomes an end rather than a means to an end.

Another important point concerning supplementary materials is that they should be collected and replaced at least by the end of the period so that they are ready for use by another class. Materials used in an experiment are not always carefully cleaned and put into their proper cabinets. Teachers and students sometimes are careless about returning materials borrowed from the library. Excerpts from newspapers and magazines may become mixed with a teacher's or a student's other papers. A good plan is for the teacher to keep a working file of pertinent materials in which he replaces material when he has finished with it.

The Assignment

A question often asked by a beginning teacher is "When and how should I make the assignment for home study?" Methods of assigning work for home study differ among teachers. Fortunately, relatively few secondary school teachers continue to assign "the next ten pages in the textbook." More appropriate and effective approaches are employed. Problems to be solved, pertinent questions to be answered, reports to be written, diagrams or charts to be constructed are among the many forms that the assignment may take.

To be effective, an assignment should motivate the interest of the student in continued learning. It is a part of teaching and serves as a transition from one lesson to the next. It never should be regarded as mere busywork. Whatever is included in the assignment should constitute a significant aspect of the total learning experience.

The assignment should be clearly and carefully explained so that no student is in doubt concerning what he should do. If the class contains students of widely differing abilities and interests, appropriate assignments can be made on an ability and interest basis rather than assigning the same task to the entire class. The assignment becomes a challenge when it has meaning for the student and is within his limits of performance.

When should the assignment be made? Opinions differ on this point. Some teachers place it on the chalkboard before the class begins. The students copy it as soon as they enter, and nothing more is said about it unless a student asks for clarification of a point. There are teachers who wait until the end of the period and then make the assignment orally. This is an unwise practice. Unless the teacher watches the time carefully, the period ends before the assignment is made and instructions concerning it are given hurriedly by the teacher as the students are gathering up their materials preparatory to leaving the room.

Probably the best procedure to use in making an assignment is to give it at that point in the lesson where it seems best fitted. That time, of course, may be toward the end of the period. You should take care, however, that you leave sufficient time for its presentation and that whatever preparation is needed for it is done carefully. At times, the assignment can be a joint effort of teacher and students. In light of what has transpired during the class period, the students themselves suggest further work that can be done outside the classroom. This is especially applicable when each lesson represents a teacher-and-student planned unit of study.

Two cautions concerning assignments are in order. First, keep in mind that the teachers of other subjects also are assigning material for home study. There is just so much time left in the after-school day for various activities in which young people should engage. All of the late afternoon and the evening should not be devoted solely to schoolwork. A young person needs a little relaxation even during the school week.

In most secondary schools, a student who is carrying four major subjects a week is expected to spend about forty-five minutes per subject per evening on his home assignments. It sometimes happens that an especially enthusiastic teacher of a subject (science or social studies, for example) may so imbue his students with interest in his subject that they are tempted to devote time to the particular subject that should be given to another. Watch out that this does not happen among your students.

A second needed caution deals with the use of the school or public library. Too many teachers assign reference work to be done in the library without making certain that (1) the reference material is available and (2) the assignment is definite enough so that the student can find the material by using the card catalog without unduly involving the librarian. If you plan to send your students to the library for needed materials, first visit the library yourself to discover whether the material is available and where it is. Then be exact in your directives to the students concerning its location in the library and its use.

The Summarization of the Lesson

A successful lesson ends with a summarization of the points covered. As you prepare your lesson plan, review your stated purpose and decide whether you have developed that aim in the listed procedures. Then, in class, summarize what has been done.

A good summarization usually is brief. Perhaps, it may be no more than asking the class a question such as "What have we tried to do today?" "What have you learned in this lesson?" or "How has today's lesson helped you to _____?" Another possible approach to the summarization is for you to list on the chalkboard words or short phrases that cover the day's work with the comment "This is what we have done today. In our next lesson we shall try to _____." This might be a good point at which to introduce the next assignment, provided you have left sufficient time for its explanation. Your students' displayed attitude toward the summarization can give you an idea concerning the value to them of the lesson's activities.

Evaluation of the Lesson

You will find after you have taught a lesson that you have ambivalent feelings toward what happened during it. You may conclude mentally that some aspects of it were worthwhile but that, in some respects, you failed to accomplish what you had planned. At the end of the lesson, make appropriate evaluative comments of the lesson on your lesson plan. Include any reactions you may have received from the students, either expressed or implied. This is a useful habit to develop.

An honest evaluation of your performance, both in planning and in execution, can help you improve your worth as a teacher. As you gain in experience, you probably will find that you become your own most severe critic. This should not discourage you, however. A master teacher, no matter how long he has been in the profession, constantly discovers new ways in which he can approach teaching-learning situations and improve his practices and techniques. You might be interested in reading suggestions offered to junior high school teachers in the Philadelphia schools. They follow:

PLAN YOUR WORK

Planning is essential. No one can do a good job of teaching without planning ahead of time, no matter how creative or experienced he may be. There is, of course, a difference between the kind and amount of planning done by the experienced teacher and the beginning teacher—but planning must be done.

Through planning, the teacher

. . . selects worthwhile activities and procedures.

. . . insures an adequate distribution of time

PLANNING DOES MAKE THE DIFFERENCE

The starting point is the course of study. The Philadelphia guides are prepared by representative committees of teachers and other school personnel. The ideas contained in the guides are useful and practical because they have been written by teachers for teachers.

The Course of Study

. . . sets the objectives and content area

. . . furnishes suggestions for building a teaching unit in line with the objectives

. . . helps the teacher organize materials effectively

. . . provides suggestions for translating philosophy into action

. . . helps familiarize the teacher with resource materials and people

The course of study suggests many ways of achieving the instructional goals, and saves the teacher a great deal of time.

One of the primary responsibilities of the teacher is to become completely familiar with the course of study. He must

. . . read the guide

. . . be familiar with the general objectives

. . . organize the information and activities into effective teaching units

Base Your Planning on the Course of Study

* * * *

It is mandatory that teachers use the Philadelphia courses of study, as is pointed out in the Policies for Curriculum Improvement, adopted by the Board of Superintendents.

". . . schools are to adhere to the objectives and to the teaching of the essentials content as set forth in instructional guides."

This may be done through wise selection from many teaching suggestions contained in the guides.

Use the Course of Study

* * * *

Planning is thinking through and getting ready for teaching. The basic long-term planning has been done by committees of teachers in writing the course of study. Each teacher must base his own long-term plan on the course. From this he works out the teaching units for shorter periods and for daily lessons.

Long-term planning is based upon

. . . probable needs of pupils

. . . the course of study

. . . school facilities—books, illustrative materials, library, audio-visual aids, resource materials, people

The long-term plan blueprints the major topics of study for the term.

Short-term planning details a segment of the long-term plan. It may vary in length from a few days to a few weeks, depending on the teaching unit.

Beginning teachers should carefully plan each week's work and write the outline in their Teacher's Plan Sheets (Form HEV 4). Many schools require that these plans be turned in each week for review.

Daily planning suggests the detailed content and activities for a class period. It tells what is to be accomplished that period and how it is to be done. Each lesson must provide for a beginning (initiation and motivation), a middle (development), and an end (conclusion).

As the teacher prepares for the lesson he decides on the aim of the lesson, knows what the guide suggests, gathers texts and other instructional materials, decides on what is to be written on the chalkboard before the lesson begins, selects the major pupil activity, and decides on the means for bringing the lesson to a proper conclusion. In this preparation he thinks through and provides for different steps of the lesson from beginning to end.

The *initiation and motivation* step gets the class ready to learn. The teacher should try to begin with the pupils' interests and develop recognition of the need for what they are to learn. Their thinking should be guided from what they know toward what they should discover. This can be done through the use of a good device to arouse their interest, such as an anecdote, a chart, bulletin board display, news clipping, filmstrip, movie, discussion, problem, text reference, or a question. It takes only a few minutes at the beginning of the period and leads right into the development of the lesson.

The *development* is the major portion of the lesson. It may be done through a variety of activities, such as audio-visual aids; developing new ideas through questions, answers, discussions, and illustrations by both pupils and teachers; reading from texts and supplementary materials; planned field trips; group work and committee reports; review, practice, or drill; remedial teaching.

Regardless of the pupil activity selected for the development of the lesson, the teacher should be certain that the pupils *know what to do* and *how to do it* before they start.

The *conclusion* summarizes the lesson and acquaints the pupils with what they have learned. It should include a forward look to the next day's work.[1]

---

[1] Consulting Teachers, "Plan Your Work: It Makes the Difference," in *Assignment: Junior High School* (Philadelphia: Curriculum Office, Philadelphia Public Schools, 1960), pp. 23–25.

A Word of Caution to the Student Teacher

A final word of caution to you as a student teacher may not be amiss. You probably are extremely interested in gaining experience in lesson planning and teaching. You are eager to "try your wings." You may be particularly enthusiastic about teaching certain aspects of your subject. You have developed a "feeling" about the way in which a lesson can be best planned and presented.

These are fine attitudes and probably indicate that you have the makings of an excellent teacher. You must keep in mind, however, that you are working with a cooperating teacher who is responsible for the learning progress of his students. The class is his, not yours. Consequently, it is your responsibility to follow his lead. For the duration of your student-teaching responsibilities in his class, your lesson plans should be patterned after his. When you are permitted to teach the class, you must fit your lesson into his general organization. It may be that your cooperating teacher may be willing for you to undertake the conduct of a unit of work that is of especial interest to you. You might ask him for the opportunity to do so; do not press the issue, however.

Be careful that you do not disrupt your cooperating teacher's established routines, even though you believe that your handling of them might be superior to his. Also, discourage any attempts on the part of students to make comparisons between your attitudes and activities and those of your cooperating teacher, especially if these comments seem to favor you.

QUESTIONS AND TOPICS FOR DISCUSSION

1. What is the value to you of observing and assisting your cooperating teacher before you begin your actual teaching experiences? Be specific.
2. Under what circumstances might a lesson be unrelated to the general context of your subject?
3. If you have planned and taught a lesson, what difficulties did you encounter?
4. Select a lesson that you expect to teach. What will you do to arouse your students' interest? How much time do you plan to devote to the motivation?
5. In what aspects of your subject can you expect students to be interested? Why?

6. Which of the various types of activities in the conduct of a lesson as listed in this chapter do you find to be most productive of student learning? Which of them do you employ?
7. As you are observing your cooperating teacher conduct a lesson, make note of his questions. How effective were they?
8. When and how does your cooperating teacher make study assignments? Critically evaluate his procedure.
9. Why is it advisable to end a lesson with a summarization of what has taken place during the period?
10. Why should you follow the lead of your cooperating teacher in lesson planning? Be specific.

SELECTED REFERENCES

ADAMS, H. P., and DICKEY, F. G. *Basic Principles of Student Teaching.* New York: American Book Co., 1951.

BROWN, T. J. *Student Teaching in a Secondary School.* New York: Harper & Row, Pub., Inc., 1960.

CARTER, W. L., HANSEN, C. W., and McKIM, M. G. *Learning to Teach in the Secondary School.* New York: Macmillan Co., 1962.

CLARK, L. H., and STARR, I. S. *Secondary School Teaching Methods.* New York: Macmillan Co., 1959.

GRAMBS, J. D. *Modern Methods in Secondary Education* (rev. ed.). New York: Holt, Rinehart & Winston, Inc., 1958.

SCHORLING, R., and BATCHELDER, H. T. *Student Teaching in Secondary Schools.* New York: McGraw-Hill Book Co., Inc., 1956.

SCHULTZ, R. *Student Teaching in the Secondary Schools.* New York: Harcourt, Brace & World, Inc., 1959.

WIGGINS, S. P. *Successful High School Teaching.* Boston: Houghton Mifflin Co., 1958.

8

LEARNING NEEDS AND TEACHING APPROACHES

An important area of teacher education is to acquaint you with various teaching approaches that can serve as effective means of stimulating successful student learning. Hence, in your college classes, you probably have considered both teaching methods in general and those techniques that are appropriate for the guidance of learning in your particular subject. Here we are reviewing some of the teaching approaches to which you should give your attention as you plan the activities to be included in classroom procedures.

THE LEARNING NEEDS OF STUDENTS

Much of a young person's learning (perhaps more than we realize) is acquired informally. As he associates with other people, he tends to imitate their behavior. As he encounters new environmental situations, he attempts to adjust to them by various trial-error-trial-success activities. He constantly is engaging in one or another form of adaptive behavior. To leave the individual to his own devices in the learning process would be a long and costly series of experiences, however. During his early developmental years, he might well acquire habits and attitudes that later would need to be revised in light of societal standards of correct behavior in the many aspects of individual participation in communal affairs.

Formal education, as exemplified by the many teacher-guided learning activities conducted in our schools, has for its purpose the acquisition by each learner of those competencies that have positive value in charting the course of his life pattern. Yet, unless an individual student is motivated to profit adequately from whatever instruction is provided for him, he achieves little that has value from his supposed participation in learning experiences. It is the teacher's function to utilize those teaching approaches that serve best to meet the learning needs of his students. Each student is expected, as a result of his schooling, to acquire appropriate knowledge, improve needed skills, and develop those attitudes, appreciations, and standards of behavior that, through their application, will benefit both himself and other people.

The Acquiring of Knowledge

Every student needs to master a body of information about the world, the people who inhabit it, and significant happenings that affected the course of history. These are facts and need to be thoroughly mastered. The date of the signing of the *Declaration of Independence,* the sequence of events in Shakespeare's *Hamlet,* the chemical elements contained in water, the relationship between parallel lines, for example, are not matters of opinion. Such items of information need to be learned so thoroughly that they become a part of the individual's habit patterns subject to immediate recall. He must appreciate their significance and recognize their importance to himself.

It is the teacher's responsibility so to present informational material that a student not only acquires accurate and clear concepts rather than merely memorizing words, possessing little or no meaning for him, but that he also can apply these concepts to new situations. The body of knowledge acquired in the study of any subject should be applicable to the student's present and future life experiences.

The Improvement of Skills

The average adult has developed many differing skills. Some of them have been acquired with little or no awareness of the manner in which they have been developed; others represent definite attempts at improvement, perhaps to serve vocational purposes.

Improvement of general skills. Every secondary school teacher is responsible for helping students improve their skill in areas of activity such as listening, reading, speaking, writing, and manipulating appropriate materials. In the so-called academic subjects (social studies, language study, science, and mathematics, for example), the students need to be able to listen carefully to what is said by the teacher and other students so that they comprehend what they hear.

Students in the secondary school should improve their ability to understand and appreciate material that is contained in books, periodicals, pamphlets, and the like. They must learn to express their thoughts, either in speaking or in writing, clearly, definitely, and in well-organized form. They must know what they want to say, orally or in writing, and present their ideas in such a way that their meaning is understood by others. Students also need to gain skill in interpreting maps, charts, diagrams, pictures, or any other form of appropriate illustrative material. These skills improve gradually as students are afforded many opportunities to engage in them.

Importance of vocationally oriented skills. The mastery of certain skills is a consciously engaged in, purposeful activity. The student elects one or another skill subject in preparation for his selected field of gainful work or as a means of helping him perform more efficiently in his study activities. For example, the primary purpose served by the commercial curriculum in the secondary school is to prepare students for participation in the business world as secretaries or bookkeepers. Yet, some young people may elect typing to enable them, as secondary school and college students, to submit written materials in neatly typed form, rather than handwritten. Again, participation in the physical activities program of the school can have as its purpose the maintaining of good physical health and the providing of interesting leisure-time activities. At the same time, athletic skill developed through the school-sponsored physical training program can be the beginning of vocational specialization.

Factors in the development of a skill. Whether you are teaching a so-called academic skill or a skill that is vocationally oriented, you need to recognize the student's degree of readiness to develop the skill, his attitude toward it, and the extent to which he is mentally and physically able to achieve adequate performance in it.

You probably have attained so high a degree of proficiency in the skill you are planning to teach that you have forgotten your first fumbling attempts to master it. You punctuate sentences as a matter of habit. Your stenographic notes offer no problem of interpretation.

Your fingers find the correct keys on the typewriter without any special conscious effort. You have achieved skill in thinking in French or in any other foreign language in which you are proficient. If your field is homemaking, you can prepare a delicious cake, plan a well-balanced meal, or organize a household budget efficiently. In other words, as a teacher you must appreciate the learning needs of your students at whatever stage of skill development they may be and proceed from that point toward improving their efficiency.

You hope your students will achieve whatever degree of skilled performance that can be expected of them in light of curriculum limitations in the subject. For example, a one-year course in book-keeping cannot make of the student a skilled accountant; yet, it may motivate him toward continued study in the field and give him a good foundation on which to improve the skill. Hence your teaching of a skill should be so geared that the students become efficient in it within the limits of their learning experience with it.

Value of knowledge of expected results. From the beginning of his mastery of a skill, a learner should know what he is trying to accomplish. He is likely to progress more successfully in his learning if he understands and is helped to apply underlying principles of performance. Good paragraph construction, for example, is based on the following of a certain format: statement of the topic of the paragraph, details, and closing summarization.

The woodworker must know the tools to use and how to handle them. The typist must recognize the value of placing his hands on the keyboard in a certain position, so that he can strike the various keys correctly. The baseball batter knows what, for him, is the best stance to take. Whatever the skill to be mastered, the learner should know what to do, step by step, and the reason for doing so. He also should be able to evaluate his own success in applying basic principles.

Value of arousal of interest. You know that interest is a strong motivator of achievement. The skilled performer enjoys what he is doing. He takes pride in mastering the techniques of his skill. You know that highly proficient instrumentalists and vocalists spend many hours daily practicing so that they can maintain their performance at a high level of perfection. Proficient athletes practice continuously to improve their performance. These individuals do not begrudge the time and effort they expend to retain their skill. Rather do they seem to experience much pleasure from the kind of activity that, to an onlooker, might appear to be sheer drudgery.

Interest in practice to improve a skill usually does not start suddenly, but is likely to be an accompaniment of active participation in the learning from the beginning. To arouse and maintain this kind of interest among your students may be one of your most difficult problems. In the introduction of skill learning, as in all other forms of learning, you need so to stimulate the imagination of your students that they can recognize the value of the learning experience to them. Each step of evidenced progress then is likely to be accompanied by feelings of pleasure in accomplishment and a desire to perform better.

Too often, secondary school students are interested only in the grades that they will receive in a subject. They are not concerned with mastery for its own sake, and probably will do little or nothing about continuing some school-required learnings after graduation unless they continue on the college level where, unfortunately, they may display a similar attitude. It behooves you, therefore, to give evidence of your own interest in the skill you are attempting to teach and of the satisfaction you obtain from performing it.

Your success may be measured by the extent to which you are able to imbue your students with some of your own enthusiasm. Moreover, you must take care that (1) you do not expect too much from beginners, (2) you recognize their difficulties and are able and willing to help them overcome errors, (3) you are liberal with commendatory comments when these are deserved, and chary with discouraging remarks, (4) you encourage consistency in practice, and (5) you vary practice sessions in such a way that they do not become unduly routinized and boring.

The Development of Creativity

Young people tend to want to do things in ways that differ from accustomed routines. They constantly are seeking new approaches to the meeting of situations that are likely to arise in day-by-day activities. They enjoy experimenting with haircombs or hairdos, their clothes, the arrangement of their room, and the conduct of their social activities. Most adolescents have the urge to create. The success of their endeavors differs, of course, with their degree of creative talent.

As a teacher, you can take advantage of this adolescent characteristic. However, you may not always recognize the opportunities that are available to you in this area of learning motivation. Some subjects seem to lend themselves more easily than others to the development of creative expression. The teacher of a subject such as music, the dance, pictorial reproduction, imaginative writing, or industrial arts is in a position to encourage a talented student to achieve well in a special field. Even the student with mediocre artistic ability can be helped to produce something that is somewhat new and different. The teachers of other subjects—the sciences, the social studies, or mathematics, for example—can stimulate their students, more or less indirectly, to give expression to their desire to create.

Carter, Hansen, and McKim describe well in the following the universality of the urge to create and the teacher's responsibility for encouraging it among all of his students:

> Creativity is not only inherent in all aspects of human activity, but it is present in all levels of intelligence and at all maturity levels. It is not limited to a few gifted persons, to the economically favored, or to the socially elite. Creative expression is not a separate entity; it is an aspect of everything we do. If we, as teachers, accept these assumptions it means that creativity, original thinking, arriving at new answers is a characteristic of all human beings—the average person, the slow, as well as the gifted. It is perhaps simply a matter of degree. One would not, of course, expect the slow pupil to be as creative, as original, as the bright student, but he does nevertheless in his limited way have a contribution to make. If an important function of the school is to make life more fruitful and worthwhile, teachers must find the creative potential of each pupil, whatever his level of ability, and develop it to the fullest in all aspects of school activity.[1]

The unit approach to teaching and learning offers many opportunities for creative activity as the teacher and students plan together for the development of the unit. In the sciences and mathematics, although these subjects are more or less logically organized,

---

[1] William L. Carter, Carl W. Hansen, and Margaret G. McKim, *Learning to Teach in the Secondary School* (New York: Macmillan Co., 1962), pp. 251–52. Reprinted with permission.

students can discover new relationships, achieve new insights, and find new ways of arriving at conclusions. Similar outlets for creative thinking also are present in the social studies and English.

What is needed in any case is a creative, imaginative teacher who can recognize possibilities for creative activities in his subject. He provides a rich learning environment. He is intelligently permissive in his attitude toward class procedures. He understands what the students are trying to do and appreciates their potentialities. He realizes that effective creative expression must be built on a solid background of appropriate knowledge and skill, and he sees to it that his students acquire and maintain these as they go about producing the relatively new and different. In other words, the extent to which adolescents adapt their creative potential to learning procedures depends in good part on your ability, as the teacher, to be a sensitive, perceptive, and creative person.

Stress High Standards of Workmanship

The building of high standards of workmanship is among the most significant learning needs of young people. The influence upon an adolescent of the standards of those with whom he associates is all-pervasive. The teen-ager tends to imitate, either consciously or unconsciously, the effectiveness of older people whom he holds in high regard. At times, he is confused by differences he observes among the standards of individuals who are supposed to serve him as models to be followed. Eventually, in light of his experiences he sets personal standards of workmanship that influence his activities.

If you are satisfied with half-learned lessons, accept sloppily prepared papers, or condone lack of promptness in meeting obligations, you are not encouraging your students to achieve high ideals of workmanship. To the extent that you are careless about the management of class routines, come to class only partially prepared for a lesson, or in other ways give evidence of low standards of efficiency, you are not a worthy model to be imitated.

You cannot expect perfection to be achieved suddenly by your students, but anything that is worth learning is worth learning correctly. Informational material must be accurate. Each step in the development of a skill should be performed correctly before the next step is attempted. One cannot build desirable work habits on a foundation of errors, or partially-mastered learning experiences. Hence, in any area of study, constructive practice is needed to help learners attain high standards of workmanship that can be expected to carry over into their many areas of life activities.

TEACHING TECHNIQUES

Earlier, we referred to some of the activities you might include in your lesson plan that could serve as ways to achieve the objectives of your lesson. By so doing, you were noting teaching techniques that might be appropriate to the development of your lesson planning. There are various methods that can be used in teaching-learning situations. You need to know what these techniques are, how they operate, and to what extent each of them has value in helping you realize your specific lesson goals.

The purpose of a particular lesson may be to increase your students' knowledge in a field of learning, improve their functioning of a skill, bring about changes in their attitudes, appreciations, or any combination of these. Your approach to the lesson will be the one that (1) seems best suited to its purpose, (2) takes into account the students' interests, abilities, and readiness for the learning, and (3) is suited to your particular teaching skills.

As you plan the various activities to be included in a lesson, you need to remember that your function is to guide the learning of your students. They are responsible for any changes that take place within themselves. It is a psychologically proven principle that one learns best by doing. Hence, whatever teaching techniques you employ, you need to involve your students mentally and physically in the learning experiences. We now shall review briefly various teaching techniques and the extent to which students can be involved in the process.

The Lecture Method

At times, an application of the lecture method may be advisable. You are introducing a new topic of study. There may be certain background material that students need to prepare them for further study. You can acquaint them quickly and succinctly with those aspects of the material that can increase their understanding of what lies ahead. Or, the students might raise a question that should receive immediate attention if the lesson is to run along smoothly. It might be more advisable to lecture briefly on the topic rather than to have the students themselves search for the answer. Again, a student, because of his out-of-school experiences, may have information about a topic that well might be shared with his classmates. You can encourage him to present a well-organized talk about it.

Elements of a good lecture. As a beginner, you may regard the lecture technique to be an easy way of presenting learning material. Some of your college instructors may utilize this teaching method almost to the exclusion of any other approach. You may have forgotten, however, how often you were bored by being a more or less passive recipient of, rather than an active participant in, the learning situation. Yet, as a mature person you should have been able to benefit from its use better than can relatively immature adolescents.

To give a stimulating lecture is not an easy task. Its content must be appropriate to the subject of study. It must be well organized and presented in an interesting and attention-holding manner. Do not attempt to lecture unless you have a pleasant voice, a good command of English, and the ability to paint vivid word pictures that will stir the students' imagination. Furthermore, you may need to engage in considerable research in preparation for even a twenty-minute lecture (rarely should it be longer). Unless you have your material well in hand, you are likely to hesitate or ramble, thereby losing the attention of your students.

You know that the attention span of many high school boys and girls is relatively short. Hence you need to vary your lecture by utilizing interest-arousing aids. You can use illustrative material, such as pictures or models. As you talk, you can place on the chalkboard, in outline form, the important points included in the lecture. Another good device is to raise a few questions for the students to consider. You then can answer these questions and intersperse your talk with a few simple questions that can be answered easily and promptly. Give the students an opportunity to raise questions about those points that may not be understood by them. You can sustain the students' interest in your lecture by providing opportunities for them to participate.

Value of the lecture method. To the extent that the lecture approach is adapted to the interests, abilities, learning background, and current needs of the students, its occasional use has educational value. Too many individuals are fluent talkers but tend to turn a deaf ear to what others say. Young people need training in attentive and thoughtful listening. For example, as you lecture, you can help them learn to distinguish between main or topic sentences and explanatory details. You can do this by emphasizing the former through voice stress, chalkboard notations, and significant voice pauses. The students can be encouraged to make mental notes or to enter briefly in their notebooks the important points of the lecture. You can judge the effectiveness of a lecture by the extent to which the students incorporate its content in their further study of the subject.

The Recitation Method

The recitation method is a traditional teaching approach to the learning of academic subject matter. It usually is based on textbook material and may follow textbook organization. In the most commonly used form of the recitation method, the teacher assigns a chapter or section of the book for home study and then devotes most or all of the class time to an application of the question-answer technique. The questions asked may be more or less pertinent; individual students vary in their preparation of the home study assignment; some of the material may not be fitted to the abilities and interests of individual students. The situation is worsened if the teacher calls upon each student either alphabetically or according to a seating chart, and then enters a grade in his record book for the student's answer.

Importance of using the recitation method. Much of your own secondary school learning may have followed the question-answer pattern. Now as a student teacher, you are tempted to employ the recitation method to the exclusion of other techniques whenever this is possible. You are accustomed to it. Basing your procedure on textbook coverage of the subject matter gives you a feeling of security. By adhering closely to it, you avoid the possible introduction of irrelevant material. The students are alerted to just what is expected of them in the way of study and, to a greater or lesser degree, attempt to fulfill required tasks.

When you use the recitation method, you supposedly have the entire class under your immediate control. Ideally, every student in turn takes part in the recitation. If one student cannot answer the question or gives an incomplete answer, you call on someone else, and continue this process until you receive a full or satisfactory response. If the material lies within the comprehension limits of all members of the class and is interesting to them, you might be able to conduct a relatively successful whole-class recitation. Unfortunately, even in a fairly homogeneous class, this situation is likely not to exist. Then you are faced with the problem of having your attention distracted from the matter at hand by those students who are engaging in activities of their own choosing, such as whispering among themselves, preparing homework for another subject, doodling, or daydreaming. An attempt on your part to recapture the attention of one of these students by asking him a question may be fatal. His response can be such as to disrupt the class completely.

What we have said to this point concerning the recitation method does not imply that material for home study should never be assigned. The students may need a background of factual material as a starting point for a lesson or series of lessons. The purpose for the study assignment and its content should be explained ahead of time. Then, some method must be found to discover whether the students have prepared themselves adequately. This can be done by administering a short quiz on the material or by a rapid oral review. Questions can be asked by the teacher and answered by volunteers. If you use this approach, be careful to include all of the students— the less able as well as the more able, the shy and retiring, as well as the outgoing and aggressive. Ask simple as well as more challenging questions. Do not allow the recitation to degenerate into a give-and-take between you and a small group of well-prepared, interested students.

As a culminating activity of a lesson or lessons, you may want to review some significant informational aspects of the study material.

A good way to accomplish this purpose is to utilize a series of pertinent questions. Student interest is heightened if the activity takes on the nature of a contest. The students form themselves into two teams, and the questions are alternated between the two groups. Your purpose is not to discover which student can stay on line the longest but to keep everyone thinking. Hence a student who fails to answer a question correctly is not removed from the team. As a means of maintaining student interest in the activity, one student can keep an account of the number of errors made by each team. Through this quick review you can discover the areas of material that require remedial work.

The Socialized Recitation or Group Discussion

One of the disadvantages of the question-answer method is that even though a student may give a technically correct answer, what he is doing is merely repeating words that he has memorized. He may have little or no understanding of fundamental concepts. A significant purpose of a socialized recitation is to encourage reflective thinking on the part of every student who is participating in the discussion of a topic or problem of the group.

The conduct of a socialized recitation. The entire class may be involved in the discussion, with the teacher as a leader, or the class may be divided into smaller groups, each of which elects a student as its chairman.

Whole class discussion. If the entire class participates as a unit, the teacher usually determines the topic or problem to be discussed. He can start the discussion with a provocative question and then "throw the ball" to the students. At times, the students themselves may decide the aspect of a unit of study that they wish to discuss. The teacher, of course, must make certain that the student-selected topic or problem is relevant to the purpose of the lesson. He also needs to keep control of the situation, lest the students digress too much from the subject under consideration. If you attempt to utilize this approach, you may find it difficult to maintain a democratic attitude toward students' participation in a discussion and yet insure their concentration on the goal to be achieved.

One of the authors recalls an experience in a senior high school

English class where the teacher was introducing the use of the socialized recitation. This teacher believed, mistakenly, that the teacher should withdraw himself completely from the class discussion. The students were supposed to be discussing the problems encountered by Romeo and Juliet because of the feud between their families.

To the amazement of this observer, the discussion turned, with no apparent reason, to the problem of modern divorce. The pros and cons of divorce were discussed in detail, with many rather gory illustrations. The teacher, standing at the side of the room, did nothing to interrupt the argument, which, by the time the dismissal bell rang, was progressing at a fast and furious rate. After the class had left the room, the teacher insisted that the lesson had been successful in that it had given the students an opportunity to follow a current interest and "give vent to their strong emotions."

We have gained considerably more insight into the proper conduct of the socialized recitation since those early days of the erroneous interpretation of John Dewey's suggestion that children learn through doing. To this teacher it meant complete permissiveness of behavior. We now appreciate the fact that young people learn best in a friendly classroom atmosphere, but that intelligently directed discussion and self-expression, not license, create a dynamic learning situation.

Small group discussion. A good procedure to follow sometimes is to have the students break up into small discussion groups. Movable furniture in the room allows for them to arrange themselves into intimate circles. Each group, with its chairman, can discuss the same topic or consider different phases of the same topic. While they are talking among themselves, the teacher moves from group to group, listening to what is being said and, perhaps, asking pertinent questions or otherwise helping to steer the group's thinking into appropriate channels.

After a sufficient amount of time has been allowed for the groups to arrive at some positive conclusions (usually not more than thirty minutes) each chairman reports to the class as a whole the reactions of his group. This procedure may result in further class consideration of the topic. The small group process is an excellent way of encouraging the participation of those students who otherwise might remain silent.

Panel Discussion, Debate, and Dramatization

The small-group approach can take the form of a panel discussion or a debate. Some educators would also include the presentation of a dramatization in this category.

Panel discussions. In the panel-discussion approach, a group of students, preferably not more than five or six, prepare ahead of time and discuss in the presence of their classmates various aspects of a topic that is of special interest to them.

It is the student chairman's function to bring all of the members of the panel into discussion and to limit in time the contribution of any one member of it. During the panel discussion, the other members of the class are encouraged to raise questions, to clarify moot points, or to add appropriate comments at its end. The teacher must so guide the project that rambling or getting away from the topic is avoided.

The debate technique. The debate follows somewhat the same format as the panel discussion except that it involves only two teams of students whose function it is to discuss the pros and cons of a problem or situation that has interest potential for the entire class. The debaters must be well prepared, speak clearly and concisely, and present their material on the comprehension level of their classmates. Enough time should be available at the conclusion of the debate for the entire class to engage in a critical evaluation of the points of view presented. This can be accompanied by a further discussion by all of the significance of the material included.

The use of dramatizations. Dramatizations of appropriate study materials, especially in the English and social studies classes, can afford students opportunities to work together cooperatively in small groups as they plan for and take part in role playing. Care must be exercised that these dramatizations are short in length and that the same students, because of their dramatic abilities, are not the only ones selected to participate. The less vocal student can be helped to gain self-confidence by participating occasionally in this form of group activity.

Aims of Socialized Recitations

The conducting of an interesting and challenging socialized recitation requires considerable preparation on the part of the teacher. He must realize that the utilization of this technique serves a dual purpose. The aim of the lesson should be to further learning in the subject matter under consideration. At the same time, the students receive training in working cooperatively with others as they exchange ideas, share one another's thinking, and learn to respect the points of view of classmates. It is a socializing experience that can help young people gain facility as members of committees or of other group activities both in and outside their school experiences.

Appropriate materials for discussion. Some learning materials can be adapted to the utilization of the socialized recitation better than others. The mastery of factual material, for example, requires that the students not only understand but also memorize appropriate content. Let's face the fact that before an individual can apply knowledge to current or future life situations, he must be thoroughly grounded in it. It is the teacher's responsibility so to guide the learning that the students recognize the value of the learning and are willing to submit to the task of acquiring a solid and accurate body of facts.

At the same time, there are many areas of learning to which the discussion approach is admirably suited. These include situations in which the purpose or goal is to stimulate students to deal with significant issues (such as in the social studies), to achieve commendable social interrelationships, to determine important policies concerning school or out-of-school activities, to participate in problem solving, or, in general, to gain skill and confidence in individual or group thinking.

Value of the discussion technique. In any form of group discussion, the students are encouraged to express their attitudes, judgments, and points of view. These then are critically evaluated by their teacher and other class members. Petty arguments among a few students must be avoided, however. The teacher needs to know when to step into a discussion that is student chaired, for example, and bring it back to a consideration of vital issues. In this connection, it is important that class or smaller group discussions be based on an adequate knowledge of pertinent subject matter. Reflective thinking cannot take place in a mental vacuum. Expressed opinions based on emotional attitudes rather than on facts have no educational value.

As a student teacher, you may want to experiment with the socialized recitation or discussion technique. You probably should not attempt to employ it until you have had an opportunity to become acquainted with your students and can recognize their strengths and weaknesses. You also must have earned their respect so that they will accept your leadership and cooperate with you in working out the details of the discussion. Your cooperating teacher and college supervisor can help you in your preplanning for the lesson.

As you and your students engage in this type of learning activity, you will want to discover the worth of the experience to each of your students as together they plan, discuss, summarize, and evaluate. Grim and Michaelis suggest a series of questions that you might ask yourself as you observe the students' reactions and note possible results of the experience:

1. In bringing his ideas to the group:
    a. To what extent does this pupil sense the aims and purpose of the group?
    b. To what extent is this pupil interested in the group and its work?
    c. To what extent does this pupil possess a background of experience that will allow him to make a unique contribution to the group?
    d. To what extent is this pupil accepted as a group member?
    e. If this pupil is not accepted by the group, what are the most probable causes of his nonacceptance? What might be done to improve the situation?

2. In sharing ideas through discussion within the group:
    a. To what extent does this pupil participate in discussions?
    b. To what extent does this pupil possess verbal skills necessary for good discussion?
    c. To what extent is this pupil willing to share time and opportunities for speaking with other members of the group?
    d. To what extent does this pupil assume an attitude of cooperation with other members?

    e. To what extent is this pupil willing to abide by the adopted guiding rules of the group?

3. In evaluating ideas and decisions of the group:
    a. To what extent does this pupil appraise the decisions of the group in terms of the group's original purposes?
    b. To what extent does this pupil eliminate his own prejudices in evaluating the decisions of the group?
    c. To what extent is this pupil able to view ideas in terms of their relative importance?

4. In applying to his own experience the results of his participation in the group:
    a. To what extent does this pupil recognize his own needs?
    b. To what extent, and in what ways, has this pupil grown through group activity?
    c. To what extent has this pupil derived satisfaction from his group experience?
    d. To what extent has this pupil learned to use self-appraisal? [2]

Problem Solving

One of the main objectives of education is to help an individual acquire a body of ideas that he can apply in his attempted solution of the many problems he constantly encounters during his life course. If he is to interpret accurately and intelligently what he hears and reads about local, national, and world happenings, he needs a broad knowledge that may cross various fields of study, such as the sciences, the social studies, and the arts. In the conduct of his affairs as a home member, a worker, and a citizen of his country, he faces problems of adjustment that can be resolved effectively only to the extent that he can apply to them the basic principles of human interaction.

School people realize that they cannot prepare any young person specifically for the meeting of all of the various problems that he may experience in the future. They do recognize, however, their responsibility for trying to teach him how to attack problems that may arise in his current experiences in various learnings, thereby equipping him with an appreciation of those principles and general-

[2] Paul R. Grim and John U. Michaelis (eds.), *The Student Teacher in the Secondary School* (Englewood Cliffs, N.J.: Prentice-Hall, Inc., 1953), pp. 158–59. Reprinted with permission.

izations that may have continued value for him. It is hoped that the kind of intelligent and accurate thinking encouraged in the classroom may have transfer value in that it helps the learner function more efficiently in his out-of-class life.

The problem-solving approach. You probably are well acquainted with the steps in John Dewey's analysis of problem solving.[3] Dewey's steps apply to a complete act of thought and include:

1. Becoming aware of a felt difficulty
2. Understanding the problem
3. Assembling and classifying data and formulating hypotheses
4. Accepting or rejecting the tentative hypotheses
5. Formulating conclusions and evaluating them

Whenever you motivate your students to engage in reflective thinking, you are attempting to help them follow Dewey's stages in an act of thought: preparation, readiness, and mental interaction. Problem solving should not be regarded as one of many teaching techniques. Rather is it a mode of approach that is characteristic of various methods of teaching.

At the beginning of a class period, you may ask a question such as: "Do you eat an adequate diet?" "What is the cause of present unrest in _____ country?" "Why did Silas Marner love Eppie?" "How can you improve your posture?" or "Does digestion occur in plants as well as in animals? Explain your answer." You have posed a problem situation that probably can be resolved during the class period by the use of one or more teaching techniques: lecture, discussion, demonstration, and experiment.

Throughout the aforementioned learning experience, you are encouraging the students to engage in reflective thinking. You help them follow Dewey's steps as you motivate them to define the problem, apply knowledge already mastered or discovered, construct possible solutions, evaluate them, and finally agree on what may seem to be the most appropriate conclusion. The actual testing of the accepted hypothesis may or may not be possible during the class session.

The problem-solving approach usually is basic to the development

[3] John Dewey, *How We Think* (Boston: D.C. Heath & Co., 1933), chap. 6.

of a larger unit of study. The sequential steps in the procedure may be somewhat as follows:

1. The problem is located and defined.
2. Under teacher leadership, the students decide on desirable approaches to be utilized, and individual and group projects are determined.
3. The students, either individually or in groups, engage in supervised study and research.
4. The various students share their findings with the class by means of individual or group reporting; dramatization or role playing; showing and explaining of illustrative material, such as diagrams, charts, or models; carrying on of experiments; and the like.
5. The class as a whole conducts socialized recitations in which possible conclusions or hypotheses are considered, and the most appropriate generalization is selected.
6. The learning outcomes from participation in the study of the unit are evaluated.

Each of these steps in the development of a unit probably will include several days of classwork, but there is evidenced a sequential pattern of activities that build up into a logical and psychological whole. This procedure is likely to hold the interest and attention of the learners.

Important aspects in problem solving. You will have many opportunities to apply the problem-solving approach. The problem may be a relatively simple matter of deciding on the best way to attack a particular bit of subject matter, to decide on a course of action; or it may represent a complex situation that necessitates the amassing of considerable research material for its solution. In either case, you need to make certain that the problem has interest appeal and is suited to the students' ability to profit from participation in the activity. The problem should not be so easy that it provides no challenge to the ingenuity of your students, nor should it be so difficult that many of them are unable to comprehend what is to be done.

The problems you set for your students or that you help them solve should be related to their experiences to the extent that they recognize the value to themselves of dealing with them. At the same time, you need to be careful lest they become so involved emotionally that they are unable to consider the problem situation objectively rather than from a biased point of view. One of the purposes of utilizing the problem-solving approach is to give young people practice in applying the scientific method in arriving at solutions of the many problem situations they are likely to encounter throughout life.

The expression of personal opinion has a place in problem solving as students seek to find possible answers to questions raised in their attempts to find a solution. Their opinions, however, must be based on known facts. For example, a group of students cannot decide by vote the present composition of the United Nations, the geographic location of Iran, the process of osmosis, the function of the red corpuscles in the blood. Facts such as these need to be discovered through research, if they are not already known, in order to solve a problem that involves the utilization of such factual source material. Moreover, knowledge gained as a means of helping in the solution of a problem often is learned more effectively than if it were acquired in the form of more or less unrelated facts to be memorized.

Your attitudes toward and the nature of your participation in problem-solving situations are very important. The classroom atmosphere should be free and friendly. Intelligent guidance on your part is necessary all along the way. Your students will need your help not only in setting up appropriate problems but also in defining them clearly and accurately. It is your function to procure source material for them or be able to tell them where they can find it.

The students should receive training in collecting and organizing data in such a way that it is easily available when they need it. As they deal with a relatively difficult problem, they may need help in dividing it into its respective units for research purposes without losing sight of the basic problem. You also have the task of guiding their critical thinking as they consider the various possible solutions, each of which should be stated clearly and definitely.

The selection of the final hypothesis or conclusion can be a challenging class project. You need to keep the students' thinking focused on the requirements of the problem and the extent to which the possible solutions meet these requirements. This is a good point at which to stress the need for objectivity of judgment in light of existing conditions. A consideration of the various ways in which the selected hypothesis can be tested offers opportunities for discussion of cause-and-effect relationships. An ingenious, imaginative teacher can stimulate much exciting and worthwhile learning experience among his students through the utilization of the problem-solving approach.

The Laboratory Technique

The conducting of experiments is a common approach to the teaching of the sciences. The laboratory technique also can be used as a means of providing opportunities for individuals to work alone or in small groups in the process of carrying on projects in an area of study that appeals to the students' current interests. The laboratory experience is a form of problem solving. As groups of students work on the same or different laboratory exercises, the teacher, acting as a consultant, moves among the members of the class and offers help wherever it is needed.

If you plan to utilize this teaching technique, you need to make certain that the problems to be solved are within the ability range of those who participate in them. Considerable flexibility is possible in that you can set up activities of varying degrees of difficulty and assign them in accord with the particular abilities of individual students or groups. Also, appropriate equipment should be available and prepared ahead of time so that needed materials can be assembled without delay. Discussion should accompany the activity. At the beginning of the class period, the students can discuss what they expect to do and why. Toward the end of the period, they should be given an opportunity to summarize their findings and compare the value to them of what has been accomplished.

The laboratory technique has various advantages. Through participation in the experience, the students can build desirable generalizations or principles. They are learning by doing. They are gaining practice in working together in small cooperating groups, thereby furthering the process of socialization in a friendly and relaxed classroom atmosphere. As the teacher confers with individual students about their activity, he is enabled to become better acquainted with them, their strengths and weaknesses, and can arrange for remedial work appropriate to their respective needs.

THE IMPORTANCE OF PRACTICE OR DRILL

We constantly emphasize the point that anything that is worth learning should be mastered completely and accurately. We also stress the necessity of students understanding what they are expected to learn. In addition, we give recognition to the fact that successful learning occurs most often when the material to be learned is interesting to the learner and related to his life experiences. How are these aspects of the learning experience related to the concept of practice or drill as a teaching-learning approach?

The Place of Practice in the Learning Situation

Psychologists and educators are placing so much emphasis (and rightly so) on the interest factor in learning and on the students' essential need to comprehend and understand learning materials that it is believed by some people that practice or drill has no place among learning experiences. Nothing could be further from the truth. Adequate mastery of learning content is not possible without well-organized practice. An individual needs to engage in intensive repetition of an item of information, a form of skill, or an aspect of attitude in order to enable him to give correct automatic responses when they are needed.

Unfortunately, in the recent past, some school people came to regard drill as a useless, boring activity that is much disliked by secondary school students. Our colleges complain that many entering freshmen come to them poorly prepared in such fundamental areas of learning as reading, theme writing, and mathematical computation. Some college entrants have brilliant ideas and mature understanding in various areas of knowledge, but they are woefully lacking in the fundamentals, such as spelling, grammatical structure, handwriting, arithmetical operations, and the mastery of simple matters of fact. Hence the lower schools have begun to assume greater responsibility for providing opportunities for students to practice intelligently those learnings that are essential to adequate mastery of significant aspects of any of their fields of study.

The Conduct of Effective Drill

Unmotivated drill can be boring. Students tend to enjoy practicing mental and motor skills, however, when they (1) understand the material that they are practicing, (2) recognize the need for repetitive activities, (3) can check their progress in improvement, and (4) come to appreciate desired outcomes of their practice. In other words, students usually are more than willing to submit to intensive drill if they are motivated to see its value to themselves.

Young people differ in the amount of practice needed to fix certain learning materials adequately. You can keep this in mind as you plan drill sessions. Those who require less drill activity can be given other interesting and challenging assignments while the slower students continue their drill activities.

You probably have learned about the spacing and duration of practice periods. Keep these points in mind as you arrange your practice lessons. Be alert to whether the students' interest in the drill process is waning. If so, change the activity. In most practice sessions there is a point of diminishing returns.

Before practice starts, make sure that the students are ready to repeat correct responses. It is better to begin by having the students practice simple elements in the total situation to which they know the correct response than to start them on a more complex operation into which errors may occur that they will incorporate in their practice. To be functional, drill should be specific.

As is true of other teaching approaches, you must prepare carefully for practice sessions. You need to take care that your students know what the correct response is that they are to practice. Do not allow so much time to elapse between practice periods that your students have forgotten what they are to practice. Insist on accuracy of performance. Be alert to those students who have specific weaknesses or disabilities and give them opportunities for special drill.

We hear much these days about the great need among secondary schools and colleges for the application of remedial learning techniques. This is an admission of insufficient or poorly organized practice experiences during the original learning situations. As teachers, we cannot disregard our obligation to make certain that our students practice learning materials in those ways that will serve them and future activities. Also, we should keep in mind that forgetting sets in as soon as practice ceases. Hence we should not be satisfied merely to see to it that a motor or mental skill has been mastered. We should provide for periodic reviews of practice materials so that the habit is maintained and strengthened.

THE UTILIZATION OF SUPERVISED STUDY

One of the learning problems of too many secondary school students arises from the fact that they have not acquired effective study habits. They seem to be unable to organize study materials. They have not learned to concentrate fully on the matter at hand. They tend to waste time in getting started on home study assignments. They fail to get thought from the printed page, or they are inadequate in their attack on a problem to be solved.

The Acquiring of Skill in Study Activities

Various books have been published that offer suggestions concerning how to study.[4] Either these are unavailable to many young people or students are uninterested in following the suggestions offered. Hence it becomes the responsibility of the teacher of any subject in which mastery of subject materials is required to help his students learn how to approach their study obligations. The various subjects may demand somewhat different approaches to their study. Teachers vary in what they expect their students to do in preparation for classroom work. In any case, secondary school students can profit from whatever help they receive from their teachers to improve their study habits.

Meaning of supervised study. The term *supervised study* implies that students participate in study activities planned by the teacher and supervised by him. This approach to learning resembles some-

[4] Lester D. Crow and Alice Crow, *How to Study* (New York: Collier Books, Inc., 1963).

what the laboratory technique. The teacher sets the problems to be solved, the project to be completed, the material to be memorized. He plans various tasks in light of individual or group learning needs. At the beginning of the period, he explains the assignments, raising questions that need to be considered and making certain that required materials are available. During these sessions, workbooks and study guides have value.

Conduct of a supervised study lesson. During the supervised study period, the teacher moves around the room, giving special attention to individuals or groups that appear to be having difficulties or who seem to have lost interest in the work. Distracting noises are eliminated, although it is permissible for the members of a small group working together on a project to talk quietly among themselves. As a student teacher, you can be helpful to your cooperating teacher by sharing in his supervision of the tasks. You can engage in remedial work with those students who need it, or find further activities for those who have completed their original assignment.

Purposes to be served in supervised study. Supervised study can serve various purposes. It can be used as a means of introducing students to effective study habits. Some teachers, at the beginning of a new term, give and explain assignments as if for home study, and then permit the class members to complete the work, under supervision, during the class period. By doing this, a teacher has an opportunity to observe individual approaches to the mastery of the material, and to give needed assistance.

The supervised study period lends itself to the completing of practice or drill activities. The assignments can be so planned that the more able students are given challenging tasks and the less able deal with fundamental concepts or skills. Also, after class discussion concerning possible approaches to the study of a unit of learning or a projected class activity, the students, either individually or in small groups, can work out the respective problems that are involved.

As a beginning teacher, you may be overwhelmed by the amount of subject material that must be covered during a school term or year. You believe that you dare not take class time for individual study. If you try this approach, however, you will find that time has not been wasted. You are affording your students opportunities to improve their study and work habits in ways that will benefit them both in and out of school.

THE USE OF TEAM TEACHING

Team teaching is not a specific method or technique. Rather is it a procedure that utilizes the abilities of two or more teachers who jointly provide instruction to the same group of students. This is a new instructional practice that appears to be rapidly increasing in popularity. For example, in a Project on Instruction sponsored by the National Education Association, it was found that, among the 948 secondary schools selected for study, only 4 per cent of large schools reported the use of teacher teams in 1956, but that this had risen to 30 per cent in 1961, with an expectation that the percentage may rise to about 50 per cent in 1965–66.[5]

Organization of Teaching Teams

The organization of the team varies with schools and purposes to be served. According to Drummond, the following five types of modifications of them are in the process of development and/or experimentation:

1. *A hierarchy of teaching assignments.* Several school systems (see Anderson, Johnson, Stone) have attempted to develop instructional teams which are based upon a specified hierarchy of teaching assignments. At the top of the hierarchy is a team leader who is a person with superior educational preparation, several years of teaching experience, and leadership qualities. The team leader often is given a lighter teaching load and a salary commensurate with the leadership responsibilities he is asked to assume. The team, in school systems developing hierarchal assignments, usually also consists of senior teachers (who receive extra pay, but not as much as that received by the team leader), regular teachers (often those without previous experience or those new to the system), part-time teaching assistants, and clerical aides. In order to cover the costs of the increased salaries for leadership and for clerical help, additional pupils are assigned to the team—usually at least one extra class section for three or four certified teachers.

2. *Coordinate- or co-teaching.* In school systems using this approach, teachers are assigned to a large group of pupils (usually a multiple of the

[5] *The Principals Look at the Schools: A Status Study of Selected Instructional Practices* (Washington, D.C.: National Education Assoc., 1962), p. 18.

number the teachers would have under more traditional assignments; e.g., two teachers to 60 youngsters, three teachers to 90) and they plan together *as peers* how best to provide for the pupils for whom they are responsible. As in the previously described "hierarchy" plan, sometimes instruction is provided to the entire group by one teacher. Sometimes one teacher works with most of the youngsters in the group while the other works with a small group of the gifted or with those needing remedial instruction. Sometimes each of the teachers has a "normal-sized" group of about 30 pupils each. Attempts are made in the planning to utilize to the fullest extent the strengths of each teacher. Such plans usually have been described as existing within established departments at secondary school levels or at grade levels in elementary schools.

3. *Team teaching across departmental lines.* In several junior and senior high schools, attempts have been made to improve the program, and hopefully to improve learning, by devising schedules for instructional teams which provide a two- or three-period block of related content (e.g., American history, American literature). Students have, normally, one period with the social studies teacher, followed by one period with the English teacher (or the reverse). Often, when desirable, the two groups are combined for the double period—as for a field trip, orientation to a new unit, lecture by an outstanding resource person, visual aids, and the like. The teachers have at least one free period at the same hour so that joint planning is possible.

4. *Part- or full-time helpers.* Many descriptions of team teaching indicate a fairly standard teaching role for the regularly certificated teacher, but seek to improve his teaching effectiveness by providing additional help of various kinds, including instructional secretaries, theme or paper correctors, laboratory assistants, learning materials coordinators, and audio-visual experts. To employ the additional personnel without substantial increases in instructional costs, teachers usually are asked to accept responsibility for a larger number of learners than normal (usually 35 to 40). The teacher retains active control of the planning and most instructional phases of teaching, utilizing the helpers on the team for particular tasks of a more routine nature.

5. *Trading groups.* In an informal way this method of capitalizing on the particular strengths of teachers has been utilized for years by elementary school teachers. The teachers have said, in essence, "If you'll take my art —you're good in it and I'm not—I'll take your music," or "If you'll take my science, I'll take your social studies." Until recently, such "trading" was rare at the secondary school level, but it may be growing now as a result of the staff utilization studies.[6]

You can realize that various modifications of these five types are possible. At the Ridgewood High School, Norridge, Illinois, for example, there are two broad area fields. "The teams are broad in scope and are classified as humanities and math-science teams. A

[6] Harold D. Drummond, "Team Teaching: An Assessment," *Educational Leadership,* December, 1961, pp. 160–61.

humanities team consists of teachers of history, English, music, art, and various foreign languages. A math-science team includes teachers of biology, mathematics, industrial arts, home economics, business education, and physical education." [7] In most secondary schools where team teaching has been introduced, however, it is customary for the team to be active in the same subject area. Where areas cross over, the two subjects included tend to be the social studies and English.

Teaching Approach in Team Teaching

There are various ways of handling the team-teaching approach. Let us assume that two teachers of the same subject are functioning as a team with a large group of students. Sometimes, particular aspects of the subject can be presented by one or the other teacher to the entire group. At other times the group can be divided according to the learning needs of the students and their learning experiences guided by one or another of the teachers.

In your student-teaching experiences, you are receiving training in the team approach in that you are working with your cooperating teacher, assisting him with many more or less routine matters, caring for teaching materials, teaching the class as a whole, and working with individuals or groups of students. You probably are finding that you are encouraged to develop aspects of the subject that have specific interest for you, or in which you are especially proficient. These experiences should have value for you if, in the future, you find yourself in a school that employs the team approach.

Assessment of Team Teaching

Administrative difficulties may arise in such matters as selecting appropriate teacher personnel to function as a team, arranging teaching schedules in such a way as to free the members of the team so that they can plan and work together, providing rooms for large groups of students, and supplying needed equipment.

Teachers need to be oriented to participation in this teaching

[7] Melvin P. Heller and Elizabeth Belford, "Team Teaching and Staff Utilization in Ridgewood High School," *The Bulletin of the National Association of Secondary-School Principals,* National Education Association, January, 1962, p. 106.

procedure. The conventional teacher whose teaching experience has been limited to working alone with a classroom sized group must learn to cooperate with other teachers whose attitudes and methods of teaching differ greatly from his own. He also may be more successful with smaller groups of students than with sixty or more. He cannot maintain the relative independence of procedure to which he had been accustomed. Yet, the sharing of teaching responsibilities provides for flexibility and variety of approach. For example, as Mitchell says:

> Three freshman English teachers, on a team, can have large-group sessions for instructions, tests, movies, dramatization, and expository lectures; they can have small-group discussion; they can regroup students according to need and ability at any time during the year. While one teacher re-teaches the lower third of the class, another teacher can go ahead with the faster group, and the third can have individual conferences with those who need personal help.
>
> When six teachers, rather than one, present the various units in Speech Arts, the students profit by the variety of approach peculiar to the temperaments of the different teachers. One uses the lecture-discussion method most of the time; another relies on demonstration; another prefers performance and critical evaluation.[8]

Team teachers can provide more adequately for students' immediate needs than can the lone teacher. As one of the team takes over the actual conduct of the lesson, the other can move around among the students and offer assistance as it is needed. Also, more and better opportunities are provided for teacher preparation. While one member of the team is working with the group as a whole in a lecture situation, for example, the other can be preparing his teaching unit. In addition, time is made available in their schedule for the members of the team to confer about their students' learning needs, material to be covered, and ways and means of conducting learning experiences. Each of the team members is challenged to utilize his special teaching skill in the teaching-learning situation.

In schools where team teaching has been attempted, the results in general have been satisfactory. The students seem to progress as well, if not better, than under the guidance of an only teacher; both students and parents are enthusiastic about the plan, and

[8] Wanda B. Mitchell, "Why Try Team Teaching?" *The Bulletin of the National Association of Secondary-School Principals*, National Education Assoc., January, 1962, p. 248.

teachers appear to be willing to participate in the cooperative venture. The supplying of instructional aids has tended to increase the cost of this procedure. Some educators still question the value of team teaching, however. They wonder whether the desirable aspects might not be achieved in other ways. For example, Drummond says concerning the worth of team teaching:

The worth of attempts at team teaching are not proven to date. The main value of the attempts which have been made thus far undoubtedly lies in the staff growth which has occurred as a result of the experimentation. Experimentation should be continued. Much more sophisticated research designs should be used, so that variables in the situations can be more carefully controlled. While team teaching is being tested more carefully, some school systems (perhaps the same ones) should also be testing other approaches to improved learning, such as: assigning not more than 20 pupils to a teacher, shortening the teacher-directed part of the school day and lengthening the pupil-directed portions of the day, utilizing more programmed materials as these become available, basing more instruction on the "workshop way of learning," orienting in-service education programs for teachers more toward materials centers and instructional secretaries in every school, and lengthening the school year for a larger number of teachers so that more time for planning and preparation is available.[9]

We cannot predict what the future of team teaching may be. At present, it is an interesting experiment in the teaching-learning approach with which you should be acquainted and for participation in which you should be prepared. It is a fact that some teachers are better suited than others for this kind of cooperative activity. Perhaps beginning teachers may gain greater facility in working with their colleagues and learn how to maintain a closer relationship with students than now is apparent in the group-teaching approach. Then we can expect real values to accrue from the adoption of team teaching.

QUESTIONS AND TOPICS FOR DISCUSSION

1. What specific skills need to be improved by students in your subject field?
2. To what extent and how does your subject field provide opportunities for creativity?
3. Evaluate your attitude toward high standards of workmanship as evidenced by your habitual performance of tasks assigned you.

[9] Harold D. Drummond, *op. cit.*, pp. 164–65.

4. What have been your reactions as a student to your teachers' utilization of the lecture method?
5. Distinguish between a regular recitation and a socialized recitation.
6. Give an example of small group discussion that would be appropriate to your subject.
7. Suggest at least five problems associated with your students. Have them present solutions for the problems.
8. Show how you could guide student thinking in one of the problems suggested in question 7.
9. Describe at least two interesting approaches to practice or drill in your subject field.
10. In what ways does your relationship with your cooperating teacher resemble team teaching? Be specific.

SELECTED REFERENCES

ALEXANDER, W. M., and SAYLOR, J. G. *Modern Secondary Education.* New York: Holt, Rinehart & Winston, Inc., 1959.

BROWN, T. J. *Student Teaching in a Secondary School.* New York: Harper & Row, Pub., Inc., 1960.

CARTER, W. L., HANSEN, C. W., and McKIM, M. G. *Learning to Teach in the Secondary School.* New York: Macmillan Co., 1962.

CROW, L. D., and CROW, ALICE. *How to Study.* New York: Collier Books, Inc., 1963.

————. *Mental Hygiene for Teachers: A Book of Readings.* New York: Macmillan Co., 1963.

DEWEY, JOHN. *How We Think.* Boston: D. C. Heath & Co., 1933.

GRIM, P. R., and MICHAELIS, J. U. (eds.) *The Student Teacher in the Secondary School.* Englewood Cliffs, N.J.: Prentice-Hall, Inc., 1953.

INLOW, G. M. *Maturity in High School Teaching.* Englewood Cliffs, N.J.: Prentice-Hall, Inc., 1963.

"Locus of Change: Staff Utilization Studies," *The Bulletin of the National Association of Secondary-School Principals,* January, 1962. (This issue contains more than twenty articles on *Team Teaching.*)

McKEAN, R. C. *Principles and Methods in Secondary Education.* Columbus, Ohio: Charles E. Merrill Books, Inc., 1962.

RISK, T. M. *Principles and Practices in Secondary Schools* (2nd ed.). New York: American Book Co., 1958.

SCHORLING, R., and BATCHELDER, H. T. *Student Teaching in the Secondary Schools* (rev. ed.). New York: McGraw-Hill Book Co., Inc., 1956.

SCHULTZ, R. *Student Teaching in the Secondary Schools.* New York: Harcourt, Brace & World, Inc., 1959.

The Principals Look at the Schools: A Status Study of Selected Instructional Practices. Washington, D.C.: National Education Association, 1962.

WIGGINS, S. P. *Successful High School Teaching.* Boston: Houghton Mifflin Co., 1958.

9

TEACHING RAPID AND SLOW LEARNERS

Teaching-learning approaches in the secondary school are pointed toward helping students master curriculum materials that have been developed in light of generally accepted educational objectives or goals suited to this school level. The teacher's task would be relatively simple if all of his students possessed equal ability to benefit from exposure to learning situations in his particular subject. As you know, this is not true, however. Individuals differ widely in the extent to which they are mentally fitted to profit from instruction that does not take into account the presence of these differences.

No two students are exactly alike in their power to deal effectively with learning materials. Ideally, every young person would be given an opportunity to proceed in mastery of subject materials at his own rate of successful achievement. Since public education must, perforce, be conducted on a relatively large-group basis, the best that we can hope to accomplish is so to organize our planning procedures that we provide in a general way for at least three categories of mental differences—the rapid learner, the average learner, and the slow learner.

THE IDENTIFICATION OF MENTAL DIFFERENCES

In your preteaching courses to this point, you probably have learned about individual differences. You know that there is no sharp line of demarcation among young people's mental capacities. Rather does each individual have a place somewhere along the line from mental retardation to high mental superiority. Hence school administrators need to establish lists of criteria in light of which they can determine the extent to which some of their students perform academically more effectively than so-termed average students and others who are inferior in learning achievement.

Commonly used criteria are the results of standardized testing instruments such as group and individual intelligence, special aptitude, and achievement tests. The results of intelligence and aptitude tests combined with measures of achievement can serve as indicators of what may be expected of a young person in respect to future academic performance. Yet, we cannot accept test results alone as our sole criteria of ability range. Concerning this point Henry Chauncey, president of Educational Testing Service, says:

> Tests, of course, have their limitations. We have no particular evidence that they measure potential creativity, original thinking, inventiveness. They certainly will not single out for us the individual who will discover new intellectual territory, as distinct from the other individuals who will settle and cultivate that territory. In short, we cannot feed results of a secondary-school standardized testing program into an electronic computer and expect a guaranteed roster of future Einsteins, Pasteurs, and other outstanding individuals to emerge. No matter how refined our techniques become, it is safe to say, with William James, "that individual . . . biographies will never be written in advance."
>
> What tests can do for us, if we use them knowledgeably, is help to identify a larger number of students who are in the score ranges from which creative scientists, engineers, philosophers, historians, economists, psychologists, jurists, educators are most likely to emerge. Thus, if we are fishing for sizable intellectual talent, standardized testing will not single out the species or net the catch for us. But it will tell us which pools are likely to contain the "big ones." [1]

Chauncey also raises the question of the degree to which tests can be used to predict success in college. Assuming that a scholastic aptitude test is administered to all students before they enter college and the progress in college work of the 20 per cent rating at the top of the scores is compared with the work of the lowest 20 per cent, Chauncey asserts:

> Typically, of the students in the top 20 per cent on the test, about 45 per cent will do honors work; an additional 52 per cent will do satisfactory work; and only about 3 per cent will fail. In other words, for every failing

[1] Henry Chauncey, "Measurement and Prediction—Tests of Academic Ability," from James B. Conant, *The Identification and Education of the Academically Talented Student in the American Secondary School,* The Conference Report of the International Conference on the Academically Talented Secondary School Pupil, National Education Association, 1958, p. 30.

student you will have 15 honor students plus 17 adequate students. Now let's look at the students in the bottom 20 per cent on the test. Of these, only about 3 per cent will do honors work; 52 per cent more will pass; 45 per cent will fail. For every honor student, 15 failures.[2]

Further, according to Chauncey, the middle 60 per cent would divide itself in this way: 17 per cent honor work, 60 per cent satisfactory work, and 17 per cent failures. Studies of this kind seem to give evidence that the results of ability tests have predictive value.

Another source of information is the recorded history of degree of successful achievement in various learning areas as this is noted on a student's cumulative record card. Much also can be learned about a young person's mental status through teachers' and parents' observation of his behavior and attitude toward school learning. The individual himself may be able to evaluate his learning potential in comparison with that of his fellow classmates.

One student realizes that he finds studying easier than do some of his friends. Another struggles to master a unit of subject material and decides that he is "dumb" because he is less successful in his study than others, in spite of his efforts to achieve desired learning goals. In addition, adolescents are quick to recognize differences in learning effectiveness among their peers. By utilization of a combination of these media, it is possible to differentiate, in a general way, among the mental capacities of individual students.

Characteristics of the Academically Superior

The rapid learner can be expected to have a high intelligence quotient. The normal or average IQ's range from 90 to 110. Since individual ratings on various intelligence tests may vary somewhat, an IQ of 115 to 120 is supposed to be characteristic of the fast learner. The mentally superior or gifted individual is expected to achieve an IQ of at least 140. Hence, although the intelligence quotient is a commonly used criterion of superior learning ability, its use as a criterion should be evaluated in light of other displayed qualities or traits.

Mentally superior young people tend to have intensive and extensive interests. They can analyze complex relationships and arrive

[2] *Ibid.,* p. 33.

at original solutions to complex problems. They can deal with abstractions and excel in independent thinking. They enjoy engaging in research, not only to achieve a learning goal but also to participate in the activity itself. They like to read, often delving into difficult reading materials beyond study requirements.

Gifted adolescents usually can express their ideas clearly and succinctly in both oral and written form, and have a rich vocabulary. They master factual information easily and apply creatively what they have learned. Such students offer a definite mental challenge to their teachers and are a joy in the classroom.

According to one analysis of the characteristics of the gifted, superiority seems to show itself in one or more clusters of traits: (1) the intellectually gifted who excel in most scholarly activities, (2) the talented and creative in areas such as music, art, and mechanics, and (3) those who have special ability in self-direction and social leadership. Each of these categories of gifted individuals tends to display certain qualities. These are listed here.

Traits that are likely to be associated with the *intellectually gifted pupil* are:

- thinks logically, reasons, generalizes, deduces
- easily grasps large concepts such as national issues, international plans, geologic time, theories of the origin and destiny of man
- deals with abstractions
- uses scientific research methods
- learns rapidly in short periods of time
- concentrates easily for long periods of time
- requires less detailed and repeated instructions; often anticipates them
- sees relationships and draws sound generalizations
- perceives trends in the past and projects these into the future
- works readily with symbols such as words and numbers in place of direct experience and the actual objects
- is interested in thinking
- is curious about meanings; continually asks why
- is interested in words and their use and soon acquires command of a fairly rich vocabulary
- enjoys encyclopedias, dictionaries, maps, globes, and other references
- enjoys reading
- reads widely

Traits likely to be associated with a pupil who has unusual capacity for wise *self-direction and social leadership* are:

- does effective work independently
- frequently concentrates on goals that are remote, poorly defined, and possibly unattainable
- shows evidence of emotional stability in ordinary behavior and in interviews with the school psychologist
- has keen sense of humor
- has a sharp sense of justice
- criticizes himself and modifies his behavior accordingly
- incorporates suggestions from others into his own thinking and actions
- assumes leadership in some situations, yet follows in others
- has leadership qualities as shown by sociometric devices
- plans opportunities for other pupils to participate in school activities
- exhibits initiative in starting worthwhile ventures
- has superior ability in planning, organizing, and promoting
- has a wide range of interests or a strong interest in a few areas

Traits likely to be associated with a *talented and creative pupil* are:

- has a sense of wonder and curiosity
- has intense feelings about the world around him
- is sensitive to fine distinctions in the structure and processes of his environment
- has vivid imagination
- visualizes actions and things from descriptions
- has unusual power to envision new structures and processes and to express his visions in speaking, writing, art, music, or some other form
- produces work that has freshness, vitality, and uniqueness
- creates new ideas, substances, and processes
- invents and builds new mechanical devices
- adjusts to and enjoys new situations
- often runs counter to tradition
- continually questions the status quo
- does the unexpected
- applies learning from one situation to different situations
- solves problems in the aesthetic field [3]

Read these lists of characteristics carefully. As you observe and work with your class, make note of those students who display any of the listed traits. Discuss them with your cooperating teacher and consult cumulative record cards to discover the extent to which reported performance agrees with your appraisal of their possessed traits.

[3] From *56 Practices for the Gifted from Secondary Schools of New York State* (Albany, N.Y.: Bureau of Secondary Curriculum Development, State Education Department, 1958), pp. 17–18. Reprinted with permission but not copyrighted.

Characteristics of Slow Learners

As is the practice in screening rapid learners, standardized tests are used in attempts to discover those students who can be expected to encounter difficulties in mastering learning materials. The intelligence quotient is a commonly utilized criterion. A few mentally retarded individuals (IQ below 70) can be found in the junior high school, but they rarely are able to continue through the senior high school years. Some slow learners, individuals with intelligence quotients between 75 and 90, are able to complete a modified secondary school curriculum. Their degree of moderately successful achievement depends partly on their own efforts and partly on the effectiveness of teaching approaches.

The validity of a low intelligence quotient is a moot question. An individual may score low on an intelligence test because of his unfamiliarity with the language or because he is unacquainted with the background knowledge needed to interpret verbal test items correctly. It is a fact that children's ratings on these tests have improved as they have been exposed to better cultural conditions. However, consistently low results on a series of performance as well as verbal tests probably indicate low mental alertness.

The slow learner is likely to exhibit characteristics that are basic to his inability to master regular learning content effectively. We must remember that, like the rapid learner, the slow learner differs from so-termed normal learners in degree of ability rather than in kind. The below-normal adolescent can think, but he is weak in abstract thinking. He needs to be stimulated by concrete situations and ideas. His study habits probably are poor. He does not know how to attack study materials quickly and efficiently. Also, his attention span is relatively short. He finds it difficult to concentrate on the task at hand and is easily diverted by distracting elements in his environment.

Since the slow learner is deficient in viewing situations and conditions in their proper perspective, his ability to find solutions to any but the simplest problems is weak. He does not always recognize appropriate relationships, and, therefore, is unable to achieve valid conclusions or generalizations. The slow student sometimes can memorize material by rote, but he may fail to understand what he has memorized.

One of the most serious problems of the slow learner is his low reading ability. He probably has had a history of poor reading throughout the elementary school and comes to the secondary school unable to put meaning into the words on the printed page. Textbooks usually are unsuited to his needs because they are written on the level of the average or superior student. He comes to class with his home assignments apparently unprepared, yet he may have tried to prepare them but achieved little, if any, understanding of what he read.

You need to understand that for a slow learner to compete with his brighter classmates is an extremely discouraging situation. He often gives up trying to succeed in his work. He is the student who may become a disruptive influence in the classroom. He may become a truant or wait impatiently for the day when he will be old enough to drop out of school.

TEACHING APPROACHES FOR THE MENTAL DEVIATES

The fundamental goal of the secondary school is to prepare all of its students for a useful and personally satisfying mode of life. School people long have tried to meet the problem of providing more or less appropriate learning situations to meet the needs of slow learners. Appreciating the mental handicaps of these students, they have attempted, although not always successfully, to offer modified programs of studies through participation in which these young people might become reasonably well fitted to earn a livelihood and become constructive citizens. In large urban communities, especially, vocational high schools have been established to meet the learning needs of the less academically minded students.

Concern for the mentally superior is a more recent development. At one time it was believed, erroneously, that the bright could take care of themselves. It was assumed that, given the opportunity to participate in learning activities, these young people would be self-motivated to achieve successfully in light of their superior interests and abilities. Community and school leaders are now realizing that modern technological and social advances demand the services of an ever-increasing number of well-trained experts in various fields of endeavor. We cannot afford to waste whatever mental superiority can be found among the youth of the land. Hence it is the function of our schools to provide appropriate learning situations that develop the individual powers of leadership of gifted young people.

Administrative Responsibility for Meeting Individual Differences

What is done for the rapid and slow learner, respectively, depends in good part on the educational philosophy of school administrators and their policy toward making special provisions for meeting the educational needs of their young people. Secondary school principals' efforts in this respect are limited, of course, by the size of the school or school system, and the money available.

Large city school systems usually are able to organize special school units to meet the educational needs of the many differing young people to be found in the school community. In New York City, for example, there are more than eighty senior high schools. These include special schools, such as the Bronx High School of Science, High School of Commerce, High School of Music and Art, High School of Fashion Industries, New York School of Printing, and Brooklyn High School of Automotive Trades, to mention a few. With proper screening on the junior high school level, individual learning needs can be met with a fair degree of successful achievement. In addition, there are differences among students in the more cosmopolitan schools.

The smaller community secondary school is not able to operate on a wide scale of differentiated offerings, mainly because of the fact that there is not a sufficient number of differentiated students to make the plan practical. Hence the principal of the school is faced with the problem of providing within the school building for differences in learning ability among the students.

A comprehensive group project in secondary education was undertaken by the U.S. Department of Health, Education and Welfare. The study deals with teaching rapid and slow learners in junior, senior, and regular high schools enrolling more than 300 pupils. One section of the report deals with administrative provisions for rapid- and slow-learning pupils. We present on pages 234-35 the summarization of the findings in tabular form.

Read this table carefully. Then evaluate procedures in your school according to the listed items. Your cooperating teacher may be interested in studying the situation with you. In what ways and to what extent is your school providing specifically for the learning needs of its students?

TEACHING RAPID LEARNERS IN THE SECONDARY SCHOOL

Various approaches are being used in modern secondary schools to motivate rapid learners to achieve successfully. As we have suggested, the procedures utilized are in keeping with administrative policy, the per cent of the student body that can be identified as mentally superior, and available materials and equipment. The purpose of the differentiated program may be *acceleration* or *enrichment,* or a combination of the two. The "gifted" may be taught in special classes or schools (homogeneous grouping) or in regular classes (heterogeneous grouping).

Value of Acceleration

School people are becoming increasingly interested in providing opportunities for acceleration of mentally superior young people. Acceleration can be justified for at least two reasons. First, since the bright student can master learning materials more quickly than is possible for less able individuals, he is likely to be bored in class or "get by" with a minimum of study effort. He may develop habits of laziness and fail to utilize his full study potential. Secondly, many of these students plan to enter a vocational field that requires five or more years of academic preparation beyond graduation from high school. This causes a delay not only in his participation in gainful work activity but also in the establishment of a home of his own.

One opportunity for students to speed up the learning process is offered on the junior high school level. Curriculum adjustments are made for selected students whereby they are enabled to complete the work of the seventh, eighth, and ninth grades in two years, thereby gaining one year of study time. No learning materials are

TABLE 8

PERCENTAGES OF SCHOOLS REPORTING THE USE OF ADMINISTRATIVE PROVISIONS FOR RAPID- AND SLOW-LEARNING PUPILS, BY TYPE OF ORGANIZATION *

Item No.†	Item	Percent using administrative provisions, by type of organization			
		All schools (795)‡	Junior high school (397)	Senior high school (135)	Regular high school (263)
1	2	3	4	5	6
	A. PROVISIONS FOR BOTH RAPID AND SLOW LEARNERS				
1	Teachers furnished guidance information pertinent to pupils	90	92	96	85
2	Teachers assigned on basis of traits and interests suitable for work	82	80	90	81
3	Regular classes furnished advanced study materials and additional learning aids	79	80	81	77
4	Space, furniture, and equipment for flexible grouping in classes and activities	62	57	64	68
5	Ability (homogeneous) classes. (Pupils grouped according to IQ, reading ability, previous grades, social maturity, etc.)	48	46	53	49
6	Individualized instruction outside of regular class hours	47	47	56	43
7	Job placement services	46	13	88	76
8	Supervised work experience	45	33	65	53
9	Summer-school sessions provided	44	46	53	36
10	Credit given for demonstrated achievement regardless of time spent in class	43	47	39	40
11	Transfer to special school encouraged	38	40	36	38
12	Flexible graduation requirements as to credits	38	45	33	30
	Mean	55	52	62.8	56

B. PROVISIONS FOR RAPID LEARNERS ONLY

13	College-preparatory curriculum	78	71	93	83
14	Pupils permitted to carry above-normal class load for graduation credit ..	57	29	81	86
15	Elective classes in advanced or specialized subjects (journalism, electronics, calculus, etc.)	48	29	74	63
16	Remedial sections for able pupils whose performance is below capacity ...	37	44	30	29
17	Teachers assigned on basis of training and experience with rapid learners .	36	34	45	34
18	Pupils sectioned in classes which do 2 years' work in 1; or 3 years' work in 2, etc.	4	4	4	2
	Mean	43	35	54.5	49.5

C. PROVISIONS FOR SLOW LEARNERS ONLY

19	Easy study materials related to pupils' interests	77	80	73	74
20	Promotion of pupils on basis of physical and social development	55	70	44	39
21	Remedial sections where performance is below capacity in basic skills	53	59	45	46
22	Low ability classes in certain subjects	52	48	54	57
23	Teachers assigned on basis of training and experience with slow learners ..	51	54	52	45
	Mean	57.6	62	53.6	52

* From A. Jewett and J. D. Hull (coordinators), *Teaching Rapid and Slow Learners in High Schools*, U.S. Department of Health, Education and Welfare, Bulletin 1954, pp. 8–9.

† Items are arranged in rank order within subdivisions A, B, and C and do not conform to original numbering on the questionnaire.

‡ Number of usable returns.

omitted or "skipped," but mastery takes place at a faster rate. Numerous school systems have utilized this plan.

Entrance into one of these "special progress" classes (SP) in New York City is based on an IQ of 130 or higher and a reading grade of at least 8.5. They report:

> The aim of the Junior High School Division's program is to give pupils with superior scholarship achievement an opportunity to follow a course of study under conditions which will:
> • challenge their spirit of inquiry
> • develop their special interests and aptitudes
> • offer opportunities for the exercise of social and civic responsibilities
> • provide acceleration of one year.[4]

Individual schools work out their programs in light of the interests and purposes of their students, although the fundamental principles of acceleration are respected. All students must be prepared to enter the tenth grade of the senior high school and participate effectively in the work of that grade. If a student in an SP class finds it difficult to maintain progress, provision is made for his transfer to a regular class. The Junior High School Division also is interested in providing for the talented individual and the young person with special interest, aptitude, or skill.

Although all of the schools in New York City adhere to the fundamental principles of SP programs, individual schools work out their own plans for the development of their rapid learners. Following is presented the plan of one school for caring for the needs of exceptional students: [5]

The Intellectually Gifted Child

How We Identify Him

Standardized tests of mental ability (a minimum I.Q. of 130)
Achievement tests (especially in reading and mathematics)
Data on health and study habits

How We Provide for Him

Through *acceleration*—three-year course in two years for pupils with an I.Q. of 130 or above, a reading grade of 8.5 and an arithmetic grade of 8.0.

---

[4] Reprinted from *Curriculum and Materials*, May–June, 1957, p. 6, by permission of the Board of Education of the City of New York.

[5] *Ibid.*, p. 7.

Through *enrichment*
1. Modification of curriculum
   a. Accent on integration of social studies and the language arts
   b. Extensive and intensive reading programs
   c. Foreign language study
   d. A more extensive trip and excursion program
   e. A more intensive research program
   f. More frequent culminating projects
   g. Student help clinic (selected students help others after school hours)
2. Modification of teaching method
   a. Larger part played by pupils in planning and carrying out class work
   b. Wider use of pupils as teachers or teacher-helpers
   c. More searching assignments
   d. Higher standards of achievement
   e. Greater stress on the "how" and the "why"
   f. More intensive participation in the evaluation of methods, materials, and activities
   g. Wider use of discussion and group process techniques (panel, forum, 6-6 method)
3. Greater opportunities for creative expression through
   a. Language arts publication
   b. Math newspaper
   c. Foreign language newspaper

Through intensive *guidance*
1. In determining interests and aptitudes
2. In personal social adjustment
3. In choosing high school and high school courses
4. In out-of-school experiences

The Talented Child

How We Identify Him

Interviews by articulation counselor
Screening by teacher-specialists
Recommendation of teachers

How We Provide for Him

Through talent classes
1. Art
   a. Sets for dramatic presentations
   b. Illustrations for school publications
   c. Posters and decorations for school events and P.T.A. activities
2. Creative writing
   a. School newspaper
   b. School magazine

   c. School reading guide
3. Dramatics
   a. Assembly presentations
   b. Evening performances for parents and pupils
   c. Presentations to individual classes over public address system
4. Music workshops (vocal, instrumental)
   a. Assembly performances
   ~ *b.* Music festival presentations

Through special talent groups
1. By joining talent classes during weekly homeroom and group guidance periods
2. By contributing to school publications
3. By participating in auditorium programs sponsored by Grade Councils

The Child With Special Interests
   (Neither intellectually gifted nor talented in the ordinary sense.)

How We Identify Him

Through interest inventories
Through teacher recommendation
Through interviews with parents and pupils

How We Provide for Him

After-school clubs
School service squads
General Organization

   Attempts have been made to encourage student acceleration on the senior high school level. In some high schools, bright students in class-sized groups engage in advanced work in subjects like mathematics and the sciences, for example. Scheduling such classes often is difficult, however. Also, a small high school may not have enough students with similar interests or abilities to form a class. In such situations, individual students may be encouraged to do advanced study on their own, with some teacher guidance.

   One of the most challenging projects in this aspect of education is the work of the Fund for the Advancement of Education. As early as 1953, they reported a study of a program in which 12 colleges and 12 high schools cooperated to the extent that the colleges involved accepted students from the cooperating high schools with credit for advanced study in the latter institution.[6] The

---

   [6] The Fund for the Advancement of Education, *Bridging the Gap between School and College,* Evaluation Report, No. 1, June, 1953.

program now is known as the *Advanced Placement Program* and is under the aegis of the College Entrance Examination Board. Any mentally superior student may take the examination regardless of the means he employed to prepare himself for it. It might be possible, in light of the extent of his preparation, for a college entrant to bypass the freshman year, starting immediately on the sophomore year program.

Another project of the Fund for the Advancement of Education is the program whereby colleges can select promising high school students at the end of their tenth or eleventh year and admit them as college freshmen. The purpose is to free bright high school students from the boredom that might be attached to their remaining in high school for a full four years. The colleges select those students who give evidence of emotional and social maturity as well as superior academic ability and scholarship.

Although programs of acceleration have definite advantages from the point of view of scholarly attainment, some psychologists question their value in the emotional and social development of a young person. As a result of participation in accelerated programs, it is possible for a twelve year old to enter the sophomore grade of the secondary school where the average age is between fourteen and fifteen. Emotionally and socially this individual may be relatively immature and at a disadvantage among his more sophisticated classmates. His problems may be lessened if homogeneous grouping is employed in the senior high school, but other problems may arise. Homogeneity of grouping is discussed later in the chapter.

The young admittee into college also experiences problems of adjustment. Although age gaps may be less significant at this level, the fifteen- or sixteen-year-old college entrant can be at a disadvantage among more world-wise eighteen to twenty year olds. The situation is worsened if the young entrant was so involved with his studies on the secondary school level that he failed to avail himself of the school's provision for participation in social activities.

The Value of Enrichment

In its most general connotation, the term *enrichment* as applied to curricular offerings includes any learning materials and experiences that go beyond the minimal essentials included in a course of study. Actually, however, by enrichment we usually mean the extent to which the superior student is provided opportunities to engage in study experiences that are in advance of what normal or average students are expected to master. "Enrichment, in whatever form, is effective only when it provides for a broader scope of activities, when it challenges and encourages special interests, and when it fosters talent, creativity, and orginality." [7]

In special schools and classes, superior students can benefit from participation in enriched curriculums. In regular classes, the teacher can encourage rapid learners to engage in more intensive and extensive study projects. It must be kept in mind, however, that able students differ in their individual interests. Enriching experiences, therefore, need to be encouraged in light of particular interests. For example, one student may respond to special challenge in the sciences or mathematics, another's concern may be that of social problems, while still another's chief interest lies in the field of the language arts.

As the members of a class select their special projects in the development of a unit of study, the more able students can be motivated by the teacher to choose those requiring the greater amount of research. They also can be encouraged to prepare and report on aspects of study material that demand the utilization of special books and equipment. Since bright students are likely to complete assigned classroom tasks more quickly than do the others, they can devote the extra time at their disposal to one or another form of advanced work. Another avenue of enrichment is membership in cocurricular clubs in which the gifted learners can explore more advanced areas of study, such as in mathematics or in the sciences. The ingenious teacher can find many ways in which to provide interesting and challenging learning situations for the rapid learners.

Types of Grouping for Effective Learning

You probably are acquainted with the two generally accepted forms of grouping students for instructional purposes: *heterogeneous* and *homogeneous*. The former term applies to that type of class

---

[7] *Administration: Procedures and School Practices for the Academically Talented Student in the Secondary School* (Washington, D.C.: National Education Assoc., 1960), p. 87.

organization whereby all of the students in a subject area, regardless of their degree of mental ability, are taught together as a group. In the latter type, some provision is made for different ability levels to be placed in classes in which they supposedly are receiving instruction with students similar to themselves in ability to profit from learning stimulation.

Many secondary schools, especially those in large school communities, either establish special schools or offer what can be called the multiple-track curriculum in the same school. These usually include a college preparatory or academic curriculum, a commercial curriculum, and a general curriculum. Selection, under guidance, by a secondary school student of one or another track presupposes a particular interest and degree of ability. To this extent, the multiple-track organization provides some ability grouping, although factors other than mental ability alone may influence a young person's decision to select a particular curriculum. Parental ambition, for example, may be at the root of a secondary school entrant's decision to select the college preparatory in spite of mediocre ability. Such a student usually is transferred, somewhere along the line, to the general curriculum. A relatively few secondary schools include another track for the specially gifted—the *honors program.*

In an increasing number of secondary schools, mentally superior students are segregated in special honors classes in one or more subjects. Selection of students for honors classes is based on demonstrated ability and interest in a particular field, such as English, social studies, mathematics, or science. A student may be in a special class for one or two subjects and in regular classes for others.

Some students have ambivalent feelings toward membership in an honors class. They may find that they are working under greater pressure than was the case in regular classes. All of the students in a special class are not homogeneous in every respect. The teacher is dealing with individuals in this type of class just as surely as he is in a regular class. Even though the members are supposedly relatively similar in scholarship ability, they may be very different in degree of emotional maturity. Hence they do not respond similarly to motivating devices. Moreover, some teachers attempt to apply the normal curve of distribution in comparative evaluation of study success. As a result, some of his students earn lower grades in this class than they would in a regular class. Ability grouping has definite advantages. At the same time, other factors may interfere with the success of its functioning. Much depends on the leadership abilities of the teacher.

The Teacher and Special Instructional Provisions for Rapid Learners

A question often raised is "What kind of person should teach the mentally superior learner?" The answer might be that this teacher should possess those qualities of leadership that are desirable in all teachers but perhaps a little more pronounced. Enthusiasm for his subject field, sympathetic understanding of the problems of the gifted in a world consisting (for the most part) of less able individuals, and ingenuity in providing challenging learning situations are among the qualities that should be possessed by men and women who attempt to guide the learning of these young people. Some of his students may possess a higher degree of mental ability than he does. This is no detriment provided he can recognize and respect their superiority.

Another question is "What are the most significant instructional provisions for use with rapid learners?" Some administrative provisions were listed earlier. The study that yielded these suggestions, from approximately 700 secondary schools, also gives highlights of instructional provision to be employed by teachers of various subjects. Of thirty instructional techniques to be used in teaching rapid learners, arranged in order of importance, we are listing the top five for English, social studies, mathematics, and the sciences:

Instructional Provisions and Procedures by Type of Organization for
Rapid Learners

English [8]
1. Encourage extensive reading of good literature outside of class
2. Require mastery of certain minimum essentials in grammar and usage
3. Teach niceties of expression, such as distinctions between *shall* and *will, between* and *among, go slow* and *go slowly, may* and *can, lent* and *loaned*
4. Emphasize reading of modern literature related to student interests and needs
5. Help students to find good substitutes for inferior comic books and magazines

[8] Jewett and Hull, *op. cit.,* p. 22.

Social Studies [9]
1. Use current events as an important part of class work
2. Teach pupils to use the layman's reference books: the dictionary, encyclopedia, World Almanac
3. Teach pupils how to register and vote; give experiences in studying party platforms and personal views of candidates
4. Encourage pupils to engage in conversation in school and at home on current events, politics, government, and views of school and neighborhood
5. Encourage pupils to use references in large library

Mathematics [10]
1. Assist students in learning vocabulary and reading skills peculiar to mathematics
2. Emphasize the social uses of mathematics
3. Provide individual supervision and guidance during class
4. Encourage study of the applications of mathematics to science
5. Encourage student self-evaluation

Science [11]
1. Insist that students report science experiments honestly and accurately
2. Encourage students to use scientific encyclopedias and references in preparing science reports
3. Include student activities to stress basic skills, such as reading tables, observing experiments, and spelling common science words
4. Guide students to note superstitions and other biases that block fair consideration of scientific evidence
5. Give students experiences in helping with science demonstrations

You may find these suggestions valuable as you plan for your teaching of bright students. Similar tables for the teaching of home economics and industrial arts are presented in the study. Also, since this study covers many aspects of teaching rapid learners, we suggest that, if possible, you procure a copy for a close study of all thirty instructional provisions for each subject.

TEACHING SLOW LEARNERS IN THE SECONDARY SCHOOL

As we have suggested earlier, the mentally retarded (IQ's below 70) are segregated in special classes and taught by specially trained teachers. You probably will not have these young people in your classes. You will find in your regular classes, however, some slow-

[9] *Ibid.,* p. 34.
[10] *Ibid.,* p. 38.
[11] *Ibid.,* p. 50.

learning boys and girls who experience difficulty in meeting successfully their study requirements. Teaching-learning approaches for slow learners are different from the procedures usually found to be effective in dealing with rapid learners.

Curriculum Provisions for the Slow Learner

Considered broadly, the needs of slow-learning students are cared for in many secondary schools through the offerings of special vocational or trade schools or curriculums. Unfortunately, in some school communities, the original purpose of this type of school is disregarded in that the administrative officers of the school vie with the more academically pointed school in their attempts to attract average or superior young people to seek admission in their school. To the extent that the slow learner is barred from entrance to a vocational school, he must be accepted by the regular secondary school where he usually is given the general curriculum with some beginning vocationally pointed learnings.

Another approach to meeting the needs of the slower learner is the trend in curriculum construction to set minimal requirements to be met by all students and supplementary experiences for the average and more able students. It is essential, of course, that the teacher of a subject know what the minimal essentials are and see to it that they are mastered.

Teaching Approaches for the Slow Learner

Since slow learners tend to be retarded in reading, each of their teachers must be a teacher of reading. He has the task of finding reading materials for them that are within their comprehension limits. He also may need to give them extra help in gaining an understanding of reading content. The utilization of audio-visual aids has value as a means of stimulating interest among these young people.

The slow learner becomes discouraged by the fact that his achievement does not measure up to that of his classmates. The teacher can encourage such a student by helping him compare his present performance with past performance. To the extent that improvement is evidenced, he can be stimulated to compete against himself, thereby attempting to better his record.

The teacher of a class that includes rapid, average, and slow learners is faced with the problem of challenging the members of each group to perform to the best of their ability. This is a difficult task and demands that the teacher be alert to existing mental differences and able to shift his emphasis on subject-matter mastery in light of these differences.

Schultz offers some specific suggestions for teaching slow learners in special classes and in regular classes. We present the substance of these suggestions here:

A. Teaching Slow Learners in Special Classes:
1. Adapt goals and explanations to situations within their immediate experience
2. Select concrete teaching examples and activities
3. Simplify activities whenever possible
4. Engage in extensive practice and review
5. Be sure they understand what you want them to do
6. Have frequent evaluations
7. Adapt reading material

B. Teaching Slow Learners in Regular Classes:
1. Adapt assignments
2. Provide opportunities for recognition
3. Have other students serve as coaches and tutors
4. Adapt reading material
5. Help them evaluate in terms of their own progress.[12]

Instructional Provisions for Slow Learners

In the study concerning learning differences that was referred to earlier in the chapter, attention is directed to thirty important instructional provisions for slow learners. These are ranked in order of value to the slow learner. As we did for rapid learners, we present the five most significant provisions for English, social studies, mathematics, and science.

Instructional Provisions and Procedures by Type of Organization
for Slow Learners

English [13]
1. Conduct drills to eliminate recurrent vulgarisms, such as "I ain't," "can't hardly," "he don't," etc.

[12] Adapted from Raymond E. Schultz, *Student Teaching in the Secondary Schools* (New York: Harcourt, Brace & World, Inc., 1959), pp. 144–54.
[13] Jewett and Hull, *op. cit.*, p. 26.

2. Help students to find good substitutes for inferior comic books and magazines
3. Emphasize reading of modern literature related to student interests and needs
4. Require mastery of certain minimal essentials in grammar and usage
5. Assign printed materials with difficulty approximating individual's reading age

Social Studies [14]

1. Use current events as important part of classwork
2. Teach pupils how to register and vote; give experiences in studying party platforms and personal views of candidates
3. Encourage pupils to engage in conversation in school and at home on current events, politics, government, and news of school and neighborhood
4. Teach pupils to use layman's reference books: the dictionary, encyclopedia, World Almanac
5. Teach basic skills in reading and writing (including map reading) to build social studies vocabulary and concepts

Mathematics [15]

1. Provide individual supervision and guidance during class
2. Assign simple drill problems
3. Assist students in learning vocabulary and reading skills peculiar to mathematics
4. Emphasize the social uses of mathematics
5. Give individual assistance to pupils after school hours

Science [16]

1. Insist that students report science experiments honestly and accurately
2. Guide students to note superstitions and other biases that block fair consideration of scientific evidence
3. Include student activities to stress basic skills, such as reading tables, observing experiments, and spelling common science words
4. Help students understand scientific reasons for fire-safety rules, sanitary standards, and/or first-aid practices
5. Discuss with students the qualities that help a person hold a job in industry

Compare this list with the five highest ranking instructional provisions for rapid learners. What likenesses and differences do you find? How would you justify these? When you compare the thirty items on each list for rapid and for slow learners, you will find some interesting differences.

[14] *Ibid.*, p. 36.
[15] *Ibid.*, p. 44.
[16] *Ibid.*, p. 54.

QUESTIONS AND TOPICS FOR DISCUSSION

1. Describe ways in which we can identify the mental deviate.
2. Select one of your students who is supposed to be mentally superior. Watch him at work and try to determine to what extent his behavior exemplifies those characteristics of the academically superior person listed in this chapter.
3. Select a slow learner and compare his displayed characteristics with those listed in this chapter.
4. Differentiate between acceleration and enrichment. Which approach do you prefer? Why?
5. Why do some bright students object to being placed in an honors class? How valid is their objection?
6. Compare the instructional provisions for rapid learners and slow learners cited in this chapter. Note specific likenesses and differences in approach.
7. What provision does your school make for meeting mental differences among students?
8. If your class is grouped heterogeneously, how does your cooperating teacher care for the needs of rapid learners? Slow learners?
9. Which group would you prefer to teach—rapid, average, or slow learners? Why?

SELECTED REFERENCES

Administration: Procedures and School Practices for the Academically Talented Student in the Secondary School. Washington, D.C.: National Education Assoc., 1960.

BISH, C. E. "The Academically Talented," in L. D. Crow and Alice Crow (eds.), *Educating the Academically Able: A Book of Readings.* New York: David McKay Co., Inc., 1963. Pp. 26–33.

CONANT, J. B. *The Identification of the Academically Talented Student in the American Secondary School.* Washington, D.C.: National Education Assoc., 1958.

CROW, L. D., and CROW, ALICE. *Educating the Academically Able: A Book of Readings.* New York: David McKay Co., Inc., 1963.

FRENCH, J. L. *Educating the Gifted: A Book of Readings* (2nd ed.). New York: Holt, Rinehart & Winston, Inc., 1964.

GOWAN, J. C. *An Annotated Bibliography on the Academically Talented.* Washington, D.C.: National Education Assoc., 1961.

HENRY, H. B. (ed.). *Education for the Gifted*, The Fifty-seventh Yearbook, Part II. Chicago: National Society for the Study of Education, 1958.

INGRAM, C. P. *Education of the Slow-Learning Child* (3rd ed.). New York: Ronald Press Co., 1960.

PASSOW, A. H., *et al. Planning for Talented Youth.* New York: Teachers College, Columbia Univ., Bureau of Publications, 1955.

SCHORLING, R., and BATCHELDER, H. T. *Student Teaching in Secondary Schools* (2nd ed.). New York: McGraw-Hill Book Co., Inc., 1956. Chap. 9.
SMITH, M. F. *Teaching the Slow-learning Child.* New York: Harper & Row, Pub., Inc., 1954.
STATE DEPARTMENT OF EDUCATION REPRESENTATIVES IN THE PROJECT, and GEER, W. C., SANDBERG, J. H., and WARD, V. S. *The Gifted Student: A Manual for Program Improvement.* Southern Regional Education Board and Carnegie Corporation of New York, 1962.

10

UTILIZATION OF TEACHING AIDS

The success of teaching is closely allied to the extent that the teacher knows his subject, understands the learner's educational needs and abilities, and recognizes and is enthusiastic about his many teaching responsibilities. No matter how well he is prepared to do a good job, however, he can improve the teaching-learning situation by utilizing the various teaching aids that now are available for his use.

You have had experience with supplementary learning materials. Your own teachers have applied some of them, and you probably have studied about them in your college classes. Here we are reviewing many of these aids to good teaching, their availability, and their proper use. As a student teacher, you can become better acquainted with them, so that you can make intelligent use of them in your teaching procedures.

GENERAL CONSIDERATIONS IN THE USE OF TEACHING AIDS

It is generally agreed among educators that learning is facilitated by the use of learning aids, such as textbooks and other reading matter, projected materials, nonprojected materials, and other resources that can be found in the school's community. Certain general principles of usage need to be kept in mind as you plan to incorporate the utilization of them among your learning procedures.

Purposes to Be Served by Supplementary Aids

Regardless of the type of material, you need to consider its usage in light of the purpose it can be expected to serve. You must keep in mind your instructional aim and your approach to the realization of this objective. Whether your goal is to increase subject matter mastery, skill improvement, or attitude development, you must make certain that the learning aid is suited to your purpose. Although it can arouse and help maintain student interest, your intent is not merely to amuse or entertain your students. Students need to recognize this fact.

Unless young people are properly guided, they may become so involved in an attention-getting experience that they lose sight of its educational significance. For example, a college instructor was accustomed to begin his class sessions with a short film appropriate to the discussion. He overheard one of his students comment on the fact that attending this class was a very enjoyable experience—that all one had to do was to relax and be entertained. Since this student rarely participated in the discussion, the instructor wondered to what extent this procedure was stimulating the student toward learning activity.

A learning aid should not be utilized as a kind of busy work. Too often, a teacher is tempted to assign book material to be read or workbook exercises to be completed in order to free himself for another activity. During the "busy work" period, the teacher corrects papers, prepares assignments, and the like. Students soon discover that the assigned task does not have a significant educational purpose. Consequently, they give it minimal attention.

Importance of Aids in Providing for Learning Differences

We know that young people differ in learning interests and in their ability to profit from learning experiences. Hence you need so to vary learning approaches that individual students can benefit from the activities in which they participate. Some students can learn much from the printed page, but many profit more from dealing with concrete materials. In fact, actual and vicarious experiences have strong learning potential for most individuals. One field trip may be worth more than the reading of many pages. A good motion picture or a series of slides can point up details that might be missed if they were the subject of an oral discussion. A chart, a map, or a diagram can present quickly and accurately facts or conditions that would take many words to describe or explain.

As you plan for the inclusion of teaching aids in your class procedures, be sure to evaluate their usefulness in light of your students' interests, learning needs, and readiness to profit from the use of particular aids. You must know something about the students' background of experience and their likelihood of regarding an aid in its proper perspective. The time element also is important.

Supplementary material must be appropriate to a specific learning experience and presented as a significant aspect of the total situation so that its relevancy can be recognized by the learners. It may be difficult for them to appreciate the significance of an audiovisual aid that is presented out of context. Used correctly, supplementary materials can (1) increase motivation toward effective learning, (2) provide for individual differences, and (3) serve to make learning more permanent.

Availability of Supplementary Learning Materials

You will find that schools and school systems differ in their policies toward the use of learning aids. For example, among the more often used audio-visual aids on the secondary school level are films, slides, and filmstrips, although some recent devices, such as tape recorders, television programs, language laboratories, and teaching machines, are beginning to receive attention. The greater use of all of these aids is projected for the future. (See Table 9.)

Schools seem to differ in their use of these aids not only in light of available money for their procurement, but also in their willingness to give them financial support. As can be recognized from a study of the table, schools are increasing the extent to which they are making such learning aids available for teachers' use.

Some materials are kept in the library or other convenient place in the school itself. Others, such as films, for example, are stored in a central depository and loaned to the individual schools. Still others are housed in community centers from which they can be obtained. More will be said about the availability of these materials as we discuss the various types of aids.

Utilization of Supplementary Aids

In the remainder of the chapter, we consider each of the more or less commonly used teaching-learning aids. Before we do this,

TABLE 9

THE USE OF INSTRUCTIONAL AIDS IN SECONDARY SCHOOLS *

Year and Descriptive Amount	Extent of Use in Per Cent for Each Aid				
	Films and filmstrips	Language laboratory	Tape recorders	Teaching machines	TV programs
1955–56					
Much use	24	0	6	0	1
Some use	72	6	70	5	17
None	4	94	24	95	82
1960–61					
Much use	58	9	33	1	6
Some use	41	26	63	12	48
None	1	65	4	87	49
1965–66					
Much use	75	40	60	10	21
Some use	24	43	39	55	65
None	1	17	1	35	14

* Adapted from *The Principals Look at the Schools: A Status Study of Selected Instructional Practices* (Washington, D.C.: National Education Assoc., 1962), p. 21.

however, we wish to add a few cautionary comments. Do not regard the utilization of teaching-learning aids as a means of relieving you of teaching responsibilities. Contrariwise, they add to your duties but are well worth the time and energy expended. Keep these points in mind when using a supplementary aid:

1. Select an aid in light of the learning interest and ability of your students.
2. Use an aid only for educational purposes.
3. Be sure that the material is integrated into the learning situation for which the aid is intended.
4. Prepare thoroughly for using the aid by familiarizing yourself with its operation and by making whatever arrangements for its use that are needed.
5. During the use of the aid, keep the students alert to its significance.
6. Engage in an appropriate form of follow-up.
7. Evaluate the use of the aid for future application.

READING MATERIALS AS AIDS

To the present and, probably, for a long time to come, the written word constitutes the one most important aid to learning. The value to the student of printed material depends, of course, on the appropriateness of its content in a particular area of learning, the appeal of the style and format of the material to the reading ability and interest of the reader, and the way in which the teacher uses the material in motivating the learning process. Reading materials commonly used in the modern secondary school classroom include textbooks, supplementary books, magazines, pamphlets, bulletins, brochures, and newspapers.

The Textbook as an Aid

The basal textbook is probably the oldest source of learning material in most secondary school subjects. Yet, too often, it serves as a crutch to the beginning or unimaginative teacher. The use of a simple textbook, to the exclusion of other teaching-learning aids, is, of course, to be deplored. If properly used, the textbook can have constructive value. Especially is this the case with many modern texts.

Publishers of textbooks are becoming increasingly aware of the factors that combine to produce a good, usable textbook as a learning guide. They select authors who know their subjects well and have had experience in teaching the subject matter of the material covered. Attention is being given to improving a book's organization and format. Much pertinent and interesting illustrative material is included. Attempts are made to adapt the style of writing to the reading comprehension level of the learners for whose use it is intended.

The selection of textbooks. In the past, textbooks usually were selected by state educational officials or by administrative officers in individual schools. The trend now is to have available textbooks in a subject field examined by a committee of teachers of the subject, either on the state or local level. Selection of the basal text is then made in light of accepted educational objectives. In some instances, individual teachers are permitted to make their own choice of books, although this procedure is more common on the college level than in the secondary schools.

Various factors are important in the selection of textbooks. In the selection process, it is suggested that the teachers involved give attention to the following points:

1. Course objectives
2. Appropriateness of text content
3. Suitability to planning and teaching procedures
4. General makeup of the book—style of writing, quality of paper, size of type, illustrative material, etc.
5. Author's reputed competence in the field
6. Recency of publication

Teachers in public secondary schools do not have complete freedom in the selection of textbooks. The school provides the books for the students. Because most textbooks are costly, they are used over and over again, often to the point that they are outdated. Current materials are omitted or presented inadequately. The teacher then needs to supplement the content or, in other ways, make certain that learners do not receive inadequate or inaccurate concepts. Perhaps the growing popularity of paperbacks may some day eliminate the use of outmoded texts.

The use of the textbook. A good text contains much material that has value to the learner and should be mastered by him. However, in some areas, such as the social studies, for example, for the learners to be exposed to the point of view of only one author would give them an inadequate background of understanding. It is much better for them to be stimulated by the differing approaches that can be realized by the use of several books in the field. In such learning situations, supplementary reading is a must.

Students do not always take kindly to much supplementary reading, even on the college level. A college senior recently complained that his instructor of political science expected the students to read parts of twelve books. "I don't understand what he wants," said this student, "I've been accustomed to having one book to study, and believe me I'd know it from cover to cover. His method only confuses me. I feel that I don't know anything." This man's attitude exemplifies the results of two extremes of book use. To master the contents of only one book has disadvantages as well as advantages; to attempt to spread one's reading too thin can result in little or no mastery. It is your responsibility, as a teacher, so to integrate reading material (either textbook or supplementary) with the whole learning experience that the students appreciate its purpose and value.

Few teachers now assign textbook reading by chapters or pages without giving needed explanation. You probably will find, even in a relatively homogeneous bright class, that your students need some help in attacking reading material. Technical terms and unfamiliar words may need to be interpreted ahead of time. A few key questions on the content of the reading unit are helpful. Recognize the fact that some members of the class may have reading difficulties that require special assistance if textbook study is to benefit them.

Be discriminating in your choice of textbook material to be used. Do not believe that you must have your students read the book from cover to cover; at the same time, be careful lest, because of time pressure, you omit significant material. Finally, remember that a good textbook is your most valuable teaching aid if you use it intelligently rather than abuse it.

Teaching-Learning Aids in Printed Material Other Than Textbooks

Appropriate reading materials can be obtained from various sources. Most textbooks include a bibliography of related readings. Some of these books may be found in the school or public library. Various bibliographies are available for your use. For example, *The Standard Catalog for High School Libraries,* compiled by Dorothy West and published by H. W. Wilson Co., N.Y., includes the titles, by subject headings, of a long list of books and pamphlets. You also may find valuable materials in your college or university that you can borrow for use with your students. Reference books, such as encyclopedias, usually are available in school libraries and often contain material that is pertinent to your subject.

The use of book material. In some schools, several sets of textbooks in the same subject are available for class use. The teacher then can vary his reading assignments so that the students are exposed to differing treatments of study material. In some instances, there are sets of three or four books, each containing material related to the subject. Individual students can be encouraged to consult these supplementary texts and report their findings to the class.

A good school library usually includes various books for each of the subjects taught in the school. These can be read in the library or borrowed for class or individual use. You may have developed a library of your own that contains books appropriate for student reading. You also may find that the parents of some students have interesting books that they are willing to lend you for class use. Whatever may be the source of available books, you need to make certain that you approach their utilization with the same care that you exercise in selecting material for study from the regular textbook.

The use of pamphlets and bulletins. Much interesting and worthwhile material can be found in current pamphlets and bulletins. Common sources of such materials are public service organizations, government agencies, and various fields of industry. They usually can be acquired at little or no cost. If used intelligently, they can help in bringing subject matter up to date and in adding interesting details. Some of these can be found in a well-stacked school library. You can obtain others by writing for them to the proper source. For example, you can contact agencies such as the American Library Association, Chicago, Illinois; the Superintendent of Documents, Government Printing Office, Washington 25, D.C.; and similar organizations.

Before you place pamphlets or bulletins in the hands of your students, you should read them carefully and evaluate their usefulness. You should evaluate supplementary aids by asking yourself such questions as:

1. Does the aid add anything to material already available?
2. Is the content of the material within the students' reading and comprehension range?
3. Should the content of the material be considered by all of the members of the class or limited in use to the more able students?

4. Does the material contain details that go beyond the educational purposes to be served at this stage of learning?
5. Is the material somewhat outdated?
6. Has the material been written to advertise a particular product or service?
7. Is the content of the material compatible with your teaching goals?

The use of newspapers and magazines. The use of clippings from newspapers and magazines or other periodicals can serve two purposes. Not only does it bring into the classroom some valuable up-to-date material related to your subject, but it also encourages the habit among your students of reading worthwhile current materials with a definite purpose in mind.

Newspapers and magazines are easily available as sources of supplementary study materials. Most school libraries subscribe to various monthly and weekly periodicals, and keep copies of the better newspapers on file. These can be referred to by the teacher and class members. You probably are alert to anything that appears in the daily newspaper or appropriate periodicals that are pertinent to your subject. Committees of students can be assigned the task of finding interesting material in magazines or newspapers that you supply them, or they can be encouraged to bring appropriate clippings from home.

Young people need training in looking for pertinent material and in their treatment of it. Younger adolescents, particularly, seem to believe that whatever is printed must be true. You need to teach them to be discriminating in their selection of valid material. In addition, some secondary school students, even college students, appear to have developed the habit of taking printed material that appeals to them and appropriating it as their own. School and public libraries find that some students clip excerpts from books and remove pamphlets, bulletins, and periodicals. Some students also cut out materials from books and other reading materials found in their homes without first receiving parental permission to do so. Do not place so much emphasis on the desirability of students' bringing interesting clippings that you, unintentionally, foster this bad habit.

The use of the library. The school, college, and local public libraries are invaluable sources of supplementary reading materials. You need to acquaint yourself with their offerings and use them. Especially should you become acquainted with the library facilities of the school in which you are teaching so that you can help your students become more proficient in their use of it. Too many young people hesitate to avail themselves of library services because they do not know how to find the materials they need.

In an increasing number of schools, students are escorted to the library by their teacher (usually a teacher of English), given instruction by the teacher or the librarian in its use, and given opportunities for practice. In some schools, supervised study periods are conducted in the library. There, either the students are permitted to browse around the room in search of material of interest to them, or they follow a prearranged plan of consulting the catalog file for assigned material, locating it, and then reading the assignment until the end of the period, at which time they return the material to the proper desk or stack. This is excellent training in library usage. When you request students to consult library materials on their own, be sure that you have first offered suggestions that will help them locate the material and use it properly.

Building a file of supplementary reading materials. For you to need to search for appropriate material each time you wish to use it in connection with the presentation of a particular topic can involve the expenditure of much time and energy. Many teachers begin early in their teaching career to build a valuable file of pertinent materials. Now would be a good time to start this procedure. In your own study of your subject, you probably have accumulated much such material. Start a working file. Be constantly on the alert for pamphlets, bulletins, and magazine and newspaper articles that may have value to you as a teacher, and file them.

Several cautions are needed. File the materials in such a way that they are readily accessible and grouped according to specific topics. Date all clippings. Remove from the file any materials that are outdated. Use the materials with discrimination. Some articles may be suitable for consideration with one class but not with another. A specific bit of information may be of interest to some young people or suited to their learning ability but inappropriate for others. A good workable file of reading material is a boon to the teacher of any secondary school subject.

COMMONLY USED VISUAL AIDS

Some materials are utilized so generally in classroom procedures that we tend to take them for granted, failing to recognize their value as teaching aids. Included among visual aids are: the chalkboard, the bulletin board, duplicated material, pictorial material, maps, charts, diagrams, graphs, the so-called realia, and exhibits. You probably are acquainted with the use of these materials. Here we are presenting some suggestions for you to consider as you employ these resources in your teaching.

The Use of the Chalkboard

In most classrooms, the chalkboard is used constantly. The teacher uses it to fulfill various purposes. He may use it to:

1. Write important notices to be brought to the attention of the students
2. List the important points of a discussion
3. Present graphs, diagrams, charts, sketches, and other illustrative material
4. Note homework assignments
5. Call attention to special items of information, summarizations, and the like

Students also can be trained in the proper use of the chalkboard. One member of the class, for example, can be selected to place a brief summarization of the points developed during the course of a discussion. Students can work out the solution of a problem or other aspects of written work, such as a paragraph on pertinent material or an outline of the significant topics in a lesson. The work placed on the chalkboard can then be evaluated by the teacher and the other members of the class. Needed corrections of work placed on the chalkboard by students should be made in such a way that everyone in the class sees and understands them.

When you use the chalkboard, be sure to comply with the following suggestions:

1. Make certain that all students can see the chalkboard. Permit them to move around the room in order to get a better view of it.
2. Take care that the writing is legible and large enough to be read easily by all students.
3. Check the lighting of the room lest there be reflected light or glare on the board.
4. Keep chalkboard and crayon trays clean.
5. Refrain from cluttering the board with much writing; organize the material in such a way that it is easily read.
6. Practice standing to the side of the board as you write so that you can watch the class as you write and avoid obstructing their view of what you are writing.

The Use of the Bulletin Board

At one time it was customary to have a classroom equipped with a small bulletin board on which were posted important official notices. The modern trend is toward having in each classroom a large permanent bulletin board, sometimes extending along the length of one wall. The board usually is made of cork or covered with magnetized material, in order to facilitate the posting and removing of materials. The function to be served by the bulletin board is to present appropriate learning aids, such as pertinent clippings from magazines or newspapers, short articles written by students, diagrams, charts, pictures, and other appropriate illustrations.

The care and arrangement of the bulletin board is important. If a teacher conducts all of his teaching in the same room and does not need to share this room with other teachers, his task is simplified. He can organize the board to meet the particular needs of himself and his classes. If other teachers use the room or if he travels from room to room for his teaching, the keeping of a useful bulletin board becomes more difficult. In any case, material placed on the bulletin board should be (1) pertinent, (2) well arranged, and (3) removed as soon as it has fulfilled its purpose.

Students can be brought into the task of keeping bulletin board material well organized and up to date. They usually experience much satisfaction from participating in a project of this kind. To the extent that the students themselves share in providing materials for showing, they are likely to watch for new items, read them, and benefit from them. Of course, the teacher should not place material on the board without directing the students' attention to it and explaining the reason for its being there.

The Use of Pictorial Representations

Included among pictorial representations are single pictures, posters, postcards, and illustrations appearing in books, pamphlets, magazines, and travel brochures. Pictured material is abundant and much of it can be obtained at little or no cost. Moreover, young people usually respond to their showing with much interest. Appropriate pictures can be used to motivate learning. Publishers of textbooks recognize this fact. Many modern textbooks are well illustrated.

Magazines like the *National Geographic, Look,* and *Life* contain pictures that serve as excellent media for the arousal of interest in various learning areas. Good pictures also can be obtained from numerous agencies, such as chambers of commerce, government departments, tourist agencies, commercial and industrial organizations. You will have little difficulty in collecting interesting and appropriate pictorial material.

The showing of pictures is a relatively simple matter, but you must be sure that everyone in the room can see a picture sufficiently well so that he can note specific details to which you direct the class's attention. The picture also can be passed around the room or projected on a screen. Be careful that you select pictures for viewing that are related to the topic or lesson being discussed and see to it that the students recognize the relationship. Encourage the students to give attention to pictures that are in their textbook by asking questions about them or by commenting on their significance.

Especially appropriate pictures and posters can be mounted attractively and used as room decorations or exhibited on the bulletin board. Even though you like certain pictures or posters very much, do not leave them in view for an entire term or year. After they have served their purpose, remove them, substituting others for them. Pictorial materials have value in arousing student interest and clarifying ideas, if these suggestions are followed:

1. Utilize pictures that present accurate images
2. Use only those pictures that are pertinent to the topic of study
3. Interpret the meaning of the picture
4. Allow sufficient viewing time for each student to comprehend the meaning, without wasting time
5. Assign certain pictures to selected students for their special study and report
6. Encourage students to contribute to the class collection of pictures from newspapers and their own magazines and to supplement class reports with illustrative material
7. Motivate specially talented students to prepare posters for class use

The Use of Maps, Globes, Graphic Materials

You probably have used these types of materials in your own study activities, and are relatively well acquainted with them. Your responsibility as a teacher is to train your students in their proper use, and motivate them to refer to the appropriate aid when the occasion arises.

Various kinds of maps, globes, atlases, and gazettes are indispensable teaching aids for the teacher of the various areas of the social sciences and physical geography. Students need to learn how to interpret these media correctly. Teachers of various subjects, especially teachers of economics and business, need to help their students read and interpret correctly such graphic materials as charts, diagrams, circle and linear graphs, and the like. Students can be encouraged to prepare their own graphic material. Such material must be correct in every detail, of course.

Good maps, charts, diagrams, and other graphic materials can be found in many modern textbooks and other reading matter. You should encourage your students to study these carefully as they read contextual material. You also can place appropriate graphic representations on large cardboards ahead of time, in preparation for class discussion; but detailed construction of charts, graphs, and diagrams should not be overemphasized.

The Use of Realia

Certain supplementary materials often are referred to as realia. They include (1) objects, such as a plant or insect, a piece of furniture (colonial, for example), or a kind of military weapon; (2) models, such as a model of the Parthenon, the human skeleton, or a spinning wheel; and (3) specimens or samples within a general classification (types of igneous rocks, of deciduous plants, or of Greek architecture).

Some teachers are ingenious in helping their students collect or make various types of realia. A field trip is an excellent medium for gathering specimens for study in biology, for example. Visits to museums enable young people to become acquainted with objects with which they otherwise would have little or no experience. Many secondary school students are interested in building models of various kinds. The building of model airplanes, spaceships, and the like seem to have a particular fascination for some boys. There is one caution here, however. The construction of a model may become a class project, but it should not be given an undue amount of class time; neither should the fundamental purpose for the model be lost sight of.

Some suggestions for the use of realia are:

1. If possible, students should have direct experience with objects and specimens.
2. The lecture-demonstration technique should be used if only one specimen is available.
3. If there is a sufficient number of specimens available, they should be studied individually by each class member.
4. In dealing with models, the teacher should call attention to differences between an actual object and its model.

OTHER FORMS OF AUDIO-VISUAL AIDS

Among more complex teaching aids can be included motion pictures, filmstrips, slides, opaque projectors, and machines used in programmed learning. We shall discuss each of these aids briefly.

The Use of Motion Pictures

A motion picture probably is the best substitute for firsthand experience with people, situations, processes, and places removed from the immediate environment of students. Many good motion pictures are now available for use with most of the subjects taught in the secondary school. Since films are expensive, the building of a film library is not possible except in large city school systems. Schools can borrow appropriate films, usually for a small fee, from college or university film libraries, commercial circulating libraries, and some state departments of education. Film catalogs that can be obtained from sources such as these give specific information concerning available films and directions for ordering them. McGraw-Hill Text-Films and Coronet films are popular sources of teaching films.

Students enjoy watching motion pictures. It is your responsibility to make certain that a film you select for viewing is pertinent to the learning situations for which it is intended. You must help the students recognize the purpose to be served by its showing, and direct their attention to its important points. Unless the students are guided in their viewing, they may attend to details that are relatively insignificant. For example, a film dealing with the treatment of tubercular patients was shown to freshmen high school students. The film had been sent to the school from headquarters without previous notice and was to be shown immediately and returned. Hence there had been no time to prepare the students for its viewing. As a result, some of these young people became so intrigued by the antics of a pet cat in the film that they missed its important aspects.

The following suggestions may be helpful for film showing:

1. Preview a film to decide what it is about and whether it is appropriate to your purpose.
2. Arrange to have the projector, screen, and film ready for showing without unnecessary delay.
3. Make certain that you can operate the projector smoothly (perhaps students can be trained to operate it).

4. Explain ahead of time the purpose of the showing and to what the students should be alert. Give them several pivotal questions to consider while they are viewing the film.
5. Refrain from interrupting the showing with questions or comments.
6. Discuss the film with the class as soon after the showing as possible. If you wait too long, details may be forgotten.

The Use of Filmstrips

Filmstrips are available in black and white and in color, and come in the form of stereopticon films and film rolls. Some filmstrips have accompanying records that are synchronized with the pictures, and others are accompanied with text material. They can be run with or without sound. Sometimes a teacher prefers to run them silently and give his own explanation or call attention to specific points. The equipment is relatively inexpensive and is simple to operate. Hence filmstrips are used more frequently than motion pictures.

Like motion pictures, filmstrips should be previewed by the teacher. He should be well acquainted with the teacher's manual that accompanies the filmstrip to make certain that he knows the purpose to be served by showing the filmstrip and that it meets his purpose. The students need to be prepared for the showing. While the filmstrip is being viewed, the teacher can make appropriate comments in order to direct the students' attention to important points. After the viewing, its contents should be discussed and the ideas incorporated in the consideration of the topic for clarification of which it was intended.

The Use of Slides

The utilization of slides is similar to that of filmstrips. A series of related slides can be helpful in bringing the attention of the class to concrete aspects of a lesson. They are available for many different kinds of learning materials. Commercially prepared slides usually are mounted on glass, but you can prepare your own pictures mounted on cardboard.

Arranging for the showing of slides follows the general pattern used for the viewing of other projected materials. Preview the slides and prepare the students for the experience. During the viewing, you can raise questions, make comments, and answer students' questions. Use a pointer to note any specific details. One advantage of using slides is that you can keep any one or more of them on view while you discuss specific points to be noted. Of course, either during or after the showing, apply what has been learned from the viewing to the topic under discussion.

The Use of the Opaque Projector

The opaque projector is a valuable and handy teaching aid. Since it projects opaque material by the use of reflected light, you can project suitable materials on a screen, the chalkboard, or a wall of the classroom. Various types of materials that can be projected are a page from a book, a chart or map, a cartoon, a song, a clipping from a newspaper or magazine, and similar illustrative material. It is advisable to have the material properly labeled for showing and filing.

TEACHING MACHINES AND PROGRAMMED INSTRUCTION

A recent innovation in the use of teaching aids usually is referred to as programmed instruction or programmed learning. In this form of learning, a series of related problem materials is presented to the student. He is required to respond to each step in the series. He is apprised immediately of the correct response and can evaluate his performance. In its fundamental concept, programmed instruction is similar to the purpose of the workbook technique (except that in the latter procedure, the student usually does not have the correct response immediately available but must seek it in a textbook or other source of information).

The Essentials of Programmed Instruction

Programmed instruction has made great strides, especially in our large cities. Much thought and experimentation already has gone into meeting the various types of problems that arise in connection with its best implementation. The following not only describes the process but also gives insight into how it can be developed and utilized in the teaching-learning process:

THE ESSENTIALS OF PROGRAMMED INSTRUCTION [1]

The essentials of programmed instruction are (*a*) presenting the student with a series of logically related problem materials; (*b*) requiring the student to make a response to each step in the series; and (*c*) immediately apprising the student of the correct response.

Together with the student the programmed material comprises a teaching-learning system with immediate feedback. The rate of learning is determined by the student's ability to absorb new bits of information.

Linear and Intrinsic Programs

There are two kinds of programming systems in current use. The *linear* method utilizes a step-by-step procedure of learner-constructed responses. Progress through the program depends on the learner's making correct responses. Incorrect responses are immediately corrected.

The *intrinsic* method of programming is also known as *branching*. It presents the student with a number of multiple-choice items. Wrong responses are corrected through branching. While in a linear program all students must read every frame in an identical sequence, intrinsic programs provide for skipping items or taking an abbreviated track.

Advocates of intrinsic programming regard the teaching-learning act as a communication process. For example, according to N. A. Crowder, the response primarily serves the purpose of informing the student as to whether or not the initial communication process was successful.

If the response is wrong the program assumes that the error in learning occurred somewhere before the response was made, and therefore directs the student into a remedial or corrective sequence. Schematically, the items (or frames) in an intrinsic program may be arranged as follows:

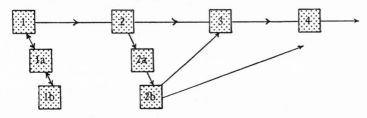

B. F. Skinner and other advocates of linear programming maintain that the act of responding tends to cause learning. This necessitates breaking-

[1] Reprinted from *Curriculum and Materials* by permission of the Board of Education of the City of New York, XVII, No. 2 (Winter, 1963), 4–5.

down and ordering information into small steps so that the student can always answer correctly. Each item in a linear program is presented in an ordered sequence. Schematically, the items in a linear program may be arranged as follows:

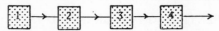

Programmed instruction makes it possible to achieve some of the critical functions of the teaching-learning process through self-instruction. It has the following advantages:

1. Each student progresses at his own rate.
2. It provides the learner with immediate feedback and reinforcement.
3. It can free the teacher from some of the less creative aspects of teaching.
4. It provides a method for the controlled study of teaching and learning.

Teaching Machines and Programmed Instruction

Until recently, the proliferation of teaching machines has overshadowed the concept of programmed instruction in the popular mind. However, it is important to indicate that a significant difference exists between the two.

Teaching machines are inherently stimulus devices and as such can be considered audio-visual aids, similar to film projectors or tape recorders. On the other hand, programmed instruction is a particular method of presenting learning material. While teaching machines are the "hardware" (with varying degrees of complexity), programmed instruction is the implementation of a number of theoretical principles of learning.

Programmed material can conceivably be presented by any number or types of machines, including film projectors and/or tape recorders. In another sense, programming can be compared to careful teaching which thoroughly analyzes materials and presents them to pupils in small, progressive steps.

The utilization of programmed instruction and/or teaching machines presents two distinct problems. The acceptance of programmed instruction in education will depend, at least in a good measure, on its theoretical soundness and practical implementation. The choice of the particular vehicle or vehicles (teaching machines) for the presentation of programmed instruction will depend on factors of economy and mechanical efficiency.

Implications for Curriculum

Programmed instruction has numerous implications for curriculum research and development. In the evaluation of curriculum materials one of the greatest sources of error is teacher variation. Porter suggests that "mechanical devices can go far toward eliminating the 'teacher effect' in educational investigations." [2]

[2] D. Porter, "A Critical Review of a Portion of the Literature on Teaching Devices," in A. S. Lumsdaine and R. Glaser, *Teaching Machines and Programmed Learning* (Washington, D.C.: National Education Assoc., 1960), p. 126.

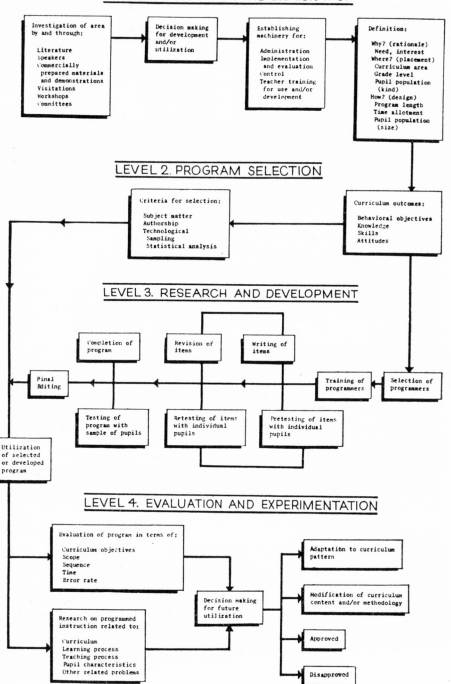

LEVEL 1. INFORMATION AND EXPLORATION

Investigation of area by and through:

Literature
Speakers
Commercially
  prepared materials
  and demonstrations
Visitations
Workshops
Committees

Decision making for development and/or utilization

Establishing machinery for:

Administration
Implementation
  and evaluation
Control
Teacher training
  for use and/or
  development

Definition:

Why? (rationale)
  Need, interest
Where? (placement)
  Curriculum area
  Grade level
  Pupil population
    (kind)
How? (design)
  Program length
  Time allotment
  Pupil population
    (size)

LEVEL 2. PROGRAM SELECTION

Criteria for selection:

Subject matter
Authorship
Technological
Sampling
Statistical analysis

Curriculum outcomes:

Behavioral objectives
Knowledge
Skills
Attitudes

LEVEL 3. RESEARCH AND DEVELOPMENT

Completion of program

Revision of items

Writing of items

Final Editing

Training of programmers

Selection of programmers

Testing of program with sample of pupils

Retesting of items with individual pupils

Pretesting of items with individual pupils

Utilization of selected or developed program

LEVEL 4. EVALUATION AND EXPERIMENTATION

Evaluation of program in terms of:

Curriculum objectives
Scope
Sequence
Time
Error rate

Decision making for future utilization

Adaptation to curriculum pattern

Modification of curriculum content and/or methodology

Approved

Research on programmed instruction related to:

Curriculum
Learning process
Teaching process
Pupil characteristics
Other related problems

Disapproved

Fig. 5.—Programmed instruction activities flow chart.

The development of curriculum under programmed instruction becomes subject to specific principles which in turn are directly related to a theoretical system. Stolurow [3] suggests that programmed instruction offers a method of reexamining the instructional process itself rather than, as is usually the case, shoring up existing procedures by adding additional activities.

Most persons associated with teaching machines and/or programmed instruction feel that they are here to stay.[4] It would be unfortunate, however, if the educational possibilities of programmed instruction were to go the way of all too many suggested innovations.

The most significant contribution that programmed instruction may be able to make to education is that of providing educators with a sound theory of teaching and learning.

Some of the ramifications of programmed instruction, and its implications for curriculum, may be seen from the flow chart that follows.

Values of Programmed Instruction

Learning material that is carefully and completely programmed enables the student to progress at his own rate of speed. A bright student is not held back, and a slower student can work as slowly as he finds it necessary for mastery and understanding of the particular learning material. This approach also enables the student to vary his speed of progress in terms of his interest and special talent.

The challenge to the teacher is to discover how best to use this new teaching aid in the teaching situation. Although it is an aid that has been constructed by educators, it is tested by students in the teaching-learning situation. Both teachers and students need to perfect ways of utilizing this new tool for the purpose intended —that of helping the learner in his pursuit of an education.

Teaching machines and audio-instructional methods and devices never can serve as a substitute for teachers, yet, in the words of Stolurow,[5] they are likely to exert a considerable influence on the future education of our youth:

With reluctance, but with the hope that they might be interesting, if not

---

[3] L. M. Stolurow, *Teaching by Machine* (Washington, D.C.: Office of Education, U.S. Dept. of Health, Education and Welfare, 1961), p. 4.

[4] *Ibid.*, p. 145.

[5] Lawrence M. Stolurow, "Implications of Current Research and Future Trends," (On Programed Instruction), *The Journal of Educational Research,* June–July, 1962, p. 526.

useful, eleven predictions were made about the future of auto-instructional methods and devices. They are:

1. These methods and devices are here to stay.
2. Several things will be done to acquaint teachers with the potentiality of these developments.
3. The comparative study of live and automated teaching will stop.
4. Future research will concern itself with discovering the important characteristics of the materials and methods.
5. These developments will lead to a theory of teaching.
6. Courses will be revised as a result of the new insights provided.
7. Basic changes in our thinking about what a course is will take place.
8. Research will demonstrate the importance of sequence factors.
9. We will see a new form of dynamic individualized programming called ability-pattern programming.
10. The devices of the future will be either books (programmed or scrambled) or computer-based machines; small devices will drop out.
11. Learning from auto-instructional programming will be shown to be capable of aiding persons to solve problems creatively.

Professor S. L. Pressey sometimes recognized as the father of machine teaching presents excellent thought-provoking observations on current methods and devices in programmed instruction. In his summary comments he says: [6]

Typically, enthusiasts carry a new idea to extremes; soon these are eliminated, and the proven residual becomes part of educational practice. The writer believes that certain kinds of changes will occur in future programed learning. (a) Enthusiastic programers will soon give up trying to replace most textbooks and other core material with thousands of "frames" viewed seriatim. Drill and rote learning may be so handled. But the larger usefulness of auto-instruction will be found in co-ordination with, not replacement of, other materials and methods. However, the programers' efforts may bring improvement in these other materials. The experiments cited . . . found that very direct and simple expository statements were better than the more formal textbook prose. It is hoped that programers, textbook writers, and teachers may combine efforts to produce co-ordinated texts, programs, and methods of using them far better than anything now available. (b) Once it is realized that most auto-instruction can use objective rather than write-in responses, new potentials as to both convenience *and* effectiveness will be reached. (c) Abandonment of the "many-easy-questions" concept will both greatly decrease bulk and increase incisiveness. (d) Devices can be far more simple and inexpensive than those now on the market—perhaps simply a

[6] Sidney L. Pressey, "Basic Unresolved Teaching-Machine Problems," *Theory into Practice*, I, No. 1 (February, 1962), 37.

3 x 5 card. Machines can also serve each learner's needs far more closely. Use should then increase greatly. (*e*) Evaluation should realistically take account of both values and costs in time and trouble as well as in money under everyday conditions. Such evaluations will show that auto-instruction can be made both far more convenient and practical, and more useful, than is now generally recognized.

RADIO, RECORDINGS, AND TELEVISION

School people are becoming increasingly alert to the value of radio broadcasts, recordings, and television programs as teaching-learning aids. The utilization of these media for educational as well as entertainment purposes among people at large has done much to enhance their worth within schools as well as outside the school. You probably are acquainted with their use as educational media. Hence we shall offer only a few suggestions for their application.

The Use of the Radio in Education

The radio probably can be used most effectively by teachers of music, English, science, and the social studies. Some commercially sponsored radio programs, for example, are excellent media for helping students (1) improve their knowledge of current happenings and other news events, (2) gain an understanding of scientific advances, (3) learn to appreciate artistic production, and (4) become acquainted with leaders in various fields as the latter relate their experiences and expound on their points of view.

Some of the larger school systems have instituted their own radio systems. The Cleveland school system was the first to experiment with radio broadcasting on a large scale. During the school year, Station WBOE operates daily from 8 A.M. to 4 P.M. Programs are broadcast for the purpose of giving demonstration lessons and for bringing to young people many stimulating and enriching programs. Other school systems also have access to radio programs throughout the school day. Some of these are broadcast by the school system, and others are commercially produced.

Many secondary schools have a sufficient number of radio sets so that they can be used in individual classrooms. Teachers need training in their utilization, however, in order to become proficient in selecting appropriate programs and in preparing students for participation in them. One advantage of the radio is that it affords students an opportunity to learn how to listen thoughtfully so that they benefit from the experience. A good radio listener gives active attention to what he hears, especially if the material included in the broadcast is discussed immediately after the listening and associated with the specific purposes of the lesson topic under consideration.

An effective learning aid is the presentation of student-planned and student-conducted radio broadcasts. These programs can include dramatic presentations, panel discussions, a survey of student activities, musical programs, quiz programs, reports of sports events, and many others. Some of these student-sponsored activities are disseminated over the school address system; others are broadcast to interested persons outside the school by way of the cooperation of the local broadcasting stations. The radio workshop has spread, and is an excellent outlet for adolescent creativity.

The Use of Recordings

Commercially transcribed or school-prepared recordings have considerable value as learning aids. Often, it is not possible for a particular group of students to listen to the original broadcast. A wire tape or disc recording then can be played at an appropriate time. At present, many commercial radio companies make recordings or transcriptions of programs that are suitable for school use. Some schools maintain a library of pertinent materials that can be borrowed by individual teachers.

As the need for it arises, an appropriate recording technique can be used as a teaching aid in various subject fields. Of particular value to the teacher of music is the recording of a musical composition. The learners are motivated to direct their attention to specific musical qualities, such as rhythm, tone quality, cadence, and theme. A class in literature can gain much enjoyment and profit from listening to a recorded excerpt from a Shakespearean play, for example. In many foreign language classes, recordings are used as the bases of instruction in the proper use of the language, voice quality, pronunciation, and organization of ideas. The language laboratory is becoming a fixture in the teaching of foreign languages in many schools.

It is becoming common practice in speech classes to record the voice and speaking habits of individual learners. It often is difficult for a teacher to convince students that they have certain speech difficulties. The effect on a young person of listening to his own voice and delivery can be an effective motivator toward his speech improvement.

The Use of Television Programs

At present, the utilization of television programs for educational purposes is receiving considerable attention from school people. In their attempts to tie in this popular medium of mass communication with school needs, educators are encountering several problems. Telecasts vary in their educational value. The installation of adequate sets is expensive. Arranging for the viewing during school hours of worthwhile programs, such as eyewitness reports of important happenings, legislative sessions, significant conferences, holiday celebrations, and the like, may disrupt scheduled class sessions. Teachers need training in the proper use of this teaching aid.

Young people are avid television viewers, but they are not always discriminating in their selections, however. Exciting programs, such as Westerns and mystery stories, and variety shows seem to have popular appeal. These often conflict in time, especially with after-school programs that teachers wish their students to view. It often is difficult to convince a young person that he should give up watching a particularly engrossing program for one that may have educational value for him but that he finds much less interesting.

In spite of high costs and difficulties of operation, some civic organizations and schools are experimenting with this medium. Closed- and open-circuit television is coming into some use. An extremely interesting experiment in educational television was begun in 1961. Known as the Midwest Project on Airborne Television Instruction, this project brings televised educational materials into hundreds of school systems in states such as Indiana, Illinois, Kentucky, Ohio, Michigan, and Wisconsin. The cost of the experiment has been carried by the Ford Foundation and various contributors from industry.

Various agencies are providing schools with appropriate televised materials for school use. For example, television cameras are now so constructed as to make it possible to project the field under a microscope onto a TV screen in such a way as to show an enlarged plant cell. Through this approach, it is possible for everyone, at the same time, to view it and for the teacher to interpret what is being observed. This is likely to be more effective than having each student in turn observe through the eyepiece of the microscope.

Opinions differ on the value of television as a teaching-learning aid. Miner calls attention to the following: [7]

Educational television has certain values which are peculiar to it. It does give the effect of a single teacher-pupil relationship; it can bring the expert teacher who has spent hours of planning and research to *every* child; it can focus attention on one tiny object which has been greatly magnified; and it can bring the home and school together as parent and pupil view the same lesson. It can motivate the learner to extend his learning far beyond the television lessons; it can also stimulate the classroom teacher to become more creative. It can be used to overcome the customary 20–30 year lag between educational knowledge and practice in the American classroom. It has many other values which could be developed into an exhaustive list.

There are, however, certain disadvantages which must readily be admitted. Instruction of high quality by the best qualified television teacher does not alone insure optimum learning; the classroom teacher does, in the final analysis, determine the success or failure of educational television in the classroom. Lessons prepared for a general grade level may not meet the individual needs of a specific class. Furthermore, all television lessons do not provide the best possible teaching-learning situations. The classroom teacher's load will not be lessened with one less preparation but may be extended as he attempts to take full advantage of the educational television lesson and its accompanying teachers' guide. The mechanical difficulties may be so great as to create a time-wasting period. Even the hoped-for relationship between home and school may fall far short of reality. . . .

The television and the classroom teachers share joint responsibility for (a) providing a more creative and challenging teaching-learning situation; (b) utilizing the best in modern research and principles of education; (c) mastering the mechanical devices; and (d) functioning as a teaching team.

The learner is required to: (a) change his habit of using TV for passive entertainment to one of active involvement; (b) adjust to more than one teacher's presentation; (c) recognize the value of televised instruction.

[7] Adah L. Miner, "Teachers, Students—and TV," *Educational Leadership,* April, 1963, pp. 444–45, 489.

Regardless of whether meager or rich televised material is available for your use, you need to follow suggestions for its viewing similar to those indicated for the use of motion pictures. Insofar as possible, acquaint yourself with the purpose and content of the telecast; prepare your students for its viewing; and discuss its implications with them as soon after they have seen it as is possible.

THE USE OF COMMUNITY RESOURCES

In the preceding pages, we have discussed the value in the teaching-learning process of students' being exposed to various audio-visual aids. Good as these media of instruction are, young people still need to experience actual situations such as they encounter in their life outside the school. Within the school's community there may be many resources that can add zest to learning. Provision should be made for students to know about and work with them.

The utilization of community resources can be handled in one of two ways. Resource people and materials can be brought into the school, or the students can go out into the community and learn about conditions and activities at firsthand. As a student teacher, you probably will have little opportunity to participate in the organization of community-pointed projects, but you can become alert to the many learner opportunities that are available in a school's community.

Bringing the Community into the School

Some community resources can be brought directly into the school for learning purposes. These include (1) visits to the school by community leaders who are experts in their field, and (2) community-sponsored exhibits and displays.

Talks by visitors to the school. You will find that in most school communities there are men and women who can offer much valuable information to students and who are more than willing to share their knowledge or experience with young people. The list of available visitors may be long and include such persons as government officials, civic leaders, business people, leaders in industry and commerce, college representatives, social workers, religious leaders, travelers, newspaper men, scientists, and, depending on the size and major interests of the community, many others. Care must be taken by the school's administrative staff and teachers, however, that an invited speaker's purpose in visiting the school. is not to spread partisan propaganda or to engage in a commercial advertising campaign.

If the talk has general value for the student population as a whole, it may be given in a school assembly. If it deals with a specific area of learning, however, it is best to limit the audience to several classes in that subject, or to a single class. In any case, the speaker should be informed ahead of time concerning the size of his audience, the background of the students, and the specific purpose that is to be served by his talk.

Students need to be prepared for the visit. They should be alerted to the relationship of the talk to their learning activities, be given some information concerning the speaker's background, and reminded of their responsibility for giving courteous attention to what he has to say. They also should be encouraged to ask pertinent questions concerning points made by him that may need further clarification. They should be warned against displaying an argumentative attitude. As soon after the visit as is possible, teachers and students should discuss the contents of the talk objectively and impersonally, relating it to their study activities.

Exhibits and displays in the school. Some community agencies, such as art galleries, museums, industrial plants, business concerns, and travel agencies, prepare and lend to schools appropriate exhibits and displays that have for their purpose the bringing to the attention of young people certain materials with which they otherwise might have little or no experience. Such exhibits or displays often are placed in a corridor for viewing by all students. Some secondary schools have "display" rooms in which pictures, objects, or specimens are housed and to which interested classes are escorted for study purposes.

The students themselves can be motivated to arrange for classroom showing of objects or specimens that they or their parents have collected. The parents of one high school student, for example, had an interesting collection of shaving mugs. Another student had collected dolls wearing clothes that represented the dress customs of national groups and of historic eras. One student might have photographs of places visited by his parents and relatives. Another could bring stamp or china collections, or specimens of leaves, wood, and the like. Viewing and discussing such collections can have considerable value as aids to learning.

School administrators and individual teachers have a definite responsibility for the care of school exhibited materials. Many articles may have monetary as well as sentimental value. They need to be handled in such a way that they are not damaged and that the same number of articles is returned as was loaned. Young people sometimes are careless in their treatment of things that do not belong to them. A student may be attracted by an article and attempt to remove it from the collection. Hence, whether a collection is entrusted to the school for a short or longer period of time, it is the responsibility of both the staff and the student body to ensure that nothing happens to the material exhibited during its stay in the school.

Taking Students into the Community

Individual students, small groups of students, or entire classes can be sent or taken into the community for various out-of-school learning experiences. Through the following of such procedures, students can be introduced to real life situations that may possess worthwhile implications for classroom learnings. Included among such experiences are interviews, field trips, surveys, and service activities. We shall discuss each briefly.

Interviews with community leaders. We have referred to bringing visitors into the school for teaching-learning purposes. At times, however, a busy representative of a civic agency, an industrial or business executive, or a member of a professional group may be willing to share his experience with secondary-school students, but finds it impossible or inconvenient to visit the school during regular school hours. It then is advisable to arrange to have several students go to him for an interview. Interviewing community leaders is an excellent learning experience for young people.

Sending students out for interview sessions requires much preplanning. The consent of the intended interviewee must be obtained and arrangements made with him or her for the time, place, and conduct of the interview. The interviewers are then selected and parental consent obtained for their participation in the project. Since an interview is primarily a question-answer situation, the teacher and class involved must decide on the purpose to be served. The kind and number of pivotal questions to be asked by the students can be determined by them. The interviewing committee also needs to be briefed concerning the proper conduct of an interview, such as beginning the interview, taking notes, asking for clarification of points made by the interviewee, and expressing gratitude for his granting the interview.

The committee then reports back to the class concerning the interview. It is advisable to encourage the students to write brief reports or summaries of the interview immediately after it is held, so that they do not forget important details when they present their class reports.

Going on field trips. Class excursions into the community have valuable educational outcomes. Students enjoy experiencing, at firsthand, those situations or conditions about which they have read in their textbooks or discussed in class. Field trips also provide opportunities for students to become better acquainted with their community and to appreciate its offerings.

Field trips can be arranged with relative ease on the elementary school level. Since one teacher is with his class for the entire day, he can plan to spend a part of the day outside the school without interrupting other class schedules. The situation is different in the secondary school. Recitation periods usually are from 45 to 50 minutes in length. Rarely can a trip be planned that will not need more time. Hence class scheduling is disrupted. Administrative approval and the cooperation of teachers of other subjects are needed to conduct a worthwhile field project. Another way to meet this problem is for the teacher and his class to take the trip after school hours on a regular school day or on a Saturday.

Visits to museums, art galleries, industrial plants, business houses, and other community centers are interesting and worthwhile projects. Much planning for their conduct is essential, however. Advance arrangements need to be made with the place to be visited, and transportation facilities arranged. The students should be alerted to the reasons for taking the trip, where they are going, and what they can expect to find when they get there. They also should have sufficient background of knowledge to make the trip worthwhile and for them to recognize its relationship to their current topic of study. A set of questions can be constructed as a guide to their listening and viewing activities on the trip.

The parents' approval of their children's going on the trip must be obtained. Some schools take care of this situation by having the parents of each student in the school sign a slip at the beginning of each term or year whereby they grant their consent for the carrying on of such projects.

Before the trip, the students need to be reminded concerning their proper behavior in public conveyances and in the place or building visited. Throughout the trip, the display of good manners must be insisted on by the teacher or teachers in charge. Younger adolescents, especially, may regard an excursion as an occasion for giving expression to their youthful energies. They require training in self-control as a means of developing habits of restrained conduct in public places.

As soon after the trip as is possible, its outcomes should be evaluated. This procedure can result in a lively and constructive discussion. The students probably will want to discuss some of their personal experiences during the trip, and their reactions to what they have heard or observed. Be sure that they understand the extent to which the trip and its outcomes are related to classroom study. They also can be encouraged to write, as a class project, letters of appreciation to their hosts and other persons who helped them benefit from the experience.

Other Avenues of Contact with the Community

Groups of students or individual students can participate in various community projects to the profit of themselves and their classmates. Among these projects are surveys, and service projects.

Surveys. As a phase of classroom study in social science, for example, students can be motivated to study kind and amount of play space available in the community, housing conditions, welfare facilities, and other community situations. Student-conducted surveys can be extremely valuable to the extent that they help develop among adolescents an interest in community affairs that carries over into their adult lives.

For a survey to have value, the students need to be motivated to enter wholeheartedly into the project, work at it assiduously and objectively, and recognize the relationship of the project to educational objectives. The findings resulting from well-planned and organized, and objectively conducted student surveys often have civic or social implications. These can be brought to the attention of community members through newspaper reports, parent-teacher meetings, public assemblies, local radio broadcasts, and similar media of communication. Then, through the combined efforts of school people, students, and parents and friends, efforts can be encouraged to effect needed civic or social changes within the community.

Service projects. Secondary school students can be encouraged to participate, on a volunteer basis, in various community activities. To be of benefit to the students, however, the participation should be related to school study. For example, girls who are planning to enter nursing as a career or who are studying home economics can serve, after school hours, as volunteer aides in neighboring hospitals. Boys can be encouraged to take part in clean-up campaigns. School bands can participate in local parades or sports events; school orchestras can share in community musical programs. Commercial students can offer their services to community welfare agencies. Older adolescents, especially those who are planning to teach, can volunteer to serve as playground assistants or help with groups of children in social agencies.

Whatever is done by young people in the community under school sponsorship needs to be carefully supervised by members of the school staff. Young people usually are extremely interested in engaging in such activities. Their enthusiasm may run away with their good sense. They need to be restrained from overdoing or from engaging in undesirable activities. For example, during a national emergency, the girl students of one high school were so eager to earn money to purchase government bonds that they canvased neighborhoods removed from their own, ringing doorbells and pleading to be given housecleaning jobs in order to raise money. So great was their patriotic zeal that they failed to recognize the possible danger to themselves of this kind of undertaking.

The school was partly to blame for this situation in that considerable pressure had been exerted to make a good showing in its contribution to the cause.

As a teacher, you will need to realize that you share with parents the protection of your students' welfare. You need to be careful that you do not encourage any of your students to engage in community projects until or unless you are convinced that such activities will bring no harm to the participants. Before you permit any student to engage in a community-pointed experience, become thoroughly acquainted with it, make all necessary arrangements for the student's participation, supervise his activities, and direct his and the class's attention to the educational significance of the project.

QUESTIONS AND TOPICS FOR DISCUSSION

1. Endeavor to discover what supplementary learning aids for your subject are available in your school. Consult your cooperating teacher about the extent of their use.
2. Evaluate the textbooks in your subject field with which you are acquainted from the point of view of coverage, reliability, authenticity, and recency. Which one seems to be most suitable to your needs?
3. How well are you acquainted with available teaching materials in your school library? Neighboring public library?
4. Look through any supplementary reading material you have collected. Appraise its value in light of the questions on pages 256–57.
5. To what extent and how does your cooperating teacher use the chalkboard?
6. List appropriate uses of graphic material in teaching your subject.
7. Which do you prefer to use: films, filmstrips, slides? Give reasons for your opinion.
8. How much training have you had in the use of teaching machines and programmed learning? What purposes do you think are best served by their utilization?
9. What difficulties can you encounter in attempting to utilize radio and television as teaching aids?
10. To what extent and how does your school take advantage of community resources as teaching aids?

SELECTED REFERENCES

CARTER, W. L., HANSEN, C. W., and McKIM, M. G. *Learning to Teach in the Secondary School.* New York: Macmillan Co., 1962.

CROW, L. D., RITCHIE, H. E., and CROW, ALICE. *Education in the Secondary School*. New York: American Book Co., 1961.

DALE, E. *Audio-Visual Methods in Teaching* (rev. ed.). New York: Holt, Rinehart & Winston, Inc., 1954.

DRAYER, A. M. *Problems and Methods in High School Teaching*. Boston: D. C. Heath & Co., 1963.

FRY, E. *Teaching Machines and Programmed Learning: An Introduction to Audioinstruction*. New York: McGraw-Hill Book Co., Inc., 1963.

GUGGENHEIM, F. *Programmed Instruction: A Resource Guide for Curriculum Workers*. Curriculum Research Report. Board of Education of the City of New York, 1963.

KINDER, J. S. *Audio-Visual Materials and Techniques* (2nd ed.). New York: American Book Co., 1959.

McKEAN, R. C. *Principles and Methods in Secondary Education*. Columbus, Ohio: Charles E. Merrill Books, Inc., 1962.

SCHORLING, R., and BATCHELDER, H. T. *Student Teaching in the Secondary Schools* (rev. ed.). New York: McGraw-Hill Book Co., Inc., 1956.

SCHULTZ, R. *Student Teaching in the Secondary Schools*. New York: Harcourt, Brace & World, Inc., 1959.

WIGGINS, S. P. *Successful High School Teaching*. Boston: Houghton Mifflin Co., 1958.

11

CLASSROOM MANAGEMENT AND OUT–OF–CLASS ACTIVITIES

The general public tends to regard teaching on the secondary level as limited to the process of guiding learning in specific subject matter fields. By this time, you probably have discovered that teaching, in its broadest connotation, includes the assuming of responsibility for various other activities that have educational implications in that they can enhance learning outcomes. In this chapter, we discuss briefly the role of the teacher in (1) classroom management and (2) out-of-class activities.

ROLE OF THE TEACHER IN CLASSROOM MANAGEMENT

In other chapters, we refer to ways in which you can assist your cooperating teacher in caring for certain routines that can facilitate learning. Here we review the significance of the various items that are generally included under the heading of classroom management.

As you observe your cooperating teacher and his class in action, you may be impressed by the fact that the room appears to be a pleasant, comfortable place and that class activities proceed smoothly and with little or no confusion or loss of time. This is not an accident; rather does it reflect the teacher's recognition of the need to provide for the management of routines in such a way that they do not interfere with the primary purpose of the class session —the mastery of specific learning materials.

Purposes Served by Good Classroom Management

The proper conduct of class routines not only frees the teacher and students for teaching-learning activities, but has educational value to the extent that thereby the students are helped to develop

284

constructive work habits. Some routine activities may have to be performed by the teacher. Others can be delegated to the students. In either case, they should be definitely organized at the beginning of the term or year, with the students participating, insofar as possible, in their planning. Then, in order to develop good habits of work, whatever procedures are selected should be followed consistently so long as they serve the purposes for which they have been selected.

Much has been said and written about the educational value of stimulating young people's interest by presenting them with the new and the different. This psychological principle does not apply to those details of management that serve as the bases for getting things done quickly and efficiently. An orderly, businesslike atmosphere in the classroom encourages the students to devote their energies to study activities and helps them maintain an attitude of desirable control of their behavior. To the extent that students understand the purposes of certain classroom procedures and have assisted in setting them up, effective and well-established routines can set the stage for a high degree of efficiency in the conduct of teaching-learning activities.

Types of Routine Activities in the Classroom

The master teacher seeks to achieve an attitude of freedom and informality in the classroom that is conducive to interested and active learning experiences on the part of the students. At the same time, certain practical routines need to be more or less formalized in order to avoid waste of time and energy. The following list of items can be regarded as routine matters. Using this checklist as a guide, evaluate routine procedures in the classroom or classrooms in which you are having your student teaching experiences. Also, keep this list in mind when you yourself become a regular teacher.

Suggestions for Performing Classroom Routines

As you read the list of items in Table 10, you discover that many of them are self-explanatory. Yet, a few suggestions concerning their use may be of value to you.

TABLE 10

INSTRUCTIONAL CHECKLIST ON ROUTINE *

(*Directions:* Mark each item of routine on the list as follows: If the item is entirely satisfactory, place a check (√) in the last column opposite it. If the item needs attention, place a cross (x) in the first column opposite it.)

Items of routine	Needs attention	Satis-factory

1. Physical Condition of the Room
   a. Adjusting shades to control light and glare
   b. Controlling artificial light
   c. Regulating room temperature
   d. Regulating room ventilation
2. Tidiness of the Room
   a. Removing waste from desks, tables, and floors
   b. Caring for blackboard appearance
   c. Caring for bulletin-board appearance
   d. Caring for pictures and other decorations
   e. Caring for appearance of storage spaces, shelves, bookcases, maps, and other equipment
3. The Movement of Pupils
   a. Entering the room
   b. Taking seats
   c. Going to and from board or other work places
   d. Getting books, supplies, or other materials
   e. Leaving the room
4. Seating of Pupils
   a. Planning for the arrangement of desks, chairs, or tables (e.g., semicircle or hollow square)
   b. Assigning seats to pupils
   c. Revising the seating to meet needs (e.g., providing seats for groups who need to work together)
   d. Providing for individual needs (e.g., adjusting seats for better seeing, hearing)
5. Systematic Procedures
   a. Beginning all activities promptly
   b. Knowing the names of pupils
   c. Making announcements
   d. Providing continuous activity
   e. Keeping everybody busy
   f. Initiating self-direction
   g. Assigning tasks
   h. Checking results
   i. Ending all activities on time		

* Raleigh Schorling and Howard T. Batchelder, *Student Teaching in Secondary Schools* (3rd ed.; New York: McGraw-Hill Book Co., Inc., 1956), pp. 113–14. Reprinted with permission.

INSTRUCTIONAL CHECKLIST ON ROUTINE (Continued)

Items of routine	Needs attention	Satis-factory
6. Handling Materials and Supplies		
a. Preparing for the use of materials and supplies		
b. Distributing materials and supplies to pupils		
c. Collecting materials and supplies from pupils		
d. Placing materials and supplies in storage		
e. Providing for uniformity in labeling and folding papers		
f. Passing or collecting notebooks or papers		
g. Providing for the display of instructional materials		
7. Making Records and Reports		
a. Checking attendance		
b. Recording pupils' marks		
c. Collecting data for the office		
d. Making periodic reports		
8. Courtesy in the Classroom: Obtaining Courtesy in		
a. Pupil-to-pupil relationships		
b. Pupil-to-teacher relationships		
c. Teacher-to-pupil relationships		
d. Reception of visitors		

Physical condition of the room. It is important that there is sufficient light in all parts of the room so that no students suffer from eyestrain. According to the direction of the sun, those students who sit near the windows may be exposed to a glare, necessitating the drawing down of the window shades; but doing this may prevent students who are removed from the windows from having enough light by which to read or write. Hence artificial lighting may be required. You can assist your cooperating teacher by caring for this detail of class management. Watch the direction taken by the sun and adjust the shades so as to avoid glare or shadows. Regulate the artificial light as needed. Also, when the class leaves the room, make certain that the electric light is turned off, especially if the room is not to be occupied during the next period. Teachers' carelessness in this matter can cost the school community a considerable amount of money.

The proper regulation of the room's temperature and its ventilation are matters that should be a primary concern of the teacher. As he and the class become involved in lesson activities, they tend to be unaware of the fact that the room is becoming overly warm and "stuffy." The temperature should range between 68° and 72° F., and the humidity should be about 40 to 50 per cent.

The teacher needs to consult the thermometer occasionally and see to it that the room is well ventilated. Care must be taken, however, that no student sits in a draft. It may be advisable to ventilate the room at the beginning of a period. If the room has regular double windows, the top one should be opened, rather than the bottom one. In many schools, the opening and closing of windows is the teacher's responsibility. Students are not permitted to handle window poles.

One matter having to do with physical conditions that is not mentioned in the list is the size of students' desks and seats. Junior high school students tend to differ greatly in height. The seats in the classroom must be so adjusted to their needs that their feet can rest comfortably on the floor. This is taken care of in most schools by having furniture of different sizes. The teacher should so seat the students that the seating arrangements are satisfactory. If this is not possible with the desks and chairs already in the room, proper adjustment of furniture may be needed.

Neatness and attractiveness of the room. In secondary schools where it is the practice for more than one teacher to hold class sessions in the same room, it sometimes is difficult to keep the room attractively decorated with pertinent material, unless the room is used by members of the same subject department who are willing to cooperate with one another in providing appropriate materials. Regardless of the number of teachers who occupy a room during the course of a school day, however, each group using the room is responsible for its neatness. Students can be delegated in turn to pass a wastepaper basket around the room toward the end of the period to gather scraps of paper or other materials from the desks or floor. This can be done quietly as a matter of habit, with a minimum of interruption of regular class activity. Students should be discouraged from leaving waste materials in their desks. An occasional inspection and cleaning out of students' desks may be necessary. The teacher should set a good example by keeping his own desk uncluttered.

The storing of needed materials also requires constant attention.

Students can be trained to take care of this routine. Classroom storage space often is inadequate, especially if several teachers use the same room. In such cases, certain shelves can be allocated to each teacher. These individual allotments should be respected by the various teachers and their students. Books, maps, equipment, and other materials should be replaced in proper storage space at the end of each period during which they have been used.

We cannot stress too strongly the need for each class to make certain that (1) all chalkboards are cleaned at the end of every period and (2) bulletin boards are attractively arranged and contain only pertinent material that is removed as soon as its purpose for being displayed has been fulfilled. Students can be delegated to attend to the care of chalkboards and bulletin boards.

Distribution of material. Much time and energy can be saved if books, supplies, and other materials can be distributed according to a preplanned system of procedure. Certain students can be named as monitors of various materials to be used during the period. At a directive from the teacher, while the class is assembling, they can obtain the materials from the closet and distribute them, and then collect and return them to the closet at the end of the period.

If written homework has been prepared for reading by the teacher, these can be *collected* by the first student in each row. This procedure usually saves more time than having the papers passed down the line. Some students, as they pass papers, stop to compare what other students have done with their own contribution. The teacher also can work out a timesaving plan for *returning* papers. Rather than calling each student by name, he can have the papers arranged according to rows, and have them returned to appropriate students by someone in each row. There is one slight objection to this mode of returning corrected papers. An adolescent may be sensitive about having other students see the mark he earned on a test, for example. He would prefer to keep this a matter between his teacher and himself.

Movement of students in the school. Some schools have relatively strict regulations about students wandering around the building during recitation periods. You need to acquaint yourself with the rules of the school in which you are working, and follow whatever its policy may be. In some schools, there is a pass card in each classroom that must be shown to the corridor student monitor by the student who has left the room for any reason. Except in an emergency, a teacher should not permit more than one student to leave the room at a time.

The teacher needs to alert his students relative to what he expects of them in his classroom. Early in the term, he can make known that he expects them to enter the room in good order, take their seats promptly, and talk among themselves quietly until the signal is given for the start of the lesson. The procedure for leaving the room should be similar to that of entering it.

The teacher needs to avoid detaining students beyond the ringing of the dismissal bell. He should be aware of the fact that his students have other class commitments and that, like himself, other teachers want their students to arrive in their classrooms promptly. Too many teachers have the failing of keeping the class for one last admonition or bit of information.

The seating of students. Teachers differ in methods of assigning seats to students. Some teachers still employ an alphabetical arrangement. This has an advantage in that it may help the teacher learn the names of his students more quickly than he otherwise might. It also has several disadvantages. It places the students in relatively the same position in every classroom, especially if most teachers place the students alphabetically by beginning with *A*'s and continuing through to the *Z*'s. No provision is made for the suitability of the furniture to individual students' sizes, or for the meeting of hearing or sight differences. Too many seating changes may need to be made after a seating chart is arranged according to this alphabetical order.

The following is an approach to seating arrangements that has proved itself to be successful with some teachers. For the first few days of the term, the students are permitted to select their own seats. Each of these days, the teacher calls the roll for attendance. Generally, roll-calling is regarded as a waste of time. At the beginning of the term, however, it can serve at least two useful purposes: (1) the teacher can learn how to pronounce individual names and (2) both the teacher and the students have an opportunity to associate names with individuals.

At the third or fourth meeting, the teacher, requesting the

students to keep the seats that they have selected, passes out the seating chart to be filled in. From then on, attendance can be taken by noting vacant seats and comparing them with the seating chart. Another good suggestion is to give each student a copy of the seating chart to enable him to become acquainted with all of the members of the class.

One difficulty associated with having students select their own seats is that two or more close friends may elect to sit together and are tempted to communicate with one another during the class session. The teacher needs to be alert to any such situation, and warn the students involved that they must desist from continuing this practice. If the warning brings about no behavior change, he may have to separate them by changing the seat of one or more of them.

The use of systematic procedures. The items under this heading in the list need little further consideration. You already have been alerted to the value of beginning and ending each class session promptly. Every student should be encouraged to feel that he has a significant share in class activities. If the lesson is well organized and is conducted in an interesting, businesslike fashion, few students will find time to engage in daydreaming or other irrelevant activities.

Study tasks should be assigned in light of individual ability to perform them. Moreover, whatever is assigned for class or home performance should be worthy of the teacher's giving it his attention. Written work, either as a class or a home assignment, should never be destroyed by a teacher before he has read and evaluated it. In fact, students like to have all of their written contributions, tests, reports, and the like returned to them with some notation (perhaps no more than a check mark) to indicate that the teacher has looked at it and has recorded something about it.

The authors recall the case of a high school senior who had spent considerable time and energy preparing a report for his English teacher. On the day on which he and his classmates had submitted their reports, he happened to pass her classroom after they had been dismissed and observed the teacher throwing the papers into the wastepaper basket. The boy became so emotionally disturbed over the incident that he attempted to leave home so that he would not have to face this teacher again. The situation was worsened by the fact that when the teacher was called to account for her act, she commented with a shrug of the shoulders, "He should not have taken the assignment so seriously. I just wanted to give them practice in writing." This woman's attitude indicated her lack of understanding of young people, and her own failure as a teacher.

Handling materials and supplies. You know that when you are planning your work, you need to prepare also for the use of any materials. You also realize that you should order supplies such as paper, pencils, paper fasteners, and the like far enough in advance so that you have them conveniently stored and on hand when they are needed. We already have considered such matters as distributing and collecting papers and providing for display of teacher-learning materials.

Your school probably has a uniform policy for the labeling of students' written work. Discover from your cooperating teacher what this policy is and make certain that your students follow prescribed formats. Also, many teachers require their students to complete and submit notebooks that contain research material appropriate to the study material of the course. These notebooks should be well organized and neatly prepared. Do not encourage your students to spend an undue amount of time on the preparation of elaborate covers. Also, warn them against including any illustrative material that represents the cutting up or otherwise defacing of books or magazine articles that do not belong to them. Some young people are so eager to submit an unsually attractive notebook that they will devote, to its preparation, time that could be used to better advantage, or include pictures, for example, that have been cut out of library books or taken from materials belonging to their parents.

The making of records and reports. You must be accurate in checking attendance, in both your homeroom and recitation classes. The class roll book is a document that, on occasions, is needed in court to verify data about a young person's presence in school on a certain day. Considerable embarrassment can be caused the school when or if teachers' records do not agree.

One of a teacher's important functions is the assigning of achievement grades or marks. These must be based on sufficient evidence so that they can be rechecked when necessary. Parents sometimes insist that their child has been treated unfairly, that he has been given a low grade because of personal prejudice, etc. You need to be able to substantiate your evaluation of a student's work by having available a series of marks that he has earned during the particular marking period under consideration. Some teachers keep samples of their students' written work until the end of the school term or year. They may return them to students to examine corrections noted, but then re-collect them, and file them for showing to parents and administrators as needed.

You probably do not need to be reminded that any reports requested by the administration should be submitted promptly and in good form. Negligence on the part of even one teacher can interfere with the smooth running of administrative routines. As a student teacher, you may not appreciate the great amount of paper work that must be prepared almost daily by the principal and his staff. The central facility of a school system constantly needs to be alerted to what is going on in the schools. Much of the required information must come from individual teachers. Hence it is essential that you accept this responsibility cheerfully and, in every way that you can, cooperate with your administrative officers.

The use of courtesy in the classroom. To the extent that you display a courteous attitude toward your students, you are encouraging them to be well mannered in their relationships with one another. Older adolescents usually treat their fellow classmates courteously and respect their achievements. This is not always true of junior high school students. The boys may tend to tease the girls or play more or less harmless tricks on other boys and girls. They are so filled with energy that the teacher often finds it difficult to relate it to learning activities. His one hope is that he can motivate them to become so interested in constructive classroom activities that they have no time to annoy others in the class.

Young people also need to receive training in being courteous to visitors. It sometimes happens that the class session is interrupted by the entrance into the room of another faculty member. The teacher should not need to do more than excuse himself to the class, perhaps suggesting that they continue the discussion, go on with a project with which they have been working, or consult their books. Upper-term students probably will not need such a reminder, but younger adolescents tend to talk more or less noisily among themselves unless they have been taught to behave courteously. In their many visits to the classrooms of secondary schools, the authors have been impressed favorably by students' courteous treatment of them. A student sitting nearby is likely to alert a visitor to what is happening in the classroom, to give him a copy of the book or other material that is being used, and in other ways make the stranger feel at home. To the extent that our schools are encouraging the development of courteous manners, they are to be much commended.

EXTRACLASS ACTIVITIES OF SECONDARY SCHOOL STUDENTS

According to the number of hours you spend daily in the school in which you are having your student-teaching experiences, you will find yourself assisting your cooperating teacher in various out-of-class activities, such as hall duty, homeroom duty, supervision of a study hall, or supervision of the lunchroom. These are regularly assigned tasks, usually shared by all or most of the members of the teaching staff, and generally following an administratively prescribed mode of procedure. These teacher activities are not our concern here. Our discussion deals rather with the teacher's role in those activities participated in by students in light of their individual interests and abilities.

Purposes of Extraclass Activities

Extraclass activities, variously referred to as cocurriculum, extracurriculum, and out-of-class projects, differ from regular class activities in that (1) they do not follow a specific course of study, (2) they do not carry academic course credit, (3) student participation is on a voluntary basis, and (4) they operate informally under student leadership and teacher sponsorship. Yet, a well-organized, interest-arousing out-of-class activity can serve definite educational objectives. Through participation in its program, a young person can learn to cooperate with his fellows, be helped to develop good sportsmanship, acquire commendable civic and social attitudes, and improve certain learnings begun in the regular classroom. Other educational goals can be achieved through these activities. Since the attitudes displayed by the teacher sponsor and the student members of an extraclass activity usually are informal and friendly, student-teacher relationships can be improved. Membership in the activity also affords opportunities for adolescents to discover and develop their special interests and abilities. Constructive leadership and followership are encouraged. Such cocurricular projects as science clubs or mathematics clubs, for example, can enrich curriculum offerings and motivate students toward improved learning in their regular classroom study. Also, healthful recreational activities may be engaged in that may serve an individual during his adult years. In general, participation in any out-of-class program of activities can help prepare young people for their present and future responsibilities as worthy, active citizens.

Out-of-class activities have value for the school itself. During their stay in the secondary school, students are more than participants in the activities of individual classroom situations. They are members of a school community that includes the administrative and custodial staff, teachers, and the student population. All of these can be brought together in a kind of team cooperation as the projects of various activity programs are planned and executed. Thereby, the morale and spirit of the school can be enhanced. Moreover, it often is through the functioning of the school's extraclass program of activities that the school is brought to the attention of parents and other members of the community, by means of its publications, dramatic and musical presentations, and sports events.

Attitudes toward Extraclass Activities

Secondary school people differ in their attitudes toward out-of-class activities. Some administrators and teachers believe that student activities should be tied to regular classroom study. Others recognize the value to the students and the school of providing opportunities outside the classroom for rich, rewarding student experiences. The present trend is toward the acceptance of the second point of view. Early in the present century, most schools did little more than to sponsor activities such as interscholastic events, musical and dramatic programs, and debating. Today, there are available for secondary school students well over one hundred different types of activity, and the number is increasing.[1]

Extraclass activities on the secondary level have an interesting history. For many years, for example, the homeroom period has been a part of the school's daily program. In the early days, the period was devoted to the taking of attendance, the reading of notices, and the preparation, by teacher and students, of the day's work. Today, insofar as time permits after the regular routines are completed, the students are likely to engage in activities associated with their various clubs or other extraclass programs.

Many cocurricular activities are more or less directly related to the curriculum. Some students in a regular subject class become so interested in the work of the class that they are motivated to continue its study outside regular periods. Hence they form a group, such as a literature, a social studies, a science, or a mathematics club, in which, with teacher sponsorship, they carry on appropriate projects. Other areas of student interest begin as out-of-class activities and find their way, partially at least, into the regular curriculum.

The beginning preparation of the school newspaper or magazine may be done in a class in journalism, although the details of its construction may require out-of-class time. A similar situation may hold for debating, dramatics, and some aspects of athletic activities. Perhaps, in the future, in-class and out-of-class learning activities may undergo an increasing degree of coordination.

Types of Extraclass Activities

Most secondary schools attempt to provide various outlets for youthful interest and enthusiasm. The number and specific types of such activities differ with administrative policy, size of school population, and availability of proper teacher sponsorship. The following types of activities usually can be found in the average school: student sponsored assembly programs, student government,

[1] See Robert W. Frederick, *The Third Curriculum* (New York: Appleton-Century-Crofts, Inc., 1959), pp. 429–35.

special interest and service clubs, school publications, and musical, dramatic, and sports programs. Since you probably had some experience with these student activities in your own secondary school, we shall limit our discussion of them to a brief presentation of their purposes and procedures.

Student participation in school assemblies. School assemblies in the past usually were conducted by the principal or by his assistant, and were devoted mainly to opening exercises, the reading of general notices, explaining of school rules and regulations, and perhaps a talk given by the principal or a guest speaker. At present, the students are much involved in the conduct of the assembly program. It is viewed as a means of bringing a large group together to experience an interesting and educationally worthwhile program.

The opening exercises of an assembly program may be conducted by a student leader. The remainder of the assembly period then may be devoted to a presentation that touches one of the many phases of school life: dramatizations, music or dance programs, sports boosting, nominations of student officers, career talks, orientation programs, honors awards, panel discussions, and the like. Instead of regarding the assembly period as a boring experience, most students now look forward eagerly to participation in it. They also are gaining practice in proper large-group behavior.

Student participation in school government. One of the most effective means for bringing about unity among a school's members and for introducing the principles of democratic living is student participation in school government. Democratic theory studied in the civics class is given practical application as students of all grades are afforded opportunities to participate in the management of those school matters that affect the well-being of everyone in the school.

Although the term *student government* often is used to designate this type of activity, rarely is the management of school affairs limited to students alone. In fact, such an arrangement is impractical, if not impossible. The principal is responsible for whatever takes place in his school. There are certain administrative regulations, such as, for example, the rule that every student is expected to be in school during the regular school day in his scheduled classes, unless legally excused from doing so. Hence students may not leave the school during regular hours of attendance or absent themselves from class in order to perform an errand associated with an out-of-class activity. This is one of the administrative restrictions that must be upheld to protect students' welfare.

Moreover, enthusiastic but immature young people cannot be trusted to manage their own affairs. They enjoy planning, organizing, and assuming responsibility for the good of their fellow students, but they often have impractical ideas. Hence their activities need to be guided by one or more members of the faculty who understand youthful ideals and can help students realize these sanely and intelligently. Realistically, the governing body of school affairs represents cooperation between students and faculty members.

The organization of student-faculty government differs somewhat with individual schools. Usually, however, the entire school is brought into the organization. The plan that is generally followed is somewhat like this one. The student council includes the elected officers (president, vice-president, secretary, and treasurer), faculty member or members, class representatives, and representatives of major student clubs and other extraclass groups.

A class representative in council is a duly elected member of his homeroom group who reports back to his group what happens in council meetings. The faculty member or members may be appointed by the principal or elected by the students. A teacher member may have a vote in council, or his function may be advisory only. Any student may become a member of the general organization by the payment of a small amount of dues—twenty-five cents, for example. A student who is financially unable to pay dues may work off his obligation through an arrangement with the faculty sponsor whereby he engages in a special service.

The student-faculty council sponsors a variety of functions and services. These include sponsoring the extraclass program of the school, issuing charters to newly formed groups; planning and presenting assembly programs; arranging social events; welcoming entrants to the school; conducting programs for parents and other interested members of the community; sponsoring various service groups; conducting campaigns for the care of the school building and grounds; and assuming other responsibilities that are inherent in the democratic way of life.

In some schools, the student council maintains a student court for the consideration of minor infractions of school rules and regulations. Although the power of the student court must be limited, its presence in the school can deter students from engaging in various forms of uncontrolled behavior. They are influenced by the fact that fellow students disapprove of their actions, and they do not like receiving penalties from their peers.

A well-organized student faculty program of school government can be an effective instrument for building group morale and furthering democratic principles. Many worthwhile decisions can be made by the students themselves with the cooperative help of their faculty sponsor or sponsors. Every student in the school has an opportunity to participate in school affairs. At a regular meeting, the council listens to reports of the interests and activities of students as these are presented by group representatives, considers these reports, and offers recommendations. These recommendations, in turn, are taken up in individual group meetings and accepted or rejected, or modifications are suggested. At the next meeting of the council, class or group suggestions concerning council recommendations are again considered and are acted upon.

At times, of course, faculty intervention is needed, but on such occasions, the students should be helped to understand why a particular plan or project is inadvisable. The administration and faculty must take care, however, that they do not dampen youthful interest and enthusiasm by demanding too strict adherence to adult standards. A few minor mistakes in judgment are likely to have good training possibilities in the development of the principles of democratic action.

Participation in interest clubs. As a secondary school student, you probably were a member of one or more interest clubs, and readily recall your experience. An interest club may be associated with a regular school subject. Some interest clubs grow out of a special hobby of a small group of students, such as stamp collecting or photography. In either case, a specific club is organized because of the special interest in its purpose on the part of a group of students. They are enthusiastic about the club activity.

To the extent that the purpose of a club is basic to young people's continuing interests and its faculty sponsor's interests, the club may flourish almost indefinitely. Yet, circumstances may be such that few if any students seek membership in it, or the original teacher sponsor may be unable to continue serving it and an effective successor is difficult to find. When either of these contingencies arises, the club probably should be discontinued, giving way to the formation of another group project of current interest to students.

Too often a school attempts to foster a long list of clubs, some of which, because of changing interests of young people, have a struggle for existence. A club, temporarily at least, may receive so many applications for membership that it is likely to become unwieldy unless restrictions are placed on membership. This procedure may defeat the purpose of the club that should be the encouragement of individual interests. Yet, a club should be relatively small so that all of its members have an opportunity to participate in its activities.

School people are faced with the problem posed by students' differing attitudes toward club membership. Some students have diversified interests and would like to join many clubs, thereby dissipating their energies. Other students are nonjoiners. For one or more reasons, they cannot be motivated to become members of any group. They want to devote all of their time to study activities; they have home responsibilities, or they enjoy a satisfying program of out-of-school social activities. Hence they take little or no part in school-sponsored clubs.

Added to the problem of encouraging the students to join clubs is that of arranging a satisfactory schedule of club meetings. In most schools these meetings are held after regular school hours. Since there are only five days available in the school week, several clubs need to meet on the same day, thereby denying students an opportunity to join two clubs of their interest if they happen to meet during the same hours. Moreover, the arranging of suitable meeting times is difficult in a large school that is on double or triple schedule. In addition, holding meetings after school hours lengthens the day for both students and faculty members.

Some schools are experimenting with ways of meeting these problems. One approach is to schedule all club meetings for a designated period each week during the regular school day, such as the last period of Friday afternoon. Every student is expected to join an activity group. This procedure usually pleases teachers but has several disadvantages from the students' point of view. A student who has several interests must choose between them since he can be a member of only one group. To the student who apparently is forced to join a club, in spite of lack of interest, the approach takes on the nature of another regular class session.

Another plan experimented with in a few schools is to lengthen the school lunch period several days during the week and to hold club meetings at these times. There are obvious disadvantages to this plan. The alloted time may need to be too short for a worthwhile meeting unless the eating of lunch and the club activity are combined. This may be difficult, since some students eat in the school cafeteria and others go home for lunch. Also, lunch should be a period of relaxation for both the students and their teacher sponsors.

Value of interest clubs. A successful interest club should represent real student interest and be sponsored by a teacher who shares that interest and who can guide the group's activities tactfully and indirectly. There should be sensible standards for admission to it— demonstrated interest rather than superior academic achievement. If there are club dues, these should be minimal. School rules and regulations must be appreciated and followed. There should be regularly scheduled meetings. The worth of the club should be evaluated periodically.

Two possible attitudes of young people in their club relationships need to be considered. One is associated with the adolescents' tendency to form exclusive cliques. For this reason, most secondary schools ban fraternities and sororities. Yet, one can find close-knit social groups operating among students. Since the meetings of these groups cannot be held in the school building, the students meet in one another's houses. In imitation of college secret societies, the members engage in secret signs and code language. They display a snobbish attitude toward those schoolmates who are considered by them to be unworthy of membership. Although the faculty members usually know about the existence of such groups among the students, there is little they can do about them except to encourage the formation of democratically organized social groups to meet the needs of all students. Some schools also have honor societies to which their high-achieving students are eligible.

Another problem is posed by the inveterate joiner, especially on the junior high school level. Most clubs are prone to devise insignia of one kind or another for their members to wear. Among younger adolescents, the larger the badge, button, or pin, the more popular the club seems to be. Some young people tend to seek membership in as many clubs as are available for no other reason, apparently, except to collect club insignia that they wear with pride. As can be guessed, these status seekers have little to contribute in the way of personal activity to any of the clubs they join. These students usually are "spotted" by serious club members and may be refused membership in desired groups. Some clubs require the return of insignia by those who join but then are inactive.

Student participation in service clubs. Secondary school students can find many opportunities for the giving of service to the school and to the community. To help others often is a strong motivator of adolescent activity. Excellent educational and social benefits are available for those young people who participate seriously in one or another form of service. However, the faculty sponsor must be aware of the fact that an adolescent may be long on promises but short on performance. Some young people are enthusiastic about participating in a service activity but tend to lose interest in carrying it on after the first thrill has passed. Most students, however, do a very good job of executing promptly and efficiently any service task that they undertake.

In most schools, service activities are sponsored by the student-faculty council and are conducted under their aegis. Some services are associated with a regular subject and supervised by the teacher of the subject; others are more general in their application. Included among the many services in which students can engage are:

1. Serving as student secretaries
2. Assisting with the school bank
3. Maintaining a lost-and-found service
4. Serving on a safety patrol
5. Assisting in the library
6. Working for the Red Cross

7. Maintaining a book exchange for students' use
8. Acting as corridor or street guards
9. Serving as lunchroom aides
10. Holding pep rallies for athletic events
11. Caring for laboratory equipment, musical instruments, or stage props
12. Conducting community surveys for the benefit of students and the community
13. Tutoring students who, because of illness or other valid reason, fall behind in their studies
14. Serving as a social committee to welcome guests and to guide them around the school, and serving as ushers at school-sponsored programs, and the like

The foregoing list represents some of the ways in which students can benefit themselves by helping others. Through their personal experiences with groups of this kind, the authors have found that participation in a service club gives a young person training in doing things for others cheerfully and efficiently. Such service can have considerable value for a student in his out-of-school personal and social relationships.

Student participation in entertainment programs. Most secondary schools afford students opportunities to participate in the production of musical, dramatic, and other entertainment productions. During the course of the school year, relatively simple programs are presented at regular assembly periods. A short play is enacted, usually by an English or speech group. The glee club or school chorus sings. Performances are given by a dance club. The school orchestra may accompany assembly singing on its own. Students enjoy listening to and watching their schoolmates in action.

At least once a year, a more elaborate musical and/or dramatic performance is presented for the edification of both the school and community. This is a large-scale production that involves the activity of students having various interests and talents. Much school spirit can be stimulated as students, both younger and older, share in the task of making the project a successful venture. Also, community members, as they view a production, develop a commendable interest and pride in the school.

One difficulty that must be met in the production of a supposedly whole-school dramatic presentation, for example, is that of assigning student roles. Since the aim is to produce an effective program, school people are tempted to use the same talented students again and again. This limits the number of young people who are permitted to participate actively. Most of the students may be mere spectators, although they do share vicariously in any honors that come to the school as a result of the success of the undertaking.

Some students may be very much hurt by the fact that they were denied desired participation in the event. Another difficulty grows out of the great amount of practice that may be needed to perfect the production. Either the students involved have to devote many hours to preparation before and after the school day or they are taken out of their regular classes. In general, however, such programs do help develop a spirit of oneness among students and faculty, and bring the school and community closer together.

Student participation in school publications. An excellent approach to the building of school spirit is the publication by the students and faculty of the school newspaper, the preparation of a student handbook, and the issuing of a school annual or yearbook. Young people like to share their thinking and experience with one another. The entire school can participate in preparing the weekly newspaper. By the way of its reporter, each homeroom class or school club can report interesting bits of news about its members to the editorial board. As he reads his newspaper, each student is alerted to what is going on in the school. The handbook gives students an opportunity to participate in the establishing of regulations concerning the management of school affairs. The annual or magazine stimulates youthful creativity, because students are encouraged to submit for publication such material as stories, poems, articles, photographs, or original drawings.

The preparation of a school publication is a tremendous task. Procuring suitable items for inclusion and arranging page proof carefully consume much time and effort on the part of both the faculty adviser and the students themselves. Also, special ability and good training are needed. Hence, as we have noted earlier, some schools offer journalism courses for interested and able students who, after a period of training, are selected to serve on the editorial staff of one or another school publication. Although the production of a publication may be undertaken in an advanced journalism class, much of the detailed work must be done during out-of-class time. However, the satisfaction they experience from producing something that gains commendation from their schoolmates and the community seems to be ample reward for those teachers and students who are involved in the preparation of school publications.

Student participation in athletic activities. Adolescents are extremely interested in sports, either as participants or as spectators. Interscholastic events on the secondary school level, especially football, baseball, and basketball, are among the earliest forms of out-of-class activities. More recently, track has been added. Successful participation in games with other schools does much to foster loyalty to the school on the part of students, the school's alumni, and the community at large. The successful school athlete is a hero among his schoolmates.

Although interscholastic contests have educational value in that they usually foster team cooperation, good sportsmanship, and school loyalty, they also give rise to various problems. A relatively few students can participate in the sports program. Since adolescents may not have acquired their full growth, injuries are possible. Time may be taken by the team members from regular class attendance, as they practice for or participate in sports events. The financing of the activity may constitute a problem. Special demands are made on the time and energy of faculty members who are responsible for the success of the undertaking. A few students may be tempted to engage in dishonest practices.

The development of strong vigorous bodies, the maintenance of good health, and the acquisition of attitudes of good sportsmanship are among the educational objectives of the secondary school. Emphasis on interscholastic sports limits the attainment of these purposes to the few. Hence many school people are stressing the value of intramural sports. Through a graded program of athletic activities in which all physically able students can participate, it is possible to help young people become physically fit and learn what it means to be a cooperating member of a team.

In some schools, physical activities are introduced that can be enjoyed by individuals during most of their adult life. Such skill activities include tennis, golf, and social dancing. At the same time, provision is being made in an increasing number of schools to encourage student participation in more academically pointed contests. Exhibitions, including the possibility of winning prizes, can be encouraged. One example of this is the 4-H Club program conducted in some high schools. Projects similar to the televised program *The College Bowl* also could be instituted.

The Conduct of Extraclass Activities

Everyone in the school system—administrators, teachers, and students—is concerned with the organization and conduct of extraclass activities. Each of these groups has a responsibility for the success of any out-of-class project.

Responsibility of administrators and teachers in extraclass projects. As we have noted earlier, the principal is responsible for whatever takes place in his school. He must take care that all school rules and regulations are upheld. At the same time, he should give attention to suggestions by teachers and students concerning possible projects that are beneficial to students. He is open-minded toward the establishment in the school of activities that appeal to student interest and that can be conducted intelligently and safely. He usually defers to the opinions of well-qualified teachers and student leaders in matters that deal with out-of-class projects and programs.

Teachers selected to sponsor student activities should be chosen in light of (1) personal interest, (2) understanding of young people, (3) ability to guide students' activities indirectly, and (4) willingness to devote extra time and energy to the fulfillment of sponsorship responsibilities. A principal may experience difficulty in finding teachers to whom to delegate his authority. Some teachers may be interested in a particular activity but lack the ability to work cooperatively with students in an informal relationship. Other teachers are inclined to direct rather than guide. The mass of detailed work associated with an extraclass activity may cause otherwise qualified teachers to hesitate accepting responsibility for it. Although the students themselves are supposed to care for the details of administration, they often are careless about such matters, leaving them to be done by the sponsor.

An important aspect of the sponsor's duties is associated with the group's finances. Club dues usually are small. Disbursals are limited, for the most part, to the purchase of club insignia, providing for refreshments, and the like. The students need training, however, in handling their money properly. In most schools, the various groups are required to deposit money received in the school bank, and then draw on the receipts as needed. In some schools, all requests for money must be signed by the club treasurer or president, and the faculty sponsor. Although the maintaining of a large bank account should not be the aim of a club, the students should receive training in spending money wisely.

The sponsor is primarily responsible for setting the tone of the club. It is he who encourages intelligent leadership and attempts to stimulate all of the members to accept responsibility for group activities. The alert faculty adviser also motivates the members to appraise the worth of their program and to bring about desirable changes or modifications.

Responsibility of student teachers. As a result of your own experiences with student activities on the secondary school and college levels, you may have developed considerable interest in them. You may have a good understanding of student attitudes toward such activities and believe that you would enjoy sponsoring a club or other project. Now, as a student teacher, you are given an opportunity to gain greater insight into the relationship that should exist between the group's sponsor and its student members.

Discover what your school's out-of-class program is like and how well it functions. Encourage students in your class who belong to clubs to invite you as a guest to one or a few of their meetings. Perhaps, your cooperating teacher is a club sponsor. He may be willing for you to assist him in its management. If you are asked by students to participate in their activities, accept their invitation insofar as your unassigned time permits. To the extent that you become acquainted with your school's offerings in this area of educational experience, you are preparing yourself for future involvement in students' out-of-class activities.

Student membership in school-sponsored clubs. The ideal situation is to have every student an active member of a school-sponsored club or other activity. What usually happens, however, is that some students seek membership in many such groups and other students join none. Another factor that needs to be considered by a school faculty is that the leaders of many groups would like to limit membership in them to academically superior students. Young people should be encouraged so to set their qualification for membership that less able but interested students are eligible. One cannot blame young people, however, for wanting to exclude from their informal groups any students who have earned for themselves a reputation of uncooperativeness, extreme aggression, or other undersirable personality quality. Yet, admission to a club of his interest can do much toward motivating a relatively undisciplined young person to change his ways.

Secondary schools use various approaches toward stimulating students to participate in a reasonable number of out-of-class activities. One of these is the *point system* whereby point value is assigned to each of the various types of membership. Membership in an activity has a value of one point if no special responsibilities are involved. The number of points earned follows a regular system of values according to the position held. In some schools where this procedure is used, the president of the student council and the editor in chief of a school publication receive the highest number of points. Each student is limited in the total number of points he may earn in any school term or year. Another approach is that of *majors* and *minors*. A position in a club that requires the assuming of a great deal of responsibility is a major, and the others are minors. These two designations are worked out carefully so that no student can be in doubt concerning his status. Membership in majors or minors is limited according to a specified listing of responsibilities.

In one senior high school known to the authors, an interesting device is used to stimulate student interest in extraclass activities. The point system is used. In addition, upon entrance into the school, each student receives a *Club Membership Card* that is so organized as to include a column for dates, another column for the name of an activity, and a third for a sponsor's signature. At the end of each term, the student fills in, with date, the record of his club membership for that term and has the various sponsors sign it.

As the student progresses from grade to grade, the card follows him, so that by the time he is ready to be graduated he has a cumulative record of his out-of-class activities. Grade counselors check these cards to note which students may be involved in too many activities and which have no or a meager record of participation. This information can be used to advantage by the counselor, as he limits the activities of some and attempts to encourage participation by others. The teachers in this school have found that many young people who at first had resisted joining clubs were motivated, by comparing their cards with those of active classmates, to change their attitude and, with teacher guidance, became active members of one or more groups.

No matter how enthusiastic we may be concerning the value of out-of-class activities, we must keep in mind that young people are in school primarily to profit from more or less formal educational offerings. Their first responsibility is to the learning experiences made available to them in regular classrooms under the guidance of well-trained and understanding teachers. To the extent that extra-class activities serve educational goals and supplement classroom learning, they should be fostered. Teachers and students alike gain much from the kind of cooperation needed to maintain a successful program of participation in whole-school living.

QUESTIONS AND TOPICS FOR DISCUSSION

1. By referring to Table 10, list the routines in your classroom that could be improved. What changes in procedure would you recommend?
2. Again with reference to Table 10, which of the satisfactory routines are performed by students? Which by you?
3. Why should students not be permitted to use window poles?
4. What type of seating arrangement is utilized by your cooperating teacher? How well does it function?
5. What is your cooperating teacher's attitude toward written work submitted by his students?
6. Keep a list of the reports your cooperating teacher submits to the administration. For each report note its purpose.
7. If, in your school, there is an out-of-class club associated with your subject, to what extent are you participating in its activities?
8. Procure a list of the out-of-class activities regularly established for student participation. Check any that you would like to sponsor if you were a full-time teacher in the school.

9. If your school has a teacher-student government program, compare its conduct with that described in this chapter. Evaluate the worth of your program.
10. Name some impractical ideas that might be suggested for adoption by student leaders.
11. When do clubs meet in your school? How satisfactory is the arrangement?
12. What services are available in your school community for student participation?
13. Evaluate the sports program of your school.

SELECTED REFERENCES

BROWN, E. J., and PHELPS, A. T. *Managing the Classroom—The Teacher's Part in School Administration.* New York: Ronald Press Co., 1961.

CARTER, W. L., HANSEN, C. W., and McKIM, M. G. *Learning to Teach in the Secondary School.* New York: Macmillan Co., 1962.

CROW, L. D., RITCHIE, H. E., and CROW, ALICE. *Education in the Secondary School.* New York: American Book Co., 1961.

FREDERICK, R. W. *The Third Curriculum: Student Activities in American Education.* New York: Appleton-Century-Crofts, Inc., 1959.

GRUBER, F. C., and BEATTY, T. B. *Secondary School Activities.* New York: McGraw-Hill Book Co., Inc., 1954.

McKEAN, R. C. *Principles and Methods in Secondary Education.* Columbus, Ohio: Charles E. Merrill Books, Inc., 1962.

SCHORLING, R., and BATCHELDER, H. T. *Student Teaching in Secondary Schools.* New York: McGraw-Hill Book Co., Inc., 1956.

SCHULTZ, R. *Student Teaching in the Secondary Schools.* New York: Harcourt, Brace & World, Inc., 1959.

WIGGINS, S. P. *Successful High School Teaching.* Boston: Houghton Mifflin Co., 1958.

12

THE DISCIPLINE PROBLEM

The ultimate goal of an individual is to develop the kind of behavior that will enable him to become an accepted member of his societal group wherever that may be and whenever it is necessary. The achievement of this goal represents a long road of learning and behaving. A person is not born a self-disciplined individual nor does he achieve that self-controlled behavior without many experiences in working with others. He literally grows into the kind of behavior that he comes to utilize in his everyday activities.

In the classroom, the teacher is concerned with the kind of behavior, both individual and group, that will enable the teaching-learning process to continue in such a way that optimum results can be obtained. Often unknown to the learners, the teacher is trying his best to provide good learning conditions for his students.

GENERAL CONCEPTS OF GOOD DISCIPLINE

Although a well-disciplined individual is the pride of the family, of any school, and of society, we are concerned here with what has happened to that individual to make him the behaving person he is and what can be done to train him to be an effective social unit in his group, regardless of its size or purpose, or whether it is within the school or outside the school.

Many attempts have been made to define discipline. We present an extended list as compiled by Peter F. Oliva: [1]

1. Discipline is the creation and preservation of conditions essential to work. *(Bagley)*

[1] Peter F. Oliva, "High School Discipline in American Society," *The Bulletin of the National Association of Secondary-School Principals,* XL, No. 216 (January, 1956), 5–6.

2. Discipline is preparation for adult citizenship with assumption of responsibilities as well as duties.   (*Bagley*)
3. Discipline is self-control.   (*Bagley*)
4. Discipline is intelligent obedience.   (*Bean*)
5. Discipline is a fundamentally re-educative process in which an individual is brought to change his attitude by a process of viewing himself as others see him.   (*Clayton*)
6. Discipline is the thwarting of impulses and short-run purposes for the sake of long-run purposes.   (*Folsom*)
7. Discipline really means training and learning acceptable behavior.
                                                                          (*Jenkins*)
8. Discipline is a necessary restraint on behavior for some specific good purpose, good for the individual disciplined and good for the social group of which he is a part.   (*Mearns*)
9. Discipline is still widely thought of as the amount of control that the teacher has of her group, or as
10. Her method of achieving and maintaining control over the group.
                                                                          (*Tryon*)
11. Discipline in a democracy means organization of one's impulses for the attainment of certain goals delineated by the philosophy of democracy.
                                                                          (*Tryon*)
12. Discipline is punishment.   (*Wiens*)
13. Discipline is enforced obedience.   (*Wiens*)
14. Discipline is training.   (*Wiens*)
15. Discipline is instruction.   (*Wiens*)
16. Discipline is education.   (*Sheviakov and Redl*)
17. Discipline is drill.   (*Sheviakov and Redl*)
18. Discipline is subjection to rule and control.   (*Sheviakov and Redl*)
19. Discipline is correction, training through suffering.
                                                          (*Sheviakov and Redl*)
20. Discipline is control and direction of energy that produces behavior.
                                                                          (*Pullias*)
21. Discipline is the name of the procedure by which we keep character qualities in mind and adopt methods to bring them about.   (*Miller*)
22. Discipline is group leadership.   (*Redl*)
23. Discipline is no longer a matter of punishment for breaking the rules, but the better adjustment of the student to society.   (*Belting and Clevenger*)
24. Discipline, then, is the device used to hold pupils to purposes which are not theirs, with which they do not agree, and which they imperfectly understand.   (*Elsbree and McNally*)
25. Discipline is obedience to the whole of which one is a part.   (*Follett*)

These definitions provide a brief glimpse at the number of ways of viewing the word, "discipline." To obtain an adequate definition of discipline for these times, the premises upon which the definition is based must first be considered. The following are the two premises upon which to found a philosophy of education suitable to democratic goals.

1. The conception of democracy held, its values, and the extent of faith in democracy as a form of government and as a way of life.

2. The knowledge of and faith in the findings concerning the nature of learning, adolescent psychology, and the improved methods of teaching.

Discipline in the school implies behavior in some form. Various types of behavior become a part of an individual as he lives day-by-day, week-by-week, and year-by-year in his home, his school, and his other social settings. The teacher usually has two general concerns in coping with the problems of discipline: (1) he wants sufficient quiet in his classroom to enable him to discharge his function as a teacher, and (2) he wants each of his students to become the kind of person who can function as a democratic citizen wherever he may be and whenever called on to set an example to others.

Impact of Earlier Training

The function of the school is greater than that of making Johnny conform to expected behavior. Parents sometimes have the notion that the development of needed inner behavior controls is the function only of the school. The parent of the preschool child often is heard to remark, "When you go to school, your teacher will make you behave." Although we are interested in the discipline problem of the secondary school, we must not lose sight of the fact that the child comes to his teachers with habit patterns of behavior that are formed either in the home or in earlier school experiences. The parents in the home do more than they realize in the way of giving direction to the ultimate behavior of the growing child. There is general agreement that the child learns more during the first five years of life than during any other comparable period. The relative weight may be even greater in the area of behavior outcomes.

Goal of Behavior Development

As our understanding of adolescent psychology increases, we are learning that there are forces at work on individuals during their developing years to determine the kind of behavior they will exhibit at any stage of their development. No longer are we attempting to impose a forced obedience; rather are we trying to effect a change in behavior through the use of sympathetic guidance. The child who is encouraged in the home to practice self-control comes to school ready to live cooperatively with others in his new environment.

The ultimate goal of the individual is to develop the kind of behavior that will serve him well in all situations—the classroom, the social situation, and the home. He is then self-disciplined. He exhibits self-control. He is under less tension when he has these inner controls that constantly work for him. His emotions then work for him because he possesses the behavior habits that are of value to him in his relationships with other people.

The individual who is able to change habitual behavior that interferes with his welfare and the welfare of others in his struggles for social acceptance becomes the kind of person who is easily accepted by others. He demonstrates traits of self-control and of self-discipline. Thus the development of self-control and of self-discipline becomes one of the most important goals toward which an individual can strive.

Need for Adjustment to Specific Situations

Any individual, of whatever age, who enters a social situation must learn to meet the needs of that situation. He soon discovers that he must adjust to the habits, thinking, and mores or general habit patterns of the group. As he enters into the activities of the group, he learns to give and take in his struggles toward self-realization. He becomes sensitive to the wishes and behavior of those with whom he associates. He often defers to the interests and wishes of the members of the group.

A teen-ager's going to school is a common practice, but the school to which he goes is a particular school and different from every other school in the country. Likewise, each classroom is different from every other classroom, not only in the country as a whole but also in the building in which it is located. Many factors account for this difference. Among the important considerations are the attitudes of the teacher and of the particular learners who inhabit the room.

In his attempt to achieve what he seems to be there to achieve, each young person learns to cooperate with the other learners present and with the leader—the teacher. To provide a good working situation and establish good working relationships, it becomes necessary to know what is expected of every member of the group. Hence there is a need for the formulation of rules to govern behavior for effective learning conditions. Not only should each learner know the rules that should govern his behavior but he should help, insofar as possible, to set them up so that he understands them and knows why their enforcement is necessary. Then, too, he should know who is given the responsibility to apply the rules whenever necessary to bring his behavior or that of others in line with established practices.

Need for Concern with Drives of Individuals

It is normal for an adolescent to strive to satisfy his drives and urges in a way that may give him the greatest pleasure. If he were the only person involved, the behavior displayed might be of little concern, but it must be realized that he functions along with other human beings in a situation. Each of the other individuals also has personal drives and urges that he is interested in satisfying. Hence a clash of expression of individual drives may ensue unless some adaptations are made in the behavior displayed by everyone. The responsibility then falls to each to check any personal drive or activity that may interfere with the approved activity of others. This attempt at self-control is needed if learning conditions are to be worth while.

A great concern of students and of a beginning teacher is associated with the problem of discipline. The student teacher may exhibit considerable fear that he will have difficulty in achieving good discipline in his class. This is not an unfounded apprehension. No matter how extensive and intensive your subject matter mastery is, you soon discover that your teaching success rests heavily on your ability to control your class to the extent that you and the students can participate in the teaching-learning activities that you have planned.

The urge on the part of an adolescent learner to test the teacher is great. The urge to give a student teacher a difficult time may be even greater. Two attitudes often prevail among adolescent learners: (1) they want to provide the best teaching conditions possible for you as a student teacher and hence cooperate to their best ability, or (2) they set about to make it difficult for you and give you what they call the full treatment. They practice all the tricks of teacher testing.

Need for Self-Discipline Rather Than Discipline in the Classroom

The implication of discipline is that obedience prevails in the classroom but that it is predicated upon the direct reaction to superimposed authority displayed by the teacher—the authority figure. Human behavior needs to be controlled either from within or from without. When the control force is from a source outside the individual, he may display disciplined behavior. However, when he responds to a force that directs his behavior from within himself, he is considered to be self-disciplined.

Individuals need disciplined behavior for their own life adjustment. How to achieve that kind of behavior is most important to the individual and to those who attempt to help him gain commendable behavior controls. Until recently, educators regarded discipline as referring to what is done in the classroom to force learners to redirect their behavior to conform to those rules and regulations as set forth by the school and/or the classroom teacher, and rigidly enforced by way of one or another drastic overt means. The ability of the teacher to gain overt obedience to his commands was believed to be evidence that a class was well disciplined.

Today there is greater emphasis on other factors in the classroom situation that contribute to disciplined behavior. We are more concerned about the teacher's attitude toward students' behavior and the effect of their behavior on the learning process. The cause of any noise in a classroom is more important than the fact that there is noise, or the amount of noise that may be present. We are especially concerned that the learning situation is conducive for every member of the group to be able to progress toward the achievement of his educational goals.

Basic Principles of Discipline

As a student teacher or a beginning teacher, you rightly can be interested in the problem of discipline. You may not have received help along these lines in your other college courses. You may not have been informed of many of the problems that you will face in your initial teaching. Hence some guiding principles here may help point the way for your thinking and planning in coping with many of the problems that are likely to arise.

You need to discover much about the policy of the secondary school in which you are doing your student teaching, the nature of the student body, and what is expected of the teacher. Of equal importance is the cooperating teacher. You need to learn how to work with him and to be given the kinds of opportunities that will enable you to cope with discipline situations on your own. Unless you have some knowledge on these points, you may find it difficult to adapt your teaching to the needs of the school, the teacher, and the learners.

The following general principles may be helpful to you in the development of self-discipline among your students. They embody elements of good teaching. When carefully followed, they may help not only you as the teacher but also your students whose behavior you are stimulating toward the kind of self-discipline that will be good in the classroom as well as in other group situations. In your attempt to guide the behavior of your learners, strive to:

1. Stimulate each learner to adopt a plan of action that will enable him to attain a worthwhile goal.
2. Follow the lead of your cooperating teacher.
3. Interpret all rules and regulations so that they are understood by all learners.
4. Make clear to your students that an infringement of rules warrants a penalty.
5. Offer teaching leadership so that your students are not expected to remain quiet for the sole purpose of being orderly.
6. Have classroom conditions reflect out-of-class life situations.
7. Help students establish habits of behavior essential to self-discipline.
8. Provide forms of activity that enable the members of the group to participate actively without the need for complete silence at all times.
9. Provide some learner activity during each classroom session.

10. Provide for individual differences.
11. Enlist the cooperation of the class in achieving good learner conduct.
12. Deal with the misdeed rather than making it personal.
13. Establish classroom routines in class management.
14. Help each learner consciously develop self-discipline.
15. Display the kinds of attitudes that will invite cooperative behavior.

BASIC BEHAVIOR DIFFICULTIES OF YOUTH

During the early years, unless care is taken, a child may develop behavior habits that are unwholesome. The young child meets his needs by displaying behavior that is aggressive and selfish. He has not yet learned that he should be polite. When he wants something he reaches for it and may grab it. Likewise, when something is taken away from him and he does not understand the reason for this, he may object vociferously. This is his way of communicating his feelings. The adolescent's attitude may be similar, but he has learned to use more subtle ways of expressing his feelings.

Why Children Misbehave

All young people have drives of aggressiveness and self-interest. These drives continue throughout life, but, as they grow older, they come to control these urges and socialize them or give acceptable direction to them. The young child may be jealous of his baby brother or sister as the mother seems to focus most of her attention on caring for the helpless infant, and he displays attention-demanding behavior.

Need for understanding. The young child needs to be helped to understand why he cannot be allowed to harm the baby and why the baby needs much care. During these experiences, the feelings and attitudes that later operate in the life of the adolescent are being set. Jealousy will take on different forms during later years, but it still is rooted in the factors of love, fear, and hate. The young child experiences jealousy because he desires the affection of his mother and believes that he is losing it or has lost it; the adolescent experiences jealousy for similar reasons, but the adored object is likely to be found outside the home, among his peers.

There are times when young children and even adolescents or adults must obey immediately without waiting for reasons. In most instances, children deserve to know the reason for requiring certain behavior and denying others. There are few instances, however, when reasons for required behavior should not be given to adolescents. If we wish to build into the individual those attitudes that direct proper behavior, we must help him understand why he is expected to behave in one way rather than in another in a given situation.

Love and attention. Young people engage in active behavior to attract attention to themselves. They love the limelight. Often they do things deliberately to attract attention, knowing that they are likely to be reprimanded. To them disapproval is better than being ignored. Sometimes it is necessary to give an adolescent the kind of attention that he *thinks* he should have. In the classroom, this is fraught with danger. His peers may expect the same treatment, or they may come to believe that the student so favored is teacher's pet.

The factor of boredom. A good program of activities tends to stave off the feeling of boredom. Idleness promotes mischievousness. Many students misbehave because they either have too little to do or dislike what they are doing to such an extent that they develop a feeling of boredom. The teacher can introduce interesting activities to overcome this feeling. An activity in which the students are interested often is the key to the establishment of a needed change of attitude that will bring about desired behavior in the situation.

The factor of frustration. The adolescent meets many situations in his home and school life that tend to frustrate him. He needs to discover that he can resolve these and move on to the mastering of more difficult problems. It is a slow process for him to learn to channel his drives into socially acceptable patterns. Yet, he is faced constantly with the choice of doing either what he pleases or what he believes will please others. Although the latter may be somewhat frustrating to him, they serve as important socializing experiences.

The factor of anger. When things go wrong it is easy to display angry behavior. The young child learned early that he could control his environment when he used this form of behavior. In some instances he went so far as to engage in temper tantrums. These experiences aggravated the problem of developing proper attitudes toward behavior during his later growing years. Nevertheless, these attitudes and behavior patterns need to be reckoned with and plans laid to eradicate them.

The angry adolescent displays the kind of behavior that tends to avoid a direct attack on the individual who arouses his anger; he may grab the first thing in sight and throw it, or engage in an entirely different form of activity. If his anger is in the form of a temper tantrum, he may use profanity in the presence of others, give the "silent treatment," attempt the use of sarcasm, or perhaps express deep self-pity and display antisocial behavior of one kind or another. He prepares himself mentally to reveal to those at whom his anger is directed that he does not like the behavior displayed toward him.

Struggle toward independence. It is not wise to deny directly to the adolescent the privilege of doing something he desires very much to do. Great care must be taken to think of a program that will give him an opportunity to utilize his energy in a substitute activity. This sometimes is a great challenge to the teacher, but when thoughtfully executed will be rewarding to the student who needs this kind of guidance.

The teen-ager especially is interested in proving his independence to himself and to those about him. The effort he utilizes to assert himself is a common cause of misbehavior. This drive is strong during the adolescent years. The adolescent often uses rebellion as his chief means of achieving independence. The achievement of independence of action is one of the greatest challenges to the teen-ager and one of his toughest problems. Teachers who understand this personality trait find it easier to overlook some of the misbehavior displayed by the individual during this period of his development.

It is not uncommon for adolescents to question the authority of their parents, teachers, or anyone else in a position of responsibility. They often doubt the wisdom of their elders and, with their increasing freedom, display uncooperative behavior. Under proper supervision they can be given practice in assuming new responsibilities. They are likely (on their own) to make many mistakes if they do not properly use procedures that, when intelligently applied, will give them a chance to grow into these new responsibilities.

CAUSES OF BEHAVIOR DEVIATIONS

The display of deviant behavior may be rooted in a variety of causes. The teen-ager may have developed many socially nonacceptable attitudes. He may have experienced numerous emotional tensions. He may have had many frustrating experiences to which he had difficulty in adjusting. No matter what the nature of the experience, the chances are that any displayed deviant behavior can be traced to physical, personal, or social factors associated with the kind of behavior the individual displays.

Usually the interaction among the various factors that cause unacceptable behavior is so subtle that we are seldom aware that one dominates others or that all are exerting an undesirable influence at any one time. It is difficult to pinpoint the physiological, the social, or the personal as the sole cause of maladjusted behavior. Any one of them may be reinforced in its effect on individual behavior by the active influence of one or all of the others. For example, glandular disturbances may alter a young person's overt behavior so as to reveal his inner state.

Influence of Physical Factors

The height or weight of an individual may play an important role in giving direction to individual behavior. The adolescent who is short for his age may participate in the kind of activities that draw attention to his success in them and thereby away from his short stature. He feels the need to engage in the kind of activities that will compensate for his height lack; they become attention-getting devices. The tall girl may engage in those activities that will help her develop a satisfactory feeling about her physical deviation. The problem of the overweight boy or girl also is that of extreme frustration. Each may try various activities in order to be accepted by his or her peers.

The factor of sex. Experiences during the span of ages (9–17) during which sex maturation takes place often account for deviant behavior associated with the sex problem. The early maturer sexually may be a slow mental developer. He may attempt to gain status among his age peers by displaying his worldly knowledge in matters pertaining to sex. Even though much of what he knows is misinformation, nevertheless it is information that many others do not have and has sufficient emotional overtones to attract and hold the attention of his peers. This situation can have an unfortunate effect on sensitive teen-agers who have not yet matured sexually.

The individual who is acquainted early with sex facts is ready mentally and emotionally for the behavior of this sexually more mature young person who believes that his role is to enlighten his peers on matters of sex. Parents and teachers early should encourage the growing individual to develop wholesome attitudes toward sexual matters. This includes the development of respect for his own body and body functions, and of positive attitudes toward members of the opposite sex. He needs to be helped to use sexual control.

Physical defects. The adolescent with physical defects of any kind may indulge in behavior that seems to be different from that of boys and girls who do not have these physical defects. Every adolescent wants to participate in activities enjoyed by his peers. Denial of this participation may cause him to become embittered and resentful. He may resort to teasing and tormenting, to temper tantrums, and to making excessive demands on others. He is unhappy and strives for attention from others in devious ways.

Influence of Personal Factors

The relative strength of an adolescent's inherent drives and urges gives direction to the overt behavior that may be displayed in any given classroom. As he lives and develops, each individual progressively acquires attitudes and action patterns that serve him in his school and social situations. There is a constant temptation to engage in behavior that deviates from the expected norm in any situation. The individual's self-interest, his interest in the imitation of the behavior of others, or his disinterest in or unawareness of consequences of his acts often causes a display of nonconforming behavior.

The factors that constitute the personality of the teacher are most important in the teaching-learning situation. The interests and attitudes displayed by him stimulate one or another form of behavior in the situation. The behavior of adolescents often is directly related to the behavior displayed by the teacher. It is not comforting for a teacher suddenly to discover that what he has been doing and/or the attitudes he has been displaying are the determining factors of behavior displayed by his students.

Factor of self-interest. Personal factors are very important to the adolescent in the development of behavior patterns. The adolescent is especially aware of himself as a person and of his real or imagined personal limitations. He is sensitive to the attitudes of his peers toward him and to the nature and extent of his learning achievement. His emotions are attuned to his ability to rate among his fellow classmates. For example, embarrassment comes to the boy whose voice squeaks, even for a brief period.

Pangs of suffering are experienced by the adolescent who cannot get himself to take part in class discussions largely because he believes that what he has to say is not worth while and that what is said by others is said so much better than he can say it if he should try. He retreats toward becoming an isolate largely because he has the difficulty of recognizing in himself the fine qualities that he finds and admires in others of his age group. He suffers further if he is extremely sensitive to adverse criticism of his behavior expressed either by his peers or by his teacher. This young person gives evidence of too great concern with self; not enough thought or energy is directed toward the welfare of others.

Self-interest is a worthy goal when it is accompanied by a sincere interest in the activities of those with whom one is associated. The very young child is expected to display self-interest. However, as the individual grows, and develops social values, he tends to outgrow the need for self-satisfaction. During these years he learns to modify his self-centered interests; he becomes more and more aware of the interests of others and varies his conduct in such ways as to earn the approval of others.

An extremely self-centered adolescent can use many and devious means to satisfy his selfish interests. He may "apple-polish" the teacher, "steal" his chum's girl friend, or "hoodwink" his parents. Behavior of this kind does not set well with the other members of the group, and often leads to the rejection of this type of person from the inner circle of the group. Too many such experiences may encourage him to become a "bully" unless he is given proper guidance toward social cooperation.

Teachers can do much to give direction to an adolescent's self-interest. He should be helped in such ways that:

1. His extreme self-interest does not dominate his behavior.
2. He becomes aware of the consequences of his behavior at all times.
3. He does not give the impression that he is stubborn or uncooperative as his displayed self-conscious behavior often suggests.
4. He controls his desire to imitate undesirable behavior.
5. He is encouraged to emulate wholesome, outgoing qualities evinced by his teacher or other adults.

Social Factors in the Environment

An adolescent's overt reactions in social situations often reflect home influences. His attitude toward the teacher, the classroom, the learning materials, and his classmates is rooted in the home. He comes to the secondary school with well-established effective attitudes toward the school and all that it connotes. He has a history of learning success or of a lack of it. His behavior patterns are ready to continue as they have in the past.

Attitude toward school. If the young person has been relatively unsuccessful in his learning he may be driven by his need for activity to do things that will overcome the boredom experienced; he is likely to participate in the kinds of activities that yield immediate satisfaction, disregarding both teacher and class disapproval. He may be tempted to throw spitballs, tear up his written work, carve his initials on his desk, or engage in similar disapproved behavior. He prefers disapproval of his behavior to being ignored.

Desire for approval of behavior. An individual of any age needs to be secure in the affection of another or of others. This is especially true of the adolescent. If he admires his teacher, he puts forth great effort to cooperate with him. If he is sensitive to the interests and wishes of others, he makes an effort to cooperate with his classmates.

He wants to belong. He tends to wear clothes that are the current "style" of his group. He defends his hero and battles anyone who says anything against him. In his struggle for peer status, his behavior is motivated by a strong desire to be an accepted member of the group. In the school situation this goal usually can be achieved best by conforming to rules and regulations consistent with freedom of activity.

The motivating desire of an adolescent is rooted in his strong drive to receive favorable attention from his associates. His efforts to achieve this goal often seem awkward and crude to his elders. Teachers and guidance counselors give recognition to these factors as they attempt indirectly to have adolescents select appropriate student leaders. The admired peer leader becomes the model for the rest of the student body. Thereby each student can be enabled to acquire qualities that may contribute to leadership.

The urge to belong to organized social groups is strong. The fraternities are built on that pulling force. Any ongoing or well-established organization becomes a status symbol. Adolescents endure great hardships in order to win acceptance in a respected club or organization. In fact, initiation ceremonies have had to be curbed in many groups because of the severity of the activities required of neophytes. It is a good socializing experience to require some form of special behavior before admitting an individual to full membership in many social and/or professional groups. However, these requirements should be in the form of constructive accomplishment.

PREVENTIVE DISCIPLINARY MEASURES (GENERAL)

The good classroom teacher is the key to preventive discipline. This is not the entire story, however. What the adolescent brings with him to the teaching-learning situation either predisposes toward socially acceptable behavior or has built-in patterns that are conducive to uncooperative behavior. Both teachers and students know the need for and the value of correct behavior. Proper attitudes toward discipline become a powerful preventive measure.

In the following pages we direct your attention to significant aspects of teacher characteristics and procedures that can encourage smoothly running learning experiences, relatively free of disciplinary disruptions. Much of what is suggested here is discussed at length in other chapters.

Importance of Teacher Activity

Pupil behavior is responsive to the behavior traits displayed by the teacher during his teaching function. The teacher, through good lesson planning, knowledge of pupils, proper use of time and equipment, and the recognition and commendation of good achievement and progress on the part of learners, does much to prevent misbehavior in his classroom.

The student teacher needs to observe what the successful teacher does to make the teaching-learning situation run so smoothly. When everything goes well, it is not easy to discover precisely what has been done to make everything so effective. You are likely to find that the successful teacher knows his subject matter, understands the capabilities and attitudes of his students, utilizes workable procedures in class management, and actively leads the discussion so that there is a realization of progress or achievement.

The beginning teacher and especially the student teacher needs to be realistic. You must work with existing conditions. These may be a crowded classroom, a student who has immediate personal problems that are home centered, or inadequate material. The preventive aspect of discipline is (1) to study the records so that you know the individual students, (2) to organize your work so that you can cope with large classes, and (3) to plan to utilize supplementary material when and if these are available.

Importance of Teacher Assets

In your evaluation of preventive measures do not forget to inspect your own assets. What you bring to the classroom in yourself and your personal equipment might be your strongest means to establish predisposing attitudes toward desirable behavior. If you know what you expect to do and proceed to carry it out, your students are likely to gain the kind of respect for you that will encourage them to follow your lead and thereby avoid getting into trouble.

Misbehavior often starts when your students begin to feel that nothing worth while is happening; they are bored. Good motivation of the learning process gives the learner the mental stimulation needed for thinking and learning. Most students prefer to be active mentally rather than to be forced to sit idly by while a teacher makes up his mind as to what he will do next.

Adolescents are keen observers of their teacher's behavior and of teaching procedures. They become outspoken critics of ineffectual teaching. Since they are likely to emulate your behavior, try to set the kind of example that is worthy of imitation. Give your administrator the kind of cooperation you expect from your students. If reports are due at a definite time, have them prepared and submit them when they should be reported. Expect the same from your students. Do not, however, expect your students to be prompt with study assignments and written reports if you have sloppy habits. Students have a way of discovering how you perform in these matters. Set a good example.

Importance of Getting the Right Start

Student teachers often decide that they are going to revolutionize discipline by treating learners like human beings and by being a good fellow from the start. They have been learners in the classrooms of a secondary school and college for many years and believe that the authority of the teacher has been too rigid. They intend to demonstrate that the teacher is and can be more human than he often is thought to be.

Student teachers often believe that the teacher can become a friend among his learners from the start. Unfortunately, they may discover that it is far easier to relax one's control than to recapture it. They usually find that once the situation has gone beyond their control they have to exercise rigid authority in order to provide acceptable teaching-learning conditions.

As a student teacher, you need to become aware of the fact that there always must be a difference between your position and that of learners. You must discover that you need to establish in the minds of the learners the fact that you are the recognized leader of the group and that your authority needs to be respected at all times, regardless of the extent of friendship that may be established between yourself and each member of the class.

Professional Factors That Can Prevent Discipline Problems

Your duty as a student teacher is that of advising and guiding students in your class. The manner in which you discharge most of the following responsibilities will determine the extent to which your discipline problems will be reduced. You are likely to find that your teaching will be more effective when:

1. You discover that a student learns best when (*a*) his mental and physical activities are appropriate for his ability and he feels confident that he can accomplish what is expected of him, (*b*) his efforts are appreciated by you and his classmates and he is free from personal distractions, and (*c*) he likes and respects you and appreciates your use of corrective measures to help him learn.
2. You observe and encourage the educational and emotional growth and progress of each of your students.
3. You provide opportunities for the development and improvement of the student's social relations.
4. You understand the individual student's role in the group, his interests, abilities, behavior patterns, goals, and family problems.
5. You use classroom practices that will further good student-teacher relations.
6. You are alert to changes in the student's pattern of behavior, work, or attitudes.
7. You utilize in a professional manner knowledge obtained from standardized tests, cumulative records, interviews, informal discussion, and observations.
8. You maintain a relaxed atmosphere that avoids tensions yet encourages each pupil to work to his maximum capacity.
9. You insist on respect for authority and the rights of others and of property, as well as on fair play, courtesy, and respect for established rules and policies.
10. You obtain the help of counselors and supervisors as needed.

Importance of Good Motivation

The arousal of learner interest in the learning material stands high as a preventive of misbehavior. Good teaching cannot be achieved without motivating the learner. The teacher who knows his learners is able to gear his teaching to their experience levels. Motivation is more directly associated with this fact than it is, for example, with the utilization of a story or novel situation to interest the learner. Some of these attempts may actually be distracters rather than motivators. If you begin the lesson with a novel approach, be sure that, as soon as possible, you direct the thinking to the problem situation with which you will be concerned during the lesson.

The good teacher begins his class promptly so that his learners become so interested in what is going on that few evidences of misbehavior are detected. This type of teacher plans his lessons on the experience level of his learners. His learners then are able to understand what is happening and get enjoyment from the learning experience. The good teacher avoids the spectacular in arousing a desire on the part of his students to learn. He challenges their thinking because he has learned to ask thought-provoking questions rather than merely factual ones.

PREVENTIVE DISCIPLINARY MEASURES (SPECIFIC)

Since the teacher is the key person to preventive discipline, what he does becomes most important. The suggestions that follow do not guarantee the elimination of discipline problems, but they can reduce the number of such by anticipating what might happen if these practices are not utilized. Read these preventive procedures carefully. To as great an extent as is possible for you to do so, try to apply them during your student teaching experiences. In some instances you will need to consult your cooperating teacher and/or your college supervisor concerning your utilization of a particular procedure. Since you are not in complete charge of the class, you do not want to do anything that goes counter to the regular teacher's disciplinary approaches. In general, however, you should find most of these suggestions helpful to you as a student teacher.

Display an Attitude That Anticipates Pupil Cooperation

Teachers and students must learn to live together and to work together in the classroom situation. This is a goal that should consciously be in the minds of all concerned. The teacher must assume the role of the leader since it is within him that authority is vested for the guidance of behavior. The wise teacher uses this authority to stimulate cooperation between himself and his students. He can impose his authority or he can invite cooperation. The same overt behavior may result in either approach; but the behavior responses that result from *a request* are more likely to be based on a cooperative attitude and hence become more functional in the lives of the students.

Your students sense the extent to which you expect them to be orderly and quiet. Once you decide that quiet must prevail in your classroom and that you will not countenance foolish or noisy behavior, this decision will be conveyed to the members of your class through the tone of your voice, your manner, and your general attitude. The students then know that you expect attentive cooperation and intend to get it from them. This attitude convinces them that you and they are there for the business of learning.

You should not beg for quiet; you should insist on it. You need to show in your voice, manner, and readiness to start the lesson that there is work to be done and that you have a plan for completing it. You cannot afford to be indecisive. You need not scold or even raise your voice as you give the members of your class the kind of mental orientation that will enable them to engage in active thinking about the study material. You must mean what you say. The will to carry through is important in the situation, and the members of the class need to discover that you are fair and just, but ready to follow through until behavior conforms to good classroom conditions.

Speak Clearly and Distinctly

The voice of the teacher is important and should be clear and distinct. It should have enough volume to reach all parts of the classroom, without being sharp or shrill. The teacher can use his voice to alert individuals to active thinking or he can use it to lull them to sleep. The teacher with a faltering voice or a timid approach is the one whom secondary school students "ride." Both through his speech and manner he should exhibit an attitude of confidence in himself so that he commands the respect of others.

Be Prepared for the Entire Class Period

A student teacher as well as a regular teacher must be prepared to continue the lesson for the entire class period. There is nothing so conducive to disorderly behavior as a teacher and a class who have finished the plan for the hour long before the end of the class period. Experienced teachers usually are able to meet this emergency, but the student teacher or the beginning teacher should guard against its happening lest he invite disorder in his class. It is too much to ask students to sit quietly when you have nothing further to offer during a class period. When you do not give the students something to do, they will provide their own activities.

Use the Names of Your Students from the Start

The proper identification of pupils can easily be accomplished by means of a tentative seating chart. It might be advisable to invite the members of the class to help you prepare this chart at the first meeting of the class. You can ask each to write his name in the proper space on your prepared chart form. This is easily done by passing it down each row. You may wish to use this as a working form to prepare your chart after seats have been selected. Also, some of the names may not be written as plainly by the pupils as you will need for your use. However, you can use this chart to call on a pupil within the first few minutes of the first recitation. The students gain the impression that you know what you are doing and begin to develop a positive attitude toward you.

Delegate Class Routine to Members of the Class

What you do in class management will set the pace for orderly activity. Each teacher has his own way of dealing with the matter of daily routines of class management. During your observation of teaching give special attention to what is done by the teacher or by various teachers. Decide on a satisfactory procedure that will be time-reducing, and use it. A fluctuation of practiced routines, even of method of passing out papers, may be upsetting to some members of your class. Decide on a method of collecting work and follow it, thereby avoiding any confusion that results from pupils not knowing what to expect. Also, give your students instructions on how to head written work and follow that plan constantly.

Students can be trained to be responsible for many class routines. When they know what is expected they are willing to cooperate in helping with many activities of class management. All students can participate in keeping the room tidy by learning to pick up paper, and the like. One trustworthy student can, under supervision, help in taking attendance. Responsibility for cleaning the chalkboard can be rotated among the pupils of the class on a definite schedule basis.

Practice Emotional Control

There are times when secondary school students seem unreasonable and unruly. These are trying times and will tax you to retain your emotional composure. There are occasions, however, in every classroom when you need to express disapproval of undesirable behavior. You must learn to deal with such situations without losing emotional control. This does not imply that you should attempt to disapprove misbehavior with a smile. It is difficult, if not impossible, to disapprove asocial behavior with a smile and be effective.

As a student teacher, it is appropriate for you to experience the feeling of anger as you deal with behavior problems, but you should show the members of your class that you can control your temper and refrain from angry blasts or temper-tantrum behavior. If you shout verbal disapproval at your students they resent you or inwardly laugh at you. Students have profound respect for the teacher who, in difficult situations, gives overt evidence of emotional control expressed in patient consideration.

Students know that misbehavior is to be corrected, and usually do not object to having you give the leadership needed to change their behavior for the better. They object less to the fact that you disapprove their misbehavior than they do to the fact that you lose your temper in so doing. Your attitude should be objective, and you should direct your disapproval toward the offense rather than make it personal. It is not easy to disapprove only offensive behavior and avoid having the offender feel that it might be personal. A silent look of disapproval often is effective, especially if the behavior is corrected thereafter.

The teacher is expected to practice emotional control in all situations. He is the leader in any emergency, such as the sudden outbreak of fire or an unfortunate accident to one of his students. His approach in meeting accidents, illness, or fire should serve as a calming influence on those with whom he works. A focus on his responsibilities usually helps him practice emotional control in trying situations. Also, although it is easier said than done, a teacher should be equally calm in the presence of his superiors. His supervisors have no more right to use fear as a disciplinary measure in dealing with him than he has in dealing with his pupils.

Remember the Human Relations Factor

Pupils of this age are individualistic and need to be treated as persons who can think for themselves. They have outgrown the mere acceptance of orders simply because these are given by someone in authority. They are concerned with the reasons that govern the request. Adolescents have a strong pull toward wanting freedom, yet they desire the protective guidance of an understanding teacher.

Adolescents enjoy teasing and tormenting. They find many ways to annoy or torment their teacher and constantly tend to tease the members of their group. The teacher who recognizes the presence of these urges and acts accordingly earns the sincere admiration of his students. Adolescents are ready to cooperate. The teacher needs to establish the kind of relationships between himself and his students that will enable them together to function at a high level in the teaching-learning situation.

Be Able to Locate the Guilty Person

If you know your students and a disturbance occurs, you should be able to identify the guilty person as soon as you locate the point of disturbance. Each member of your class is deterred somewhat from engaging in uncooperative behavior by his knowledge of the fact that you are alert to everything that takes place in class. Your attention to any and every distracting influence is paramount. This does not mean that you make an issue of each one, merely that everyone knows that you understand what is happening.

Plan to Keep Every Student Busy

A resourceful teacher finds ways to keep all members of the class busy. He keeps an eye on incipient troublemakers and arranges to keep them occupied. There are some students who cannot be reached by you when you are doing your student teaching. In these cases you should enlist the help of your cooperating teacher and, when you are a regular teacher, the help of the guidance counselor.

Give Attention to the Seating of the Students

Much continued disturbing behavior can be prevented by reseating those students who have too much to say to each other and who may have less to talk about if seated alongside another student. It is known that one student may have a bad effect on another and excite him to excessive talking. When you discover this, you can rearrange your seating plan to alleviate some of the problems that seem to be arising in the present situation. Often, one pupil will become mischievous if he is near a friend; if he is removed to another section of the classroom, he will be quiet.

Practice Calling on the Less Attentive

It is satisfying to carry the discussion on the level of those who are eager to participate and are raising their hands. You need to stimulate the thinking of all, especially those students who give evidence of daydreaming, show an interest in friends, engage in excessive doodling, and the like. With careful planning, it is easy to bring them into the discussion. It will not happen, however, unless you do something about it. Be aware of the less vocal, and direct questions to them that they probably will be able to answer.

Make Constant Use of Your Eyes and Ears

It is interesting to study the behavior of students in a classroom. Usually when one of them wishes to engage in deviate behavior he first takes a quick look at you before he starts his act. You can do much at this moment to alter the student's behavior by "catching" his eye and continuing to look at him. You thereby are letting him know that you suspect what he is about to do. He then is likely to desist from a planned bit of mischief, an attempt to cheat on a test, or any other form of undesirable behavior.

As you move your eyes around the room, the members of your class begin to realize that you are aware of them and of what they are doing. You will find that this is more easily done when you are standing or moving about in the room, rather than remaining seated at your desk. You need to develop skill in writing on the chalkboard so that you are not separated from your class. Your recognized ability to see and hear what is happening in your classroom enables you to prevent much deviant behavior from starting.

Display a Sense of Humor

Amusing incidents are likely to occur in the classroom. Consciously or unconsciously, a student may say or do something that arouses laughter among his classmates. Show that you are a good sport by joining briefly in the merriment. If a student seems to be baiting you deliberately, ignore it at the time and direct the attention of the class to an activity that they will find interesting. Avoid a sharp retort, or any indication of the fact that you have been hurt or angered by what he has said. Later, in a private conference with him, you can attempt to discover why he acted as he did and bring about a better relationship between him and yourself.

Avoid Public Conflict with Students

Try to avoid criticizing a student or arguing with him in the presence of other members of the class. Display patience and show the poise that is expected of a teacher. When suggestions for improvement are necessary, make them to as great extent as possible in a private personal conference. Always be as supportive as possible to the student. Whenever it is possible give him the benefit of a doubt.

Help Students Who Tend to Interfere with Others

When a student interferes with the study or learning of his classmates, request his cooperation by a quiet approach. Whatever you do should be done with calmness, dignity, and firmness. Try to help the individual before you decide to send him to a counselor or administrator for assistance in dealing with his problem.

Display a Personal Interest in Students

Adolescents like to believe that their teacher is interested in them as persons. Getting this idea over to them works wonders in gaining their cooperation with you. Attend as many of their school meetings as your time permits. They appreciate your cooperation with their special assembly programs and their school athletic events. Also, students develop a warm feeling toward you if you listen sympathetically when they tell you about some of their problems and if you respect their confidences. They also thrill to receiving a short message of sympathy—a telephone call or, perhaps, a visit when they are ill.

Be Well-Organized and Businesslike

When you are well-organized, it implies that you know what you intend to do and that you have a plan to implement your purpose. If you have worthwhile material for each lesson you can provide your pupils with a program of action that tends to deter the start of most behavior problems. Make it a point to start a lesson on time and with enthusiasm for the subject—and be sure to end the lesson promptly with the bell. Each student is entitled to his full time to get to his next class. You should not detain a student from meeting his next appointment on time. If a personal conference is needed, make an appointment for that purpose at a time that is convenient for the student as well as for yourself.

You have responsibilities for discipline between class periods. Supervise the behavior of students near you. If there is crowding in passageways, let your presence and influence be known. It is your duty also to keep a careful record of attendance and tardiness and to submit this record to the administration when due. Laxity in these matters may be a causative factor of your own discipline problems.

Encourage Student Cooperation

You will find it helpful to involve the students as much as possible in class activities. The extent to which they know what is expected of them and what procedures are to be utilized will determine the nature and willingness of their cooperation. Bring the students into your planning. They like to comply with procedures they have helped to develop. This was discovered many years ago when the junior high school pupils in New York City were invited by the Superintendent in charge of Junior High Schools to draw up a "Code of Behavior" for their group. This became an excellent experience for them. However, it has no more value to present junior high school pupils than a code of behavior drawn up by educational experts. For such a code of behavior to be most effective, each generation of pupils needs to develop one of its own. As the young people work on it, they achieve an understanding of its purposes and a willingness to live by its provisions.

Strive to Be Impartial

You need consciously to try to avoid a display of favoritism toward one or more members of your class or classes. Although you want to be impartial in your attitude toward your students, human nature is such that partiality may tend unconsciously to creep into your teaching-learning situation. Sometimes students are aware of your behavior long before it occurs to you that you may have given one or more students the kind of attention and/or consideration that you have not given to the others.

You wonder how it is that partiality tends to creep into your practices. One student reacts toward you in a way that another does not. This starts a chain of human interactions that is different from what it is between you and another or even every other member of the class. You must guard against displaying greater interest in this individual as a person than in others in the class. You need to evaluate fairly the attitudes and behavior of your students and treat each according to his personal needs and his ability to meet his responsibilities. Individual differences are present and should be reckoned with, but not to the extent of giving excessive attention to the interests of one or two students.

Students have the right to expect fair treatment at all times. You are wise to examine, from time to time, your relationship with the members of your class. If you find that you are giving undue attention to one or more of your students or if several of them are taking an overabundance of your time after class, you might try to bring this into line with what you do for and with other members of the class.

Need to Cooperate with Parents

Parent-teacher relationships are closer on the elementary level than on the secondary level. However, more and more parents are being brought into the situation in the secondary school when behavior problems arise. Adolescents usually are not interested in having their parents come to school to discuss their behavior problems with their teachers. Yet, as we indicated earlier, behavior problems do not suddenly start in high school. There usually is a long history of their development. Hence there is need for cooperation between the parents and the secondary school teacher to get at the root of the problem and to help the adolescent develop a change of attitude that must be the forerunner of any change of behavior. The parent, the teacher, and the guidance counselor working together may be needed to give greatest assistance.

Learn to Work with the Guidance Counselor

The relationship between the teacher and the counselor should be a reciprocal one. Some teachers have not yet developed the confidence in counselors that should prevail in our schools, but most teachers want to cooperate with guidance counselors. They are unhappy, however, when the guidance counselor has information about a learner that is not made available to sympathetic and understanding teachers.

Teachers are handicapped by the pressure of time and crowded classrooms. Counselors must be sensitive to these facts and try to make it easy for the teacher to work with them. They must be ready to help the teacher eliminate such causes of arguments as "I do not have the time to give to that extra work for one student." They need to convince teachers through tact, diplomacy, and artful persuasion that the guidance function can go forward only when both teacher and counselor work together for the good of the student.

The counselor can help you realize that there are some adolescents so emotionally disturbed that they cannot be given sufficient help in the classroom. With this reassurance from the counselor, you are encouraged rather than discouraged when he attempts to provide satisfying and enriching experiences for this kind of student. You then are willing to accept the assistance of the counselor.

QUESTIONS AND TOPICS FOR DISCUSSION

1. Read the definitions of discipline as compiled by Oliva. Select the five definitions that you consider to be most applicable to the secondary school. Justify your choices.
2. List at least five rules or regulations that are intended to govern students' behavior in your classroom.
3. What is your cooperating teacher's attitude toward any student who fails to respect such class rules?
4. Differentiate between discipline and self-discipline.
5. To what exent do discipline problems arise when you are in charge of the class? How do you handle such situations? How should you?
6. Study those students in your classroom whose behavior is undisciplined. Try to discover the reasons for their lack of cooperation.
7. List some of the frustrations often experienced by adolescents.
8. Cite examples of displayed self-interests among the students in the class. How does your cooperating teacher handle such situations?
9. List teacher characteristics that are effective in encouraging good discipline among students.
10. Which of the procedures for preventive discipline listed in the chapter do you consider most significant? Give reasons for your choices.

SELECTED REFERENCES

ATKINSON, J. W. *The Assessment of Human Motives*. Princeton, N.J.: D. Van Nostrand Co., Inc., 1958.

BARUCH, D. *New Ways in Discipline*. New York: McGraw-Hill Book Co., Inc., 1949.

CROW, L. D., and CROW, ALICE. *Mental Hygiene for Teachers: A Book of Readings*. New York: Macmillan Co., 1963.

CUTTS, N. E., and MOSELEY, N. *Better Home Discipline*. New York: Appleton-Century-Crofts, Inc., 1952.

HAVIGHURST, R. J. "The Functions of Successful Discipline," *Understanding the Child*, XXI (1952), 35–38.

HESTER, H. "Beginning Junior High School Teachers May Benefit from a Sermon on Discipline," *The Clearing House*, January 1963, pp. 311–12.

HYMES, J. L., JR. *Discipline*. New York: Teachers College, Columbia Univ., Bureau of Publications, 1949.

KRUG, O., and BECK, H. L. *A Guide to Better Discipline*. Chicago: Science Research Associates, Inc., 1954.

LEONARD, C. W., *Why Children Misbehave*. Chicago: Science Research Associates, Inc., 1952.

PHILLIPS, E. L., WEINER, D. N., and HARING, N. G. *Discipline, Achievement and Mental Health*. Englewood Cliffs, N.J.: Prentice-Hall, Inc., 1960.

REDL, F. *Understanding Children's Behavior*. New York: Teachers College, Columbia Univ., Bureau of Publications 1960.

SHEVIAKOV, G. V., and REDL, F. *Discipline for Today's Children and Youth* (rev. ed.). Washington, D.C.: Association for Supervision and Curriculum Development, NEA, 1956.

STRANG, RUTH. *The Adolescent Views Himself: A Psychology of Adolescence*. New York: McGraw-Hill Book Co., Inc., 1957.

13

THE DEVELOPMENT OF SELF–DISCIPLINE

Constructive discipline is concerned with motivating the utilization of correct behavior at all times and in all situations. A student's classroom behavior should be judged on the basis of his reasons for behaving as he does, and the effect of his behavior on other young people in the learning situation. For example, the cause of noise in a classroom may be more important than the fact that noise is heard. What may be considered to be confusion in one situation may represent orderly procedure in another. Most important is whether all members of the group are busily progressing toward the goals they have set for themselves.

NEED FOR STANDARDS OF CONDUCT

Adolescents need standards to govern their conduct. They want to know the general principles that are to be used to guide their behavior. They are entitled to understand the rules and regulations that are to be used to govern their behavior. These serve as stabilizing influences for them.

Each adolescent should be stimulated toward the achievement of a particular goal. He should work under a set of rules that he understands, and he should know that an infringement of these rules will result in some form of penalization. Quiet should not be expected for its sake alone but for the purpose of getting on with the work of the day. Classroom conditions should be conducive to thinking and, insofar as possible, reflect life situations.

Desirable behavior habits should be trained into each individual to such an extent that they become habitual. Each student should be encouraged and expected to participate actively in every learning situation of which he is a part. The nature and extent of his self-discipline is evidenced in group situations in which there is a minimum of teacher supervision.

Pupil behavior should be a joint function and responsibility of both the student and the teacher. The person with the authority, the teacher, should transfer the responsibility for behavior to the students individually and collectively whenever they demonstrate ability to use the responsibility intelligently. This approach helps young people function effectively in all social or group situations in which they find themselves.

Constructive discipline is based on active participation, cooperation, and social awareness, as these operate to bring about changes in student behavior. The aim is not to have a classroom in which nothing ever goes wrong, but rather one in which the students and the teacher alike know when something has gone wrong and are able and willing to effect needed changes for good social living.

There is a fine balance between an adolescent's *rights* and his *responsibilities* in the home and/or the school. We illustrate these for the teen-ager in the school. You might draw up a similar set for his rights and responsibilities in the home.

RIGHTS   *and*   RESPONSIBILITIES

of Adolescents [1]

In School Relationships

1. To be provided with proper facilities to gain an education	1. To cooperate with teachers and schoolmates
2. Not to be compared unfavorably with classmates	2. To attend school regularly
3. To have curricular offerings and teaching methods suited to one's ability level	3. To obey school rules and regulations
4. To receive teacher recognition of successful study achievement	4. To appreciate and utilize the right to a free, public education
5. To have reasonable freedom in choice of subjects to be studied	5. To take an active part in school affairs
6. To receive help in vocational selection and planning	6. To respect school property
7. To have freedom in the expression of one's opinion in class	7. To uphold school standards: honesty in examinations, attention in class, etc.
8. To have the opportunity to join clubs or to participate in extracurricular activities in terms of one's interests	8. To accept deserved disapproval of one's work or conduct
	9. To respect the rights of other students

[1] Alice Crow, "Three R's for Teen-agers: Rights, Responsibilities, Relationships," *The High School Journal,* May, 1958, pp. 370–71.

RIGHTS   *and*   RESPONSIBILITIES (*Cont.*)

9. To ask pertinent questions in class
10. To receive expert counseling when it is needed

10. To meet school obligations by completion of homework, proper grooming and dress, etc.

In Social Relationships

1. To join groups of one's own choice
2. To have status in a group
3. Not to be discriminated against because of creed or race or nationality
4. To choose one's hobbies and other activities, such as sports, dancing, etc.
5. To be accepted for one's self rather than for another's worth
6. To lead or to follow, depending on one's ability and interest, and the situation
7. To develop a normal interest in the members of the opposite sex
8. To exact loyalty and justice from group members
9. To have such prestige as one merits
10. To be permitted sufficient time each week for constructive and relaxing activities

1. To conform with desirable group standards but maintain proper individuality
2. To be a good sport
3. To share in group activities
4. To trust parental guidance of one's social activities
5. To abide by all safety and sanitary codes of the community
6. To manifest no superiority or prejudiced attitudes
7. To avoid influences and situations which might lead to trouble, such as gang war, vandalism, loitering late at night
8. To respect the opposite sex (for boys especially)
9. To be careful of one's language
10. To be loyal to friends

PRACTICES FOR CONSTRUCTIVE DISCIPLINE

Always plan to use the entire class period for teaching-learning experiences. Do not expect good order if you use class time to assign lessons that are to be learned outside of class and in the classroom only listen to and check on the extent to which the assigned material has been learned. You should become involved in real teaching. You should work with ideas in such a way that all learners in the group are gaining in understanding of the problems under consideration.

Secondary school pupils enjoy hard work if it applies to worthwhile tasks. There is deep satisfaction that comes with doing high-quality workmanship if it has a purpose. This does not imply that a student always should be permitted to work only at that in which he is interested at the moment. Rather does it mean that the teacher has an obligation to motivate the learning in all situations to the extent that interest may be aroused in each and every worthy learning activity. This may be facilitated by providing a variety of functional activities. Lessons can be individualized or respective students can be assigned a responsibility for a particular phase of a project.

The teacher is one unit or cog, but an important one, in the class and school setting. What each teacher does individually becomes important collectively in building what is known as *esprit de corps*. The rapport and spirit that permeates the school is something that is built up over a period of years.

The standards of a school help build the reputation of the school; the school's tradition, in turn, works for the benefit of the school. It is easy to develop self-discipline in situations in which, for years, good behavior has been the accepted practice. The going is rough if the school develops a reputation of laxity; it is difficult also for a teacher who has the reputation that anything goes in his class.

REMEDIAL MEASURES FOR IMPROVING STUDENT BEHAVIOR

We can all agree that misbehavior should be corrected. The means by which this is accomplished is less clear. There is no one panacea or recipe for correcting misbehavior of individuals. As a student teacher or a beginning teacher, you may express the desire to be furnished with a simple formula to help you deal with disciplinary problems. It will not take you long to discover that general principles are all that can be supplied. Their application almost always needs to be modified to meet the particular needs of the individual and the situation in which the misbehavior arises.

Suggestions for Correcting Misbehavior in the Classroom

The measures to be used to correct misbehavior are never simple and are never the same for two teachers or for two different classes of the same teacher, nor for two individuals in the same class. A problem may arise in one class of a teacher and never arise in another class. Then, too, one teacher may be able to apply one technique effectively and be unable to get satisfactory results from the use of another, or another teacher may find corrective measures working in reverse. It seems clear then, that although a method works in one situation, this does not, in and of itself, make the method a psychologically good one. Merely to change overt behavior does not insure effective behavior patterns; much depends on how it was done.

Indirect control is usually the better approach, yet there are times when direct control is necessary. A technique used effectively with one student in one situation may fail when used by the same teacher to achieve its purpose with another student or in another situation. Hence you will find it necessary to vary your methods of dealing with uncooperative overt behavior. The effectiveness of a measure depends on the way it is used and on the extent to which it applies to the individual and his particular offense.

Be Impersonal in Your Approach

The teacher should make any disciplinary measures he uses as impersonal as possible. It should be a matter of correcting the offense and not abusing the student who has misbehaved. Whatever measures are used should be understood by the student and should be accepted by him as reasonable. It is important that extreme measures be administered in private and that they be adjusted to the nature of the offense. When administered, the teacher should not be in a state of anger or displaying a temper tantrum. All measures should be effective, yet not be physically harmful to the individual.

The guilty person should be penalized in such a way that there is no interference with the learning opportunities of the members of the class. Care should be taken that the entire class is not penalized for the misbehavior of one or two misbehaving members of the group. The important consideration is to enlist the cooperation of the class in developing desirable behavior practices of all the members of the group.

If an entire class is punished for the misdeeds of one or two wrongdoers, they are not likely to want to cooperate in developing a good spirit in the group. When you get the members of the class to laugh at, rather than with, the culprits, you are making headway in having the members of the class help in providing conditions necessary to good learning.

Use Praise When Warranted

You will find it most helpful if you use the positive approach in whatever you do. Think constructively. Do not criticize your superiors. Be careful of your criticisms of your students. Your words get back to your students in ways you little expect. Practice using praise whenever and wherever you can. This applies both to your students and to your colleagues. Be fair, generous, and willing to ask students to display acceptable behavior.

Many behavior problems that develop might have been avoided if you had made wise use of approval and given recognition to respective individuals and their achievement. When they fail to win approval for acceptable achievement, adolescents often turn to other less desirable approaches as attention getters and become problems to their teachers. They prefer your disapproval to lack of recognition of what they have done or are doing.

You are likely to find it profitable to evaluate the achievement progress of each student and thus convey to him the fact that you are interested in what he is doing. If your evaluation is meaningful to him, he then understands that you appreciate whatever difficulties he may be encountering with it.

Behavior problems often arise when there is conflict between teacher and student. The giving and receiving of desired approval is a continuous process that enlists the interests of both the teacher and the students. You should learn early to make judicious use of this effective means of directing student behavior. Praise based on evaluation and disapproval directed against all misbehavior without favor are helpful factors in the development of those attitudes that govern good social behavior.

Remedial Measures Based on Definite Causes

In his discussion of "High School Discipline in American Society," Peter F. Oliva presented excellent *Remedial Measures* that might be used in the treatment of behavior caused by such factors as physical factors, social and emotional factors, home and community influences, and society in general. We present his recommendations here:

Physical Factors. Possible remedial action which can be taken in the treatment of causes of behavior problems resulting from physical factors are:
1. Thorough medical examination will provide data on the nature of physical difficulties.
2. Provision of minimum medical and dental attention in school is a necessity.
3. Extra milk and opportunities for extra rest can be provided by the school.
4. Reports to parents from the school physician and school nurse should be sent and followed up.
5. Enlisting the help of social agencies to assist poor children in obtaining needed medical and dental attention is a responsibility of school leadership.
6. Provision of corrective therapy for the physically handicapped is important. There are many schools which have corrective therapy rooms used to no extent or for such purposes as storage.
7. Seating and scheduling of the child's program should be such as to conform to his physical abilities.[2]

Social and Emotional Factors. Action which may be taken in dealing with social and emotional factors includes:
1. Affection and sympathy from the teacher to help satisfy needs of affection, approval, and security.
2. Provision for guidance services to help the pupil solve some of his many problems.
3. Placing responsibility on the pupil in keeping with his abilities in order to satisfy his need of approbation, independence, and new experiences.
4. Social functions and training in social manners to give the adolescent the necessary confidence and skills to establish good relationships with the opposite sex.
5. Group projects to develop group morale and to satisfy the desire for gregariousness.
6. Praise and publication of achievements to satisfy the need for success.
7. Part-time work to give added opportunities to fulfill adolescent needs for security and independence. The school can assist in this training through diversified work-experience programs and through placement services.
8. Provision for outlets for excess energy and for talents not brought out in the academic phases of the curriculum. This can be done through extracurricular activities and athletics.[3]

[2] Peter F. Oliva, "High School Discipline in American Society," *The Bulletin of the National Association of Secondary-School Principals,* January, 1956, p. 21.
[3] *Ibid.,* p. 24.

Factors Originating in the Home and Community. Approaches to the treatment of causes of behavior problems originating in the home and community may be outlined.

1. Visits to the home establish rapport and furnish necessary information about the pupil's background.
2. Part-time work may solve some of the family's economic difficulties.
3. Adult education can provide parents with help in the problems of growth and development of their boys and girls.
4. Retraining of youth from underprivileged environment must be handled tactfully and patiently.
5. Adequate and available physical recreation facilities in the school can do much to counteract neighborhood conditions and provide a healthful environment under adult supervision.
6. Cooperation with outside agencies, such as Boy Scouts, Girl Scouts, community centers, churches, *et al.*, attacks the problem of unfavorable home and neighborhood environment.
7. Teachers have discovered that in many cases little can be done by the school about home environment. They have the responsibility of seeking any measures which may be helpful and, negatively, by not augmenting the pupil's conflict by mentally unhygienic treatment.[4]

Factors Originating in the Larger Social Order. No one, of course, can blame all the ills of society on the public schools. Home and community environment are extremly potent factors in the development of such evils as delinquency and crime. Yet, it can be said that schools have not done all they can to recognize symptoms of disorder and to prevent and correct these disorders. Possible approaches to the treatment of behavior problems resulting from causes originating in the larger social order can be outlined.

1. Orientation to youth problems will help adolescents understand the reasons for military service, the problems of democracy, and the reasons for the necessity for participation in democracy. Courses in orientation to school and community living and in personal and social adjustment should be a part of the general education of all youth.
2. Vocational education and guidance are essential to provide the youth with salable skills.
3. Instruction in school needs to encompass some of the pressing, controversial issues of democracy in search for solutions. Avoidance of this attempt to solve some of democracy's most difficult questions is an injustice to the nation. Too often educators are timid about permitting discussion of controversial problems. Yet, these are the problems which distress youth and the nation and which must be faced.
4. Discussion of the individual's role in an industrial society must be emphasized in secondary education. In this way the adolescent is made to consider his place in society, his obligations, and to sense his responsibilities.

[4] *Ibid.,* p. 28.

5. Counteracting prejudices and special-interest narrowness can be accomplished by providing opportunities for heterogeneous groups to live and work together. Objective teaching of information to dispel irrational discrimination is a function of schools in a free society. The school can combat social class divisions by nourishing the young in a truly democratic atmosphere of social cooperation.
6. Adapting the curriculum for the locality will serve to resist alien urban influences on the small localities.
7. The school can provide opportunities for the development of the social skills of manners, cooperation, and teamwork. The United States is high in technical skills, but notoriously low in the social skills.
8. Attention should be given in every course to citizenship from the local level to world responsibilities.
9. As much attention should be given to the imperative needs of society as is given to the imperative needs of youth.[5]

SPECIFIC REMEDIAL SUGGESTIONS FOR TEACHERS

Different approaches have been tried in the past with varying degrees of success to effect a change in behavior. The more common corrective or remedial measures include a long list of practices. Among those often used can be mentioned: change of seat, apology, demerits, deprivation of privileges, detention, assigning extra work, ignoring, isolating the offender, scolding, time for meditation, providing incentives, payment for property damage, appeal to members of class, advice of experienced teachers, personal conferences.

You help establish the attitudes and habits in your classroom. You must learn to live with them. It is helpful to have rules to guide your own conduct and decisions in matters of behavior control and the development of self-discipline. For example:

1. You should avoid publicizing offenses and parading them before your class. This is likely to create more problems than it deters.
2. You should avoid punishing the entire class for misconduct of a few members.
3. You should avoid the use of ridicule or sarcasm as a means of punishment.
4. You should not make threats. You must carry out all plans that you announce. Idle threats are of no value to anyone.

[5] *Ibid.*, p. 37.

5. You should not assume authority that is not yours. For example, you should not announce a make-believe suspension. It can only be an unrealistic, undesirable threat since you do not have such authority.

You should avoid making an issue of situations or behaviors that are trivial. You must decide what behavior is permissible for good teaching-learning procedures and what needs to be corrected. You need to know what is going on, but you also need to decide when and where to stop what is happening. As you gain confidence in the situation, you will become attuned to this and realize better what ought to be done in each situation. For example, neither permit students to congregate around your desk during class time, unless you invite them to do so, nor allow uncontrolled movement of them in the classroom.

Value of Changing Student's Seat

If two or more students indicate by their behavior that they cannot work quietly when seated together, you might find it helpful to change the seat of one or both of them. The individual student must be aware of the reason for your changing his seat. The authors make it a practice in college classes never to assign definite seats to the members of their classes. Yet, they reserve the right to reseat any member who, for one reason or another, should be seated elsewhere. During these many years, there have been very few occasions when the reassignment of the seating of one member seemed advisable for the improvement of learning conditions. In those instances the reseating was promptly done.

Students who are close friends often have a great deal to talk about. They may have developed habits of teasing one another when out of school, and this may carry into the classroom unless you do something to terminate its continuation. Separation is helpful since it enables these students to give attention to what is happening in class rather than to each other. It is good for the other students, since it has removed one of the irritants in the situation and has subtly put them on notice that action will be taken when needed.

Factor of Using Apology in Correcting Behavior

The use of apology with adolescents to correct misbehavior is fraught with danger. An adolescent should never be forced to apologize for his misdeeds. Of course, your interest is to bring about a change in the attitude and behavior of the individual. Your motivation should be that of helping him *want to behave properly*.

You want to help him achieve more than an expression of regret —you want him to mean what he says. It is so easy to verbalize the words in a statement of regret. The expressed regret is of little value unless it is accompanied by deep feelings of regret and a resolution that such behavior will not be repeated. You are succeeding in correcting misbehavior only to the extent that the student actually regrets his mischievous behavior whether he utters a formal apology or not.

Factor of Using Demerits

If administered judiciously, demerits can serve a helpful purpose. A system of demerits may have value if, when used, there is a resulting loss of privilege of a desired activity. The worth of demerits can be measured in terms of the attitudes engendered toward successful pursuit. If they serve to encourage the young person to avoid loss of prestige, they have meaning for him. Also, for demerits to be effective, the demerit used must be considered as a penalty and must be associated with the offense.

Use demerits sparingly since an accumulation of them can have adverse effects. If the student receives a large number of them, he realizes that he is in a situation that cannot be remedied by displaying good behavior. He becomes discouraged and often decides to defeat the teacher with the teacher's own weapon by accumulating as many demerits as possible. The teacher should have some flexibility in the utilization of demerits that enables him either to take away a coveted privilege or to assign a demerit. This flexibility allows for better treatment of individual problems and enables the students to appreciate its application better.

Factor of Denial of Student Privileges

Behavior changes for the better can be achieved through the denial of certain school privileges to individual students. If a student does not perform his duties efficiently, he can be helped immeasurably by calling on another student to take them over at the time. For example, if a student is assisting the teacher with lateness and absence records and is either late himself or, in some other way, inefficient, he should be replaced by another student who will discharge his duty faithfully. If a student cheats to gain a higher standing in class, he should be denied the recognition that accompanies the higher achievement.

Care must be exercised to utilize only those forms of deprivation that are valuable to improvement of behavior without injury to health or safety. An uncooperative young person should not be deprived of organized health-giving exercise that may be planned for all students. To deny him the needed physical activity may further aggravate the behavior problem when next he appears in either your class or that of another teacher.

Deprivations that may encourage the adolescent to engage in other and perhaps more serious misbehavior should not be used. Corrective measures that temporarily deny a misbehaving student his rights and privileges in a particular situation may be applied if the individual is helped to understand the relationship between the denials and his uncooperative behavior.

Factor of the Use of Detention

Every student must be taught the value of being punctual. Some young people are not encouraged in the home to give close attention to time. Adolescents like to dawdle. Parents must keep after them, and school people must spend a great deal of energy to teach them that time is important. Not only do latecomers interfere with classwork when they enter the class, but they lose educational experiences that cannot be recaptured.

Secondary school students need to be impressed with the importance of the time factor. Hence the use of detention as a penalty might be limited to cases of tardiness. Students who lose time can be asked to make up that time. They cannot compensate for the experience they lost, but they can learn to understand the importance of *doing things on time*. However, they should be provided with learning materials on which they can work during their stay in the detention room.

The student's time should not be wasted in the detention room. He should be given tasks to perform that are educational rather than purely punitive in nature. This experience should be one of educational worth and should be planned with learning goals in mind or the detention program altered or dropped. Ideas are not taught by the imposition of penalties. Learning takes place in a situation that is relatively free from fear-inducing factors. Provide worthwhile activities in the detention room or do not send the student there.

The Factor of Requiring Extra Work

Seldom, if ever, should additional work be assigned to change undesirable behavior into desirable behavior. This approach is likely to instill more negative attitudes than any possible good that can result from the work completed. If you wish to reward a student, give him the *privilege* of doing extra work or study; never *impose* extra study on him as a penalty for misbehavior.

You are interested in having your students learn as much as they can. You need to do what you can to activate the learning process. Although you may believe that you are requiring added exposure to new learning material, you should be concerned with those learning outcomes that may result from enforced extra study as a correction for disciplinary problems. If you use this technique, you are likely to arouse dislike of the subject.

Factor of Awareness of All Behavior yet Separating It from the Personal

You need to detect all misbehavior but to be careful that you do not make your disapproval of it personal. To the extent that you can separate the misbehavior from the individual and focus on it when you reprimand him, you are likely to succeed in working with adolescents. It is a fine line between the two that can be appreciated by the learner when he realizes that you are willing to accept him as a functional member of the group so long as his behavior is in line with acceptable social standards for the situation. He then realizes that you will not discredit him because of his misdeeds, but that you will not countenance any nonconforming behavior either.

The student should be helped to realize that any misbehavior is not acceptable in a particular situation. As the teacher, you have many ways of acquainting him with this fact. You may disapprove with your eyes; you may deny him the privilege of participating in the discussion by not giving him an opportunity to enter into it; or you may openly reprimand him. Most of these are positive and dynamic acts, although the denying of privileges is an overt expression of ignoring him. There are other extreme measures that can be taken in the ignoring process.

The Factor of Isolation of Offender

There are various ways in which the student can be isolated from the members of the class. He can be physically removed, or he can be denied the opportunity of participating in any group activity that may be in progress. When a student is isolated, he should be denied special privileges until his case is settled. If the span of time between the offense and the final settlement is long, he may need to be readmitted into group activities pending a decision concerning the settlement of his problem.

The Factor of Scolding

Scolding implies oral reprimand in the presence of peers. Take care that you do not become a nagging teacher. Petty faultfinding is an indication of a lack of self-confidence. Adolescents dislike this approach. The overly faultfinding teacher loses the respect of secondary school students. Moreover, too often, scoldings are not followed by constructive action. If they continue, regardless of the school rules that have been broken, adolescents soon become insensitive to their application. Whenever it is necessary, however, call attention to any infraction of school rules, but be judicial. Use the question approach. It is better to have the student tell you what he intends to do to correct his behavior than it is for you to thrust it at him.

Misbehavior among adolescents often is the result of a striving to gain approval from members of the social group. Every young person has a strong desire to belong and to have his behavior approved by both his peers and his teachers. If you can so direct the influence of the class as to cause an adolescent's misbehavior to be made a matter of class disapproval, you will be spared the need for scolding or reprimanding. Genuine changes in behavior are the result of such social pressures. The skillful teacher learns how to make effective use of this corrective measure.

Value of Lapse of Time before Dealing with Penalty for Offense

When it is known that the individual has committed an act that warrants corrective action, it often is wise to give the offender some time to think it over before you attempt to resolve the problem. When an offender has an hour or more, for example, to meditate on his wrongdoing, he is likely to resolve that he will try not to repeat the offense. During a composition lesson, for example, a high school freshman, in playful mood, accidently spilled ink on his seatmate's composition paper, necessitating its being rewritten. The victim of the prank was much annoyed. The teacher, however, remarked quietly, "We shall settle this matter later." At the end of the period, the offender came to the teacher's desk with his seatmate. Expressing his regret for the accident, he offered to rewrite the spoiled paper at the end of the school day, and assured the teacher sincerely that in the future he would avoid engaging in pranks of this kind.

Incentives That Stimulate Change in Behavior

Not all students go to school because they want to go. Some are sent to school. As you realize the importance of the implied difference, you come to appreciate the fact that your job of motivating the learning process for all of them is a sizable one. It is not enough to hope that the success achieved in knowledge, skills, and attitudes will furnish the momentum for your students to want to continue in the learning situation. Many of them will need special incentives to spur them to greater study activity. You can help them acquire the desire of self-improvement. This in itself can be an intrinsic reward that will give direction to individual behavior.

The age and the interests of the students are important to the form of incentives that may be useful for them. Learning for the sake of gaining an education is an intrinsic reward of great value. Many students, however, need forms of incentives that are extrinsic in nature. Our system of grades or marks represents a type of reward that serves as an incentive for some students, but not for all.

A slow-learning student often finds it difficult to compete with his more able classmates in study activities that go beyond his ability to master. Hence he is likely to receive lower grades than the others. Your emphasis then should be on this student's attempts to improve his achievement in comparison with his own past record rather than in comparison to the grades earned by other students. In addition, you should set learning tasks for him that are in accord with his intellectual level. You also should attempt to discover any phase of the learning situation in which the young person may display interest and for which he has some aptitude, and then reward his efforts in this area by words of approval. A fundamental educational principle, of course, is to avoid exposing less able students to unfair competition with those who are much more able than they are.

The bright underachiever poses a problem of adjustment. For one or another reason, he displays little or no interest in his schoolwork and performs inadequately. The offering of extrinsic awards may fail to improve his attitude toward study. It is then the responsibility of the school people involved, in cooperation with parents, to attempt to discover the cause of the student's failure to conform to learning requirements. This may be a difficult task, requiring patient working with the student by teachers and counselors. If they persist, however, they usually can bring about a change of attitude that will result in the young person's devoting his energies toward achieving academic success that will serve as an intrinsic reward for his efforts.

Payment for Property Damaged

It is difficult to hold all students to a requirement of paying for property deliberately damaged by them. The economics of the home does not always make this possible. The attitude of the student is important. He should present a willingness, within his ability to do so, to pay for damaged property, or to restore it or repair it. Whatever promises are made should be carried out.

Value of Appeal to Members of Class

If you are not certain of the guilty person you may make an appeal to the entire class. In so doing, you may shield the guilty person and gain his cooperation by saving his face and at the same time setting the class against the repetition of that particular kind of activity. You will find that there are times when you need not identify the wrongdoer.

Value of Getting Advice of Experienced Teachers

In your observation of teachers, you are afforded an opportunity to discover how various situations are handled by them. Yet, you know that, when you are teaching, the class reacts differently under your leadership than when another person is guiding the learning process. You discover that the students are the same students but that they behave differently when you are in charge. This is characteristic of all learners; they behave differently in the presence of different teachers. More than they realize, teachers are responsible for differences in student behavior in the classroom.

You might make it a point to ask teachers about the development of self-discipline in students. Ask them what they do to deter problems from arising and what their attitude is toward various types of behavior problems. Sometimes, they find it difficult to advise you. They have developed certain habits of dealing with such difficulties and now use them almost unconsciously. They may tell you that they are alert to all that transpires in the classroom but that they try not to be petty about it. They avoid making an issue of something that is trivial. You will discover after a talk with a teacher or teachers about dealing with discipline problems that the best way for you to learn to deal with them is for you to develop these skills in the classroom.

Experienced teachers will tell you that the problem of discipline is one that is ever present. They know that they must be alert to the problem at all times and not "let up" on their standards lest confusion begin in class. Recently about 3,400 classroom teachers were asked about this problem in a study made by the National Education Association. It was revealed that the problem of discipline continues to be their major concern. The beginning teacher also places discipline high on his list of classroom situations to master, but the kind of discipline problems he meets are often somewhat different from those met by the experienced teacher.

When you are in doubt about how to handle a particular discipline situation, it is wise to seek the counsel of an experienced teacher, guidance counselor, or administrator. First you should use your own resources to correct the behavior. Do not hesitate, however, to enlist the assistance of more competent persons in the resolution of behavior problems. Avoid letting the situation get out of hand before calling for assistance. You may find that suggestions coming from experienced teachers or from other trained experts are most helpful.

Value Associated with Holding a Personal Conference with a Student

Most student teachers do not get sufficient training in the use of the personal conference with individual students. When skill is developed in the use of a personal conference, it can become one of the most effective means of bringing about a readjustment of recalcitrant behavior. In a face-to-face talk with a student before or after the regular school day, during the lunch period, or at any other convenient time, much can be accomplished by way of having the learner understand what is meant by good classroom attitudes and behavior. To be effective, these talks need not be formally planned but may grow out of a need that arises in the classroom. Your preparation for them should be based on an acquaintance with whatever information may be available about the habits and record of the student.

The personal conference should not be used as a scolding session. If properly conducted, you as well as the student can gain from a personal conference. For you, it can serve as a medium through which you gain insight into the student and his problem; for the student, it affords an opportunity to strengthen his self-confidence and his urge to belong.

If you talk privately with a student who has been extremely uncooperative, instead of scolding him publicly, you gain in stature— the members of the class respect you for it. Sometimes, during these face-to-face conferences, the student tells you things that you otherwise would not be able to discover but that are pertinent to his displayed behavior. At the same time, you find that you are more successful with some students than with others in these conferences, since some students tell you many things that other students tend to withhold from you.

In these personal conferences, you should learn to listen and to ask the kind of questions that will elicit information pertinent to the individual's problem. Your role should be that of establishing a warm, permissive, informal atmosphere that will promote the flow of personal information. Once obtained, this information should be treated as confidential.

THE STUDENT TEACHER AND DISCIPLINE

Many student teachers and beginning teachers claim that the most difficult aspect of teaching is the maintaining of good discipline among their students. As we have suggested earlier, some secondary school boys and girls fail to recognize the authority of a man or woman who is not much older than themselves. Hence they engage in uncooperative behavior that they would not dare to display with an older, more experienced teacher. You should be concerned about discipline, but you should not be afraid to meet the problems that arise. Perhaps, more than you realize, your own attitudes are potent instigators of the kind of behavior evidenced by the members of your class.

Mistakes Made by Student Teachers

Because of your inexperience, you are likely to make mistakes in dealing with your students that later you will know how to avoid. You are likely to find that your own errors tend to contribute to the discipline problems that arise in your classroom. A primary purpose of your engaging in student teaching is to learn from your mistakes at this time when you have help in overcoming them rather than when you are on your own as a full-time teacher.

More often than many beginning teachers realize, they provide the stimuli that are basic to the chain of misbehavior that ensues. For example, a student teacher was teaching reading to a third grade class. In her preparation of the lesson, she attempted to learn all about the picture on which the reading was based. While inspecting the contents of the picture with the class, one child reported seeing something in the picture that had escaped the student teacher during her preparation. Unconsciously, the teacher said "Gee! I didn't see that!" Some minutes elapsed before the child bouncing in her seat, called out, "Gee! Gee! Gee!" She was promptly reprimanded. Yet, the teacher actually was responsible for stimulating this behavior. Until her college supervisor told her what she had said, she was unaware of the fact that she had said "Gee! I didn't see that!"

There are various mistakes that you can make that account for students' misbehavior. We already have referred to some of these. They include:

1. Coming to class unprepared or poorly prepared for the lesson.
2. Failing to start the lesson promptly.
3. Wasting time trying to locate materials that should be at hand.
4. Repeating an indistinct answer rather than requiring the student to speak clearly.
5. Oversimplifying explanations or stating them in terms beyond students' ability to comprehend.
6. Wording questions vaguely or indefinitely.
7. Utilizing inappropriate motivation.
8. Failing to adjust lighting and heating conditions and seating arrangements according to students' needs.
9. Interrupting a lesson to harangue a student for misconduct.
10. Engaging in emotionalized behavior or "throwing a temper tantrum" when things go wrong.

11. Assigning the class "busywork" in order to complete reports, etc.
12. Failing to return students' written work that has been properly evaluated.
13. Standing with back to class while writing on chalkboard.
14. Assigning work for home study hurriedly or without proper explanation.
15. Failing to provide for ability differences among the students.
16. Employing the question-answer technique of recitation to the exclusion of other more interest-arousing approaches.
17. Caring for all class routines personally rather than delegating some of them to students.
18. Permitting students to leave the classroom at will.

You should try assiduously to refrain from committing any of the foregoing errors. Moreover, your whole classroom manner exerts a powerful influence on your students' attitudes. They react unfavorably toward a teacher (1) who indicates by a low voice and hesitant manner that he is afraid of the group, or (2) who, by the use of loud tones and an aggressive attitude, seems to give evidence that he expects trouble and is ready for it. Try to assume an attitude of self-confidence and of a belief in your students' desire and ability to cooperate with you in achieving worthwhile learning outcomes.

Special Suggestions for Dealing with Factors of Poor Discipline

You know that slides to be used as teaching aids usually are accompanied by study guides to assist you in their presentation. One such guide is presented here that accompanies slides on "Discipline in the Junior High School," for use in education classes. It contains pertinent suggestions concerning discipline.

I. Recognizing Danger Signals
   A. Inattention
      1. Making-up in class
      2. Comic books
      3. Daydreaming
      4. Boredom
   B. Teacher faults
      1. Remains seated at desk

    2. Permits pupils to congregate around desk
    3. Tolerates uncontrolled movement by pupils
    4. Lacks direction
    5. Ignores physical factors that contribute to misbehavior

II. Contributing Factors to Poor Discipline
    A. Poor lesson planning
        1. Starting classwork late
        2. Absence of directions
        3. Lack of motivation
        4. Monotony of presentation
    B. Lack of pupil participation

III. Setting Up a Trouble-Free Classroom Climate
    A. Procedures set up cooperatively by pupils and teacher
    B. Pupils comply with procedures they helped to develop
        1. Entrance and exit from room
        2. Distribution and collection of materials
        3. Proper disposal of litter
        4. Initiating activities
        5. Controlled pupil movement
    C. Teachers share in responsibility
        1. Plan good lessons
           a. Be interesting and detailed
           b. Use a variety of techniques
           c. Follow courses of study
        2. Know your pupils
        3. Use your time and equipment efficiently
        4. Use praise and recognition
        5. Assign responsibilities to pupils

IV. Treating Trouble Immediately
    A. Pause and look at person(s) meaningfully
    B. Gestures
    C. Move closer to disturbance
    D. Confiscate material
    E. Separate offenders
    F. Isolate within room
    G. Deprive pupil of privileges
    H. Admonish or reprimand
    I. Confer after school
    J. Refer to other school personnel

V. Getting Help
    A. Keep records
    B. Study previous records
    C. Ask other teachers

D. Refer for counseling and other specialized services
E. Contact home
F. Confer with vice-principal [6]

The Building of Good School Spirit

It should be comforting to you to appreciate the fact that you are not alone in your attempts to develop well-disciplined behavior among young people. In reality, student discipline is the responsibility of every member of the school staff—the principal, the department chairmen, the guidance counselors, and the teachers. Building student morale is an important function of the school's personnel who work with learners. Some principles that should characterize the building of good school spirit and, in turn, of acceptable behavior are summarized below. As they apply to you they include:

1. Your awareness of a student who has a problem and who needs help; opposed to here is a problem student.
2. Your acceptance of the immediate problem as a learning experience that can be used to help the student meet his future problems effectively.
3. Your eagerness to get the student's side of the story, including listening to his ideas regarding what should be done about it.
4. Your willingness to display an attitude of acceptance of the student even after he has violated regulations.
5. Your fairness, consistency, firmness, and understanding.
6. Your willingness to commend a student for partial success rather than to condemn him hastily for failure to achieve.
7. Your ability to build or to restore a student's self-respect rather than to destroy or remove his feeling of security.
8. Your desire to assist a student to work out a plan that may ameliorate the immediate situation, preclude the occurrence of unfavorable responses, or find constructive activities that give direction to his behavior.
9. Your willingness to give a student a vote of confidence

[6] Allen Wetter, *Discipline Study Guide* to accompany slides on "Discipline in the Junior High School," Philadelphia, 1961. (Allen Wetter is Superintendent of the Philadelphia Schools.)

by giving him a second chance in the form of new responsibility.

10. Your interest in providing favorable conditions that will enable a student to achieve successful performance.

11. Your willingness to discuss established ground rules for classroom recitation sessions.

12. Your willingness to keep records of disciplinary infractions for future reference as a means of helping individual students improve their behavior.

THROUGH DISCIPLINE TO SELF-DISCIPLINE

Throughout this discussion we have stressed the value of your employing constructive techniques that have as their primary purpose the restraining of students from engaging in various forms of misbehavior. To the extent that you are achieving your goal, you are building habits of control among young people that can function when your students are removed from your physical presence. Your own well-disciplined behavior can serve as a model that they are likely to imitate more or less consciously. Your encouragement of student cooperation can carry over to situations outside the classroom.

Some people seem to believe that the well-disciplined person does not fear the consequences of asocial behavior. This is an error. We all tend to avoid engaging in socially unacceptable acts because we are unwilling to face the aftermath of such behavior. The difference is one of motivation. The child refrains from being "bad" because he fears that a penalty for his deed will be administered from the outside in the form of physical punishment, loss of privileges, isolation from his group, and the like. The administration of such penalties probably is needed in the beginning stages of his training. Gradually, however, the young person can be guided to think through the effects on himself and others of his displayed attitudes and behavior. This broadened concept of discipline motivates him to behave toward others as he would like them to behave toward him.

As you, in your dealings with your students, give approval to evidences of controlled behavior and show disapproval, with reasons, of uncontrolled activity, you are helping the members of your class recognize the value of cooperation. Especially as you commend improved behavior on the part of former recalcitrant young people you are assisting them in developing those inner satisfactions that are experienced by well-disciplined individuals.

One of the chief areas of learning for the adolescent is the acquisition of ideals and standards of behavior that shall enable him to meet present and future responsibilities constructively so that he is a worthy participant in the activities of the various groups of which he is or will be a member. If he is to earn the respect of his associates, he needs to exercise control of his emotions and appreciate the rights of others as well as his own. In other words, he becomes a self-disciplined individual in all of his various relationships. To the extent that you can help an adolescent develop such self-control or self-discipline, you are fulfilling one of your most important teaching functions.

QUESTIONS AND TOPICS FOR DISCUSSION

1. Draw up a set of rights and responsibilities of the adolescent in the home similar to those for the school presented in this chapter.
2. Enumerate specific ways in which individual teachers can build *esprit de corps* in a school.
3. Which of Oliva's suggested remedial measures are you in a position to apply with your students?
4. Carefully read the rules presented in this chapter for guiding your own conduct. How well are you succeeding in applying them to your own class behavior? Note the ones that need improvement.
5. How can you ascertain the sincerity of a student's verbal apology for a misdeed? Illustrate.
6. List constructive deprivations that would have value in helping your students achieve self-discipline.
7. Give the psychological factor involved in avoiding the requirement of extra work for misbehavior.
8. What are some examples of the "ignoring" process in dealing with a student's lack of cooperation?
9. How can your cooperating teacher assist you in developing self-discipline among your students?
10. Reread the list of teachers' errors and check those that you tend to commit. Try to avoid them.
11. Summarize the ways in which you can help your students develop self-discipline.

SELECTED REFERENCES

BLOCH, H. A., and NEIGHEHOFER, A. *The Gang: A Study in Adolescent Behavior.* New York: Philosophical Library, 1958.

CROW, L. D., and CROW, ALICE. *Readings in Guidance.* New York: David McKay Co., Inc., 1962. Chaps. IV, VI, IX, XIII, and XIV.

Helping Delinquent Children. Washington, D.C.: U.S. Department of Health, Education and Welfare, Children's Bureau, 1953.

MILLER, D. R., and SWANSON, G. E. *Inner Conflicts and Defense.* New York: Holt, Rinehart & Winston, Inc., 1960.

MOSS, H. "Standards of Conduct for Students, Teachers and Parents," *Journal of Consulting Psychology*, 1955, pp. 39–42.

OLIVA, P. F. "High School Discipline in American Society," *The Bulletin of the National Association of Secondary-School Principals*, XL (January, 1956), 1–103.

OLIVER, W. A. "Teachers' Educational Beliefs versus Their Classroom Practices," *Journal of Educational Research*, XLVII (1953), 47–55.

REDL, F., and WINEMAN, D. *Controls from Within.* New York: Free Press of Glencoe, Inc., 1952.

ROTHNEY, J. W. M. *The High School Student: A Book of Cases.* New York: Holt, Rinehart & Winston, Inc., 1953.

SCHAIN, ROBERT L. *Discipline: How to Establish and Maintain It.* Valley Stream, N.Y.: Teachers Practical Press, Inc., 1961.

SCHORLING, R., and BATCHELDER, H. T. *Student Teaching in the Secondary Schools* (3rd ed.). New York: McGraw-Hill Book Co., Inc., 1956.

SHEVIAKOV, G. V., and REDL, F. *Discipline for Today's Children and Youth* (rev. ed.). Washington, D.C.: National Education Assoc., 1955.

STRANG, RUTH. "What Discipline Means to Adolescents," *Nervous Child*, XXV (1951), 125–46.

ZAPF, R. M. *Democratic Processes in the Secondary Classroom.* Englewood Cliffs, N.J.: Prentice-Hall, Inc., 1959.

14

EVALUATION OF STUDENT PROGRESS

Everyone in the school is interested in and concerned with the evaluation of the student and his progress. The teacher, however, is the school person who is most directly involved with the responsibility of measuring and evaluating student achievement. He is better able to assess this progress when he knows something about each student's capacity to learn, and the extent to which each has mastered significant concepts or skills basic to an understanding of the next learning unit. In other words, knowledge of experience background is beneficial to teacher effectiveness in evaluating extent of learning.

Evaluation has value to the extent that goals of instruction are known and understood. Evaluation is the final step in the education process. It is important to know the objectives of education that are to serve as the basis of evaluation of teaching-learning outcomes. It is as these are known by you and your co-workers that your teaching will be directed toward meaningful purposes and that you will know what learnings are to be evaluated.

Objectives of education of which you were aware prior to the period of instruction serve as guides against which to measure the extent of learning resulting from your teaching efforts. Too often these objectives are assumed rather than set forth or even consciously conceived. You might refer to the goals of secondary education that we presented on the national, state, and local level in Chapter 6. These can serve as possible educational outcomes against which to measure educational or learning progress.

EVALUATION OF PERSONAL QUALITIES

Various types of well-organized tests have been constructed to yield results that give one or another measure of student ability, competence, or personality. Intelligence tests, both individual and group, are widely administered. Some of these yield results that give information concerning both abstract and mechanical ability. Individual and multifactor aptitude tests also provide helpful data for the teacher.

Various other tests have been standardized to measure such qualities as personal traits and interests. These include numerous self-administering tests as well as those in which an individual is rated by others. Some personality and interest tests are locally constructed and do not have norms available for comparative purposes. Projective techniques such as the *Thematic Apperception Test* and the *Rorschach Inkblot Test* have norms that add to the worth of these tests.

We shall consider the various types of standardized tests that are available for the evaluation of students' personal qualities. Many of these tests have been in use since the beginning of this century. Their worth depends on the extent to which you are able to make professional application of available scores or upon the accuracy of the data obtained by their administration.

Information from Record Forms Filled Out by Students

Valuable personal data such as are found on a questionnaire often are available to teachers. Although this information is especially useful to the guidance counselor, you will find that you can use it to gain a better understanding of your students. Studying such questionnaires will not take as much time as you may think, and is likely to increase your understanding of the personality patterns of your students. Here is a sample of a record form that is to be filled in by a student.

INDIVIDUAL RECORD FORM

The purpose of this questionnaire is to bring together *all of the information* that we can get about *you*. It is for our confidential use only, so *please answer the questions as honestly and completely as you can.* After this information has been obtained we will be able to *know your problems and assist you in your school life while at* _____ High School.

Name _____

     (Last)   (First)   (Middle)

Sex: Boy _____ Girl _____ Age _____ Date _____
Address _____ Telephone _____
School   List here the schools you have attended.
Name of school   What grades?

_____   _____
_____   _____

Which school have you liked best? _____
Why? _____
Place a circle around the school subjects you like best. Draw a line through
   the ones you like least.
English, Social Studies, Mathematics, General Science, Foods, Clothing,
   Blueprint, General Metal, Auto Shop, Mechanical Drawing, Woodshop,
   Glee Club, Chorus, Instrumental Music, Art, Latin, Business Training,
   Gymnasium (others) _____
Underline *once* all the activities you have belonged to in the past. Underline
   twice all the activities you are now taking part in.
Girl Reserves, Hi-Y, Scouts, Stamp Club, Astronomy Club, Dramatic Club,
   Airplane Club, Noon-Hour Service, Morning Service, Traffic Patrol, Lost
   and Found, Library, Em-Ju-Hi Staff, Paper Weighing, Noon-Hour, Chorus,
   Auditorium Service (others) _____
What hobbies do you have?
What clubs do you belong to outside of school? _____
Other activities outside of school _____
What activities would you like to take part in at school? _____
Do you find that you need help in: (check)
   Arithmetic _____ Reading _____ Personal appearance _____
   Spelling _____ Writing _____ Reciting in class _____ Storywrit-
   ing _____ Study habits _____
Do you mind if someone else makes a better mark or does something better
   than you do?
   Quite a bit _____ A little _____ Not at all _____
Do you think you have as much ability as most of the people you know?
   Yes _____ No _____
How do you get along with your teachers?
   Very well _____ All right _____ Not well _____
How have you gotten along in school?
   Very well _____ All right _____ Not well _____
What is the nationality of your father? _____ Mother? _____
How do you get along with your father?
   Very well _____ All right _____ Not well _____
How do you get along with your mother?
   Very well _____ All right _____ Not well _____
What languages are spoken at home? _____
Is the family interested in your success at school? Yes _____ No _____
Does your family listen to the radio?
   Often _____ Sometimes _____ Seldom _____

Underline your father's special interests.

Golf, cards, gardening, reading, church activities, P.T.A., Rotary, Kiwanis, I.M.A., Y.M.C.A., movies, clubs, dancing, bowling, hunting, fishing, camping (others) _____

What books are read in the home? _____

What magazines are read in the home? _____

Underline your mother's special interests.

Golf, cards, sewing, knitting, reading, gardening, church activities, P.T.A., music, movies, Y.W.C.A., dancing (others) _____

Underline which of the following live in the same house with you: Mother, father, stepmother, brothers, sisters, grandfather, grandmother, aunt, uncle, cousins, roomers, boarders.

Does your father have regular employment? Yes _____ No _____

Are all members of your family in good health? Yes _____ No _____

If not, tell who is ill, and give the nature of the illness. _____

Complete the following table:

	First name	Age	Last grade completed	Country of birth	Where employed	Kind of work
Father						
Mother						
Brother						
Sister						

Have you any physical defects? Yes _____ No _____ What is it?_____

At what age did it become noticeable? _____

Give the date of your last illness _____ What was it? _____

How often are you absent from school because of illness?

Frequently _____ Seldom _____ Never _____

Height _____ Weight _____

Vision: Good _____ Average _____ Poor _____

Do you wear glasses? Yes _____ No _____

Hearing: Good _____ Average _____ Poor _____

Are your friends mostly your own age? _____ Younger _____ Older _____

What do your friends do for a good time? _____

Do your parents approve of your friends? Yes _____ No _____

Are you permitted to bring friends into your home? Yes _____ No _____

Do your parents let you go out on school nights? Yes _____ No _____

What time do you have to get in nights? _____

What recreation takes place in your home? _____

How many movies do you attend each week? _____

How much do you work each day outside of school?

	Hours	Where	Work done
Monday			
Tuesday			
Wednesday			
Thursday			

Friday _____

Saturday _____

Sunday _____

In what way do you get the money you need? _____

If your parents give you an allowance, do you have jobs at home that you
are expected to do? Yes _____ No _____

If so, what are they? _____

How do you get along with people your own age?

Boys: Very well _____ All right _____ Not well _____

Girls: Very well _____ All right _____ Not well _____

Do you make friends: Easily _____ All right_____ With difficulty_____

How do you get along with other people?

Very well _____ All right _____ Not well _____

Do you usually let yourself go when angry? Yes _____ No _____

Do you say or do things for which you are sorry afterwards?

Often _____ Sometimes _____ Seldom _____

Do you run away from unpleasant things which you should face?

Usually _____ Sometimes _____ Almost never _____

Do you mind being criticized?

Quite a bit _____ A little _____ Not at all _____

Have you had more trouble than most boys and girls? Yes _____ No _____

If you get into trouble, whom would you ask for help? _____

What did you do each evening last week? Monday _____

Tuesday _____ Wednesday _____

Thursday _____ Friday _____

Saturday _____ Sunday _____

Are there any other things about yourself that you think the homeroom
teacher should know? _____

Intelligence Tests

During recent years, many instruments have been devised to
measure the mental capacity of learners. The general intelligence
of individuals is variously referred to as mental ability, academic
aptitude, or scholastic aptitude. The index that roughly represents
level of mental ability is the IQ. This index is obtained by dividing
the mental age of an individual as obtained from a standardized
intelligence test by his chronological age, and then multiplying by
100. The IQ is relatively constant throughout the developing years
of the individual. Many valid and reliable tests (both group and
individual) have been devised to measure mental ability. An intelligence test with high reliability is one administered to one student
at a time (individual intelligence test), such as the 1960 revision of

the Stanford-Binet or one of the several Wechsler tests of intelligence.

Multifactor Aptitude Tests

The measurement of aptitude, of necessity, is an indirect outcome of the measurement of achievement in various areas. Hence a multifactor test such as the *Differential Aptitude Test* has come into extensive use since it measures achievement in various areas of learning. The *Differential Aptitude Test* attempts to measure such abilities as verbal reasoning, numerical ability, abstract reasoning, space relations, mechanical reasoning, clerical speed and accuracy, and language usage—sentences and spelling. Other available multifactor tests include *General Aptitude Test Battery, Holzinger-Crowder Uni-Factor Multiple Aptitude Test,* and *Scholastic Aptitude Test.*

The *Scholastic Aptitude Test (SAT)* given by the College Entrance Examination Board is one of the best aptitude examinations administered to college entrants. It is taken by many high school seniors prior to entrance into college. Due to its wide administration, much is known about (1) the relationship between the scores made on this test and later success in academic work, and (2) the relationship between school grades and scores made on the *SAT.* For example, girls usually have higher high school averages than boys, but the results on the *SAT* do not support the grade differential made by girls in their respective high schools. We present the Verbal and Mathematical scores made by both boys and girls on a recent *Scholastic Aptitude Test.*

A study of Table 11 reveals that on verbal ability 72 per cent of the boys attained scores below 600, while 88 per cent of the girls scored below 600. Also, on mathematical ability 72 per cent of the boys scored below 600, while 89.2 per cent of the girls scored below 600. It is interesting to note that, although school averages of girls usually are higher than those of boys, when both take the same standardized achievement test under similar conditions the results often are reversed. These results indicate greater achievement of boys than of girls in both verbal and mathematical learning.

You should make use of whatever test results are available to

TABLE 11

SCORES ON VERBAL AND MATHEMATICAL PARTS OF THE SAT MADE
BY HIGH SCHOOL SENIORS WHO TOOK THE TEST *

Verbal			Mathematical		
Boys Per Cent	Score	Girls Per Cent	Boys Per Cent	Score	Girls Per Cent
0.2	750–800	0.1	2	750–800	0.2
2.0	700–749	2.0	4	700–749	1.0
5.0	650–99	5.0	9	650–99	3.0
9.0	600–649	9.0	13	600–649	7.0
12.0	550–99	13.0	15	550–99	10.0
14.0	500–549	15.0	17	500–549	16.0
17.0	450–99	18.0	14	450–99	17.0
16.0	400–449	15.0	13	400–449	19.0
13.0	350–99	12.0	8	350–99	15.0
8.0	300–349	7.0	4	300–349	9.0
3.0	250–99	3.0	1	250–99	3.0
1.0	200–249	1.0	0.1	200–249	0.2

* Reproduced with permission from *Your College Board Scores: Scholastic Aptitude Test, Achievement Tests,* published in 1960 by the College Entrance Examination Board. This booklet is revised annually and is supplied to secondary schools for distribution to students with their College Board test scores.

enable you to understand your students better. To do this it is important that you understand the meaning of these test results. It is sad to report that too many prospective teachers do not understand the meaning of either *Differential Aptitude Test* scores or the intelligence quotients furnished by the school. Many do not know what use can be made of such results, or perhaps use them to the detriment of the student.

Personality Evaluation

Any effort to measure an individual's interests, drives, and behavior is an attempt to evaluate personality. You must not be misled, however, into thinking that personality can be measured by a compilation of scores obtained from tests of intelligence, aptitude, and achievement. The measurement of any one of these traits represents only a phase of personality. It is the integrated functioning of all the aspects of the individual that represents his total personality pattern. Hence personality evaluation is concerned with the measurement of all qualities that reveal the individual as a unique functioning entity.

There now are available numerous measuring instruments that give some indication of an individual's attitudes toward himself and others; his fears and worries; his likes and dislikes; his degree of adjustment as revealed on pencil-and-paper tests; and his understanding of socially acceptable behavior in general. Observable evidence of an individual's behavior suggests something concerning (1) the ways in which he behaves in school or other social situations, and (2) the extent to which he is liked by others. If he displays a cooperative attitude and other students seek his company, he appears to have desirable personality qualities adequate for the social needs.

You must keep in mind that personality patterns, although somewhat stable, are not static but continue to respond to influences within and outside the individual. Hence some personality measurement may yield personality ratings that vary with the time and conditions of the testing. Factors such as the emotional state of the individual and his attitude toward the administrator of the test may influence his responses at the time of its administration. In spite of other limitations, such as deliberate falsification of responses or inability to recall past experiences, it is possible from the results of personality tests to discover certain inherent attitudes, emotional states, and behavior patterns that otherwise might not be revealed to you or another person.

Personality-rating approaches can be used to supplement the direct and personal evaluations of an individual. The techniques that are constructed for use in measuring various personality traits include: self-evaluating questionnaires or inventories, rating scales, and projective techniques. The functioning of each is briefly explained here.

Self-evaluating questionnaires. Self-evaluating questionnaires are measuring devices that require the giving of answers on a prepared form. Much can be learned from having a student react to specific questions that have been devised to help him evaluate his behavior. Many such questionnaires have been developed and norms prepared for them. It is recognized, of course, that these results cannot be as reliable as other more exact measures. They serve to give a profile about the individual, however, as he introspects or views himself. They are more valuable when supported by evaluations of his personal characteristics that are submitted by other persons who know him well.

Some of the tests in which the individual rates his own personality include the *Bernreuter Personality Inventory;* Woodworth's *Personal Data Sheet; Study of Values; Minnesota Multiphase Personality Inventory; Kuder Preference Record; Mooney's Problem Check List;* Bell's *Adjustment Inventory; Bonney's Socio-Graph;* and *Miller Analogies Test.* In addition to using these standardized questionnaires and inventories, many schools prepare forms for students to use in self-appraisal and for teachers to utilize in student evaluation.

You need to exercise great care in interpreting and using data obtained from any self-evaluating personality test or inventory. For example, the *Bernreuter Personality Inventory* yields six different aspects of personality by the application of six keys to the answers of the 125 questions in the test. The phases of personality measured include: neurotic tendency, self-sufficiency, introversion-extroversion, dominance-submission, confidence in one's self, and sociability.

The *Minnesota Multiphase Personality Inventory* has been devised to use in evaluating adolescents. It consists of 550 questions that help to evaluate the extent to which the individual deviates from normal persons in such areas as, health, social, civic, and religious attitudes; family; educational and occupational relations; the presence of abnormal drives, phobias, or other neurotic tendencies.

Rating scales. When an instrument is constructed for the purpose of rating another person, it usually is called a *rating scale.* Some self-rating questionnaires can be used both by the individual to rate himself and by another to rate the individual. Usually, however, a rating scale is used by a teacher or a supervisor to evaluate the student's attitudes, interests, or other personal qualities.

You are likely to be asked to cooperate in the evaluation of the personal characteristics of your students. You no doubt have been introduced to the use of rating scales. Personality reports have been completed for many years by instructors at Brooklyn College. The general items to which they give responses on these reports are:

Appearance, Responsibility, Social Adjustment, Emotional Stability, and Professional Promise. Each of these is briefly interpreted by descriptive comments on the report form. The scale extends from 1 (poor) to 5 (outstanding), with a place for 0 (no judgment).

The authors have prepared a personality rating scale to be used by students in secondary schools. The scale is organized according to eleven categories to enable students to appraise themselves, and teachers to rate students in the same areas of behavior. The categories included in the scale are: Personal Attractiveness, Emotional Control, Social Adaptability, Attitude toward Others, Mental Capacity, Initiative and Industry, Trustworthiness, Capacity for Leadership, Service to Others, Speech and Voice, and Health. As a guide to the evaluator, descriptive interpretative statements are provided for the respective categories. We illustrate the general layout of the scale here:

Personality Trait	Excellent	Above Average	Average	Below Average	Poor
A. Personal Attractiveness	Exceedingly attractive, well-groomed	Pleasing appearance	Acceptable appearance	Careless about appearance	Unkempt, not tidy
B. Emotional Control	Exceedingly well-poised	Controls self with ease	Usually has emotional control	Displays emotional behavior	Lacks emotional control

Projective techniques. Some techniques are used for the prime purpose of affording the individual an opportunity to give free expression to his attitudes or ideas. In the classroom you can employ such informal approaches as the keeping of a diary or log, and the writing of an autobiography. The *Rorschach Inkblot Test* and the *Thematic Apperception Test* are standarized projective tests about which you need to know, but for the administration of which you are not trained. Although you may have learned about these instruments in a college course and have seen them demonstrated, we report on them briefly here.

Projective techniques as evaluative instruments of personality are based on the concept of the unity of the whole of personality. In these tests the emphasis is on the measurement of the individual's attitudes and thinking as he reacts freely to the specific materials that are presented to him. Through his responses in these situations, the administrator is enabled to gain insight into his personality pattern.

Rorschach Inkblot Test. This technique is widely used with adolescents and adults. Ten inkblots on cards (see Figure 6) are presented to the individual, one at a time, for his interpretation. Some of these cards are colored. The administrator records the responses given by the subject. The former then evaluates these responses according to established norms, and reports on the subject's attitude and creative insight. The most difficult part of this total testing experience is the interpretation of the responses. Because of the problems involved in maintaining standards of interpretation, no one except a highly trained person should undertake to administer and interpret the responses.

Fig. 6.—Inkblot sample similar to those used in the *Rorschach Test.*

The Thematic Apperception Test. The *TAT*, as this test is commonly called, consists of twenty cards; nineteen have pictures and one is blank. This test provides for a free flow of ideas about the picture on the card. As these cards are given to the individual, he is asked to look at the picture and tell a story that includes what has gone before, what is happening, and what is likely to happen. When he is handed the blank card he is expected to use his imagination to construct a story.

During this storytelling process, the subject presumably is giving expression to his attitudes, dominant drives, emotions, and conflicts. Stories told about these pictures vary with individuals. The administrator gains insight into the testee's personality to the extent that adequate responses are made and mistakes in interpretation are avoided. This is not an easy task in spite of the fact that there are instructions and standards for scoring and interpretation. This technique also should be employed only by trained experts.

EVALUATION OF LEARNING PROGRESS

The individual most directly affected by evaluation procedures is the student. He feels more at ease in his study when he has confidence in the approach that is used in judging his learning achievement. An evaluative system that is fair and is administered uniformly to all students tends to give the student security and helps him become more certain about his progress. The kind of measuring instruments you use and the way in which you utilize the results obtained are the concern of every learner in your class.

During the term, you are likely to utilize many evaluating devices such as oral recitations, short quizzes, written reports, teacher-constructed short form and essay examinations, and standardized achievement tests. Your success from the viewpoint of your students will be determined, in part, by your skill in using effectively these instruments in evaluating their learning progress.

Daily Oral Recitation as an Evaluative Instrument

Although there are advantages to entering a mark in your class record for student responses during the daily recitation, the disadvantages seem to outweigh the advantages. The students come to class presumedly prepared to participate in the discussion. When you make it a point to evaluate in written form every remark made by them during their attempt to answer questions, you provide conditions that are threatening and not conducive to the production of creative thinking. You should attempt to use the class period as an opportunity to develop ideas based on the background of your students, and thus stimulate the thinking process. To the extent that you provide thought-provoking questions, you will stimulate the kind of thinking that is likely to enable them to arrive at solutions of problems that you pose.

Several factors militate against the value of recording grades for participation in class discussion. The questions that you ask respective students to answer are likely to vary in difficulty. Also, some students become so involved in guessing what the next question will be that they fail to listen to what is being said by a student who is discussing the present question. Then, too, the shy student is at a disadvantage in comparison with the more aggressive or outgoing student who often talks without having much to say on the topic.

Written Reports as Evaluative Instruments

You have a responsibility to evaluate all written work that you require students to submit to you. This includes such written materials as themes, term or project reports, and notebooks. As a student, you probably always have looked forward with anticipation to the return of your written work. You have appreciated a teacher's evaluating and grading it carefully and fairly. Now you have the responsibility of returning written work as quickly as time will permit your careful evaluation of it.

In some subjects, workbooks and notebooks are necessary. When either is used, it is your duty to encourage your students to keep them neat and to make careful entries in them. A workbook or notebook is for the student's use, but you need to supervise the writing to insure its accuracy of contents and usability at a later date. Encourage students to make only those entries that have a bearing on the subject. An elaborate cover design may satisfy the ego of the student but does not contribute to worthwhile content. The nature of the material and its applicability to the topic are of prime importance. You become skilled in helping students prepare worthwhile notebooks by giving time and attention to this kind of project during your student teaching experiences.

The Use of Tests in Measuring Achievement

The tests with which you are likely to have the closest relationship from the point of view of application are the various forms of tests that are used to measure extent of achievement. You will use many short quizzes and either prepare or help prepare questions for administration to evaluate small units of study. You also will be involved in the preparation of end-term or final examinations.

You are likely to use the results of certain standardized achievement tests that were administered earlier. Scores made by your students in such learning areas as reading and mathematics will be found on most cumulative records. In addition, you may participate in the administration of standardized tests that are devised to measure extent of achievement in the subject or subjects that you are preparing to teach or are teaching. You should be acquainted with reliable tests in your subject area and know how to interpret the results of their administration.

The use of short quizzes. Rather than rate each oral contribution of your students, it might be a better policy to plan short quizzes that cover the assigned work and, using no more than five or ten minutes of the class period, get weekly statements that can be rated and recorded. You need to encourage home study and to know something about the extent to which it has been completed. The remaining time can be devoted to the solution of problems that challenge the thinking of your students and, at the same time, make them feel more at ease in the learning situation.

You need to develop skill in using some form of short quiz that can be administered, at the beginning of recitation periods, as a check on completeness of home study. You might even bring the members of the class, on a rotating basis, into the administration of this quiz project. A social studies teacher, known to the authors, for example, gives the responsibility of daily quizzes on assigned home study to rotating student committees. Each of these committees (numbering three students) in turn prepares ten appropriate short-form questions or one essay question, and administers it. Sometimes the committee corrects the papers; sometimes the students exchange papers and rate them; at other times the teacher collects the papers and marks them. A record of the students' performance is kept in a special notebook for the teacher's use. Of course, a project of this kind requires careful teacher supervision, but the students' participation in testing procedures helps them recognize the difficulty of preparing adequate questions and of rating them accurately and honestly.

Teacher-Made Tests and Examinations

You will want to make use of many types of written tests to measure student achievement, since you will need much information to assist you to determine the grade to be placed on a report card. Of course, these paper-and-pencil tests serve purposes other than that of aiding in the determination of grades. They can be regarded as devices that reveal something about the success of the teaching-learning process. You should not lose sight of the fact that effective teaching as well as extent of learning are reflected in these measurements.

Objectivity in testing. Teachers need measuring instruments that will help them measure learner achievement more objectively than can be done by using only the essay-type questions. Numerous experiments have been made that reveal the wide range of scores assigned to answers on essay questions even when they are evaluated (marked) by experts. This holds not only in subjects like English and the social sciences but also in the physical sciences and mathematics. For example, 142 teachers rating one English paper assigned scores that ranged from 64 to 98; 118 teachers who rated a final examination paper in mathematics gave scores ranging between 28 and 92. Objective type tests tend to correct this fault even though they have faults of their own.

Good objective test questions are difficult to formulate. The challenge to the test constructor of the short-form objective type test is (1) to select questions that completely cover the material to be tested, and (2) to prepare questions that are clear, thought-provoking and ranging from the simple to the relatively difficult. A variety of objective-type tests are in wide use. Included among them are true-false tests, multiple-choice tests, completion tests, matching tests, identification tests, and controlled essay-type tests. We present sample questions of each type from several learning areas.

Examples of True-False Questions. Directions: Place a plus sign (+) before each statement that is true or essentially true; place a zero (0) before each statement that is false.

1. Success, even in a simple activity, is a powerful interest motivator.
2. Bright young people always tend to be interested in all of their school subjects.
3. Interests are acquired in the sense that feeling becomes associated with the activity.
4. The preadolescent experiences little conflict between independence and dependence.
5. Self-realization connotes more than self-awareness.
6. Discipline, in general, refers to control of an adolescent's behavior by forces outside himself.

Multiple-Choice Questions. Directions: In each question, select the best ending and place its identifying letter before the number of the question.

1. A chemical change is represented by the (*a*) burning of coal, (*b*) dissolving of sugar in water, (*c*) melting of ice, (*d*) evaporation of gasoline.
2. The incorrect sentence is (*a*) Mary is lying on the couch.
   (*b*) I know the boy whom you mentioned.
   (*c*) None of them are here.
   (*d*) Did you see the sun rise this morning?
3. Radar makes use of the principle of (*a*) refraction, (*b*) reflection, (*c*) divergence, (*d*) regression.

Matching Questions. Directions: On the line before each gland in the left column, write the letter of the right-hand column that describes its function.

Endocrine Gland	Functions of Gland
___ 1. Adrenal glands	*a.* Cortex secretes cortin
___ 2. Gonads	*b.* Causes dwarfism and gigantism
___ 3. Pancreas	*c.* Function not known
___ 4. Parathyroid	*d.* Lymphoid tissue
___ 5. Pineal gland	*e.* Regulates calcium metabolism of body
___ 6. Pituitary gland	*f.* Regulates sugar metabolism
___ 7. Thymus	*g.* Secretes sex hormones
___ 8. Thyroid gland	*h.* Secretes thyroxin

Identification Questions. Directions: On the lines below, write the names of the states for the numbers given.

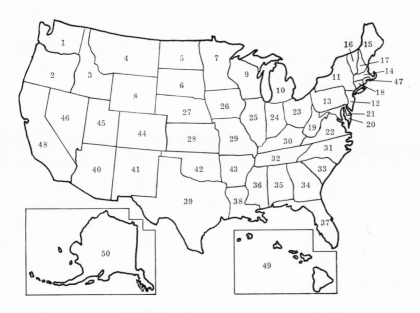

Fɪɢ. 7.—States in the United States.

44 _____	3 _____
32 _____	33 _____
22 _____	16 _____
38 _____	6 _____
8 _____	25 _____

Same or Different Meanings. Directions: Differentiate between *Same* or *Different* meanings of words by placing an *S* or a *D* before each set in this list.

__ 1. maturation—learning __ 5. projective test—*TAT*
__ 2. diagnostic—prognostic __ 6. motive—purpose
__ 3. test—scale __ 7. character—personality
__ 4. mental age—IQ __ 8. norm—standard

Controlled Completion. Directions: In the blank space provided, place the proper word from those given below.

1. When learning takes place _____ are produced in the _____.

curves   changes   plateaus   retention   organism   diagram

Controlled Essay. Directions: Answer each question as indicated in the space provided.

1. Five characteristics that describe adolescent behavior are:
   a.
   b.
   c.
   d.
   e.
2. State three advantages of the cross-sectional study approach over the longitudinal approach in the study of individuals.
   a.
   b.
   c.

Principles of Test Construction

When you construct questions to measure the achievement of your students, you can be guided by some basic principles such as:

1. The questions should be drawn from the material to be learned without attempts to use trick questions.
2. The questions should be stated clearly so that they can be comprehended by each student.

3. The questions should become progressively more difficult in the test, especially if it is a short-form test.
4. Most of the questions should be geared to the ability level of the less able, but a few should be difficult enough to challenge the mentally superior students.
5. The test should be long enough to keep the students busy during most of the time set for the test or examination.
6. Each student should be given a copy of the questions. When questions are placed on the chalkboard, you must make certain that they can be read easily by every student in the room.
7. If for any reason you need to read the questions to the class, your reading must be clear, distinct, and slow enough for each student to grasp the meaning of the question.
8. The questions should be so worded that they permit of only one correct interpretation.
9. The students should be given the correct answers to the questions they missed on the tests. This can best be accomplished by returning corrected papers and discussing them.
10. Evaluative judgments of students' success in the test should be made by you in relation to the relative performance of each member of the class.

Special Considerations

You should make certain that material included in the test is pertinent to the material that was to be learned. As you correct test papers you can note such things as (1) the errors that are common to the majority of the learners, and (2) errors made by various individual students. The first procedure will help you evaluate your teaching effectiveness; the second is diagnostic in that it gives you insight into individual weakness.

As you go over test papers with your students, you may find it advisable to assume the responsibility for the common errors made by them and have these errors become the bases for further class discussion. Each student should recognize his errors and understand the correct answer when it is supplied to him. Often a student will need additional instruction before he comprehends sufficiently so as to make the material useful in his educational progress. You will find that if you use test results constructively, students do not fear tests but are glad to have them administered so that they may know the extent of their achievement in the subject.

STANDARDIZED ACHIEVEMENT TESTS

Standardized achievement tests are usually of the short-form type. Most of them have multiple-choice questions with four or five options from which to select the *correct* or *best* answer. These tests are constructed by test experts who follow definite rules of construction. When the term *standardized* accompanies a test it means that, after wide administration of the test in a particular learning area, norms have been established for the test. A manual usually is provided that offers carefully prepared directions for the administration and scoring of the test.

During the process of standardization, the preliminary form of the test contains more items than will be included in the final form. Through proper elimination of questions and rearrangement of those retained, the test usually is scaled—i.e., the least difficult questions are placed near the beginning and the more difficult ones toward the end of the test.

The worth of a standardized test depends on its *validity* (measures what it is supposed to measure) and its *reliability* (yields consistent results after repeated administrations). A test that has high reliability is one that gives comparable results when used to test the same group of students after an interval of time or that yields consistent results whenever administered.

Standardized achievement tests are not to be used to measure achievement in learning units as you progress in your teaching of the subject, but rather for comparative purposes with other students who have completed the study of the subject for which the test has been constructed. Results obtained from the administration of standardized achievement tests can be used properly to compare the achievement of your students with established norms. Note that standardized tests other than achievement tests are administered to evaluate individual students in comparison with large numbers of same-age groups in areas such as (1) intellectual capacity, (2) interests, and (3) emotional adjustment. Standardized tests should not be administered as a kind of busywork. Once administered, the results should be studied and serve as a basis for adjusting teaching procedure to learner difficulties.

EVALUATION FOR PURPOSES OF MARKING AND GRADING

One of the most difficult responsibilities of a teacher is to deter-- mine a mark that represents extent of achievement, record it, and perhaps justify it to the student. More and more, teachers are coming to realize that teacher-assigned marks are not as absolute as once had been believed. At best, marks represent no more than a teacher's estimate of student achievement. Usually, they are indicative of the extent to which, in comparison with others in the class, an individual student has succeeded in the learning of assigned material in the course.

Need for Competence in Marking

You will need to develop skill in the use of various kinds of tests so that you can use the results obtained in your assessment of a student's standing in his work. This necessitates (1) the construction of valid short-form tests and (2) the using of acceptable procedures in the marking of essay-type papers. You know about the variability among the marks from one teacher to another. You also need to realize that, during your marking process, you should maintain the same rating standards for all students. For example, it is better to complete a set of essay papers for a class once you start marking them so that you use one standard for all the papers. It is known that marking standards are likely to vary, on the same question, from one marking period to another.

Scores obtained from the administration of classroom tests and examinations serve as a significant basis for term marks or grades to be entered on report cards. These assigned marks will be as valid and as reliable as are the scores obtained from the tests used. In a short-form test, for example, the number of items included, the extent to which they cover the subject matter, and the care exercised in its construction are factors that influence school marks. Essay questions should be so worded that students understand exactly what they are expected to include in their answers. Students are interested in the marks they receive and the basic considerations used in their determination.

Method of marking important. The index that you use to evaluate the extent of student learning is the mark that you give, whether it is in the form of a *per cent* or of a *letter*. The former represents, in the mind of the student, an exact number such as 85 per cent; the latter represents a step interval including several percentage points —A = 90 to 100 per cent.

There are several methods that you can use to indicate level of achievement of your students. You may reveal the degree of achievement in relation to that of the other members of the class; you may attempt to give an absolute measure of achievement; you may compare individual performance with norms of available standardized achievement tests in your subject. What most students are interested in is, "Where do I stand in my class?" Each student wants to know something about his achievement in relation to that of other members of his class, or of other classes in the school.

Importance of having standards understood by students. In your evaluation of student achievement you will make use of criteria in arriving at a mark. Students and parents need to know the standards that are used by you. You should utilize every available evaluating source, such as individual reports, daily recitations, weekly tests, notebook work, special projects, and final examinations. Not only should the students know that these are the criteria used by you, but it is of further value to them to know something about the relative weights assigned to each.

Factors Causing Variability in Marks

You must be on guard not to let student behavior influence your evaluation of achievement. Some teachers have a tendency to give higher marks to cooperative students than to troublemakers. A mark given to a student should represent your most accurate judgment of his learning progress and not be influenced by his attitudes or behavior. It should indicate your estimate of his accomplishment in the learning situation in relation to the achievement of all other students in your class. Evaluation of his other personal characteristics can be reported in other ways.

The fact that teachers do not agree upon nor use precisely the same standards in marking, accounts in part for the divergence among teachers' marks. Your set of values enters into marking more than you realize. A simple example can illustrate this point. Suppose you assign a grade to the following example on the scale from 0 to 10. What score did you assign to it? Do you give him credit for

$$
\begin{array}{r}
786 \\
+249 \\
\hline
1025
\end{array}
\qquad \text{Grade\_\_\_\_\_}
$$

knowing the principle of addition even though his answer is incorrect? We have given this type of example to college juniors and seniors and to graduate students. It is never possible to get agreement on what the score or grade should be. The scores usually range from 0 to 9. Each student wants to explain his reason for his rating. What he means is that he has his standard that guides his evaluation. The purpose of this example is to enable you to understand that grades are based on your own mental standards and are far from being absolute.

Earlier in the chapter we reported that the marks of specialists on specific papers varied widely. Some teachers believe that minor errors should carry heavy penalties and are known as teachers who give low marks; other teachers are willing to overlook certain minor mistakes and accordingly assign higher marks. The latter become known as easy markers. Ironically, these standards vary from school to school and from subject to subject within a school, as well as from teacher to teacher.

SUGGESTIONS FOR DISTRIBUTION OF MARKS

In an unselected group of learners there will be found a distribution of marks that follows closely that of a normal curve of distribution. (See Figure 3, p. 76.) Even in a class of students already equated on some ability basis or level of achievement, the scores earned by them tend to range from a low to a high with the larger number of scores falling near the middle of the distribution. In other words, when the achievement of a group of students is measured, you are likely to find a wide distribution of scores with which to deal. You then are confronted with the problem of using these scores in assigning midterm or endterm marks.

Classes that are organized according to learning achievement and ability to perform constitute an excellent teaching-learning situation. When the learners have experiences that are somewhat comparable, your burden as a teacher is eased from one point of view. However, for the purpose of assigning marks, it is easier for you when you have an unselected group of learners. Here you have no difficulty in knowing what grades to give to the few at the low end and the few at the high end of the scale. When you have a class of "honor" students, you find a shorter range of scores, and you are less certain about the marks to assign the students.

Midterm marks or endterm marks should reflect all of the evaluations that have been made by you during the course of the training period. There are various schemes of percentage distributions that you might use. You may have a school policy on this. If so, be sure to follow it. We present here several distribution schemes that represent the percentage of students who might be assigned respective marks.

TABLE 12

TYPES OF DISTRIBUTION SCHEMES FOR REPORTING MARKS

Letter Grade	Percentage Range	Per Cent of Students in Each Range			
A	90–100	10	7	5	10
B	80–89	20	24	25	25
C	70–79	40	38	40	55
D	65–69	20	24	25	10
F	Below 65	10	7	5	0

If they are available, you might study the distribution of marks already given by teachers to different classes in your subject. Much can be gleaned from these data. Also, you might be provided with the marks given by your college instructors in one or more of the subjects you are taking there. You are likely to find that college instructors vary in their marking procedures and standards in the same way as do teachers in the secondary schools.

Even though the students who attend college are highly selected, the marks representing their achievement in any subject area vary with instructors and are distributed from low to high in any one class. In Table 13, we present representative marks given in three courses including child development, adolescent development, and educational psychology.

TABLE 13

DISTRIBUTION OF MARKS IN THREE COLLEGE COURSES

Course	Marks				
	A	B	C	D	F
	Number of Students				
X	30	180	80	25	9
Y	35	103	64	24	6
Z	61	332	162	52	9

THE USE OF VISUAL GRADING

As a student teacher you are filled with enthusiasm. You want to be fair in your appraisal of student achievement and want to correct some of the grading abuses that you have observed. You want to put meaning into the marks that you assign. You proceed to construct an acceptable test and administer it to prevent cheating or any other abuse. You score the papers accurately and conscientiously. Once you have the raw scores, you are confronted with the problem of distributing them according to school policy. K. L. Russell [1] provides us with four criteria of a meaningful grading system. He says:

FOUR CRITERIA OF A MEANINGFUL GRADING SYSTEM

1. The grade for achievement in a given subject should be based on a comprehensive and extensive measurement program. There should be many measurements; they should be scattered over an extended period of time; and they should represent a number of different testing procedures.
2. The grade must be a symbol of comparison between student status and

[1] K. L. Russell, *Visual Grading* (Huntsville, Tex.: Educational Filmstrips, 1959).

known and fair standards. The parent and the student want to know what the standard is. A standard in the mind of the teacher is not enough. The teacher must be able to describe these standards to both parents and students. Parent education is an absolute necessity.

Fairness needs no justification, but fairness does not just happen. The grade level and maturation of the student must be considered in establishing a fair standard. Fair standards are derived from a combination of performance of students in the local school with a definition of competence by experts in the subject or field in question.

Percentage standards of and in themselves are of little or no value. A score of 80 per cent on a test has no meaning until we know something about other scores made by other students assigned the same subject matter and who took the same test. Without knowing the scoring practices of the individual teacher, we know little or nothing about the real meaning of percentage grades. A percentage score of 80 may represent the best achievement in the class or it may represent the worst. One teacher gives tests of a difficulty level designed to be a challenge to bright students with the result that 80 may be an above-average score. Thus we find that a percentage standard is not a standard at all since it can vary from day to day, from teacher to teacher, and from year to year.

3. Grades and reports should be realistic. Much has been written about frustrating the student with too much emphasis upon grades. Grading in such a way as to prevent frustration is impossible. "Over-grading" is certainly a disservice to the student because he will tend to over-rate his ability and be frustrated when he tries his skill in a non-school atmosphere. To under-rate the good student with low grades in order to prod him to more accomplishment may frustrate him and keep him from achieving as high as he should. Believe it or not, most of the progress of the world has been made by individuals who were frustrated in some way or another and set out to do something about it.

Some schools grade upon effort. Slow students are given good grades because they "try hard." Excellent students receive good grades for superior achievement. Without knowing whether the grade is for effort or for achievement, we know nothing about the effort or the achievement of the student. To average an *A* for effort and *F* for achievement, and report a *C* as the grade may indicate little about either effort or achievement.

There are good reasons for grading on effort, and where this is done there should be two grades—one for achievement and one for effort. The poor student is encouraged by his good grade for effort, yet recognizes his poor accomplishments. The good student may be reprimanded with a poor grade for effort and still be told that his achievement is of high quality.

4. The grade symbols must be understandable to students and parents. The meaning of grades should be clear and constant from year to year and from teacher to teacher.

Dr. Russell carefully explains the meaning of "Letter Grades" and defines what achievement is expected for each category:

LETTER GRADES

Letter grades provide a method of classifying achievement into meaningful groups. Experience suggests that teachers can place student achievement into approximately five groups. Finer divisions than this are impractical.

No two school systems define letter grades exactly the same way. The important thing is that schools clearly specify to all concerned what their letter grades mean. One such description is given here as an example.

The letter *A* is reserved for *very superior* achievement. It means that the student is prepared for high-quality advanced work in the field of study and usually represents a small number exhibiting outstanding accomplishments.

The letter *B* is representative of *highly satisfactory* achievement. It indicates that the student is prepared for above-average quality advanced work. The group receiving this grade is usually larger than the *A* group but much smaller than the *C* group.

The letter *C* represents *competent, satisfactory, average* achievement. It should mean that the student is prepared for advanced work. The *C* group is usually larger than the *A* and *B* groups combined.

The letter *D* signifies *poor* achievement. It represents work which is marginal for advanced work in the field of study. The group is similar in size to the *B* group.

The letters *E* and *F* are reserved for *very poor* achievement. The group is usually similar in size to the *A* group.

It is utterly futile to argue what per cent should be assigned the various grades. The proportions will vary from class to class, from semester to semester, and from community to community. However, over a two-year period or after 250 grades have been assigned, the distribution should be about 25–35 per cent *A*'s and *B*'s, 35–50 per cent *C*'s, and 25–35 per cent *D*'s and *F*'s. To be more exact than this is misleading. To stray too far from these figures, however, denies the definitions stated above. A teacher who persists in giving more than 50 per cent *A*'s and *B*'s or *D*'s and *F*'s has changed the definitions of the grades to fit his own purpose and thus his grades are meaningless to the rest of the school and the community. There may be exceptions to this where homogeneous grouping is attempted.

Many schools now use the mark of *E* for reporting very poor achievement. The *E* should be used when it seems advisable to "pass" or "promote" most children each year because of social, psychological, or economic reasons. This allows the teacher to report low achievement without the implications of failure and non-promotion. The *F* should be used when it seems advisable to "fail" or "retain" approximately 5 to 10 per cent of the students each year.

Five to 10 per cent of the students will generally fall in the very low group. No amount of juggling or adjusting of test scores can change this fact. If the school wishes to be realistic and report this fact to the parents, the school, and the community, it should adopt a system which makes it possible without implying failure and non-promotion. Parents will accept accurate reports of achievement. They will not accept arbitrary failure and non-promotion for their children. If the school is prepared for 5 to 10 per cent of its students to "fail" and is prepared to adhere to its decision, in spite of parental pressures, then it should use the *F*. If the school is unwilling for 5 to 10 per cent of its students to be in the process of repeating courses and grades, then it should use the *E*.

Advantages of Visual Grading

The advantages of visual grading as given by Russell are presented here:

The plotting of scores on cross-section paper for visual interpretation is one method of making grades more meaningful. It is a well proven fact that when a large number of unselected cases of any natural phenomenon are measured and plotted that a bell-shaped curve results. This fact has been the basis for improving grading practices for many years, but in practice the plans have proven inadequate. Most authorities who propose the "curve" as a background for grading forget that classroom teachers do not have the time to apply complicated statistical interpretations to student achievement. Moreover, the scores in any one class provide too small a sample to follow the statistics of the curve in daily practice. As a result the "curve" is extremely unpopular as a foundation for grading.

Visual grading adapts the phenomenon of normal distribution to small groups. This is done through visual interpretation rather than through a statistical one. Experience has shown that the visual interpretation of small groups of scores results in grade distributions which meet the criteria for meaningful grades. The following advantages can be attributed to visual grading:

1. Visual Grading makes it easy to include all types of evidence. Large groups and complicated statistical interpretations are unnecessary. It is not limited to any given number of measurements, to a period of time, or to any particular testing procedure.

2. Visual Grading provides a uniform basis of comparison regardless of the differences in scoring practices. The standard is verified by student achievement in any given area of learning. The system is fair to all students, while at the same time helping to provide a challenge to the bright students at all grade levels.

3. Visual Grading helps to keep grades constant from teacher to teacher and from year to year. Meaningless percentages are not used. Rigid "curve" grading is avoided. Achievement is classified into meaningful groups, not into artificial patterns dictated by blind percentages.

4. Visual Grades are realistic. There is no need to water-down the content of examinations. There is no need to be lax in evaluation procedures.

5. Visual Grading can be easily explained to students and parents in many ways. For convenience in explaining Visual Grading, a series of

three filmstrips has been prepared for use with teachers, students, and parents.[2]

6. Visual Grading is less time-consuming than many other methods. No complicated mathematical computations are involved. No averaging or percentage calculations are necessary.

Charts That Illustrate Visual Grading

We now present four charts from Russell's *Visual Grading* that illustrate some of the ways that visual grading is used:

You are now ready for your first experience in the visual interpretation of test scores. Fairness seems to dictate that the same grade be assigned to similar scores.

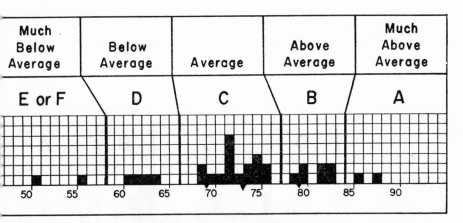

Fig. 8.—Assigning the grade.

The following is suggested as a beginning approach to the problem of visual grading with homogeneous groups. Experience is very limited in this area and the author will appreciate receiving distributions of scores from teachers who have been assigned homogeneous groups.

Assume a group of students selected from the upper 33 per cent of the student body. *A* and *B* students.

[2] Kenneth L. Russell, *Grading Student Achievement,* Three Color Filmstrips (Huntsville, Tex.: Educational Filmstrips).

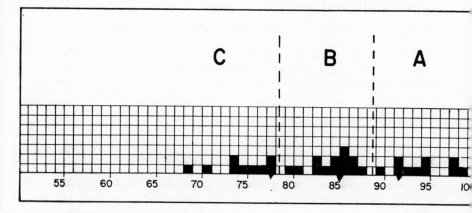

Fig. 9.—Grading homogeneous groups.

This chart illustrates a method of combining scores from several sections of the same course taught by the same teacher.

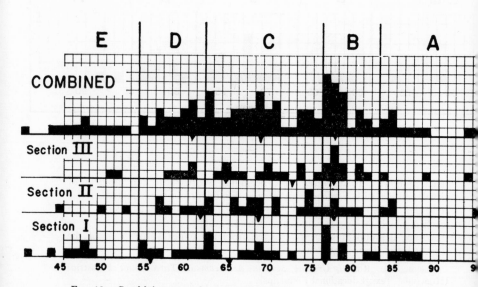

Fig. 10.—Combining scores from several sections.

If the school requires the reporting of a percentage grade, in addition to a letter grade, the following procedure is suggested:

1. Chart the scores and grade according to the concept of visual grading.

2. Assign the lowest grade in each letter group the lowest percentage specified by the school for this particular grade. Adjust the other scores accordingly.

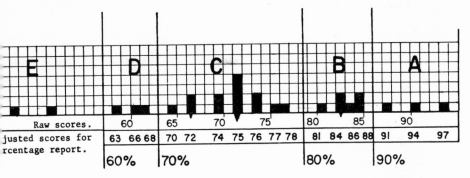

FIG. 11.—Adjusting to percentage scores.

This adjusted percentage will now agree with the definition of the grade. This adjustment appears more desirable than to say that a score of 70 is average when in reality it may be above or below average.

REPORTING MARKS TO PARENTS

The student's report card of which we presented samples in Chapter 5 represents an important medium for reporting student progress to parents. It is one of the most important documents that the student receives during his school life; it is important not only to him but to his parents, to colleges, and to employers. On the report card is presented the story of the student's achievement according to the standards of the teacher of every subject he takes. The student deserves to have his grade represent fairly his degree of achievement. At the secondary level there has been less experimentation on the form that these report cards should take. High schools tend to use either the percentage or the letter grade, both of which have come to have meaning for most parents of secondary school learners.

Parents often are uninformed concerning what has gone into the mark that appears on the report card. The student and the parents should know the basis of the grade assigned. If the teacher uses different weights to evaluate different types of class activities, this fact should be known to students and parents. For example, a teacher may follow a definite plan to determine his grades. He may assign different weights to various types of activities, as in the following:

Special reports	25 per cent
Daily recitation	15 per cent
Notebook work	15 per cent
Weekly tests	15 per cent
Special projects	5 per cent
Final examination	15 per cent

Parents' cooperation is more easily attained in school projects when they understand what is going on and how they can assist in encouraging their children to participate actively in their schoolwork.

QUESTIONS AND TOPICS FOR DISCUSSION

1. Reread the Individual Record Form presented in this chapter. Are there any items which you think should be omitted? Which? Why?
2. What intelligence test or tests are administered to the students in your school?
3. Compare the results of intelligence tests administered to the students in your class with their achievement ratings. To what extent do they agree? What specific differences do you find? How do you explain these differences?
4. If you have taken a personality test, report on your attitude toward it and your reaction to individual items.
5. With your cooperating teacher's approval, experiment with having your students prepare some daily quiz questions. What difficulties do the students encounter?
6. Which type of short-form questions do you prefer? Why?
7. Why should questions in a test become progressively more difficult?
8. What are the implications of item 10 of the principles of test construction?
9. What are some of the difficulties involved in assigning end of term grades?
10. Which of the types of distribution schemes in Table 12 seems to you to be the most equitable? What factors can influence your opinion?
11. What have you learned about grades from reading Russell's comments? In what ways has he helped you in assigning marks?

12. How might your method of weighting different learning activities vary from the one presented in the chapter?

SELECTED REFERENCES

BRAFIELD, J., and MOREDOCK, H. *Measurement and Evaluation in Education*. New York: Macmillan Co., 1957.

EBEL, R. L. "Measurement and the Teacher: Ten Useful Principles," *Educational Leadership*, October, 1962, pp. 20–24.

GARRETT, H. E. *Testing for Teachers*. New York: American Book Co., 1959.

GREEN, J. A. *Teacher-Made Tests*. New York: Harper & Row, Pub., Inc., 1963.

GREENE, H. A., JORGENSEN, A. N., and GERBERICH, J. R. *Measurement and Evaluation in the Secondary School* (2nd ed.). New York: David McKay Co., Inc., 1954.

JORDAN, A. M. *Measurement in Education*. New York: McGraw-Hill Book Co., Inc., 1953.

LINDVALL, C. M. *Testing and Evaluation: An Introduction*. New York: Harcourt, Brace & World, Inc., 1961.

NOLL, V. *Introduction to Educational Measurement*. Boston: Houghton Mifflin Co., 1957.

ODELL, C. W. *How to Improve Classroom Testing*. Dubuque, Iowa: W. C. Brown, Co., 1953.

REMMERS, H. H., and GAGE, N. L. *Educational Measurement and Evaluation*. New York: Harper & Row, Pub., Inc., 1955.

RUSSELL, K. L. *Visual Grading*. Huntsville, Tex.: Educational Filmstrips, 1959.

SCHWARTZ, A., and TIEDEMAN, S. C. *Evaluating Student Progress in the Secondary School*. New York: David McKay Co., Inc., 1957.

THOMAS, R. M. *Judging Student Progress* (2nd ed.). New York: David McKay Co., Inc., 1960.

TRAXLER, A. E., *et al*. *Introduction to Testing and the Use of Test Results in Public Schools*. New York: Harper & Row, Pub., Inc., 1953.

WENDT, E., and BROWN, G. W. *Essentials of Educational Evaluation*. New York: Holt, Rinehart & Winston, Inc., 1957.

WRIGHTSTONE, J. W., JUSTMAN, J., and ROBBINS, I. *Evaluation in Modern Education*. New York: American Book Co., 1956.

15

TEACHER PLACEMENT AND ORIENTATION

During your student teaching experiences (probably earlier), you gave attention to the problem of securing your first position as a regularly assigned teacher. You will want to devote sufficient time and thought to this task so that you finally select and are accepted by a school in which you can achieve personal and professional satisfaction, and, through participation in the activities of which you are stimulated, grow in your chosen career. Too many teachers-to-be who make this decision hastily discover that, for one or more reasons, they are unhappy in their work. They may even come to believe that they are unsuited for teaching.

SEEKING EMPLOYMENT AS A TEACHER

Before you start to seek your first position, you need to ask yourself certain important questions concerning your teaching interests. For example: Do you want to teach in your home community or are you willing to accept a position in another community or even state? Do you prefer teaching in a large or a small school community? Can you teach another subject in addition to the one for which you have primarily prepared? To what extent will size of salary affect your decision? How important to you are opportunities for professional growth and advancement?

Your answers to questions such as those given in the foregoing will determine in part the kind of school or school system in which you will attempt to secure employment. Fortunately for you, the student population on the secondary school level is increasing. Hence teacher demand is greater than teacher supply. Yet, since the number of young people preparing to teach on this level also is increasing, you will have stiff competition. You may need to compromise somewhat in regard to what you consider to be an ideal teaching situation. Too, you must make certain that you meet the certification requirements of the kind of school in which you may be interested.

Certification Requirements for Teaching

Each state has established certain requirements that must be met by an applicant for a teaching position before he can be given consideration by a school system in that state. For example, here is a summarization of the minimum preparation for teaching required by states for initial certification. Various states are tending to increase the minimum years of preparation for high school teachers from four to five years. Some states interpret the fifth year as 30 credits beyond the bachelor's degree; other states demand the completion of a master's degree.

States differ in the number of semester hours of professional education required as well as the semester hours of directed practice or student teaching. (See Table 14.)

TABLE 14

SUMMARY OF MINIMUM PREPARATION REQUIREMENTS BY STATES FOR LOWEST REGULAR INITIAL CERTIFICATE (AS OF JULY, 1961)*
(Includes District of Columbia and Puerto Rico)

College Years of Preparation Required	Number of States Requiring High School Teachers
5 years	3
4 years	48
3 but less than 4 years	0
2 but less than 3 years	1
1 but less than 2 years	0
Less than 1 year	0

* W. Earl Armstrong and T. M. Stinnett, *A Manual on Certification Requirements for School Personnel in the United States* (Washington, D.C.: Commission on Teacher Education and Professional Standards, National Education Assoc., 1962), p. 7.

Some states are tending to change or upgrade their requirements. California, for example, is planning to increase the number of semester hours in many academic fields from science to the humanities. They are proposing not to accept applicants if their chief training is in the methodology of teaching.

In order to determine your accrediting status, it would be wise for you, before you apply for a position, to consult the latest edition of the National Education Association *Manual on Certification Requirements for School Personnel in the United States,* which publishes a revised edition about every two years. We quote from the latest edition. (See Table 15.) A college placement officer also may be able to help you check your eligibility in various states. In some states, the schools will employ you provisionally, giving you a period of grace in which to fulfill a specific requirement.

Approaches to Teacher Placement

There are various avenues of approach to securing a teaching position. You may have a friend or relative in a school in which you might be interested in teaching. If there were an appropriate vacancy in that school, the person could speak in your behalf and perhaps arrange an interview for you with a member of the administration. You might decide on geographical areas that would be convenient for you and visit locations in order to discover possible vacancies. These informal approaches may yield uncertain results, however. More formal approaches to seeking a position usually are to be preferred.

Value of a college placement bureau. Most colleges and universities maintain a placement bureau for the use of their students and graduates. Many schools and school systems report their faculty needs to certain selected institutions of higher learning that are engaged in teacher education. These vacancies are kept on file in the placement offices of the colleges, and attempts are made to fit graduates to available positions. Your first approach to finding a position might be to register with your college bureau. You will find that the director or one of his assistants will be more than willing to discuss with you any opportunities for placement that may be available. The bureau also will help you organize your credentials. Some secondary schools send recruiting officers to various colleges to review the credentials of possible teacher applicants and to meet them for interviewing purposes.

TABLE 15

MINIMUM REQUIREMENTS FOR LOWEST REGULAR TEACHING CERTIFICATES *

| | High School | | |
| | Degree or Number of Semester Hours Required | Professional Education Required, Semester Hours (Total) | Directed Teaching Required, Semester Hours (Included in Column 6) |
State			
1	5	6	7
Alabama	B	24	3
Alaska	B	18	C
Arizona	5 [a]	18	6
Arkansas	60 [b]	12	3
California	5	22	6
Colorado	B	AC	AC
Connecticut	B	18	6
Delaware	B	18	6
District	5	18	6
Florida	B	20	6
Georgia	B	18	6
Hawaii	B	18	AC
Idaho	B	20	6
Illinois	B	16	5
Indiana	B	18	5
Iowa	B	20	5
Kansas	B	20	5
Kentucky	B	17	8 [d]
Louisiana	B	18	4
Maine	B	12	0
Maryland	B	18	6
Massachusetts	B	12	2
Michigan	B	20	5
Minnesota	B	18	4
Mississippi	B	18	6
Missouri	B	20	5
Montana	B	AC	AC
Nebraska	B	18	3
Nevada	B	18	4
New Hampshire	B	21	6
New Jersey	B	24 [h]	6 [h]
New Mexico	B	18	6
New York	B [i]	18	6
North Carolina	B	18	3
North Dakota	B	16	3
Ohio	B	17	6
Oklahoma	B	21 [j]	6
Oregon	B [k]	24	6
Pennsylvania	B	18	6
Puerto Rico	B	29	5
Rhode Island	B	18	6

TABLE 15 (*Cont.*)

MINIMUM REQUIREMENTS FOR LOWEST REGULAR TEACHING CERTIFICATES *

State	Degree or Number of Semester Hours Required	Professional Education Required, Semester Hours (Total)	Directed Teaching Required, Semester Hours (Included in Column 6)
	High School		
1	5	6	7
South Carolina	B	18	6
South Dakota	B	20	5
Tennessee	B	24	4
Texas	B	24	6
Utah	B	22	8
Vermont	B	18	6
Virginia	B	15	4–6
Washington	B [n]	AC	AC
West Virginia	B [o]	20	5
Wisconsin	B	18	5
Wyoming	B	20	C

Legend: AC means approved curriculum; B means bachelor's degree of specified preparation; 5 means bachelor's degree plus a fifth year of appropriate preparation, not necessarily completion of master's degree; C means a course.

* W. Earl Armstrong and T. M. Stinnett, *A Manual on Certification Requirements for School Personnel in the United States* (Washington, D.C.: National Commission on Teacher Education and Professional Standards, National Education Assoc., 1962), pp. 24–25.

[a] *Arizona.* Secondary certificate: master's degree or 30 semester hours of graduate credit. Presecondary certificate (valid for grades 7–12): bachelor's degree plus 6 semester hours of graduate work; valid for 2 years; may renew for 2 years by having a total of 18 semester hours of graduate credit.

[b] *Arkansas.* Bachelor's degree will be required in 1963.

[d] *Kentucky.* A teacher who has taught successfully 4 or more years is required to take only 4 semester hours in practice teaching or a seminar of 4 hours. A teacher who has had 2 years of successful experience may take a seminar dealing with professional problems instead of the 8 hours in practice teaching.

[e] *Massachusetts.* Completion of bachelor's degree or graduation from an approved 4-year normal school.

[h] *New Jersey.* Practice teaching requirement is 150 clock hours, 90 of which must be in actual classroom teaching.

[i] *New York.* A provisional high-school certificate is issued for the academic fields based upon completion of bachelor's degree with 18 semester hours in education, including 6 semester hours of supervised practice teaching; valid for 5 years; nonrenewable; holder must complete requirements for permanent certificate; permanent certificate requires an additional 6 semester hours in education or in advanced study in the subject field.

[j] *Oklahoma.* For standard certificate; for temporary certificate the requirement is 12.

Other teacher placement services. There are commercial teachers' agencies to which you can apply. Although college placement officers usually do not charge a fee, commercial agencies exact a fee for placement of about 5 per cent of the first year's salary. Most of these agencies conduct a reputable business, but you should consult someone who knows about these agencies before you sign up with one. In some states there also are state sponsoring placement services or services offered by state teachers' associations. These usually charge a small fee.

Other ways of locating a possible position are (1) to send letters of inquiry to selected schools to discover whether there are any vacancies in your field of interest, and (2) to apply by letter to schools in which you have heard that there are available positions. The *Education Directory,* published by the U.S. Office of Education, can be used to find the names and addresses of all school superintendents. Also, the names of superintendents of all large school systems in the United States are published annually by American Book Company on the back pages of a calendar that they prepare for distribution to schools.

Some of the larger school systems (New York City, for example) select their teachers by way of licensing examinations. Any qualified citizen of the United States is eligible to enter one of these examinations that are held at stated intervals. If you pass the various parts of the test (including a physical examination and a speech test) your name is placed, in rank position, on an eligible list from which appointments are made. One difficulty of this procedure is that many months may elapse between the taking of the examination and the date of the appointment.

Table 15, Footnotes (*Cont.*)

ᵏ *Oregon.* Provisional certificate only; 5 years required for standard certification. Fifth year must be completed within 5 years after provisional certificate is issued.

ⁿ *Washington.* Provisional certificate only; 5 years required for standard certification. Fifth year must be completed within 6 years after provisional certificate is issued.

º *West Virginia.* Issues only 1 standard certificate, the Professional based on the bachelor's degree. The 1957 Legislature repealed law providing for certificates based on 2 and 3 years of college preparation. The State Board of Education still issues some temporary certificates below the degree level.

Data to be included in an application. Any materials that are needed in applying for a position must be accurate and carefully prepared. You need to be sure that your credentials are properly stated. Someone in your college placement bureau can assist you in their preparation. File a set of credentials with the bureau for present or future use. Be sure that what you file is kept up to date.

Your college probably has a form for the listing of credentials. Fill in all items. These usually include identifying data, the position for which you are qualified, your personal qualifications, your training, and any experience you have had with young people, including your student teaching. Give specific dates and places. You usually are required also to include the names of at least three persons who can serve as references. Avoid using the names of close friends or relatives. The names could include those of (1) a college instructor, (2) your cooperating teacher in a school, and (3) your clergyman or other community leader. You should name individuals who will give a fair and impersonal evaluation of your personal qualities, your skill in working with young people, your scholarship, and the like.

Most schools require a transcript of your college record of scholarship. This is furnished by the college upon request. The first transcript is sent without charge. You may be asked to pay a small fee for others. Also included with the credentials should be a small photograph of yourself (about 3 × 5 inches). Snapshots are not desirable. When you sit for the photograph, wear conservative business clothes, and be sure that your head and shoulders are in view. Avoid a "posed" expression.

The letter of application. A letter of application should be clear, brief, and to the point. This is a business letter and should follow the proper format. Type the letter, unless a school administrator prefers that you write in longhand. If so, make certain that you write legibly and in black or blue-black ink. Take care that your signature can be read easily. Be specific. State the position for which you are applying, and your training and experience. Either enclose a brief statement of your qualifications or refer the reader to the placement agency from which your credentials may be obtained. Specify when you will be available for appointment and indicate your desire to be called for an interview. End your letter by expressing appreciation of whatever consideration you may receive. Also, enclose a large self-addressed, stamped envelope for any forms that may need to be sent you.

The letter of application is an important document. Administrators often are shocked by the carelessly written and poorly organized letters of application they receive from college-educated young men and women. An attractively and properly prepared letter is a point in favor of your candidacy. After you have written your letter, proofread it, noting any errors of form, spelling, grammatical structure, typing, and the like. If possible, submit it to a college instructor for criticism. Rewrite when any errors are found.

Many school systems require the completion by the candidate of a regular application form that requires the submitting of pertinent data. The application blank of the Westport Public Schools, Westport, Connecticut, for example, includes the following area items:

Teaching Position for Which You Are Applying

1. Personal Data
2. Employment Data
3. Military Service
4. Educational Preparation—Undergraduate Level
5. Educational Training—Graduate Level
6. Educational Credits
7. Teaching Experience
8. Student Teaching Experience—If New to Teaching
9. Other Work Experience
10. Other Professional Experience
11. References
12. Name and address of the Placement Office where your credentials are on file
13. Write a brief statement of your reasons for wanting to teach in Westport and your satisfactions in teaching thus far.
14. What do you consider your strongest and weakest characteristics as a teacher?
15. What reading have you done in the past six months?
    a. General Magazines
    b. Professional Magazines
    c. Books

16. List the professional, civic, and social organizations in which you hold membership.

Your interview with school administrators. School officials usually want to meet a candidate before deciding on his eligibility for a vacancy. This can be accomplished in one of two ways. The candidate is invited to the school on a particular day and at a specified time convenient to the interviewer and interviewee; a recruiting officer of the school may interview possible candidates at the college. In either situation, your displayed attitude during the interview is extremely important.

Your first interview probably will be a trying experience. Especially will this be true if the position for which you are being interviewed is one in which you are very much interested. You may tend to be "nervous." You may break out in a cold sweat and seem to be losing control of your voice. You may be inclined to fidget or to sit in a rigid position. You may be impelled either to overplay or underplay your qualifications for the position.

You need to become mentally set for the interview before you arrive. It is imperative that you be prompt, courteous, and honest. Before the interview, try to learn something about what might be expected of you. Avoid telling the superintendent how to run his school. Be willing to assess your own ability to meet the needs of the position. Reveal your interest in students and your interest in teaching as a profession. Somehow reveal the fact that you can be relied upon to discharge your obligations as a teacher when they are due and in the way they should be done. Convince the superintendent that you will reflect credit on the faculty and the school by your presence in the community.

Remember that the interviewer probably has had considerable experience in interviewing candidates for their first job and is able to recognize the symptoms of your inner perturbation. Hence he will make allowances for it. He is likely to prefer a modest young person to one who appears to be brash and overconfident. Listen attentively and answer questions simply and truthfully. Indicate by your manner that you appreciate the opportunity to be interviewed and that you hope that your qualifications are satisfactory. Although it is helpful to ask questions for clarification of the needs of the position, avoid any seeming attempt to interview the official.

Your final decision. The chances are good that you will receive at least several offers of positions. Deciding on the one to accept may constitute a problem. You do not want to be hasty. The first offer you receive may meet all of your expectations concerning teaching conditions, attitude of the administrator and other faculty members, salary schedule, kind of community, and living conditions. You probably will accept this position and look no further. It may be, however, that you have a question about one or more aspects of the vacancy. It is best then to wait for other offers. Yet, this procedure may give rise to difficulties of placement.

You cannot expect a school to hold a vacancy open to you indefinitely. You may need to meet a deadline for acceptance. Also, later offers may be less desirable than the one about which you are hesitating. Some schools do not object to your accepting the assignment tentatively, provided that you give your final decision within a reasonable period of time. It is unethical to accept several offers of employment and then to withdraw applications with no regard for the inconvenience caused to an employing school. Consult with the director of your college placement bureau concerning the ethics of dealing with employment practices.

Your teaching agreement. A teaching contract is a formal legal agreement between the employing school system and the teacher being employed. The form and interpretation of such contracts differ somewhat with states. Before you sign a contract you should read it through carefully. Make certain that you understand its provisions and are willing to abide by them. The contract includes specific information concerning length of tenure as specified in the contract, as well as the terms under which the agreement can be terminated by either party.

A teaching contract is binding on both the board of education and the teacher. Just cause must be shown by either for breaking the contract. If you are performing conscientiously and effectively, you need have little fear of being released from the contract. Likewise, you are expected to live up to it, except in the case of an emergency.[1]

Beginning teachers do not always appreciate the seriousness of

[1] See *Code of Ethics for the Education Profession,* National Education Assoc., 1963, Principle IV, pp. 440–41.

contractual agreements. For example, a graduating senior of an institution for teacher preparation made application for a teaching position in several school systems in his state. During May, he signed a contract with the superintendent of school A. In early summer, he received what seemed to him to be a more favorable offer from school B. Thereupon he signed a contract with that school but neglected to notify school A of his changed plans until the end of August. When this matter was called to the attention of the head state authority, this young person's teaching certificate was suspended for a period of six months, starting in September of the following year. This meant that, although the teacher was permitted to teach in school B for one year, he then was denied accepting a position in a public school in that state for the following September.

Starting Your First Teaching Position

After you have made your final decision concerning the school in which you will teach and have signed the contract, you need to prepare yourself for entrance into your new field of responsibilities. Whether you have completed your plans before or after college graduation, various matters need to be attended to before you begin your actual teaching.

One of your first considerations is where you will live. If you are to teach in your hometown or close to it, this presents no problem. You probably will live at home and travel to and from school. If your new school is so far removed from your home that travel would be difficult or impossible, you need to find a temporary home for yourself. The school officials usually have a list of appropriate homes for their teachers. Obtain a list of such vacancies and investigate the possibilities in light of your interests.

Some characteristics of available quarters can be judged on inspection; others need to be lived with to be evaluated. For example, distance from the school; size, furnishings, and general appearance of the room; size of family, number of other roomers and boarders, and cost can be determined by means of a visit to the home, accompanied by tactful questioning. Such matters as kinds of meals, heating facilities, and extent of personal freedom and privacy can be discussed in advance, but no conclusions can be arrived at concerning them until you have lived with them. It probably is wise to make tentative arrangements that can be changed later if necessary.

You also should attempt to acquaint yourself with the community. Visit the town to discover its available facilities, such as libraries, religious organizations, community centers, educational and recreational facilities, and the like. Some schools send their prospective new teachers maps and other interesting material about the community. Try to become as well acquainted with the community as is possible before you become a member of it.

Another area of preparation, of course, is the preparation of teaching-learning materials that will be helpful to you on the job. Here again the school can be of assistance to you by giving you, ahead of your arrival for duty, whatever in the way of curriculum materials, courses of study, and lists of available aids that you will need. You also can visit the school, preferably before you sign the contract, to discover something about the school's policies, types of students, teaching schedules, available teaching-learning equipment, and similar matters. The better prepared you are to start your teaching, the greater will be your chances of successful accomplishment.

PROGRAMS OF TEACHER ORIENTATION

Modern school administrators are becoming increasingly aware of the value to all concerned of helping beginning teachers in a school system adjust with a minimum of tension to their new responsibilities. Most schools sponsor orientation or induction programs at the start of the school year and continue to offer assistance to new teachers throughout their first year in the school. Where this is possible, an experienced teacher of the school, usually in the same subject, is assigned to help the latter in the meeting of his various school-and-class, management-and-teaching obligations.

As interpreted by most school officials, the term *new teachers* can refer either to beginning teachers or to more experienced teachers who have transferred from other school communities. Although orientation or induction procedures are conducted for both groups, beginning teachers receive whatever additional sympathetic help that may be needed.

Assistance in adjustment is rendered either through the issuance of teacher handbooks and other information materials, or through the conducting of workshops or meetings before the regular school year begins, or both. We shall present briefly some examples of orientation procedures that have been selected from school systems in various sections of the country.

Handbooks and Brochures for Teachers

Written materials dealing with information of value to the teacher tend to be attractively organized and arranged. They vary in length in terms of their specific purpose. For example, the Omaha Public Schools have prepared a well-illustrated ten-page brochure entitled *You'll Like Teaching in Omaha.* It contains brief comments on the environment, possibilities of professional growth, orientation, opportunities for advancement, salary and benefits, professional associations, and living conditions. The purpose is to attract qualified teachers to Omaha.

Various types of such publications are illustrated by the orientation booklet of Syracuse, N.Y., *Welcome to Syracuse,* Rochester's *Now That You Are with Us,* and the two booklets of San Diego, California—*San Diego City Schools Secondary Education* and *New Teachers' Handbook.* These handbooks include detailed information concerning policies, credentials, regulations, schedules, tenure, special services, and other types of data with which teachers in the particular school system should be acquainted.

Teachers' handbooks are generally intended for use by all the teachers of the school. Some schools include materials for new teachers in the same booklet; others prepare a separate pamphlet, as is the case with the San Diego schools. In fact, this school system goes a step further by presenting to new teachers an extremely attractive booklet entitled *San Diego Today,* which contains snapshots of some of their teachers at work with young people at various grade levels or in special subject areas. The St. Paul, Minnesota Schools publish *A Handbook for Teachers* and a brochure *Welcome Aboard,* which includes information that is of special interest to the new teacher. You might be interested in reading the foreword of the brochure.

Welcome to the staff of the Saint Paul Public Schools!

You are now a member of a most congenial, skillful, and helpful staff. May I express the hope that you will find genuine enjoyment in your new work in Saint Paul and that out of the ensuing school year will come much of lasting benefit to you as a result of your personal and professional associations.

The role of a teacher in our present-day society is not an easy one, and the first year of teaching, or the first year in any new school situation, is always beset with special problems. It is within our intentions, throughout this rather difficult period of adjustment, to render you every possible assistance. Your principal, the directors and supervisors, and your fellow teachers are ready to help you. Do not hesitate to call on them. Your contributions and your successes will be the source of much satisfaction to us, in the same way that these successes will contribute to your own feelings of personal satisfaction and well-being.

Good Luck!

Forrest E. Conner
Superintendent of Schools [2]

Schools and school systems throughout the country are accustomed to list in writing certain definite materials concerning your professional relationships. The City School District of Syracuse, New York, for example, issues administrative bulletins that deal with teachers' orientation information. The current bulletin includes the following items:

Absence from your classroom
Absence (excused), request for
Certification
Change of name, etc.
Discipline, classroom
Helping teachers
Hospitalization, medical benefits
Leave of absence
Policies and regulations
Probational reports
Probational status
Professional record, personnel file
Retirement
Salary adjustments

[2] Forrest E. Conner, *USS St. Paul Public Schools; Welcome Aboard* . . . (St. Paul, Minn.: Board of Education, 1962), foreword.

Sick leave
Social Security
Termination of employment, notice of
Time schedule, daily
Transferral

Similar materials prepared by the Tenafly, New Jersey, public schools include brochures, *Tenafly Invites You* and *Let's Get Acquainted,* and a salary guide dealing with matters such as salary range, salary increase, credit for previous experience, recognition for professional improvement, sick leave, pension and retirement, insurance, and sabbatical leave.

You also may be interested in reading answers to probationary teachers' questions as presented by the San Diego school officials. They deal with matters that concern you, regardless of the school system in which you have accepted an appointment. You need to discover what the policies of your school are in these respects:

For Probationary Teachers:

ANSWERS TO YOUR QUESTIONS ABOUT YOU AND YOUR JOB [3]

ED. NOTE: Each year, our growing number of probationary teachers ask questions concerning matters which affect them directly as certificated employees of our district. The following questions and answers, prepared by the Personnel Department, are set forth in a sincere desire to improve understanding and communication on tenure, leaves, retirement, service evaluations, third-year physical examinations, and similar matters.

Ratings or Service Evaluations

Q. *How often am I to be evaluated as a probationary teacher?*

A. Each probationary teacher is rated by his principal twice during the year. These ratings are due in the Personnel Department not later than Nov. 15 and Feb. 15. The principal will discuss both ratings with the teacher and the teacher will sign the forms as an indication that he has seen them.

Tenure

Q. *What is the legal basis for tenure in California?*

A. *Education Code Section 13304:* "Every employee of a school district of any type or class having an average daily attendance of 250 or more,

[3] From *San Diego City Schools: Secondary Education* (San Diego, Calif.: Personnel Department, 1962), pp. 14–15.

except a joint union or union high school district maintaining eight or more schools lying not less than six miles apart, who, after having been employed by the district for three complete consecutive school years in a position or positions requiring certification qualifications, is reelected for the next succeeding school year to a position requiring certification qualifications shall, at the commencement of the succeeding school year be classified as and become a permanent employee of the district."

Education Code Section 13328: "A probationary employee who, in any one school year, has served for at least 75 per cent of the number of days the regular schools of the district in which he is employed are maintained shall be deemed to have served a complete school year. In case of evening schools, 75 per cent of the number of days the evening schools of the district are in session shall be deemed a complete school year."

Education Code Section 13331: "Service by a person under a provisional credential shall not be included in computing the service required as a prerequisite to attainment of, or eligibility to, classification as a permanent employee of a school district."

Q. *If I am absent for illness does my absence count toward the 75 per cent of the regularly scheduled teaching days in the school year which I must teach in order to have it count for tenure and a salary increment?*

A. No. According to legal opinions received by the Personnel Department, absence because of illness does not constitute service under the meaning of the Education Code section. Anyone absent more than 25 per cent of the school year for illness or other noncreditable reasons loses credit for that year toward tenure and must be considered "first-year probationary" again the following year. No salary increment is received for that year.

Q. *What are the standards for permanency?*

A. New teachers in the San Diego Unified School District are selected on the premise that they will achieve sufficiently high standards of service to become permanent. Prior to permanency, however, probationary teachers must demonstrate high professional competence and good physical and mental health.

Q. *How is the pre-permanency health exam handled?*

A. In the spring, health questionnaires are obtained from second-year probationary teachers and their principals. These are screened by the school physician, and those teachers who have no apparent health problems are exempted from the pre-permanency health examination. Appointments are scheduled with the Medical Board the following fall for those teachers not exempted. The expense for the routine exam is borne by the district; however, if any special report or medical care is necessary, the teacher obtains such from his personal physician at his own expense.

Leaves of Absence

Q. *Are probationary teachers eligible for leaves?*

A. Leaves of absence are granted only to permanent teachers with the one exception of leaves for compulsory military service.

Q. *May a teacher who is recommended for permanency after three years but who has not served the fourth year be granted a leave?*

A. Teachers who are recommended for permanency and who accept a contract for the fourth year of service are considered, for all practical purposes, as permanent employees. Therefore, such a person would be entitled to all the rights and privileges of a permanent employee, including leaves. However, because of the teacher shortage, all leave requests will be critically reviewed.

Q. *What job protection do permanent teachers have if their request for leave is not granted and they wish to resign?*

A. Under Education Code Section 13402, any certificated employee who is permanent and who resigns may apply for reemployment; and *if he is reemployed within 39 months* from the last date of *paid* service with the district, he is reinstated as a permanent employee with all the usual rights and privileges.

Sick Leave

Q. *What sick leave privileges do I have as a probationary employee?*

A. Full-time, 10-month, probationary employees during their first year are immediately eligible for 10 days of full-time sick leave at full pay. In addition, they are eligible for 100 days sick leave at half pay. Second-year probationary employees who have not used any sick leave during the first year are eligible for 20 days of full-time sick leave at full pay and 90 days at half pay. Full-time sick leave for which the employee is compensated by full salary is accumulative indefinitely under California Law. The sick leave policy appears on page 113 of the district *Rules and Regulations* available in the principal's office.

Absence on Personal Business

Q. *May I be absent to attend to personal business?*

A. Yes, if the business is of an urgent nature. The request should be submitted to the Personnel Department at least 3 days in advance on the "Personal Business Absence" form. Such absence entails loss of salary.

Administrative Examination

Q. *How do I achieve eligibility to be considered for administrative appointment?*

A. Administrative appointments are made from candidates who have qualified on the administrative examination. This exam is given once a year, usually near Christmas vacation, and the date is announced in the *Superintendent's Bulletin.*

Q. *What are the general requirements for taking the exam?*

A. Candidates must be permanent teachers or third-year probationary teachers who are being recommended for tenure, must hold a Master's Degree and the proper administration credential.

Transfer Requests

Q. *May I request a transfer from one school to another or from one level to another?*

A. Yes, any employee may fill out an Assignment Preference Request indicating his desire for a change in assignment. The deadline is Dec. 18 for changes desired the following September. In general, however, employees are expected to stay with a particular assignment for a full school year.

Retirement

Q. *Do probationary employees participate in the retirement program?*

A. Yes, all certificated employees must participate in the State Teachers Retirement System. Deductions for the employees' contributions to the program are made automatically by the Accounting Department.

Q. *If I resign, may I get back my retirement contribution?*

A. Yes, any employee resigning from the district may apply immediately for refund of the retirement contributions, plus interest, which the employee has made.

Q. *May I receive credit for teaching experience outside the State of California for retirement purposes?*

A. No. Under present legislation, there is no provision whereby an employee may obtain credit for teaching service outside the State of California.

Death Benefits

Q. *In the event of the death of an employee, are there any benefits to the estate or the beneficiary?*

A. Yes. There are four types of death benefits immediately available to the beneficiary of a deceased employee: (1) A refund of all contributions plus interest. (2) A lump sum death benefit of 1/12 of a year's salary for each year of service to a maximum of six years or half salary. (These benefits are paid to any beneficiary named by the employee.) (3) A survivor benefit of $90 for each dependent survivor to a maximum of $250 a month. These benefits are remitted to the immediate family of the deceased. Consult the Retirement Section for more details. (4) If the employee has reached age 55, the widow or orphan children of an employee may elect a retirement allowance of half the retirement allowance to which he would have been entitled had he retired at the moment of death. This benefit is paid in lieu of benefits (1) and (2) listed above.

Q. *In the event of a prolonged illness prior to the death of an employee, are sick-leave benefits available to the beneficiaries?*

A. Yes. Sick-leave benefits due an employee for days absent because of illness are available if claims for such benefits are made by the authorized executors.

Health Insurance

Q. *What provisions are made for participation of employees in health and accident insurance plans?*

A. Payroll deductions to cover the premiums for the Washington National Insurance Company income protection plan may be arranged. In addition, all employees who qualify are covered without cost by the Pacific Mutual Life Insurance Company's major health and accident group policy. Qualified employees may arrange for a salary deduction to cover dependents under this plan. Complete details of the coverage offered may be found in the handbook issued by the Pacific Mutual Life Insurance Company.

Even before you become attached to a particular school you can benefit from acquaintance with the policies and regulations that are common, to differing degrees, in most schools and school systems. Note the various areas of information that usually are regarded as being significant to the beginning teacher. Include them among the points to which you will give attention as you consider the pros and cons of service in any schools that may offer you a position. Perhaps your college placement office has copies of the handbooks of particular schools that you may consult to alert yourself to teaching conditions in them.

Orientation Practices

A common school practice, in addition to distributing pamphlets and brochures, is to bring teachers together for a day or more before the beginning of the regular school year in order to afford them an opportunity to prepare for the year's work. This preschool session usually includes general information meetings and special panel discussions of the teachers of respective subjects. New teachers attend such meetings and, in addition, are briefed in other ways concerning their status and responsibilities. To acquaint you with what you can expect to have happen at such orientation sessions, we are presenting a few programs conducted in specific schools or school systems.

Seattle, Washington Public Schools. The Seattle public schools have an extended preschool program. Five-day summer workshops are conducted toward the end of August. Attendance at these workshops is voluntary. New teachers are invited to participate. A one-day induction session for new teachers also is scheduled. This begins with two general sessions held in a specified school, with a coffee break between sessions. The general sessions are followed by subject area meetings. After lunch, the new teachers leave for the school buildings to which they have been assigned.

Topics discussed at the general meeting have included the following:

Opportunities in the Seattle Schools
School Medical Services
Your Personal Record and Its Importance
Greetings from Various School Officials

Atlanta, Georgia Public Schools. In his reply to our request for what is done in orienting new teachers in Atlanta, the Deputy Superintendent of Schools wrote as follows:

Our program for orienting new teachers has several facets which are not "contained" in a single brochure or mimeographed bulletin. I shall attempt, however, to set forth in broad outline what we are doing.

1. All new teachers are convened to general meetings in which various personnel explain briefly certain aspects of the school program, particularly such matters as attendance accounting and pay, sick leave, insurance, pensions, Board regulations, etc. Many of these are explained more fully by special bulletins or booklets.
2. Area meetings (our large system is subdivided into school districts, which we call "Areas") in which subject- and Area-wide matters are presented by the Area Superintendent and his staff.
3. Television presentations are made to new teachers utilizing facilities owned and operated by the local Board of Education.

4. Local school orientations are conducted by the building principals.
5. In-service training courses are conducted by instructional supervisors. These courses carry through most of the fall.

All in all, these orientation programs are of 20 hours duration, a fact which must be certified to by the Area Superintendent in order to enable the teacher to move to the second step on the salary schedule.[4]

Philadelphia, Pennsylvania Public Schools. In Philadelphia a one-day orientation session is held for new teachers. Teachers on all levels attend an opening session. Following this, senior and technical high schools have another general morning session. The afternoon is devoted to group meetings by subject areas. New teachers in the junior high school attend a two-day orientation program, during which are treated topics such as adolescence, discipline, lesson planning, and the like. The afternoon of the second day is devoted to a consideration of specific courses of study. A pamphlet, *Assignment: Junior High School,* prepared by consulting teachers, also is distributed. It contains the following chapters:

Know Your School
Study the Pupils
Provide the Atmosphere
Plan Your Work
Be Professional
Off to a Good Start

The purposes of the orientation conference are stated in a letter sent to newly appointed junior high school teachers, as follows:

You will be given a brief explanation of the organization of the Philadelphia Public Schools. You will be shown how you can obtain various kinds of assistance. You will receive help in interpreting the courses of study that you will use. You will be given guidance in the solving of problems of classroom management and discipline. You will get help in the practical considerations of lesson planning. You will meet the Consulting Teachers and Supervisors who work with new teachers throughout the school year. Throughout the conference, the practical considerations of teaching will be stressed—you will get answers to the questions, "What do I do next week, and next month?" and "How do I do it?" [5]

[4] From a letter written to the authors by Rual W. Stephens.

[5] Part of a letter by Clayton E. Buell, assistant to the Associate Superintendent, Helen C. Bailey.

NEOPHYTE NEWS

Special Edition   Philadelphia Junior High Schools   September, 1963

THE FIRST DAY

You, the teacher, *for* the class
1. Be businesslike
2. Make a good personal appearance
3. Speak softly, calmly, firmly
4. Deal with nonconformity immediately
   a. Avoid shouting
   b. Avoid threats
   c. Ask deviates to return after school for brief conferences
5. Have work carefully planned
   a. A prepared roll
   b. A seating chart
   c. An outline of term's work
      (1) Physical defects
      (2) Psychological records
      (3) Disciplinary records
      (4) Achievement records
6. Make room reasonably attractive
   a. Panels above blackboards
   b. Bulletin boards
   c. Bookcases
   d. Teacher's desk

You, the teacher, *with* the class
1. Be at the door to receive pupils
2. Direct pupils to temporary seats
3. Direct class to start written work on board
   a. Work should be brief, simple, and clear
   b. Suggested topics
      (1) Subject matter
      (2) Requirements
      (3) Class rules (main points only)
      (4) Personal information
   c. Distribute paper and pencils where necessary
4. Give permanent seats as class does written assignment
   a. One row at a time
   b. Check roll as seats are distributed
   c. Make adjustments for size and physical defects
5. Follow written work and seating with short discussion of boardwork
6. Continue period
   a. Diagnostic test
   b. Introduction of the subject matter
   c. Review

7. Conclusion of period (last five minutes)
   a. List of required materials (itemized on board), e.g., assignment book, two sharpened pencils, notebooks

AFTER THE FIRST DAY

You should have obtained all courses of study and other materials that you will need. A written plan of your program of a day-to-day basis is essential. The daily lesson plans should include:

Purpose of the lesson	End-of-period activities
Content	Summaries
Method of presentation	Final instructions
Texts and other materials needed	Preparations for the next day

You should have a procedure for:
1. Entering and leaving the room
2. Organizing notebooks and written work
3. Making assignments
4. Distributing and collecting materials
5. Cleaning up prior to the dismissal bell

Greenwich, Connecticut Public Schools. The Greenwich schools conduct a fairly elaborate program of teacher orientation. Two days of meetings are held before school opens in the fall.

The purpose of the preschool orientation program is intended to assist the new teacher in these ways: first, in becoming acquainted with your new school; second, in learning more about the purposes and programs of the Greenwich Public Schools; third, in getting to know your co-workers who, with you, will be so important to the quality of our schools this next year and thereafter.[6]

These before-school orientation meetings are followed by either three or four other general meetings held after school hours. The final meeting of each year is on the topic: "Pleasures and Problems of Teaching in Greenwich." This meeting is one of great value. They prepare for it by having each teacher new to Greenwich list what he believes to be the pleasures of teaching in Greenwich and the problems of teaching in Greenwich. On a given afternoon, all new teachers meet and are subdivided into small interest groups where, under the leadership of the chairman selected from the group in advance, they discuss these pleasures and problems. A re-

[6] From a report given to all teachers new to Greenwich by the Assistant Superintendent, Dr. Kenneth C. Coulter, 1962.

corder from each group then reports to the entire group of new teachers.

New Jersey Educational Association. According to a circular issued in 1963, resulting from a study of New Jersey's public schools, the following practices were reported as constituting *Teacher Orientation Programs:*

PART I: "New Teacher" Orientation Programs

One hundred seventy-six school districts reported special "new teacher" orientation programs. A large majority of these meetings (86 percent) were held prior to the official opening of school in September.

However, at least fifteen school districts indicated that briefing sessions were also held after school began for these new personnel. Such sessions usually were after-school meetings, sometimes held in addition to preschool meetings and sometimes as a substitute for the special training sessions held in the summer. Examples: One district held six mandatory Monday afternoon meetings for new teachers. New teachers in one district met with various service people from 8:00 to 8:30 A.M. each morning for one and one-half weeks to discuss services and problems. One district set aside time before school opening in the fall as well as seven afternoons for subjects important to new teachers. One district allotted one to five days in the spring and one day in September for these sessions.

Even though one district in six did not specify length of orientation session, it was evident that one- and two-day sessions were most frequent. One-day meetings were held in at least 64 school districts and two-day meetings in 46 districts. Administrators in districts which did not specify length of meeting time commented that these meetings were held at the convenience of administrator and teacher, individually set, held at time of employment, held sometime during the summer, etc.

General Observations on "New Teacher" Orientation Programs

Local groups such as board of education, teacher associations, P.T.A. council, service clubs, and chamber of commerce often participate in "new teacher" meetings. They sponsor luncheons, dinners, and other social functions.

Many programs combine business with pleasure. They include one or more social functions such as breakfast, luncheon, social hour, reception, or dinner. One program featured luncheon in a local plant, guided bus tour, and reception and buffet supper at a local hotel. Other types of social gatherings mentioned were picnics (board, chamber of commerce, or teacher-association sponsored) and boat ride.

Many programs include tours of the community. At least 33 school districts included this activity on the agenda. Such tours are sometimes sponsored by local chambers of commerce and local teacher associations.

The major emphasis in "new teacher" orientation programs is effective adaptation to school environment and educational offerings within the district. To achieve this purpose, most programs include discussions of school philosophy, policies, curriculum, report cards, personnel policies, testing programs, and professional organizations. New teachers are alerted to available equipment, educational services, and special projects in operation. Programs often include departmental meetings (high school), separate building meetings with principals, classroom demonstrations, workshops, etc. Outside consultants such as State Department personnel, representatives from teachers colleges and universities, and other leading speakers are often used in more formalized programs.

Some districts use the person-to-person approach in their new teacher programs. The "buddy" system in which each new teacher is assigned to an experienced one for help and guidance is one technique used. One district holds individual meetings between the new teacher and principal and between the new teacher and the old teacher.

In a special effort to help new teachers, some districts prepare packets of information for this group. One district specified advance summer mailing of professional information.

Some districts invite teacher association representatives to speak on teacher welfare (retirement, legal rights, etc.).

Other ideas incorporated into new teacher orientation programs include the following:

—County helping teachers are sometimes used to help in setting up these programs, especially in rural counties.

—In one district, new faculty members and department chairmen worked during the summer in preparing courses of study, visual materials, library assignments, and audio-visual aids.

—Several districts stress public relations. One district spends considerable time on "quality" of teaching and salesmanship of education.

—One district devotes three days of its briefing session for teachers with provisional certificates, less time for new teachers with limited certificates, and one day for teachers with experience.

—After one month of service, one district invites new teachers to a dinner to evaluate their work and receive suggestions on improving the orientation program.[7]

Detroit, Michigan Public Schools. Approximately nine hundred new teachers are employed annually in the Detroit Public Schools. Hence much of their orientation is done by the administration of the individual schools. Each fall, however, receptions are held in each of the nine districts, at which time the beginning teachers meet the Superintendent, the Board Members, and other administrative staff people. In addition to these meetings, the supervisors hold regular meetings at the Division of Staff Orientation for the Improvement of Instruction for the various subject areas.

[7] *Teacher Orientation Programs for the 1962–63 School Year* (Circular No. 87), New Jersey Education Association, Trenton.

At the end of each school year, a questionnaire is completed by each first year teacher. This is returned to the office of the Division of Staff Orientation, unsigned by name of school or individual. This questionnaire is presented here. More is said about it later.

The responses obtained to items on the questionnaire are summarized. The findings in the form of a report are then submitted to principals and supervisors. The main purpose of the study is to examine various aspects of the orientation program, its scope, its strengths, and its weaknesses, to aid in planning activities in the future.

DEPARTMENT		DETROIT
OF STAFF		PUBLIC
ORIENTATION	ATTENTION—FIRST YEAR TEACHERS	SCHOOLS

Dear Teacher:

You are just completing your first semester or year of teaching in Detroit. We are glad to have you with us and would like to profit from your experiences. The Department of Staff Orientation needs your help in planning specific aspects of the program for new colleagues who will join the Detroit teaching staff next year.

Will you please give your reactions to the following items? Your answers will guide us in knowing how to help other teachers. *You need not sign your name.*

Please return the completed form via the school pick-up to Room 738, Schools Center Building, 5057 Woodward, *on or before June 14, 1963.*

Florence Kuhn

Assistant Superintendent

DIRECTIONS: Please check or fill in the blanks in accordance with your experience. Use the margins and the back of the last sheet for additional comments.

A. Is this your first or second semester as a Probationary I teacher in Detroit?
    1. First   _____
    2. Second   _____   (1)

B. What previous teaching experience have you had?
    1. As contract teacher in Detroit   _____
    2. As contract teacher elsewhere   _____
    3. As substitute teacher in Detroit   _____   (2)
    4. As substitute teacher elsewhere   _____
    5. None except as student teacher   _____

C. At what school level are you doing most of your teaching?

    1. Elementary   _____
    2. Junior High   _____   (3)
    3. Senior High   _____

D. Are you teaching in one of your fields of specialization?   1. Yes _____   2. No _____   (4)

E. Is there an official department head in your school for the subject which you are teaching?   1. Yes _____   2. No _____   (5)

F. Were you given your school assignment early enough to enable you to visit the school before your first day on duty?   1. Yes _____   2. No _____   (6)

G. Did you have a conference with your principal before you started teaching in his school?   1. Yes _____   2. No _____   (7)

H. Were you on duty the first day of your first semester?   1. Yes _____   2. No _____   (8)

I. Where did you do your student supervised teaching, last contact?

    1. School to which I am now assigned   _____
    2. Some other Detroit public school   _____   (9)
    3. A school other than a Detroit public school   _____

J. Did you do substitute teaching in the school to which you were assigned?   1. Yes _____   (10)   2. No _____

K. Did you receive help from your school's handbook of school policies and procedures?   1. Yes _____   2. No _____   (11)   3. None available _____

L. How much help were the following handbooks to you?

	Much	Some	Little	Did Not Receive	
THE HUMAN TOUCH	1. _____	2. _____	3. _____	4. _____	(12)
IT TAKES TEAMWORK	1. _____	2. _____	3. _____	4. _____	(13)
TEACHER'S BULLETIN NO. 3	1. _____	2. _____	3. _____	4. _____	(14)

M. Who, among the following, observed your teaching long enough or often enough to make an evaluation of your teaching?

District Administrator_____ (15)   Assistant Principal   _____ (18)
Supervisor   _____ (16)   Department Head   _____ (19)
Principal   _____ (17)   Other (specify)   _____ (20)

N. From which *one* among the following did you
    receive most help on your professional prob-
    lems? *Check only one.*

District Administrator   1. _____   Department Head   5. _____
Supervisor   2. _____   Counselor   6. _____   (21)
Principal   3. _____   Teacher   7. _____
Assistant Principal   4. _____   Other (specify)   8. _____

O. Did you visit classes in your building to ob-   1. Yes   _____ (22)
    serve the teaching of others?   2. No   _____

P. Did you visit other schools for half a day or   1. Yes   _____ (23)
    more to observe teaching?   2. No   _____

Q. How helpful were the following to you?

	Much Help	*Little Help*	*None*	*Attended*
Supervisors' meetings	1. _____	2. _____	3. _____	(24)
Summer or Saturday workshops	1. _____	2. _____	3. _____	(25)
Demonstration lessons	1. _____	2. _____	3. _____	(26)
Department meetings in the school	1. _____	2. _____	3. _____	(27)
School's teachers' meetings	1. _____	2. _____	3. _____	(28)
Committee meetings	1. _____	2. _____	3. _____	(29)
Building orientation meetings	1. _____	2. _____	3. _____	(30)

R. Which *five* of the following sources of help or
    service do you think are *most* important to
    a teacher new to Detroit? *Check only five.*

Assistant principal   _____ (31)   Principal   _____ (39)
Counselor   _____ (32)   School secretary   _____ (40)
Demonstration lessons   _____ (33)   Supervisor   _____ (41)
Department head   _____ (34)   Teacher-sponsor   _____ (42)
District administrator   _____ (35)   Teacher's handbook   _____ (43)
District reception   _____ (36)   Teachers' meetings   _____ (44)
Observation of other   Other (specify)   _____ (45)
  classes   _____ (37)   _____
Other teachers   _____ (38)

S. What do you feel was the reaction of the
    teaching staff toward you as a new colleague
    of theirs?

        Most of them were friendly and made me   1. _____
        feel welcome.

Some of them were friendly and made me feel welcome.	2. _____
Only a few of them were friendly and made me feel welcome.	3. _____ (46)
They seemed to be too busy to pay attention to me.	4. _____
They made me feel uninvited and left out.	5. _____

T. Would you, in general, recommend the Detroit 1. Yes _____
system to a friend or acquaintance as a good 2. No _____ (47)
place to work so that you would encourage 3. Doubtful _____
him to file an application for a position?

U. What is your reason for your answer to question "T"? (Your answer to this question will be most helpful.)

(48)

V. What further comments or suggestions do you wish to make? (Use the back of this sheet if you need more space.)

(49)

Please return this form to Room 738, Schools Center Building, 5057 Woodward, via the school pick-up. Thank you for your help.[8]

Comment. The various examples of orientation programs cited give you some idea of what you probably will experience on your entrance to your first teaching job. Regardless of what a school does to help its new teachers adjust to working conditions, real benefits accrue to the individual teacher in terms of his own attitude toward the program and his own efforts to profit from the assistance offered.

QUESTIONS AND TOPICS FOR DISCUSSION

1. In which states are you eligible for certification?
2. If you already have your teaching placement, how did you receive your position? If not, what are you doing about it?
3. Write a letter of application for a position and ask one of your college instructors to criticize it.
4. Compare the application blank of the Westport public schools with some that you have received. In what ways are they alike and different?

[8] Courtesy of the Detroit Public Schools.

5. What has been your experience with interviews? What changes, if any, do you need to make in your attitude toward them?
6. If you have accepted a position, on what factors was your decision based?
7. Why do the regulations concerning teaching contracts need to be strict?
8. What are you doing to become acquainted with the community in which you expect or hope to teach?
9. What have you learned about teacher status from reading the answers to the San Diego Schools to teachers' questions?
10. Which of the orientation programs described in this chapter do you think would be the most helpful? Give reasons for your opinion.

SELECTED REFERENCES

ARMSTRONG, W. E., and STINNETT, T. M. *A Manual on Certification Requirements for School Personnel in the United States*. Washington, D.C.: National Commission on Teacher Education and Professional Standards, National Education Assoc., 1962.

MASON, W. S. *The Beginning Teacher: Status and Career Orientation*. Washington, D.C.: U.S. Department of Health, Education and Welfare, 1961.

RICHEY, R. W. *Planning for Teaching* (3rd ed.). New York: McGraw-Hill Book Co., Inc., 1963.

Teacher Orientation. Washington, D.C.: American Association of School Administrators, National Education Assoc., 1956.

Teaching Career Fact Book. Washington, D.C.: National Education Assoc., 1963.

VAN DALEN, D. B., and BRITTELL, R. W. *Looking Ahead to Teaching*. Boston: Allyn & Bacon, Inc., 1959.

Welcome to Syracuse: Teachers' Orientation Booklet. Syracuse, N.Y.: Board of Education, 1963.

16

YOUR PROFESSIONAL GROWTH

Your teacher-education program has prepared you for entrance into your chosen profession. Your student teaching experiences will enable you to put into practice the various aspects of theory that you learned in your college classrooms. You have been appointed to a school in which you hope to apply the principles of good teaching that you conscientiously have attempted to master. Through the orientation program offered to new teachers by your school, its administration and other faculty members have assured you of their sympathetic understanding of and friendly cooperation with a beginning teacher. They have alerted you to the many details of school organization and management that you need to know.

Now you are started on your career as a teacher and are more or less on your own. Your co-workers probably will continue to aid you in meeting effectively all of your many teacher responsibilities. Yet, what actually takes place in your classroom and the extent to which your students cooperate with you as you attempt to guide their learning activities depend in good part on your (1) knowledge of proper classroom procedures, (2) understanding of young people, and (3) ability to plan, organize, and present effectively the learning materials of your subject field.

You probably are starting your teaching activities with much enthusiasm and a strong desire to be a successful teacher. It is likely, however, that at first you will have some misgivings concerning your ability to handle the situation. These early fears usually are overcome as you gain confidence through continued experience. Your question could be "What kind of teacher will I be five, ten, or fifteen years in the future?" The answer to this question can be contained in another question, "What can I do to foster my professional growth?" It is with the matter of professional development that the remainder of this chapter is concerned.

YOUR FIRST YEAR OF TEACHING

Your first year of teaching can serve as a kind of proving ground. You will need to become acclimated to new living and working conditions. You will be attempting to develop friendly and cooperative relationships with your students, the school faculty, and members of the community. With the assistance of the school administrators and your fellow teachers, you gradually will improve your teaching techniques and procedures. You will acquire an increasing understanding of your responsibilities and rights as a teacher.

Developing Friendly Relationships with Students

Much that was said about your interrelationships as a student teacher applies to your experiences as a beginning teacher. However, these relationships are on a more permanent basis and you must chart your own course. You do not have a college supervisor and a cooperating teacher available to ease the way for you.

Most adolescents admire young teachers. They seem to feel that a beginning teacher is close enough to them in age and experience that he will understand them and their problems. They also may catch some of his enthusiasm for his subject. You usually can afford to be friendly with them and let them know that you are interested in their activities. At the same time, you should maintain an attitude of dignity and objectivity as befits your position.

A few of the less well-controlled students may attempt to "test" you. They may submit poorly prepared home assignments, talk out of turn in class, act the clown, and in other ways try, as they express it, "to get your goat." Difficult as this may seem, you need to keep calm in situations such as these, indicating by your attitude that you want to be fair in your treatment of them but that you will tolerate no nonsense.

The more cooperative students in your class often come to your rescue by handling the situation in their own way. For example, a newly appointed young woman was in charge of a study room in an all-boys high school. A few of the boys started to heckle her by clearing their throats in rhythm and by dropping books, and then in loud tones apologizing for doing so. One of the school's leaders, a tall well-developed boy, announced to these troublemakers privately that he would meet them, one at a time, in the schoolyard after school. There were no further recurrences of the "testing" process.

Beginning teachers sometimes are hesitant about referring to the authorities a student whose behavior in class is troublesome. They believe that doing so is a sign of personal inability to maintain proper discipline. You would not, of course, report minor infractions of school or classroom rules or regulations. These lie within your domain of authority. If a student by his display of uncooperative behavior persists in interfering with the work of the class, drastic measures may need to be employed.

If your efforts at control are ineffectual, first consult teachers who are acquainted with the student concerning their experiences with him. Follow suggestions they offer. If these fail to work, admit to his guidance counselor or another school official that you are unable to reach him and that you need help. If you utilize this last approach sparingly, the administration will respect your recognition of the limits of your power to treat recalcitrant youth. In some secondary schools, there is an attempt to avoid assigning a newly-appointed teacher any student who is known to be difficult in classroom situations.

Relationships with Faculty

Experienced teachers differ in their attitude toward a newcomer. For the most part, remembering their own neophyte experiences, they are sympathetic toward him and his problems. They are quick to recognize his needs and give him whatever assistance they can. Members of his department offer him the use of their instructional materials, help him in lesson planning, and introduce him to faculty members outside the department. He is invited to join a lunchroom group and encouraged to participate in small- and large-group social events.

You are likely to find in the school a few teachers who seemingly resent you. If the students appear to like you, some teachers will be jealous of your popularity, perhaps claiming that you are trying to undermine school discipline. To the extent that you utilize more modern methods than they do, they may accuse you of adding "fads and frills" to the program. Usually, these persons have lost confidence in their own teaching effectiveness, and make you or any other beginning teacher the target of their insecurity.

In your dealings with your co-workers you must face up to the fact that they are evaluating your potential worth as a teacher. They are willing to make allowances for any minor lacks in your ability to function efficiently because of your inexperience. They are extremely sensitive, however, to your displayed attitudes toward them, school policies, and your various school duties. There are various forms of behavior that you should avoid. Some of these are the following:

1. Even though you believe that the teaching approaches taught you at college are more effective than those commonly employed in the school, do not say so. Quietly introduce as many newer techniques as you can with administrative approval and without disrupting school-accepted procedures. You may find that some teachers gradually will come to follow your lead.

2. Do not complain about the kind or number of routine duties to which you are assigned in comparison with other members of the faculty. The more experienced teachers probably are carrying other responsibilities that you are not yet prepared to assume. Be willing to take your share of responsibilities for good school management.

3. Avoid participating in unfavorable criticism of administrative officers or other faculty members. As members of a faculty, teachers sometimes possess what may seem to be a peculiar kind of loyalty. They feel that it is their privilege to question the rightness of what is done by members of their group, but take umbrage at attempts of a comparative outsider to follow their example.

4. Refrain from any display of superiority among your fellows. Be modest. Do not boast about your college, your family, or your hometown. Let the members of the group discover for themselves that you are a fine person with an excellent background. You may find yourself talking too much about yourself without meaning to make invidious comparisons. One young teacher was accustomed to recount, with pride, stories about the accomplishments of family members. She was much chagrined one day when a fellow teacher

responded to such a story with this old saying, "He who boasts of his illustrious ancestors is like the potato; the best part of him is underground."

Relationships with the Community

Your relationships with the community should follow a pattern similar to that which is desirable for school relationships. Be courteous and friendly with parents, enlisting their aid in helping their children fulfill their potentialities. Attend parent-teacher meetings and show by your attitude that you are interested in the welfare of young people and their families. Accept invitations to participate in community-sponsored activities insofar as doing so does not interfere with the meeting of school responsibilities. Avoid listening to or taking part in gossip concerning members of the teaching staff, students, or community leaders. If you are living in the home of one of the school's students, be careful to refrain from discussing anything about the school with family members. You know that an innocuous remark can be much exaggerated.

At one time, school communities tended to exercise considerable control over the behavior of the members of the school staff. Community leaders attempted to decide what a teacher should or should not do in personal matters such as religious affiliation, recreational activities, dating, time to arrive home at night, marital status, and the like. These community attitudes have undergone considerable modification, especially in the larger urban areas. Some small communities, however, still prescribe certain restrictions that the teacher is expected to respect. It would be advisable for you, therefore, to ascertain, before you accept a teaching position, what the community's attitude is toward a teacher's private life. By so doing you can avoid the experiencing of considerable frustration while you are on the job.

Desirability of Teaching in Your Home Community

A question often raised is whether a teaching candidate should accept a position in a school that he attended as a student or in the neighborhood in which he was reared. Whether or not this should be done depends on the kind of person he is and his reputation and that of his family in the community.

To some people, a child never grows up. If you accept a position in a school that you attended, you may find that some of your former teachers may embarrass you by describing to others in detail some of your adolescent feats of accomplishment or other less desirable activities. They may treat you as though they still hold a position in regard to yourself of *in loco parentis*. They may overwhelm you with attention or feel called upon to criticize your every activity. Neighborhood friends and acquaintances may give evidence of a similar attitude toward you.

In spite of these apparent disadvantages of teaching in your home community, there are many advantages. You know the school and the community. You do not need to become acquainted with it and perhaps commit social blunders while you are doing so. A feeling of belonging is quickly and easily established. Because you grew up in the neighborhood, you are likely to understand the young people whom you are teaching. Consequently, you probably are better able to motivate their learning activities and to share their interests. Your former teachers and neighborhood friends are proud of your achievements. They are ready to accept you and to do what they can to help you earn success in your chosen profession. Teaching in your home school and community can be a rewarding experience.

Improving Your Teaching Procedures

No matter how much success you achieve as a student teacher, you will find that assuming full responsibility for the learning progress of your students gives rise to problems of planning, organizing, and presenting learning materials that you did not encounter in your earlier experience. You will meet five or six classes daily. The respective classes may represent different levels of your own subject, or perhaps another subject in addition to your field of specialization. You will need to prepare differing lesson plans. You must adjust your utilization of teaching aids to the materials and equipment available in the school. You will need to adapt your teaching approaches to school-accepted courses of study, class organization, and teaching procedures, as well as to the learning needs and abilities of the student population.

If you participate in a well-organized preschool program of orientation, you receive many worthwhile suggestions concerning the school's teaching policies. At the beginning, however, you are likely to find the going to be rough. You may try some of your "pet" procedures only to find that they do not produce desired results. You will realize that you need both to improve your teaching techniques and to receive the assistance of more experienced individuals. Two of the more commonly-used procedures to help beginning teachers are (1) intelligent and sympathetic supervision and (2) observation of the teaching of master teachers.

Value of Constructive Supervision

It is a common plaint among teachers that they fear and dislike supervisory observation. This teacher attitude probably is the result of experience with the kind of supervision that was too prevalent in the past—destructive rather than constructive (emphasis on what is wrong with the lesson rather than recognition of its commendable aspects). As a beginning teacher, you should welcome supervision as the primary means of helping you develop professional competence and improved satisfaction in your work.

In most secondary schools at present, the purpose of supervisory observation is to bolster your morale rather than to tear it down. During your first year of teaching, you can profit much from this experience. At first, members of the administrative staff, especially the head of your subject department, probably will visit your class for short periods of time in order to discover your teaching attitudes and needs. Later, at your invitation, a supervisor will visit you for longer periods, observing complete lessons. Such a visit should be preceded by a conference in which you talk over your plans for the lesson, indicating to your supervisor what you hope to accomplish. You receive an evaluation of the lesson as you later discuss it with your supervisor.

Your reactions to supervision exercise a potent influence on the extent to which it can assist you in improving your teaching techniques. Your attitude should be positive rather than negative. Insofar as the supervision is friendly and constructive and you give evidence that you are eager to learn, good rapport can be established between you and your supervisor.

Value of Observing a Master Teacher

Your observation of the presentation of a lesson by an experienced teacher in your subject field is a valuable experience. You know that your observation of your cooperating teacher enlarged your concept of the teaching process. Now that you have begun to recognize some of your faults, you are ready to apply to your own work some of the approaches used by the master teacher.

You can give evidence of your desire to improve by requesting that opportunities be arranged for you to observe other teachers at work. When permission to do so is granted, enter into the experience with an open mind. Look for those elements in the lesson that are an improvement over what you have been doing. A short conference with the observed teacher has value. In it you can express your appreciation for the help he has given you and stress the points of the lesson that were especially worthwhile. In addition, of course, throughout the year you should constantly evaluate your own performance and strive to make whatever changes in techniques that seem to be advisable.

Learning about Your Responsibilities and Rights

During your preteaching educational experiences you probably became somewhat acquainted with your responsibilties and rights as a teacher. Now, as a regular teacher, you are becoming concerned in a practical way with ethical standards in teaching and a teacher's legal status. You should discover early in your teaching career what is expected of you as a member of the profession and in what ways your legal rights are protected.

Ethical standards. In common with other professional and business groups, members of the teaching profession are limited in their activities by certain generally accepted dicta to which they should adhere. The most widely known set of ethical standards for teachers is *The Code of Ethics of the Education Profession* that was constructed by the *NEA Committee on Professional Ethics* and adopted by the *NEA Representative Assembly*, Detroit, Michigan, July 1963.

The Code of Ethics of the Education Profession

PREAMBLE

We, professional educators of the United States of America, affirm our belief in the worth and dignity of man. We recognize the supreme importance of the pursuit of truth, the encouragement of scholarship, and the promotion of democratic citizenship. We regard as essential to these goals the protection of freedom to learn and to teach and the guarantee of equal educational opportunity for all. We affirm and accept our responsibility to practice our profession according to the highest ethical standards.

We acknowledge the magnitude of the profession we have chosen, and engage ourselves, individually and collectively, to judge our colleagues and to be judged by them in accordance with the applicable provisions of this Code.

PRINCIPLE I

Commitment to the Student

We measure success by the progress of each student toward achievement of his maximum potential. We therefore work to stimulate the spirit of inquiry, the acquisition of knowledge and understanding, and the thoughtful formulation of worthy goals. We recognize the importance of cooperative relationships with other community institutions, especially the home.

In fulfilling our obligations to the student, we—

1. Deal justly and considerately with each student.
2. Encourage the student to study varying points of view and respect his right to form his own judgment.
3. Withhold confidential information about a student or his home unless we deem that its release serves professional purposes, benefits the student, or is required by law.
4. Make discreet use of available information about the student.
5. Conduct conferences with or concerning students in an appropriate place and manner.
6. Refrain from commenting unprofessionally about a student or his home.
7. Avoid exploiting our professional relationship with any student.
8. Tutor only in accordance with officially approved policies.
9. Inform appropriate individuals and agencies of the student's educational needs and assist in providing an understanding of his educational experiences.
10. Seek constantly to improve learning facilities and opportunities.

PRINCIPLE II

Commitment to the Community

We believe that patriotism in its highest form requires dedication to the principles of our democratic heritage. We share with all other citizens the responsibility for the development of sound public policy. As educators, we are particularly accountable for participating in the development of educational programs and policies and for interpreting them to the public.

In fulfilling our obligations to the community, we—

1. Share the responsibility for improving the educational opportunities for all.
2. Recognize that each educational institution may have a person authorized to interpret its official policies.
3. Acknowledge the right and responsibility of the public to participate in the formulation of educational policy.
4. Evaluate through appropriate professional procedures conditions within a district or institution of learning, make known serious deficiencies, and take any action deemed necessary and proper.
5. Use educational facilities for intended purposes consistent with applicable policy, law, and regulation.
6. Assume full political and citizenship responsibilities, but refrain from exploiting the institutional privileges of our professional positions to promote political candidates or partisan activities.
7. Protect the educational program against undesirable infringement.

PRINCIPLE III

Commitment to the Profession

We believe that the quality of the services of the education profession directly influences the future of the nation and its citizens. We therefore exert every effort to raise educational standards, to improve our service, to promote a climate in which the exercise of professional judgment is encouraged, and to achieve conditions which attract persons worthy of the trust to careers in education. Aware of the value of united effort, we contribute actively to the support, planning, and programs of our professional organizations.

In fulfilling our obligations to the profession, we—

1. Recognize that a profession must accept responsibility for the conduct of its members and understand that our own conduct may be regarded as representative.
2. Participate and conduct ourselves in a responsible manner in the development and implementation of policies affecting education.
3. Cooperate in the selective recruitment of prospective teachers and in the orientation of student teachers, interns, and those colleagues new to their positions.

4. Accord just and equitable treatment to all members of the profession in the exercise of their professional rights and responsibilities, and support them when unjustly accused or mistreated.
5. Refrain from assigning professional duties to non-professional personnel when such assignment is not in the best interest of the student.
6. Provide, upon request, a statement of specific reason for administrative recommendations that lead to the denial of increments, significant changes in employment, or termination of employment.
7. Refrain from exerting undue influence based on the authority of our positions in the determination of professional decisions by colleagues.
8. Keep the trust under which confidential information is exchanged.
9. Make appropriate use of time granted for professional purposes.
10. Interpret and use the writings of others and the findings of educational research with intellectual honesty.
11. Maintain our integrity when dissenting by basing our public criticism of education on valid assumptions as established by careful evaluation of facts or hypotheses.
12. Represent honestly our professional qualifications and identify ourselves only with reputable educational institutions.
13. Respond accurately to requests for evaluations of colleagues seeking professional positions.
14. Provide applicants seeking information about a position with an honest description of the assignment, the conditions of work, and related matters.

PRINCIPLE IV

Commitment to Professional Employment Practices

We regard the employment agreement as a solemn pledge to be executed both in spirit and in fact in a manner consistent with the highest ideals of professional service. Sound professional personnel relationships with governing boards are built upon personal integrity, dignity, and mutual respect.

In fulfilling our obligations to professional employment practices, we—

1. Apply for or offer a position on the basis of professional and legal qualifications.
2. Apply for a specific position only when it is known to be vacant and refrain from such practices as underbidding or commenting adversely about other candidates.
3. Fill no vacancy except where the terms, conditions, policies, and practices permit the exercise of our professional judgment and skill, and where a climate conducive to professional service exists.
4. Adhere to the conditions of a contract or to the terms of an appointment until either has been terminated legally or by mutual consent.
5. Give prompt notice of any change in availability of service, in status of applications, or in change in position.

6. Conduct professional business through the recognized educational and professional channels.
7. Accept no gratuities or gifts of significance that might influence our judgment in the exercise of our professional duties.
8. Engage in no outside employment that will impair the effectiveness of our professional service and permit no commercial exploitation of our professional position.

Read the code thoughtfully. Note that its provisions deal with a teacher's responsibility to his students, the community, the profession, and professional employment practices. Each of these areas of commitment includes practices that should be known to and followed by all members of the teaching profession, since the principles apply to all persons engaged in the professional aspects of education.

Legal aspects. As a teacher, you have certain rights and responsibilities that are granted or implied by law. The legal status of a teacher may be decided in light of federal and state constitutional provisions, statutory enactments, and judicial decisions.

Various aspects of a teacher's professional relationships have legal implications. We already have referred to their application to employment and contractual practices and their possible effect on a teacher's private life. Other areas of possible legal controversy include the political activity of a teacher, academic freedom, and collective bargaining. The law also has something to say about proper disciplinary approaches and student sustained injuries. You should acquaint yourself with the legal provisions that apply to teachers, especially those of the state in which you are teaching.[1]

Teachers sometimes tend to resent what they consider to be too strict legal restrictions on their professional rights. They fail to recognize the fact that the law also protects their rights as citizens and teachers. The following statement concerning censorship is a case in point:

Legal Safeguards for Teachers

Legal safeguards for teachers in dealing with censorship can be discussed only in a general way, but the underlying legal question in any instance is

---

[1] For a more complete discussion see Warren E. Gauerke, *Legal and Ethical Responsibilities of School Personnel* (Englewood Cliffs, N.J.: Prentice-Hall Inc., 1959); and *Classroom Teachers Speak on Professional Negotiations* (Washington, D.C.: National Education Assoc., 1963).

whether or not the teacher is carrying out the obligations of his contract of employment.

A teacher who fails to carry out the orders of his superiors runs a risk of committing a breach of contract in proportion to the specificity and reasonableness of the orders. Thus, a teacher who insists on using a book in his classes after his board has specifically banned it will have little chance to defend himself successfully against an action of dismissal.

Even if the board acted unwisely in banning the book, this is not likely to constitute a defense for the teacher. If his immediate superior, however, has approved his use of the book, he may be able to pass the responsibility up the line.

On the other hand, a teacher who offers instruction about a significant event in religion despite orders to use no materials containing sectarian religious ideas will find the test of reasonableness more in point. To apply such a test, the teacher would be obligated to show that in a particular instance the learning objective was primarily social or historical, rather than religious.

The teacher who himself becomes a censor risks breaching his contract. If he is ordered to use a health text during a specific fifteen-minute period each week and he fails to do so, he will have breached the usual form of teacher contracts. If, however, he omits portions of a prescribed textbook, the matter of reasonableness may be applicable again. He may be able to show extenuating circumstances—such as lack of time to cover the entire textbook—which would lawfully justify his action.

The teacher's best legal safeguard in matters involving censorship is to observe all lawfully enacted rules which do not shock his conscience and to use proper channels to deal with those matters which he feels compelled to oppose.

—OWEN LOVE, *legal counsel, NEA Commission on Professional Rights and Responsibilities.*[2]

A generally law-abiding citizen and a conscientious member of the teaching profession is unlikely to become embroiled with the law because of his own participation in illegal activities. Hence any legal problems that arise and in which he becomes involved are likely to be initiated as the result of undesirable or outmoded statutory enactments or the incorrect interpretation of the law by school officials. It is advisable that you refrain from challenging a particular law as it is upheld by your superiors as long as it is on the statute books. If you believe that it is unjust or no longer mandatory, join with other school people in efforts to have it removed or changed to meet existing conditions more adequately.

[2] Owen Love, "Legal Safeguards for Teachers," *NEA Journal,* May 1963, p. 26.

Evaluation of Your Professional Progress

During your first year of teaching, you should attempt periodically to appraise your effectiveness in and attitude toward teaching. The end of that year is a good time for you to evaluate your progress as a teacher in the particular school in which you have been functioning. Some school officials help you in your self-evaluation by making available for your use questionnaires similar to the one prepared by the Detroit school system and presented in the preceding chapter.

By the end of your first year in the field, you probably will question the effect on you of your year's experiences. Do you still believe that your selection of teaching as a career was a wise decision? What satisfactions have accrued to you in your work? Recently, the United States Office of Education published its final report of a survey of beginning teachers.[3] Among the many areas of beginning teaching surveyed was one that concerned teachers' satisfactions with various aspects of their positions. The items included in this part of the questionnaire are listed here:[4]

Your Satisfaction with Various Aspects of Your Position: Please write the code number which best expresses your feeling about each item in the space to the left of each item. Use the following code:

4 - Very satisfactory
3 - Fairly satisfactory
2 - Fairly unsatisfactory
1 - Very unsatisfactory

—— Adequacy of your school building
—— Adequacy of supplies and equipment furnished to you by the school
—— Your present salary
—— Maximum salaries for classroom teachers in your school system
—— Time needed to reach the peak salary in your school system for teachers with full qualifications for their positions
—— Provisions for sick leave
—— Provisions for retirement
—— Your salary compared to that of other occupations in your area open to people with your level of education

[3] Ward S. Mason, *The Beginning Teacher: Status and Career Orientation* (Washington, D.C.: U.S. Department of Health, Education and Welfare, 1961).
[4] *Ibid.*, p. 195.

—— Your teaching load
—— Your non-teaching responsibilities
—— Total time you spend on school duties, including both teaching and non-teaching responsibilities required or definitely expected of you
—— Helpfulness of the supervision you receive
—— Fairness with which duties are distributed in your school
—— Your relations with your superiors
—— Your relations with fellow teachers
—— Your relations with students
—— Your relations with parents
—— Pupil attentiveness and discipline
—— The amount of interest shown by your students
—— General community attitude toward teaching as an occupation
—— Your position as a whole (except salary)
—— Your position as a whole (including salary)

The resulting data, representing responses from about 7,000 beginning teachers, is presented in Table 16.[5]

The report includes these comments concerning the rank order of the satisfactions:

> Given a generally high level of satisfaction, we may still ask which aspects of teaching are most satisfactory and which are least satisfactory. A glance through the ordering of items quickly indicates some clear-cut patterns in this regard. The items with the top four ranks all have to do with the teacher's social relationships—with fellow teachers, superiors, students, and parents. There is a nearly unanimous feeling that all these relationships are satisfactory, and in each case a majority of teachers say "very satisfactory." This finding would seem to indicate that the attention often given to orienting the new teacher to his job and integrating him in the organization and community tends, on the whole, to be successful.
>
> At the other end of the rank order is a clustering of four items all having to do with salary, and a fifth item in which the influence of salary is undoubtedly very large. Here is strong evidence to the effect that beginning teachers find their salaries the least satisfactory aspect of teaching. They say this about three separate aspects of salary: the salary currently received, the maximum salary, and the time needed to reach the maximum salary.[6]

A study of Table 16 and accompanying comments may be fruitful. Where would you rank yourself in the satisfaction items? In regard to attitudes expressed toward salary and salary schedules, keep in mind that this study was completed in 1957. Much has been done

[5] *Ibid.*, p. 80.
[6] *Ibid.*, pp. 79–80.

TABLE 16

Satisfaction of Beginning Teachers with Selected Aspects of Their Job, with Items Ranked in Terms of Mean Satisfaction Expressed, by Teaching Level and Sex: 1956-57

	All beginning teachers							Per cent saying very or fairly satisfactory, by teaching level and sex			
	Item scores			Per cent by degree of satisfaction				Elementary		Secondary	
Satisfaction item [1]	Rank	Mean [2]	Total [3]	Very satisfactory (Wt.=4)	Fairly satisfactory (Wt.=3)	Fairly unsatisfactory (Wt.=2)	Very unsatisfactory (Wt.=1)	Men	Women	Men	Women
1	2	3	4	5	6	7	8	9	10	11	12
Your relations with fellow teachers	1	3.77	100	79	20	1	(4)	98	98	99	99
Your relations with your superiors	2.5	3.65	100	70	26	3	1	98	97	95	95
Your relations with students	2.5	3.65	100	67	31	1	(4)	98	100	97	98
Your relations with parents	4	3.57	100	61	35	3	1	96	98	95	95
Fairness with which duties are distributed in your school	5	3.41	100	55	35	7	3	93	93	85	83
Your position as a whole (except salary)	6	3.40	100	48	46	5	1	93	96	91	91
Provisions for sick leave	7	3.20	100	43	42	9	7	84	84	83	85
Provisions for retirement	8	3.19	100	36	51	9	4	84	91	80	90
Amount of interest shown by your students	9	3.14	100	29	58	10	4	88	94	78	82
Your nonteaching responsibilities	10.5	3.12	100	35	47	13	5	82	84	79	80
General community attitude toward teaching as an occupation	10.5	3.12	100	34	48	13	5	79	90	69	83
Pupil attentiveness and discipline	12	3.08	100	26	59	11	4	88	90	81	78
Helpfulness of supervision you receive	13	3.04	100	38	37	15	9	77	77	73	72
Your teaching load	14	2.99	100	30	47	15	8	75	81	71	77
Adequacy of supplies and equipment	15	2.98	100	28	49	16	7	78	82	68	73
Adequacy of your school building	16.5	2.96	100	31	44	14	10	74	80	73	73
Total time you spend on school duties	16.5	2.96	100	25	53	17	6	78	81	57	74
Your position as a whole (including salary)	18	2.83	100	17	55	21	6	59	83	50	76
Your present salary	19	2.63	100	12	52	22	13	46	75	52	69
Time needed to reach peak salary	20	2.62	100	13	49	23	14	56	71	49	62
Maximum salaries	21	2.61	100	14	47	25	14	54	70		61
Your salary compared to that of other occupations in your area open to people with your level of education	22	2.36	100	13	34	28	24	28	62	27	52

[1] The wording of some of the items is abbreviated; for complete wording see item 53 of the questionnaire in app. D.
[2] The mean is based on the weights as indicated in cols. 5 through 8.
[3] Because of rounding, detail does not necessarily add to total.
[4] Less than ½ of 1 per cent.

445

since then in many school systems to place teachers' salaries on a more equitable basis. Hence greater satisfaction can be expected to prevail among beginning teachers now than was the situation at the time of the study.

CONTINUING YOUR PROFESSIONAL DEVELOPMENT

Let us assume that you have made a good beginning as a teacher. Your first year of teaching has been rewarding and satisfying. For the most part, your students are responding well to your guidance of their learning. You have developed good rapport with the school's administrative staff and your fellow teachers. You have found a place for yourself in the school's community. Where do you go from here?

You cannot rest on your laurels, believing that continued success will be yours if you do no more than maintain the status quo. New educational demands will be made upon you. Changes constantly are taking place in teaching-learning approaches as a result of experimentation. Research brings to light new aspects of your subject field with which you need to be acquainted if you are to continue to perform adequately in the classroom. Public interest is increasing in providing effective teaching and teaching facilities for young people. You dare not stand still amid all of the many factors of change that are characteristic of progress.

Perhaps there is no more pathetic individual than the teacher who began his professional career with enthusiasm and relative success and then became so bogged down by the mass of detail inherent in his work that he found no time or energy for self-improvement. You probably have encountered teachers who have become routinized to the point that they seem unaware of the changes that have taken place in education. They attempt to meet their teaching responsibilities according to a pattern that they found effective ten, fifteen, or more years ago. You can avoid getting into a rut by taking advantage of all the opportunities that now are available to you.

General Approaches to Teacher Growth

As an active member of your school's faculty, you will continue to engage in various activities that can strengthen your teaching skills. You will be expected to participate in faculty meetings and departmental conferences. Your classroom work will continue to be supervised. You may be invited to participate in the development of curricular materials and the planning of teaching approaches.

At the same time, you can utilize other growth media on a more or less voluntary basis. Regardless of the program of self-improvement that you select, it is essential that you continue to engage in periodic self-evaluations to determine, as best you can, your outstanding strengths and your particular weaknesses.

Membership in Professional Organizations

Many and varied educational organizations have been established on the local, state, and national levels. These professional groups are intended to serve both general and specific needs of school people. Membership in these organizations is voluntary, but their value usually is so great that you cannot afford to refrain from joining those that meet your interests and that can benefit you professionally. These associations have periodic meetings, some of which you could attend with profit to yourself. Most of the professional groups publish periodicals for their members. These publications can keep you informed concerning what is happening in the field of education, both generally and specifically.

As a beginning teacher, you would be wise to affiliate with the local teachers' association. Here you will have an opportunity to cooperate with your colleagues in attacking and attempting to solve educational problems that have local and immediate significance. Also worthy of consideration is affiliation with statewide professional organizations that bring together teachers from all parts of the state and from various fields of professional activity. The state organization usually is primarily concerned with the important aspects of teacher welfare, such as the legal status of teachers in matters dealing with teachers' salaries, tenure, and retirement, although other professional areas are not neglected.

The National Education Association (NEA), with a membership of about one million, exercises a potent influence on American education. It has 33 departments, serving all educational levels and professional ranks. Its monthly publication, the *NEA Journal,* keeps association members informed concerning all aspects of educational development. The *Research Bulletin* reports studies and investigations conducted by its research division. The bulletin contains many articles dealing with teacher welfare and the improvement of teaching and teaching conditions. The association sponsors a general meeting every summer. Also, the various special departments and divisions publish bulletins and yearbooks, and conduct annual meetings.

Associations have been organized, at the national level, to serve the teachers of practically every subject area on the secondary school level. Some of these are affiliated with the National Education Association; others are organized independently. You can learn much from membership in an appropriate group. Some of these groups have local branches whose meetings you can attend with a fair degree of regularity. The summer meetings of the NEA and its affiliates usually are rotated from one geographical location to another, thereby enabling its members in various parts of the country to attend occasional meetings. Even though you may find it difficult to attend organizational conferences, you can keep abreast of educational happenings through the reading of their publications.

Value of Continued Study

Not only is preteaching education increasing in extent and depth, but considerable emphasis is being placed by school people on a teacher's need to participate in one or another form of in-service education. When you are graduated from college and start to teach, you probably will feel that for a year or so you will want to devote your time and energy to your teaching job. This usually is a good decision, but you should not delay study activities to the point that you find it difficult to resume the student role.

Some school systems require teachers to take appropriate courses in order to be eligible for their annual salary increments. In school systems where there is a three-year probationary period, a teacher may be excused from engaging in in-service education until he is preparing to enter his fourth year of teaching. In addition, some large school systems provide nonfee in-service courses for their teachers. These courses usually are staffed by administrators, supervisors, and experienced teachers of the system. New York City sponsors over six hundred such courses.

Many colleges and universities offer graduate courses, either on campus or at off-campus centers, to meet teachers' educational needs. If you are teaching in a community that contains an institution of higher learning or in one of its off-campus centers, opportunities will be provided for you to study after school hours and/or on Saturdays. Many teachers devote some of their summers to study, perhaps also taking a leave from their school for a term or a year in order to complete the requirements for a higher degree.

One purpose for continued study is to complete advanced study in one's subject field or to keep up-to-date concerning changes in educational policies, curriculum development, and instructional methods. Another purpose is to prepare oneself for entrance into a field of specialization, such as administration, supervision, counseling, and the like. Whatever your purpose is, plan ahead for your educational progress, and stay with it. Be careful, however, that you do not become so involved in your study activities that your teaching responsibilities are neglected.

In-service education is an important area of professional growth. Your growth as a teacher depends in good part on the effect of continued education on your attitudes toward your work. The expanding body of knowledge and the increasing complexities of teaching literally require continuous study to keep abreast of the new developments in the teaching-learning situation.[7]

Other Media of Professional and Personal Growth

Some school systems and institutions of higher learning, and educational organizations foster the formation of summer workshops. Groups of teachers having similar educational interests gather together (usually from two to six weeks) under the auspices of the sponsoring agency. Here they consider their common problems and attempt to work out tentative solutions to them. Recommendations arrived at during a workshop session are then applied, insofar as this is possible, to the next year's teaching activities and evaluated in light of results. The workship approach is an excellent means of encouraging creative activities among school people.

Another way in which you can keep up-to-date, of course, is to

[7] For an excellent discussion of "Continuous Growth for the Teacher," consult *Educational Leadership*, November, 1962.

follow a planned program of professional reading. Both public and school libraries are giving increased attention to the need for supplying good reading materials in the various areas of general world affairs and in education. Also available are many professional periodicals. As a beginning teacher, you should develop the habit of becoming acquainted with offerings in your subject field and in educational literature.

It may seem to you as you reflect on the foregoing that we have stressed unduly the various aspects of professional growth to the neglect of your development as an individual. That is not our intent. You cannot grow professionally—in the best connotation of the term—unless you also are constantly developing your personal interests and activities.

Many avenues of personal growth are open to you. As a teacher you have relatively long summer vacations. Some of that time can well be spent in travel. Do not confine your reading to professional literature. Become interested in the arts, perhaps developing a hobby. Take time out for recreational activities. Select some of your friends from among people who are engaged in occupational fields other than your own. Devote a reasonable amount of time and energy to participation in community affairs. Engaging in wholesome out-of-school activities can take you back into the classroom with renewed vigor and enthusiasm for your professional responsibilities.

QUESTIONS AND TOPICS FOR DISCUSSION

1. Why should you begin now to consider ways in which you can grow personally and professionally?
2. To what extent and in what ways do you think that your present experiences with adolescents will help you as a beginning teacher?
3. What should be your attitude toward a teacher who seems to resent you?
4. What is your attitude toward teaching in your home school or home community? Be explicit.
5. Which of your experiences as a student teacher do you think will help you most as a regular teacher?
6. As a student teacher, what has been your attitude toward supervision? Give reasons for it.
7. Differentiate between an ethical standard and a legal enactment.
8. If you already have contracted for a teaching position, how well

satisfied are you with the salary you expect to receive? If you have not accepted a position, what salary is your goal?

9. Name professional organizations that you could join as a student teacher. As a regular teacher. In what ways could you benefit from membership in them?

10. Name the books, in addition to your textbook, that you have read during the past year. How have you benefited from reading them?

11. What are your favorite recreational activities? How can participation in them encourage personal and/or professional growth?

SELECTED REFERENCES

A Handbook for Teachers. St. Paul, Minn.: Office of Research, St. Paul Public Schools, 1962.

BROWN, T. J., *Student Teaching in a Secondary School.* New York: Harper & Row, Pub., Inc., 1960.

CARTER, W. L., *et al. Learning to Teach in the Secondary School.* New York: Macmillan Co., 1962.

MASON, W. S., *The Beginning Teacher: Status and Career Orientations.* Washington, D.C.: U.S. Department of Health, Education and Welfare, 1961.

Proceedings: Conferences on Professional Rights and Responsibilities of Teachers in Relation to the Newer Educational Media. Washington, D.C.: National Education Assoc., 1962.

SCHULTZ, R. E., *Student Teaching in the Secondary Schools.* New York: Harcourt, Brace & World, Inc., 1959.

Teacher Orientation. American Association of School Administrators, Washington, D.C.: National Education Assoc., 1956.

Teaching Career Fact Book. Washington, D.C.: National Education Assoc., 1963.

APPENDIX

RECOMMENDED MOTION PICTURE FILMS

The 16 mm. films listed here can be used to supplement the material in the text as indicated, chapter by chapter. The running time is given for each film. We recommended that the instructor preview each film before showing. The names and addresses of the producers and publishers are included at the end of the list of films.

Audio-Visual Aids to Learning (United World Films, 11 minutes). Shows how audio-visual aids can be used in class. Chapter 10.

Broader Concepts of Curriculum (McGraw-Hill, 20 minutes). Presents ways in which four important needs of youth may be met in the secondary school. Chapter 6.

Broader Concepts of Method (McGraw-Hill): Part I, *Developing Pupil Interest* (13 minutes); Part II, *Teacher and Pupil Work Together* (19 minutes). Chapters 7, 8.

Developing Self-reliance (Coronet, 11 minutes). Shows the importance of self-reliance in successful endeavor. Chapters 12, 13.

Discipline during Adolescence (McGraw-Hill, 16 minutes). Illustrates the effect on adolescent behavior of too much and too little parental control. Chapters 12, 13.

Discovering Individual Differences (McGraw-Hill, 25 minutes). The teacher learns about each pupil and adapts his teaching to the needs of each. Chapters 4, 9.

Feltboard in Teaching (Wayne University, 9 minutes). Presents various ways of using feltboard in teaching. Chapter 10.

Getting Yourself Across (McGraw-Hill, 21 minutes). Shows effect of a speaker's personality on his audience. Chapters 2, 8.

Importance of Goals (McGraw-Hill, 19 minutes). Suggests the value of meaningful goals. Chapter 6.

Individual Differences (McGraw-Hill, 23 minutes). Presents the case of the teacher dealing with a shy pupil. Chapters 3, 9.

Introduction to Student Teaching (Indiana University, 20 minutes). Presents many aspects of the problems encountered by the student teacher. Chapter 1.

Learning Democracy through School-Community Projects (University of Michigan, 21 minutes). Presents ways in which students can become involved in numerous extraclass activities. Chapter 10.

Learning from Class Discussion (Coronet, 11 minutes). Portrays the importance of stimulating learning through questions. Chapter 8.

Learning to Understand Children (McGraw-Hill): Part I, *A Diagnostic Approach* (21 minutes); Part II, *A Remedial Program* (23 minutes). Chapter 3.

Making Learning More Meaningful (McGraw-Hill, 12 minutes). Shows how a teacher can assist learners to integrate learning. Chapters 2, 6.

Maintaining Classroom Discipline (McGraw-Hill, 14 minutes). Presents two approaches in meeting discipline problems. Chapters 12, 13.

Motivating the Class (McGraw-Hill, 19 minutes). Presents the problem faced by a student teacher in a geometry class. Chapters 8, 10.

Planning for Personal and Professional Growth (McGraw-Hill, 18 minutes). Presents some of the problems faced by teachers in professional growth. Chapter 16.

Preparation of Teachers (United World Films, 20 minutes). Presents the need to stress personality traits in teachers. Chapters 2, 15.

Principles of the Art and Science of Teaching (Iowa State University, 55 minutes). Concerning the assignment, this film presents the setting up of objectives, selecting content and activities, and adapting procedures. Chapters 7, 8.

Problem Children (Penn State University, 20 minutes). Presents the ways in which home and school experiences affect the personality of two adolescents. Chapter 12.

Problem of Pupil Adjustment (McGraw-Hill): Part I, *The Drop Out: A Case Study* (20 minutes); Part II, *The Stay-In: A School Study* (19 minutes). Chapters 8, 9.

Promoting Pupil Adjustment (McGraw-Hill, 20 minutes). Shows how the classroom teacher promotes social and emotional adjustment. Chapter 4.

Speech: Group Discussion (Young American Films, 10 minutes). Shows how a group can be organized for group discussion. Chapter 8.

Student Government at Work (Coronet, 11 minutes). Shows what a student council can do to be of help in high school. Chapter 11.

Teacher and Pupils Planning and Working Together (McGraw-Hill, 19 minutes). A teacher and pupils work together to develop plans for the day's work. Chapter 7.

Teaching (Mahnke, 11 minutes). Presents the qualifications and characteristics of teachers in this country. Chapter 2.

The Problem of Method (McGraw-Hill): Part I, *Defining the Problem and Gathering Information* (18 minutes); Part II, *Using Information to Solve the Problem* (16 minutes). Chapter 6.

The Teacher as Observer and Guide (Teachers College, 20 minutes). Suggests ways in which the teacher can help pupils with their learning and adjustment problems. Chapter 3.

We Plan Together (Teachers College, 20 minutes). Presents ideas for teacher-pupil planning. Chapters 6, 7.

What Greater Gift (National Education Association, 28 minutes). Shows the teacher as a professional person, as well as something about the nature of teaching. Chapter 16.

Producers and Suppliers of Films

Coronet	Coronet Instructional Films, 65 E. South Water St., Chicago, Ill. 60601
Indiana University	Indiana University, Bloomington, Ind.
Iowa State University	State University of Iowa, Bureau of Visual Instruction, Iowa City, Iowa
Mahnke	Carl F. Mahnke Productions, 215 E. 3 St., Des Moines, Iowa
McGraw-Hill	McGraw-Hill Book Co., Text-Film Department, 330 West 42 St., New York, New York 10036
National Education Association	National Education Association, Press and Radio Section, 1201 Sixteenth St., N.W., Washington, D.C. 20036
Penn State University	Pennsylvania State University, State College, Pa.
Teachers College	Teachers College, Bureau of Publications, Columbia University, 525 West 120 St., New York, New York 10027
United World Films	United World Films, 1445 Park Ave., New York, New York 10029
University of Michigan	University of Michigan, Ann Arbor, Mich.
Wayne University	Wayne University, Audio-Visual Materials Bureau, Detroit, Mich.
Young American Films	Young American Films, Inc., 18 East 41 St., New York, New York 10017

INDEX

Index

DATE DUE